James Atlas

The Shadow in the Garden

James Atlas is the author *of Bellow: A Biography, Delmore Schwartz: The Life of an American Poet* (nominated for the National Book Award), and the memoir *My Life in the Middle Ages: A Survivor's Tale.* The founder of the Lipper/ Viking Penguin Lives series, Atlas was for many years an editor at *The New York Times,* first at the book review and later at the magazine. His work has appeared in *The New Yorker, The Atlantic, The New York Review of Books, Vanity Fair,* and other periodicals. He lives in New York City.

The Shadow in the Garden

The Shadow in the Garden

A BIOGRAPHER'S TALE

James Atlas

VINTAGE BOOKS
A Division of Penguin Random House LLC
New York

FIRST VINTAGE BOOKS EDITION, NOVEMBER 2018

Copyright © 2017 by James Atlas

All rights reserved. Published in the United States by Vintage Books, a division of Penguin Random House LLC, New York, and distributed in Canada by Random House of Canada, a division of Penguin Random House Canada Limited, Toronto. Originally published in hardcover in the United States by Pantheon Books, a division of Penguin Random House LLC, New York, in 2017.

Vintage and colophon are registered trademarks of Penguin Random House LLC.

Portions of this work have originally appeared, some in different form, in *The New Yorker*, *The New York Review of Books*, *The New York Times Book Review*, *The New York Times Magazine*, *Vanity Fair*, and *The Atlantic*.

Owing to limitations of space, permissions to reprint previously published material can be found following the index.

The Library of Congress has cataloged the Pantheon edition as follows:
Name: Atlas, James, author.
Title: The shadow in the garden : a biographer's tale / James Atlas.
Description: New York : Pantheon, 2017.
Includes bibliographical references and index.
Identifiers: LCCN 2016057846.
Subjects: LCSH: Atlas, James. Biographers—United States—Biography.
Biography as a literary form.
BISAC: BIOGRAPHY & AUTOBIOGRAPHY/Personal Memoirs.
BIOGRAPHY & AUTOBIOGRAPHY/Literary.
BIOGRAPHY & AUTOBIOGRAPHY/Editors, Journalists, Publishers.
Classification: LCC CT34.U6 A85 2017 DDC 920.073—dc23
LC record available at https://lccn.loc.gov/2016057846

Vintage Books Trade Paperback ISBN: 978-0-525-43182-4
eBook ISBN: 978-1-101-87170-6

Book design by Iris Weinstein

www.vintagebooks.com

for Anna

The Shadow in the Garden

Delmore Schwartz, from *Vogue*

I

It's late afternoon on Christmas Eve 1974 and growing dark. I sit alone at a long wooden table in the Rare Books and Manuscripts Room of the Beinecke Library at Yale. On the table are six large cardboard storage boxes. I take the top off of one and peer inside: chaos. Manuscripts, letters, loose papers, and manila envelopes, all jumbled together as if they'd been tossed in the box by movers in a hurry—which, as it happens, they had.

The boxes contain the accumulated detritus of the poet Delmore Schwartz, who died of a heart attack at the Columbia Hotel in Times Square on the night of July 11th, 1966, while taking out the garbage. His body lay unclaimed in the morgue at Bellevue for two days, until a reporter noticed his name on a list of the dead. The next morning a lengthy obituary, accompanied by a photograph of a tormented-looking Schwartz, appeared in *The New York Times*. He was fifty-two.

It was his friend Dwight Macdonald, one of the great critics of that era, who salvaged the papers strewn about Schwartz's hotel room at the time of his death. They would have vanished forever if it hadn't been for a chance encounter in a bar between Macdonald's son Michael and the owner of a moving company in Greenwich Village called the Covered Wagon. Macdonald lost track of them and would write me later: "I find in my files a note on 'Delmore, re. White Horse days' w. places the C.W. as being over Bradley's restaurant, University Place at 11 st." Schwartz's papers were at the Covered Wagon.

Macdonald took on the role of Schwartz's literary executor—no one else had volunteered—and for years afterward the papers were stored at Hofstra University on Long Island, where Macdonald was teaching at the time. But three months before my visit, in the fall of 1974, he arranged for them to be transferred to his own alma mater, Yale. I would be the first person to examine what Macdonald had rescued—barely—from oblivion.*

It was nearly five now, and the library would soon be closing for the holidays. There wouldn't be time for more than a brief look at Schwartz's papers, but I was eager to see them. I was twenty-five and had signed a contract with the distinguished publishing house Farrar, Straus & Giroux, committing me to write a biography of Schwartz without having any idea whether, in fact, there was enough material to do so.† What was in these boxes—they could have been the junk of a college student moving out of his dorm—would determine the course of my life.

I pulled out a letter from the top of the pile. It was typed on the stationery of Faber & Faber, the English publisher of T. S. Eliot, who had also worked for many years as the firm's poetry editor.

The letter was from Eliot himself. It was brief but significant. Acknowledging receipt of an article by Schwartz in the *Kenyon Review* on Eliot's journal, *Criterion,* the great man had written: "You are certainly a critic, but I want to see more poetry from you." The letter was dated October 26th, 1939. Schwartz would have been twenty-five, the exact age I was at this moment.

As I stared at Eliot's signature, I felt like Keats in his poem about discovering Chapman's translation of Homer, "some watcher of the skies / When a new planet swims into his ken." I was there with the young poet, tearing open the envelope with eager hands, tipped off to the identity of its author by the return address, scanning it quickly, breathing hard as he came to the sentence about his poems, then setting the letter down gently on his desk and smoothing it out to read again and—or so I imagined—again and again and again. *T. S. Eliot!*

I rummaged through a sheaf of discarded drafts and notes for poems until a letter in a schoolboy's neat blue script caught my eye. It was six pages long and addressed "Dear Delmore Schwartz"—the stiff salutation of someone who didn't know him very well. I flipped to the last page. The letter was signed "Wystan"—W. H. Auden.‡ I raced through

---

* The second actually, the first having been a "graduate student at Hofstra" to whom Macdonald had given access to the papers. I never learned the identity of this precursor, destined to remain forever unknown, like the anonymous "person from Porlock" who interrupted Coleridge while he was writing *Kubla Khan.*

† And if so, whether I could do it; but that is a whole other story—in fact, *the* story.

‡ When I was seventeen, I had gone to hear Auden read at a local college. Hunched over the podium, he muttered incomprehensibly, his face cracked with deep wrinkles

its contents with the nervous fervor of an heir reading a will. Which in a sense I was. Only my inheritance would turn out to be, instead of worldly goods, the custodianship of an obscure poet whose unlikely name would resonate through my life like a mournful bell.

The letter's subject was a two-hundred-page poem by Schwartz entitled *Genesis*. Written in biblical-sounding prose alternating with long passages in blank verse, it told the story of Hershey Green, a "New York boy" born to Jewish-immigrant parents, and his efforts to find his way in the bewildering New World of America:

> *O land*
> *Whence come chiefly the poor hurt peoples*
> *Who for a reason good or bad cannot endure*
> *Or be endured by the old Vaterland.*

Published in an edition of three thousand in 1943, when Schwartz was thirty years old, it was a hugely ambitious effort, and he hadn't quite pulled it off, in Auden's view—at times the tension between "high" language and pedestrian detail was forced, and the epic conceit grew tiresome. Still, it had a kind of crazy energy, spilling forth in a hypnotic rhythm unlike anything ever seen in American poetry.

Not wanting to pour cold water on such a heroic effort, Auden concluded on a solicitous note: "This is a muddled and priggish letter I fear, but I really am both hopeful and anxious about your future development, as you have been given great gifts which, like all of us, you are turning against yourself."

The brass lights on the table flicked on and off. I put the folder back in the box and shrugged on my puffy winter coat. As I headed out across the dark campus, snowflakes swirling around the lamps' white orbs, I knew that I would soon be back in that hushed room, spending long days in the company of someone I had never met but would come to know better than anyone else in the world.

Schwartz's story had lingered in my mind since I was in high school. I recall the exact date when I first encountered this exotic name:

---

like the mud floor of a dried-up lake. Poetry makes nothing happen, he had famously declared. As far as I was concerned in those days, poetry made everything happen.

October 9th, 1966. My father, a book-mad physician who subscribed to *Encounter* and *The Saturday Review,* liked to pick up the New York newspapers' Sunday editions from the out-of-town newsstand a few blocks from our home in Evanston, Illinois. (He found the book reviews in the local papers "primitive.") On that particular Sunday, leafing through the *New York World Journal Tribune Book Week*° in the breakfast nook of our kitchen, I had come across a front-page article about a poet who had died that summer at the age of fifty-two, his once-promising career cut short by drugs and alcohol.

The article was by Alfred Kazin, the author of a memoir, *A Walker in the City,* about growing up the child of Jewish immigrants in Brooklyn during the great Diaspora; I had read this book in high school, excited by its passionate voice. Kazin was lavish in his praise of Schwartz, describing him as a figure of "immense intellectual devotion" whose poems "astonished everyone by being impeccably, formally *right* in the prevailing Eliot tradition—emotional ingenuity tuned to perfect pitch by gravity of manner." But his long descent into madness had begun early. By the time he was thirty, he was exhibiting signs of erratic behavior, and his last years were a tale of squalor: he drifted from the Twin Elms Hospital, a sanitarium near the campus of Syracuse University, where he had been on the English faculty, to a desolate apartment in Manhattan, and finally to the seedy Times Square fleabag where he died.

The photograph on the cover of *Book Week* showed the poet on a park bench in Washington Square in a dark suit, his cigarette held outward between thumb and finger, Russian style. (I recognized this grip from my uncle Grisha, one of the old Russians who used to gather in my immigrant grandparents' living room on Saturday nights for pinochle.) His eyes were wild. His gaze was averted from the camera. A scrap of the *Daily News* with the bold headline HEIRESS KEEPS HER MILLIONS lay beneath his feet. Over a quarter of a century, Schwartz had gone from a literary Adonis to a derelict stumbling in the street.

It was a haunting story, and after my Sunday morning encounter with this strangely named poet, I began to encounter references to Schwartz from time to time, experiencing that jolt of recognition one gets when registering the existence in the world of a person one hadn't

° The elongated name was the result of an ill-considered merger that lasted less than a year.

been aware of before. Oscar Williams had included him in *Immortal Poems of the English Language,* his face staring out from one of the oval portraits of contributors on its cover. Hair brushed back, eyes gazing off-camera in a sensuous stare, he looked like a movie star. But it wasn't until I came across the story that had made Schwartz famous in his day that I understood Kazin's preoccupation with this curious, self-doomed figure. It was called "In Dreams Begin Responsibilities."

I first read this beautiful, deeply unnerving story during my sophomore year in college, while taking a course on American literature in the 1930s. I was deep in the stacks, reading back issues of *Partisan Review* to get a sense of what our professor liked to call the "intellectual currents" of the period, when I noticed Schwartz's name in the table of contents of the autumn 1937 issue. His story was the first piece. "I think it is the year 1909," it began. The narrator is sitting in a darkened movie theater, watching a newsreel of his parents as they stroll on the boardwalk at Coney Island, four years before his own birth. As the film unfolds, Schwartz listens to his father boast of how much money he has made, "exaggerating an amount which need not have been exaggerated," and starts to weep, overcome by his father's suspicion that "actualities somehow fall short, no matter how fine they are." The son, transfixed by the tragedy unfolding before his eyes—his parents' unhappy marriage, his father's lost fortune in real estate, his mother's lonely widowhood—leaps up from his seat in the darkened theater at the very moment his father is about to propose to his mother and shouts, "Don't do it! It's not too late to change your minds, both of you. Nothing good will come of it, only remorse, hatred, scandal, and two children whose characters are monstrous." When I got to the end, I had the experience described by the critic Irving Howe upon encountering the story for the first time: "I felt my blood rise."

In his masterwork, *World of Our Fathers,* Howe would note with tolerant irony "the sing-song, slightly pompous intonations of Jewish immigrants educated in night schools, the self-conscious, affectionate mockery of that speech by American-born sons, [and] its abstraction into the jargon of city intellectuals." I was deeply familiar with that world, one in which the Jewish elders, ashamed of their provincial homeland, boasted of belonging to "the right class of people" and enjoying "the finer things in life." As for the bookish characters I had encountered in Schwartz's stories, "suspicious, rejected, ambitious to win more than most human beings desired"—I recognized them, too.

There were five titles listed in the library's card catalog: Schwartz's first collection, *In Dreams Begin Responsibilities*, which contained, apart from the title story, a series entitled "Poems of Experiment and Imitation," and a strange play, "Coriolanus"; *The World Is a Wedding*, a collection of stories; *Shenandoah*, a pamphlet-size play whose eponymous protagonist, Shenandoah Fish, possesses one of those supposedly haughty "American" first names combined with an ordinary Jewish surname that were a Schwartz trademark (note Bertholde Cannon and Belmont Weiss); *Genesis*, the two-hundred-page poem in "biblical verse" that Auden had written him about; and *Vaudeville for a Princess*, a collection of poems and eccentric prose pieces that provided evidence of the rapid decline Alfred Kazin had charted in his eulogy to Schwartz.

It was a modest but impressive body of work by my estimate: three stories—"The World Is a Wedding," "New Year's Eve," and "In Dreams Begin Responsibilities"—and five or six lyric poems that routinely show up in anthologies of American poetry, along with Whitman and Frost, Longfellow and Poe. The titles were often the first lines: "I am to my own heart merely a serf"; "Tired and unhappy, you think of houses"; and "In the naked bed, in Plato's cave," where the insomniac poet gazes out the window at "the stony street," awaiting dawn as he listens to a bird's first call:

> *So, so,*
> *O son of man, the ignorant night, the travail*
> *Of early morning, the mystery of beginning*
> *Again and again*
> *While History is unforgiven.*

When I first read this poem, I was too young to understand what it was about: the depredations of time, the innate will to survive, the way life crushes us in its inexorable march toward oblivion. But there was another poem I *did* understand, or thought I did, even at the age of seventeen. It was a poem so piercing in its insight into the human condition that it made me want to learn more about the author. How could he have known what he knew so early? It was called "The Heavy Bear Who Goes With Me," and Schwartz was twenty-four when he wrote it—the same age at which he wrote "In Dreams Begin Responsibilities":

Breathing at my side, that heavy animal,
That heavy bear who sleeps with me,
Howls in his sleep for a world of sugar,
A sweetness intimate as the water's clasp,
Howls in his sleep because the tight-rope
Trembles and shows the darkness beneath.
—The strutting show-off is terrified,
Dressed in his dress-suit, bulging his pants,
Trembles to think that his quivering meat
Must finally wince to nothing at all.

The sexual imagery—"his quivering meat . . . bulging his pants"—was hard to miss, and to describe orgasm as a "wince" was genius. But there was something else—vulnerable, guarded, inaccessible even to himself—that made the poem memorable. It was the presence of the poet's double, the self from which he could never escape. The poem bespoke a loneliness of unfathomable depth. You could never get away from who you were.

Richard Ellmann

I I

I can trace my obsession with biography back to the fall of 1971, when, armed with a B.A. in English literature that offered few prospects of future employment, I headed off to Oxford on a fellowship for study abroad. The turmoil of the sixties hadn't reached England's shores. In America, protests against the war in Vietnam were shutting down college campuses all across the country; every time you went to a comp lit seminar, you felt as if you were crossing a picket line. But Oxford was still defiantly archaic. Students who elected English literature had to begin at the beginning—the summer before my departure, I was sent a handbook of Anglo-Saxon grammar.°

I was affiliated with New College ("new" when it was founded in 1379 with a grant from Richard II), but rather than live on campus, as most students from America did, I found "lodgings" in a Victorian redbrick house on Boars Hill, miles from the center of town. My days were a dreary expanse of dead time. There were no requirements, few lectures, no seminars—or none discoverable by the uninitiated. One's only hope of establishing some formal connection with the university was through a tutor. I had been assigned J. O. Bayley, the husband of the novelist Iris Murdoch—and in later life, under the de-initialed name of John Bayley, a memoirist who pitilessly recorded his illustrious wife's descent into Alzheimer's.

Bayley, alas, had no interest in teaching, or at least in teaching me. A distinguished critic, he was preoccupied with his "pieces" for this journal and that—and would dismiss me with a wave of the hand on the

---

° Half a century later my Anglo-Saxon vocabulary, modest even then, has dwindled to a single word: *sweord-jiefu*, "sword-giving." It's not a word that often comes in handy, but once in a while it still pops into my head, as it did one night when I happened to catch a rerun of Robert Zemeckis's *Beowulf*. (Anthony Hopkins was terrific as Hrothgar, but I don't believe he made any mention of swords.)

few occasions when I wandered into his office in search of an assignment or, at the very least, human contact. "Go read George Eliot, my
boy. And not just *Middlemarch* and *Daniel Deronda*. The whole lot.
That ought to keep you busy."

I did as I was told, spending my afternoons loitering in Blackwell's
Bookshop on Broad Street, where—to the detriment of my stipend—
I was allowed to purchase books simply by signing my name in a ledger. In
this manner I also got through Stendhal, ten or twelve Balzacs (*The Black
Sheep, Cousin Bette, Lost Illusions*), Laclos's *Dangerous Liaisons*, and
Manzoni's *The Betrothed;* the major Russians; most of Dickens; and the
entire works of Hardy, Forster, and Henry James, all in Penguin paperback editions. Their spines were color-coded according to period and
nationality—black for nineteenth-century European literature, orange
for the English Victorians, gray for the twentieth-century Moderns—
and that was how I shelved them in my perpetually cold "bedsit," where
the only heat was from an electric coil in the sealed-up fireplace.

Four decades later it troubles me that I spent hundreds—
thousands!—of hours absorbed in books that now spark not a single
memory neuron, but I've grown comfortable with this recollective nul-
lity. Somehow the experience of reading as a priestly task—a calling—
has stayed with me. Whenever I pass through the dining room of my
New York apartment and see these old companions on the shelves, I
feel a certain pride: I may have nothing to show for all my efforts, but
I didn't waste my time. It was from books that I learned the imagination is real: I knew Julien Sorel and Lucien de Rubempré and Frédéric
Moreau better than I knew my own friends.

A t the beginning of my second year at Oxford, my luck changed.
Richard Ellmann, the renowned biographer of James Joyce, was
in residence at New College as the Goldsmiths' Professor of English,
and he had agreed to supervise me, though with the gracious defer-
ment of ego that I would later come to recognize as an element of his
character. In answer to the importuning letter I'd written him upon
learning he was there, Ellmann replied, "You may well prefer to have
an Englishman rather than an American so as to savour* Oxford more

---

* Note the English spelling, the only Anglicism I ever detected in anything Ellmann
wrote or said.

completely." I didn't. Steven Dedalus had stumbled upon his Leopold Bloom.

I spent my days and nights that year working my way through Joyce's allusion-stuffed behemoth with the help of Ellmann's own book, *Ulysses on the Liffey,* a genial guide that I referred to constantly, like a disoriented tourist navigating the streets of a foreign city, Fodor's in hand. I was often lost, but I plunged ahead anyway, reassured by the analogue of *The Odyssey* that trotted alongside it, chapter by chapter, and by Ellmann's erudite yet amiable crib. I grew to love *Ulysses.* I was defeated, though, by the hermetic stream-of-consciousness of *Finnegans Wake,* a book to which Joyce expected his readers to devote their entire lives. I didn't have that kind of time.

For Ellmann, the book was as clear as Trollope. Sometimes, while he read aloud from that mellifluous and daunting text—"Untie the gemman's fistiknots, Qvic and Nuancee . . . Tez thelon langlo, walking weary! Such a loon waybash—wards to row!"—I would study the row of pale-green Dublin phone books* on the shelf behind his desk and wonder what had drawn him to his subject.

Outwardly Joyce and his eminent biographer could hardly have been more different. Joyce was, in his own words, "a man of small virtue, inclined to extravagance and alcoholism." Ellmann was a man of large virtue (though for many years he had a mistress in London) and a moderate drinker, if he drank at all; I remember only the odd glass of sherry. Joyce had a trim mustache, bottle-thick glasses, and in his later years, an eye patch; he was going blind. Ellmann had a receding hairline and a flat midwestern accent that years of dining at High Table with snobbish dons had failed to soften. Maybe it was his seemingly effortless fidelity to his own nature that made him such a shrewd interpreter of others. Ellmann treated his subjects with a benign, avuncular tolerance. He remarked upon, and forgave, their failings.[†] He was fascinated by genius, yet was himself in outward aspect an ordinary man. I often wondered if, like Leopold Bloom, he feasted on the inner organs of fowl.

Many years later I came across a memoir of Ellmann by a former

---

* Their color reminded me of Joyce's evocation in *Ulysses* of "the snot-green sea."
† Even the title of his collection of biographical essays on the major Modernists, *Golden Codgers*—the phrase is from Yeats—reflected Ellmann's affection for the writers whose lives he interpreted so deftly.

student, Henry Hart, in *Sewanee Review;* the title, "Richard Ellmann's Oxford Blues," gives a sense of its mournful tone. Hart, who arrived in Oxford just three years after I left, floundered there, too; having been turned away by other prospective tutors, he was taken in by Ellmann and spent seven years writing his Ph.D. thesis (known at Oxford as a D.Phil.) on the British poet Geoffrey Hill. His recollection of Ellmann—"a plump, slightly balding man wearing black-rimmed glasses, baggy pants, and running shoes"—corroborated mine, except for the shoes. Hart reminded me of details about Ellmann's life at Oxford that I had forgotten, such as the ancient narrow house on St. Giles, near the center of town, where he lived with his wife, Mary, the author of a lively book of essays called *Thinking About Women.* (She was confined to a wheel-chair, the result of a stroke.) But he also told me a great deal I *hadn't* known: that Ellmann had started out as a poet, publishing his work in "little magazines" like the *Hudson* and *Kenyon* reviews until he decided to follow "the gods of biography"; that his London mistress had written an autobiographical novel about him; and that, like Bloom, he "brooded on his sins." I also learned the extent to which Ellmann felt like "a loner" at Oxford, excluded even from his own college's social life because he was an American Jew who specialized in "Modern" (that is, twentieth-century) writers: a deadly triad that could spike your chances of happi-ness in that city of dreaming spires. No wonder I was drawn to him.

There was another connection, too. Like Ellmann, I had once aspired to be a poet and had published my work in various little magazines; I had even "placed" a poem in *The New Yorker* when I was nineteen.[*] But poetry didn't consume me—a requirement for anyone determined to follow that forbidding path. I was beginning to sense that the lives of poets interested me even more than the poetry. I could recite Robert Lowell's "Skunk Hour" in its entirety ("I myself am hell; / nobody's here"), but I was also curious about the car crash that nearly killed his first wife, Jean Stafford, while he was driving. I thrilled to the onomato-poetic mutterings of Eliot reading "The Waste Land" on the Caedmon album[†] I owned, but I still wanted to know why he had locked away *his*

---

[*] It was called "Lighting the Lamps," and I got paid ninety-eight dollars, a mysterious sum that didn't add up by either word or line count. I've kept the check stub to this day.
[†] Albums were played on a "record player," a machine with a spindle onto which you lowered the "record," a grooved vinyl disk, which in turn dropped down onto a spin-ning wheel, causing the arm of the needle to position itself over the record and lower itself onto its outermost groove. You can still find these in antique shops.

first wife, Vivienne Haigh-Wood, in a mental institution. Art and life didn't just coexist: they enriched each other.

Like a promising pianist who discovers that he's not good enough to get to the top, I gave up my dream of becoming a poet without much regret (not having learned yet that life is about giving up dreams). In a poem dedicated to Schwartz, Lowell had quoted Wordsworth's lines:

We poets our youths begin in gladness;
But thereof in the end come despondency and madness.

It wasn't just a matter of talent: I didn't have the mental stamina. Why chance it?

Besides, poetry wasn't the only path to immortality. How many books of any kind could rival Ellmann's biography of Joyce? To say that it was "magisterial," as so many have, didn't begin to explain its power. You could admire its stolidity, the eight hundred pages of closely packed type, the dense columns of footnotes. But lots of biographers had produced books that were just as big. It was the *way* Ellmann told the story that enthralled me. Despite its length, his Joyce (as far as I was concerned, Ellmann's Joyce *was* Joyce) managed to avoid the tedious march of facts and data that made these brick-weight biographies such a chore to read. He sought to bring us close to the man. He made his intent clear from the first sentence, assuring us that he would be our companion on the journey through his subject's life, not an intimidating authority but an intimate guide. "We are all learning to be James Joyce's contemporaries," he wrote.

In order to understand Joyce, we had to inhabit the world he had known. June 16th, 1904—the day that Joyceans refer to as Bloomsday—was the day before Joyce's landlords, the McKernans, "encouraged him to leave until he could pay his rent" (note the verb choice of "encouraged," a sly ironic touch that lends character to the otherwise unobtrusive narrator). It was also the day that, walking down Nassau Street, Joyce "caught sight of a tall young woman, auburn-haired, walking with a proud stride"—Nora Barnacle, soon to become Nora Joyce. We even learn the weather: "June 16 was a fine, breezy day, with four hours of sunshine, and a clear night."*

° Biographers take justifiable pride in pinning down the exact weather on a significant day in their subjects' lives. One obvious motive for this ostentatious display of

The product of this factual density was a book that recorded its subject's life as if the biographer were living it alongside him. Recounting Joyce's efforts to find a flat in Trieste, Ellmann reports that his subject moved into "squalid" quarters at 1 via Santa Catarina, where he and Nora were joined by Joyce's brother Stanislaus: "To reach their own room James° and Nora had to go through Stanislaus's." Eventually he found a more suitable flat, at 8 via Scussa, for 600 crowns: "($120, £25)." Ellmann helpfully converts the sum; for a diligent biographer, no job is too small. "One pupil, Ettore Schmitz, was willing to put up 200, but no more, and Nicolas Santos, a Greek fruit merchant with a buxom wife, also would have helped."† How did Ellmann discover that the wife of a Greek fruit merchant who in the end loaned Joyce no money was "buxom"? (The source was Stanislaus's diary.) And why did it matter? Because, we learn a hundred pages later, the wife's ample bosom would become a synecdochic feature of Molly Bloom.

Ellmann's *Joyce* didn't read like a biography: it read like a work of art. It had the authority of great fiction; it was scholarly but not academic; and behind its facade of objectivity you could detect, if you listened closely enough, the biographer's own voice. This was the kind of book I aspired to write. Ellmann—though I didn't know it then—had made me want to be a biographer.

---

archival labor is to show that the biographer has rummaged through almanacs, old newspapers, and nautical records with impressive, even irrational assiduity; but the case can also be made that these feats of meteorological research really do provide an atmospheric sense of what a particular moment in time *felt like*. Brian Boyd, in the first volume of his massive and entertaining biography of Vladimir Nabokov, isn't satisfied to give us the date of his subject's birth; he must furnish us with the climate conditions: "St. Petersburg. Dawn, April 23, 1899. A day ago the ice began breaking up on the Neva, but at this early hour—already the sun rises at 4:30—the air temperature has dropped again well below freezing." The information doesn't seem superfluous; it sets the scene for the opening act of the novelist's life with the kind of precision Nabokov himself made a fetish of. Or this, from volume one of George Painter's *Proust*: "The sky above Paris had never seemed so blue or crystalline—for the factories were closed, and their chimneys had ceased to smoke—as on the Sunday of Mobilisation Day, 3 August 1914, when Proust saw his brother, Robert, off to Verdun at the Gare de l'Est." The cloudless sky at once foreshadows and obscures the terrible event about to occur.
° Why did Ellmann resort to the familiar James here? My guess is that it was out of deference to the first-name basis he was on with Nora. Ellmann was a courtly man.
† Why the conditional? Perhaps the Greek fruit merchant's help was proffered but declined—or more likely, turned out for one reason or another to be unnecessary. A biographer can't explain everything: the story would never get told.

One afternoon I was hurrying through the narrow streets of Oxford, the old cobblestones slick with rain—did it ever *not* rain in this beautiful but perpetually cloud-shrouded town?—when a sharp pang of homesickness shot through me. I had been in Oxford for two years and had never acclimated myself to its strange ways: the closing of pubs from three to six ("HURRY UP PLEASE ITS TIME"); the odd Oxford vocabulary (*vivas* and *swots*); and the weird food (spotted dick, bubble-and-squeak, toad-in-the-hole). I had bought a used Wolseley Hornet, so dank and old that the carpet had rotted away; after a while I mastered driving on the left, but I could never distinguish between dual carriageways and pelican crossings or bonnets and boots. I might as well have been in Finland.

As I stood on the drizzle-darkened sidewalk in front of Blackwell's, stirred by the new books in the window—there were always new books—I realized that I would never be at home here. Perhaps I would never be at home anywhere. Life seemed to me indecipherable, except in books, where you could make of it what you would. "Cityful passing away, other cityful coming, passing away too: other coming on, passing on." Only where was my Dublin? Who my Joyce?

I headed over to the Bodleian Library, that hushed, high-ceilinged cathedral of books, and sat down at one of the long tables, hoping to make some progress in *Finnegans Wake* (I was still only fifty pages in) when, on a sudden impulse, I got up and hurried over to the "card catalog"—in reality, a counter of atlas-size leather-bound black volumes containing age-buckled pages of entries written out in spidery longhand on strips of paper and pasted in with glue. I looked up Delmore Schwartz. The library had all his books. I filled out the slips and waited patiently for the librarian to bring them over to my table; books at the Bodleian had to be retrieved from some ancient cellar and hoisted up to the front desk by a pulley-operated device like a dumb-waiter. I had learned to wear gloves in the library. It was so cold I could see my breath.

All afternoon I sat beneath the centuries-old portraits of Oxford great men, faint light filling the tall windows, and immersed myself in Schwartz's books—the stories, with their troubled young protagonists; the sad, eloquent poems; the hyperrhetorical *Genesis*—marveling at the way he had managed to transform the idiom of immigrant Jews into the formal, echoic language of the English literary tradition. His poetry resonated with a primal depth; it shook literature awake for me in a way that made it seem like something I could actually produce, could *do*. I wanted to return to my own language and my own people, to hear a voice that spoke to me.

I left Oxford near the end of my second year—I had neither the temperament nor the patience for academic life. I couldn't even satisfy the demands of the tolerant Ellmann, who was always willing to cut me some slack: at the top of a twenty-page paper on Joyce's use of the Renaissance philosopher Giambattista Vico's theory of historical cycles in *Ulysses*, he had penciled a "good start."

III

Back in the States, I found a room in a rambling old house in Cambridge, not far from Harvard Square, and settled in to an aspiring writer's life, pounding out essays, collecting rejection slips from various magazines, and chipping away at the modest trust fund I'd inherited from my immigrant grandfather, who had arrived penniless from Russia, sold postcards door to door, and eventually parlayed a job as an itinerant wool salesman into a thriving business. Once in a while I got a break: the literary editor of *The Nation* let me write book reviews for thirty-five dollars, but other journals paid even less. The fee at the local "alternative" newspaper, *The Boston Phoenix*, was, I recall, twenty-five dollars; and I once received a check for ten—payment for a painfully convoluted essay on Beckett in *The Minnesota Review* that ran to some seven thousand words and must have taken weeks to write.°

I had wangled an assignment from Stephen Berg, the kindly editor of the tabloid *American Poetry Review*, who gave me a shot when I proposed—an unknown writing about a no-longer-known—a biographical essay on Schwartz. It appeared, studded with errors (he died at the age of fifty-two, not fifty-three; it was his aunt, not his uncle, who attended his funeral; etc.), in the January–February 1974 issue. Whatever its flaws, it would serve me well.

It was around this time† that I had lunch at Benihana with Tom

---

° The fact that such a humiliating fee could even be countenanced by either editor or contributor should have raised a red flag about the penury in which a freelance writer could expect to live.

† How glad I am to be spared at last the biographer's flustered rummaging among papers for the exact date; the licensed uncertainty of the memoirist feels liberating after a life spent in the fact-constricted prison of biography.

Poetry, my stern step-mother, perhaps I will depart from your

house. ##
           At night, when the hair grows on your face, and your body

grows longer, and dinner is changed to blood, and your nails grow

longer, you ought to remember, however empty your sleep, how much

is untouched by the conscious mind. ##

           If the glow of the first hour of the morning lasted, I would

give myself utterly to thought and art.##

           There is a big red-brick house on the corner. Mansard roof

and dormer windows are on top, and the right and the left of the

house present their windows in Bullfinch embon point. And in the

late light, when the sun goes down, the redbrick front gains a sing-

ular glory of solidness; the solidness of red.

           The black slates of the mansard roof cover each other like

fish scales on front, with the forms of shields; but on the roof,

they are straight oblongs, and laid in a plane.

           The lamppost curves at the top, like giraffe, and the green

mailbox is hunched and squat. A yellow sign says flatly in red

capitals, STOP, and the mailbox at the shoulder's height looks

like a *big lock—*

*When the poet comes, let your hand to a tapping
finger on a fountain pen or a pencil, not only
let the dark influences rise and be in light.*

*Let the room die and let your body be
placed in the closet with the overcoat*

*Let your mind not be deceived by joy, nor
by freedom of thought. Do not let his free actions
commit you the heartful object scrawled on
the page. His not*

*If a marriage with mystery of joy, and it is, then
he put is the mystery of having and possessing the having.*

A page from Delmore's journal

Stewart, a college classmate who had just landed a job at the acronymic FSG—as Farrar, Straus & Giroux was known to those who managed to penetrate its dingy sanctum on the fourth floor of a nondescript office building facing Union Square. Tom had read and liked my essay, and as the chef on the other side of the counter flipped shrimp off the sizzling griddle, he suggested I consider writing a biography of Schwartz.

Thus began a correspondence that dragged on for months. "There are crates and crates full of papers,"° Tom reported: Bob Giroux, the legendary editor of T. S. Eliot, had learned of their existence from Macdonald. The main obstacle, apart from my inexperience, was the unremitting dolor of Schwartz's story, which "starts at the top and moves inexorably toward the bottom," Tom noted, quoting Hobbes. "The problem of writing about a life that is 'nasty, brutish, and short' is how to avoid a nasty and brutish book." ("Short" probably wasn't desirable either; biographies were supposed to be long.)

I wrote a proposal, and eventually Tom persuaded Roger Straus, the house's famously parsimonious founder, to put up a three-thousand-dollar advance—a small but not unreasonable sum for someone two years out of college whose only published prose consisted of the essay on Delmore and a few book reviews.[†]

If Roger didn't exactly shell out the dough (as he might have put it in the tough-guy idiom he affected), he was an enthusiastic supporter of the project in other ways. He was a great prowler, and whenever I came into the office to see Tom, he would stop me in the corridor to offer some tip.

"What about Malamud?[‡] Is he a black hole?" Had I thought of applying to Bread Loaf, the summer writers' workshop in Vermont? He could get me a grant. And so it was.

The most important thing Roger did was send me to Dwight Macdonald. In the spring of 1974 I went to see him at *The New Yorker*,

---

° It would be impossible to craft a sentence capable of bringing greater joy to a biographer.

† Let's not forget "The Prose of Samuel Beckett: Notes from the Terminal Ward," the long-winded piece in *The Minnesota Review*.

‡ Do I need to identify this once-famous novelist? There was a time when Bernard Malamud, Philip Roth, and Saul Bellow constituted—so Bellow joked—the Hart, Shaffner, and Marx of American literature. (It occurs to me now that I should probably explain that allusion, too: a Jewish clothing company.) At least we no longer need refer to him as a "Jewish-American" writer, a term as obsolete as calling Ralph Ellison a "Negro" writer.

where he kept an office, though he hadn't written a word for the magazine in years.

The thought of facing Macdonald intimidated me. Yale-educated, from a family of now-slightly-worn gentility, he had been a vivid figure in the literary life of the 1950s and '60s, when he wrote the essays that would be collected in *Against the American Grain*. What stirred people up about Macdonald was his defiant certitude: he was always sure of the rightness of his position. Even if he often changed his mind, he didn't regard consistency as a virtue. And he was utterly without pretension—a highbrow but not a snob. He made a distinction between "serious" literature and the productions of such "middlebrow" writers as John Steinbeck and Pearl S. Buck, but he did so in a comic spirit, spluttering like Elmer Fudd. One of his most famous essays, "By Cozzens Possessed," eviscerated James Gould Cozzens, a once-popular novelist, long forgotten now, his descent into oblivion no doubt hastened by Macdonald's opprobrious attack; in a particularly memorable sally, he likened the novelist's sex scenes to "a *Fortune* magazine account of an industrial process" as described by "a tongue-tied Dr. Johnson."

But Macdonald wasn't chiefly a literary critic. He was what would now be called a public intellectual. Politics was his main preoccupation—no, his obsession. A Trotskyite in the 1930s (when it was the fashion to be a Stalinist) and an isolationist during World War II, he liked to think of himself as a "conservative anarchist"; he achieved his greatest prominence as a leader of the anti–Vietnam War movement, playing a major if somewhat clownish role in the 1967 March on the Pentagon. In *Armies of the Night,* that masterpiece of fanciful but dead-on reportage, Norman Mailer expressed admiration for his compatriot's fanatical probity: "Macdonald was forever referring the act of writing to his sense of personal standards which demanded craft, care, devotion, lack of humbug, and simple *a fortiori* honesty of sentiment."

The man who ushered me into his office wasn't outwardly imposing—he would have laughed at the very idea. His white hair and goatee were streaked with yellow; his skin had a ruddy flush; his Caribbean-blue tropical shirt shimmered in that dusty cubbyhole.

Smoking a long cigarette in a holder, his shirt riding up over his big belly, he gave me a sly smile. "So you want to write about Delmore," he said, slouching over his desk as if he were protecting an exam from a neighbor's prying eyes. "But why did you come to me?"

His voice, a high-pitched stutter, was incredulous. He found the whole scene—the young man in his office, the idea of a biography of Delmore, the fact that he was Delmore's literary executor—comical. Didn't I see the joke?

"Well, no one else has done it," I said, provoking another outburst of merriment. The stern critic was nowhere in evidence; he was vague, good-natured, uncomprehending—a shrewd peasant playing dumb.

It was out of the question, he assured me. Delmore's papers were scattered all over the place, no one knew where; besides, Delmore's brother had the last word, and he was nowhere to be found. And who was I, anyway? "What makes you think you could write his biography?"

Still, Macdonald conceded, waving his cigarette at me, maybe something could be worked out. He had promised the papers in his possession to Yale and was arranging for them to be transferred there. He'd let me know as soon as they arrived. My effusive thanks cracked him up again, and he gave me a pat as he walked me down the hall.

"By the way," he said. "No one ever called him 'Schwartz.' If you're going to do this book, you'd better start thinking of him as 'Delmore.'"

My sharpened pencil and pad for taking notes were at the ready.* Like a detainee under questioning, I had stored all my other belongings in a locker. After an interval that seemed as long as the wait for a job interview (in a sense, I was interviewing myself: Was I the right person? Did I have the experience? Was I up to the task?), the librarian at last arrived bearing the papers I had ordered ten minutes—it felt like ten hours—before.

Since my last visit, they had been cataloged and put in some kind of order. Taut with anticipation, I opened a manila folder, and there, on the table before me, was a stack of typed pages, the brittle yellow sheets riddled with Braille-like holes where the period key had punched through the tissue-thin paper. Now and then a corner would flake off, crumbling like a moth's wing.

I removed a page and set it down gently on the table, smoothing out the edges. No event in a biographer's life has such electrifying intensity. It's the moment of contact, when you travel in a startling instant

* No pens are allowed in these sanctums, lest some malevolent scholar end up defacing a manuscript.

from the present to the past, your subject suddenly alive before you on the page, redeemed from oblivion—real. Lucasta Miller, on her first glimpse of Charlotte Brontë's journals in the Morgan Library, felt her eyes filling with tears: "This scrap of paper, covered in tiny writing, recorded the minute-by-minute secret fantasies of a woman who had been dead for nearly a century and a half. I was overwhelmed by an almost necromantic sense of the past coming to life, and could understand for the first time the emotional lure of relics."

It was thrilling, yes, but there was a nagging question here—the first of many that would trouble me in the years to come. Should I—should anyone—have been looking at these journals in the first place? Did their content "belong" to me? I'd been given permission by the estate—that is, Dwight Macdonald—so there was no criminal malfeasance. Nor was it an ethical matter: I wasn't here to uncover dark personal secrets (as far as I knew). Not that Delmore was aware of the drama about to unfold. But he was still implicated, even if posthumously. Otherwise why would he have kept his journals? For whom was he writing them? Were they simply for himself, to keep track of his moods? Or were they for posterity—for his biographer? Surely he believed there would be one. How else interpret this ambiguous journal entry of 1942: "Biographies written of you. It is different with everyone; with the great poet. NOT moral."

After a lifetime of thinking about this declaration, I'm still puzzled by it. Did Delmore mean that biography wasn't moral, or that it was only moral "with the great poet"? That if you were a mediocre poet, a biography would be intrusive, but if you were a great one, all bets were off? Delmore was only twenty-nine when he wrote this entry—not old enough to be sure if he would be great. (Obviously, he thought he had a shot.) That was the thing about writing a biography: you knew more than your subject could ever know about his fate.

Delmore's journals (yes, for me, he was now Delmore; I was pouring my own life into the resurrection of his, and taking Macdonald's advice, I felt free to be on first-name terms with him) were written both for posterity and to keep himself company. They were gossip as internal monologue. Surrounded by scholars laboring away over Dryden variorums in the basement of the windowless, marble-walled library, I investigated John Berryman's philandering and tensions in the marriage of Lionel and Diana Trilling; I wrote down in my notebook the philosopher Sidney Hook's opinion of Mary McCarthy: "People do what they want anyway. She at least admits it." It all belonged to what Bellow's friend Isaac Rosenfeld called, in a comic euphemism, "social history."

Despite his garrulous disposition, Delmore had lived mostly alone between his two marriages. Talking to himself, he was talking to me. "January 16: I almost wept into my Hungarian goulash at the Georgian in the cold blank winter evening." I thought about this passage while refueling at a vending machine in the bowels of the Beinecke. Hunched over a microwaved turkey sandwich, a two-day-old copy of the *Yale Daily News* open before me on the Formica table, I found his loneliness consoling. He was good company: witty, sympathetic, observant. The simplest note—"July 1st, to Falmouth & Truro; cocktail ecstasy; moonlight summer country evening"—brought back Delmore's once-living presence. And I was touched by his sorrowful ruminations. "Snubbed by waitress, consoled by sandwiches"—this entry somehow made my own mealy, plastic-wrapped sandwich more palatable. (How I would have loved the presence of a waitress, even at the price of being snubbed.) "I drank in the darkness, arose, looked at my picture, & drank more." *I drank in the darkness.* Nice.*

There was also a lot of tedious circumstantial detail: saw this one, saw that one; went here, went there. Habitually short of cash, Delmore would obsessively review his tottering finances:

REVISED BUDGET SEPT. '53–'54

Certain or almost certain:

Bank	1,700
ND [New Directions]	600
Saul [Bellow] textbook	750†

I was fascinated by these calculations of chronic insolvency. Even at his most mundane, Delmore was interesting. He was present—

---

* Notice, first of all, the consonance of *d* [drank] and *d* [darkness]; and (even if unintentional) the ambiguity of the line: Did he drink from his bottle of gin in the dark; or did he "drink in" as a figure of speech, the way one "drinks in" a beautiful landscape? Also, the colloquial way of putting it would have been to write "I drank in the dark"— not "darkness." It was as if Delmore couldn't *not* write poetry.

† An intriguing line item: Bellow and Delmore had gotten a contract from Viking for a textbook on "What the Great Novelists Say About the Novel." It came to nothing.

there—in all his confusion and humanness. I could see him at his desk, desperately monitoring cash in/cash out, the folds of his already furrowed brow deepening as he contemplated the precariousness of his situation. ("The teething anxiety, the gnawing nervousness that wastes so many days and years of consciousness"—I wonder if Delmore wrote that memorable line, from "Seurat's Sunday Afternoon Along the Seine," after one of his futile exercises in drawing up a budget.) But the raw numbers, so bland and innocuous, also signaled his desperation; he never had enough money, never would have enough money.

I also had to slog through terse sketches of ossified, long-forgotten events that, decades later, lay dead on the page: "Jay [Laughlin, Delmore's publisher], Bellow, Jean [Stafford, the writer], and [David, a critic, alas, forgotten now] Bazelon in Ticino's"; "Tuesday morning, breakfast at the Dicksons'." But even these entries could resonate with a poignant lyricism ("Kissed Rose's cheek. Fatigued, depersonalized. The thick lamb sandwich") or blossom into strange fragments of poetry ("Passes the path of the downing sunlight and is charred, among burning silver"). Flipping idly through the pages, I stumbled upon profound aphorisms buried beneath the detritus of daily life: "Every dream is an illness, and every fantasy from conflict flows." I was chilled by Delmore's psychiatric self-appraisals: "I lie in the coffin of my character." But he was funny, too: "She was frigid, he was rigid: what a marriage."

Delmore's journals were the spillover of his genius:

August, a country house
A dry bright day
Summer already waning

Birds—shears & the trimming of hedgerows
A recurrent splash
Above which
Whistlers warblers trillers

He could rattle on for pages at a time in loose blank verse about the events of his day: whom he'd seen, what he'd read, what he'd done and hadn't done. One night, deliberating about whether to go to a party, he worked out the alternatives in his journal:

Shall I go there tonight, not Dickens read
Who is so large, says [Edmund] Wilson, almost Avon's°
Great height (desiring this man's gift, and that
Man's scope and hope) who might teach much,
And give much joy. (He also had bad taste,
Was maudlin and, says Wilson, "pretty bad"
Are the short stories shoved in "Pickwick Papers")

He wrote about Wordsworth, Tolstoy, Blake; philosophy and politics; his parents' marriage and their stories of the Old World. He exhorted himself to produce ("A page a day! No day without a page!"); recorded his friends' dialogue; and registered the vicissitudes of consciousness:

This is the way
My mind works. From peak to peak, I read
The purple passages of prose and verse,
Having only the stumbling stamina
Of one who comes back after each defeat.

These "excurses"—as Delmore called them—were a joy to read. I admired the galloping rhythm, the rapid alternation of colloquial and formal style, a faux-stentorian tone that was at once pompous and self-deflating. He was playful, audacious, funny.

But I found the meticulous record he kept of his daily alcoholic and pharmacological intake unsettling. He alternated between highs ("Xmas Eve: a lively happy active day, causeless happiness") and lows ("Dead day, dead Sunday") that he regulated with an increasingly steep intake of alcohol and amphetamines. By the time Delmore hit thirty, he was already in trouble, drinking too much ("rum at 4"; "two glasses of Zinfandel before noon") to counter the effects of his truly alarming consumption of Dexedrine, gobbled at the rate of up to twenty a day. May 27, 1952: "Calm after two Dexs." December 21, 1953: "16 pages of U[lysses]—at 5 Flem.† & back, no liquor, no cigarettes & bubbling of ideas."

° Stratford-on-Avon, Shakespeare's home—a fresh substitute for that now-threadbare metonym, "The Bard."
† Flemington, New Jersey, the rural town where Delmore lived in the early 1950s, when he was teaching at Princeton.

That Delmore was aware of what was happening to him ("This life-long sickness which robs me of myself, which takes away my power") didn't mean he could do anything about it. As he reached his forties, his condition had worsened to the point where he could no longer function without massive quantities of uppers and downers, with predictably deleterious effects that he recorded in his blank verse journals: "How many years have I shortened my life / By barbiturates and alcohol?" Quite a few, as he must have known—and as I knew for certain, reading these prescient words two decades after he wrote them in his journal.

Why did Delmore's decline feel so inevitable? In part, perhaps, because only limited help was available. Psychiatry in the 1940s, when his condition was in its incipient phase, was still in the pre-pharmacological era: mental turmoil could be resolved or mitigated only by the conventional form of "talk" therapy. But Delmore had little faith in this method, which he saw as a threat to his powers of imagination. In his essay "The Vocation of the Poet in the Modern World," published when he was only twenty-eight, he declared that his job was to remain "indestructible as a poet until he is destroyed as a human being."

Delmore himself was the apotheosis of this myth. The artist was by definition alienated: it was his job to be alienated. In his verse journals, he celebrated the secret fraternity

> *who find in art*
> *What exile is: art becomes exile too,*
> *A secret and a code studied in secret,*
> *Declaring the agony of modern life.*

When I first read these lines in the mid-1970s, I felt stricken—what an ordeal life had been for Delmore. Reading his journals over now, it's hard to miss the diagnosis. When he writes of "running up and down the hills and dirt roads of sensibility," or refers to "the roller-coaster" of his emotions, he's describing what has come to be recognized as a biological condition: Delmore was bipolar.[*] I knew none of this then.

---

[*] It's instructive to compare this attitude toward mental illness with David Lipsky's *Although of Course You End Up Becoming Yourself,* his account of accompanying

All I knew was that he had suffered. Now I see his anguish, perhaps too simply, as a symptom of faulty wiring, a physical disability no different from diabetes. But knowing—or believing—that there is a creative component to one's depression perhaps makes it easier to bear. Besides, to medicalize his genius would have been to steal its magic. For Delmore, poetry was a death sentence. But it was also divine.

One afternoon, ready to pack up my notebook for the day—I was copying out in pencil the passages I might need—I came across the following entry, written when Delmore was forty-five:

December 31 [1958]
Alone—alone but free of all bondage to anyone but myself—on the
    last night of
the year of 1958—save for weaknesses and temptations—
Who knows—BUT GOD—what the future may hold . . .

God and the biographer.

David Foster Wallace on a book tour around the country. In his introduction, Lipsky offers a detailed chronicle of Wallace's history with various antidepressants; his suicide is treated purely (though nonreductively) as a psychopharmacological problem. It's a given that Wallace was a genius, but how contributory that genius was to his illness isn't raised as an issue and is either beside the point or hasn't even occurred to the author, who belongs to a generation—and I say this with envy, not disparagement—for whom literary talent was a gift, not a curse.

Leon Edel

IV

Not long after my return to Cambridge, I had looked up a girl I used to "court"—probably not the right word to describe my habit of periodically showing up stoned at her dorm in the middle of the night, eager to babble on about Herbert Marcuse and Norman O. Brown. I was drawn by her sharp intelligence, her reserved manner, and her elegant features. She seemed even more striking now that we were in our mid-twenties and our lives were beginning in earnest. Annie was in medical school; I was a writer, or trying to become one. We got married in 1975, when I was a year into my book, and moved into an old wooden three-flat in Cambridgeport.

Annie quickly became what I called a biographer's widow, the spouse of someone who is not strictly speaking dead but not entirely present either. I spent much of my time in the company of another—my subject, who demanded vast amounts of my time, my energy, and my mental attention, and with whom I also had an actual relationship, even though Delmore really *was* dead. I loved Annie's company, but Delmore was always there.

It was strange to be living in the city where Delmore had lived. Everywhere I went, I could sense his shade—"the heavy bear"—by my side. He had spent three years in the 1940s teaching at Harvard; loitering in the Grolier Bookshop, a quaint establishment that stocked only poetry; dining in the Hayes-Bickford cafeteria in Harvard Square ("the Bick"), long since replaced by a Chinese restaurant; and staring morosely out the window of his apartment on Ellery Street. I have a photograph of him in front of the building, a standard three-decker, leaning against a telephone pole in a winter coat, behind him piles of snow—the same frigid tableau I encountered as I trudged past his door (number 47) on my way to the Out of Town newsstand in the Square to flip through *Kenyon Review* after a long day of clacking away on my Olympic electric typewriter.

When we visited Annie's family house in Vermont, I discovered that Delmore had beaten me to North Bennington as well. I would drive past the Overlea Inn, where he and his first wife, Gertrude Buckman, swam in the goosebump-inducing waters of Lake Paran, where we swam in the years I was writing my book, and where, a decade later, our children would swim.

The Overlea Inn was on a dirt road that has since been paved; now a private home, it belonged to "Mrs. Stanwood," whose name for some reason doesn't appear in the index. What I really wanted to write about here was the heat: the boiling summer days when the air shimmered on the asphalt in front of Powers Market and the sun beat down with a furnace intensity. Delmore must have experienced this heat—he was in Vermont all summer—but I would need a *Farmers' Almanac* to prove it.

Nothing, however, prevented me from identifying with Delmore's conduct on the college tennis courts, where, he confessed in his journals, one day he would lose his temper and the next behave like "a tennis Christian" who gives his wife a chance: "After playing long and well, he tempers the wind to the shorn lamb, he plays pat-pat lightly with her and not only does she enjoy it but he enjoys it also." I behaved the same way with Annie, whacking forehands cross-court; it wasn't until she pointed out my bad manners that I recalled Delmore's conversion and let up.

As I pored over Delmore's journals, I was haunted by the familiarity of his voice, which I seemed almost to *hear* as a ghostly emanation from the page. I was dimly aware, as of a voice from one's past heard over the phone after many years (a high school friend, an old lover), that I knew him, knew his torment, his sense of squandered possibilities, in some deep and fundamental way. Writing a biography was like being a psychiatrist with a single patient, and though Delmore had "terminated" long before I "took him on," the thousands of hours I spent trying to understand him gave me the kind of insight into his character that often eluded me in my relationships with the living.

Biographers are invariably drawn to the writing of a biography out of some deep personal motive," noted Leon Edel, the great biographer of Henry James. For many, this affinity with their subjects is

overt. They're from the same place (Theodore Roethke and Allen Sea-
ger both grew up in rural Michigan); they write in the same genre (the
poet Andrew Motion on the poet Philip Larkin); they've embarked
on the same religious quest (A. N. Wilson, a writer preoccupied with
the sturdiness of his Christian faith, and C. S. Lewis, its tortured
questioner)°; or they belong to the same profession (Charles Strozier, a
psychoanalyst, and Heinz Kohut, the founder of self-psychology): what
binds them is their life experience.

E. M. Forster's tribute to his beloved professor Goldsworthy Lowes
Dickinson was a model of overt biography (whether acknowledged or
not). Published when Forster was fifty-five, it was, to employ a psychoanalytic term, "experience-near." Reflecting on Dickinson's first
impressions of Cambridge, Forster wrote: "He had no idea of what
Cambridge meant—and I remember having the same lack of compre-
hension about the place myself, when my own turn came to go up
there. It seems too good to be real." His description of King's College,
Forster's own, is permeated with a bone-deep familiarity:

> Nearly everyone knows what King's College, Cambridge, looks
> like; it has been depicted and described since curiosity began.
> But as we return, as we recross the bridge, as we ascend the gen-
> tle slope of the lawn, note how the buildings of Gibbs dominate,
> how they set their seal upon the composite beauty of the scene.

Goldsworthy's world is Forster's, so much so that by the time the
biographer himself enters the picture, a hundred pages in ("From his
classes and essay-talks we slide onwards into social intercourse and
familiarity, and this is the moment when I want to introduce myself"),
it's as if we have been expecting him all along.

There was another significant parallel. Dickinson, like Forster, was
"worried by sex"—a euphemism for *gay* (in the parlance of the time, an
"invert"); it was the primary conflict of Forster's own life. His intimation
that Dickinson suffered from a kind of general unrequited love ("He
had for many years been offering affection where it was not needed")
is given authority by Forster's own romantic solitude (assuaged, finally,
by a policeman who became his lover). What better way to deal with
his own sexual conflicts than by exploring someone else's?

° Also—is this insane?—they share two-initial names.

At other times, however, the biographer's motive is covert:[*] he develops an emotional bond with his subject or attaches his own character traits and preoccupations to a figure whose outward circumstances could hardly have been more divergent from his own.

It was this covert form of identification, barely (if at all) conscious, I suspect, that Walter Jackson Bate brought to his life of Samuel Johnson. Bate's biography is a supreme effort of sustained empathy, yet it's based on no perceptible resemblances between biographer and subject. The two men belonged to different historical periods and nations; they diverged in sexual orientation—Bate was homosexual, Johnson heterosexual; they had no religion or geography or family circumstances to bind them. But as I watched Bate climb the steps of Widener Library on a chilly winter morning, huddled against the cold in a Gogolian overcoat, I thought of a passage from his biography: "the dark bewildered prison house of the isolated subjective self."

Leon Edel was another covert biographer. A child of Jewish immigrants who grew up in the remote Canadian province of Saskatchewan, where his father owned a general store, he seemed to have little in common with Henry James, the urbane, fastidious, and worldly novelist to whom he devoted his life. James was at ease in European aristocratic circles, whether he was visiting Edith Wharton's estate, the Pavillon Colombe, or dining with the popular novelist Horace Walpole at the Reform Club. And yet after years of living in close proximity, many biographers tend to identify with their subjects even as they're turning their subjects into versions of themselves. Edel, initially a stranger to James's world, soon made himself at home in it; he studied literature at NYU and the University of Paris, traveled widely abroad, and would become adept at the kind of mild snobbery for which his subject was famous.[†]

---

[*] *Covert* or *overt*: I like the rhyme of this dyad, the second term an orthological truncation of the first. It reminds me of Auden's sly observation that the word *cosmic* is separated by only a single letter from *comic*.

[†] I once interviewed Edel at the Century Association, a venerable arts club that has been around in New York since the mid-nineteenth century. It was Memorial Day weekend, and the place had a deserted feel. Over coffee, he explained that Saskatchewan wasn't as provincial as it appeared. "In that town, all Europe seemed to be gathered," he said. "It may have been a frontier, but it was cosmopolitan, steeped in a nostalgia for culture." He showed me the club's portrait of Henry James—also a member of the Century. Superficially, there was little resemblance between the two men. And yet despite the biographer's pencil-thin mustache, his slight frame and American

In my Cambridgeport apartment I made my way through Edel's two-thousand-page epic. I loved the book but eventually tired of his adulatory, even slavish tone. In Switzerland, he wrote, James "seized the romance and the ruin of Europe, the contradictions of old and new, the symbols human and material of the old feudal order." And all by the age of twelve! A volume later, the biographer compared the novelist to Marcus Aurelius: "He would offer the world the countenance of a conqueror who was, as Arnold said, tender and blameless—*tendentemque manus ripae ulterioris amore.*"* That Henry James was a figure of great stature, that he moved through the world with inordinate gravitas, no one doubts, but he was a novelist, not a Roman emperor.

Still, if at times he elevated James to an unnatural height, Edel possessed uncanny insight into his subject's life and mind. One of the most devastating episodes in his biography concerns the reception of James's play *Guy Domville*, a work that James had hoped would bring him money and fame but instead brought him public humiliation. In a letter to his friend Morton Fullerton, James reported that he had been driven off the stage by "a howling mob"; Edel saw the "brutish rumpus" as one of the precipitating causes of the nervous breakdown James suffered near the end of his life.

Edel's chapter on the "black times" brought on by the debacle of *Guy Domville* and the disappointing sales of the New York edition of his novels is one of the most eloquent in his massive book. Remorselessly he quotes James on "the black devils of nervousness, direst damndest demons," "the sick inanition and weakness and depression," the "beastly solitudinous life" he leads at Lamb House. The novelist sobs in his bedroom, frets over his dwindling checkbook, and submits to "electrocutions." (Today we would call it ECT.) Edel reports all this with such empathic acuity that it's as if he's in the room with James, having his own nervous breakdown.

Were my intimations of a deep subliminal connection between Edel and James plausible, or were they mere speculations based on the thin-

---

accent, I had the unsettling sense that Edel had *become* the novelist he was writing about. So thorough, so total was his identification with his subject that he had virtually erased himself. The biographer Janet Adam Smith, in her obituary of Edel in *The Guardian*, confirmed this impression: "I really believe that Leon—wearing a ring that had once belonged to the Master!—felt that by immersing himself so deeply in James's life and thought something of their essence had been transmitted to him."
* My seventh-grade Latin has evaporated, so I don't know what this means.

nest of evidence—or on no evidence at all? Only many years later did I come across a long interview in *The Paris Review* in which Edel confessed that before embarking on his James project, he had gone into analysis out of "confusion and despair."

My connection with Delmore was overt—so much so that I sometimes wondered if I was writing my autobiography. The circumstantial similarities between us were pronounced: he was born in 1913, the same year as my father; his parents had come over from Russia in the great wave of Jewish immigration that crested around the turn of the last century and brought my own grandparents to these shores; we were both poetry-besotted adolescents, drunk on Eliot, intoxicated by the strangeness of Wallace Stevens, and groping our way through the opacities of Ezra Pound.

As dramatic (and sometimes creepy) as these parallels were, they were incidental. The real ones ran much deeper. Delmore's attachment to the innocence of early childhood, his unrealizable expectations, his piercing loneliness, his book hunger, his literary ambition, his dread of failure, his sense of the sadness of life . . . these were traits and longings we shared.

There's a saying in the psychiatric profession: the specialty you choose is your own disease. If so, I had chosen my subject wisely.

V

Journals are the log of the inner life; letters are the life presented to the world, the face prepared to meet the faces that you meet. I traveled across the country on a dogged recovery mission, tracking down Delmore's correspondents and ransacking library archives—I marveled that so many letters had survived the ruthless onslaught of time, which in the end disperses all. Why these and not others? Like the torn scrolls of Greek and Latin poetry that survive the depredations of history, from which we struggle to reconstruct a vanished civilization in its barest outlines, the letters painstakingly collected by the biographer reflect only a shadow of his subject's life as it was actually lived.

The record, I discovered, is inevitably partial.* There are always more letters: they show up after the biography is written, discovered in some overlooked archive or library; tucked away in a drawer and forgotten; withheld for whatever reason by the recipient. If only I'd had in my possession the letter that turned up at an auction three years after I finished my book, the whole story would have become clear!

Why this feverish quest? Letters are the foundation of biography.

---

* Philip Larkin's letters to his girlfriend Monica Jones provide a vivid example of how precarious the whole letter-collecting enterprise can be. Jones had bought a house in Northumberland but spent most of her time with Larkin at his home in Hull, where she stayed on after Larkin's death. Eventually, following years of amicable negotiation, she granted Larkin's biographer Andrew Motion access to the letters, but by that time she was too ill to accompany him to the Northumberland house. Motion drove up alone, only to discover that it had been ransacked by burglars. The furniture was broken; cans of food oozed their contents on the steps; and—what nervous joy this must have brought the biographer—there were letters from Larkin strewn about everywhere, in boxes, cupboards, and closets, stuck in books. Motion gathered them up, locked the house, and drove off, "exhilarated and ashamed" by the cache he'd salvaged. A week later thieves again broke in and took everything left: "If the letters had been there, they would have gone too."

Gotham Book Mart sign

Uncensored and unscripted, they often reveal a great deal about their author that the author may not have wanted known—or didn't know he was revealing. A letter may contain evidence of a secret assignation or identify a lover unlisted on the roster of the author's known inamorata;[*] it may disparage a friend or engage in "the mere twaddle of graciousness," as Henry James called the genre of the tossed-off, jocular, sometimes inane missive one writes to thank a host for dinner or wriggle out of a date. They're not intended for the *Collected Letters*—though they may end up there if the recipient decides to sell them to a private collection or a library. If you don't want your letters to be read, don't send them.

Or don't write them at all. Letters are vessels that bottle up the fluidity of the self; they capsize your expectations and turn your subject into someone else, one of the infinite selves contained within us. Delmore's letters recounted the same events to different correspondents in different voices, changing their tone, their intent, even the facts when it suited his purpose.

I loved Virginia Woolf's letters; I owned two volumes and would eventually own all six. "Letter writing is one of the gifts which was kept back when fairies stood at my cradle and gave me an affectionate heart," she wrote the novelist Hugh Walpole. Hardly. She was a master of the vivid image, the wry detail, and could depict a scene with fine satirical verve. "Oh I'm so furious!" she complained to her sister Vanessa: "Just as we'd cleared off our weekend visits, the telephone rings, and there comes to lunch late, hungry yet eating with the deliberation and mastication of a Toad, Mr. Gillies of the Labour Party. It's 5:30. He's still there, masticating."

Her bipolarity is on vivid display; moods fluctuate with an almost dangerous versatility. Toward importuners—young novelists, pushy acquaintances, literary editors—she is polite but firm; toward the Bloomsbury circle, she vacillates between subtle shades of intimacy;

---

[*] See Flaubert's letter to a friend in which the novelist, apparently fresh from a tumble with the governess, signs off, "*Votre géant qui f . . . comme un âne.*" A noncommittal footnote in the Pléiade edition suggests, "Perhaps an allusion to Juliet Herbert." The tactful *perhaps* hints that an omission in Flaubert's sexual history has been rectified, though at a cost to one of the parties concerned. "It is hard not to wonder what the Herbert family would have made of this," Julian Barnes notes wryly in a review of the *Correspondance.* I suspect Flaubert would have been pleased by the revelation of his sexual prowess.

toward her aristocratic friends, she's engaging, flattering, and disarmingly attractive but never unctuous. Welcoming a visit from Lady Sibyl Colefax, she warns: "(1) View is ruined (2) No room for chauffeur in house (3) the smallest possible doghole for you (4) Village char is cook." Returning from a visit to Vita Sackville-West at Sissinghurst, one of England's great houses, she writes her friend Ethel Smyth: "The whole place was a magnificent proof of our old English aristocratic tradition. When I got back here I was positively ashamed of my middle class origin. It was a wet night and the kitchen was damp and my room all strewn with old clothes."

Smyth, a strong-willed composer and memoirist in her seventies who had become infatuated with Woolf, made her impatient. The novelist's hectic, stilted letters to her elderly friend are ill tempered to the point of comedy. "And you now," she writes, "now drop your trumpet, which by the way is upside down, and tell me: about the opera; about the orchestra"—and about a lot of other matters that Woolf makes it clear don't interest her in the slightest. She is forever putting off her aggressive admirer, bestowing on Smyth praise so extravagant that it verges on hostility; to others she's snippy: Ethel is a "termagant," a "catastrophe." "Ethel's new dog is dead," she writes Vita. "The truth is, no dog can stand the strain of living with Ethel."

But then, writing to her sister Vanessa about her unshakable marriage to Leonard Woolf, she sounds an elegiac note:

> We get snatches of divine loneliness here, a day or two; and sanguine as I am I said to L. as we strolled through the mushroom fields, Thank the Lord, we shall be alone; we'll play bowls; then I shall read Sevigne; then have grilled ham and mushrooms for dinner; then Mozart—and why not stay here for ever and ever, enjoying this immortal rhythm, in which both eye and soul are at rest?

This is the Virginia Woolf whose voice captivates us in the novels. It's eerie to hear it in a letter, where, as nonfiction, it gives us a vivid sense of the life—the *real* life, in which the Woolfs have grilled ham and mushrooms for dinner—behind the work. The biographer mines letters for addresses and dates, but if we read carefully, we can glimpse in the dense underbrush of footnotes the living—or once-living—figure, in all its erratic reality.

A theme runs through the stories of writers pursued by their biographers: call it epistolary pyromania. Henry James was one of the worst offenders: he lit a match to his correspondence with defiant gusto on more than one occasion. "I kept almost all my letters for years," he wrote to a friend, "till my receptacles would no longer hold them; then I made a gigantic bonfire and have been easier in mind since."

James was obsessed with fending off predatory biographers. In his story "Sir Dominick Ferrand," a struggling writer, Peter Barron, discovers a cache of letters by a major literary figure of the recent past, now deceased, in the hidden compartment of a desk that Barron has purchased from a secondhand furniture dealer. He resists the temptation to sell them to the "hungry little editor" of a literary journal called *The Promiscuous,* choosing—out of pride and honor—to burn them instead. (James was undoubtedly providing a lesson in how biographers *should* behave.) And in "The Aspern Papers," reflexively invoked by masochistic biographers as a damning critique of their profession, James's narrator, a journalist named Geoffrey Aspern, moves into the desolate Venetian palazzo of an elderly woman who had once been the lover of a famous poet, hoping to ferret out letters he suspects are in her possession; she surprises him in the act of opening a desk where he supposes them to be hidden and denounces him as "a publishing scoundrel."*

For James, biography was a sport, a game designed to set biographer against subject. In an essay on George Sand, he addressed the issue with a pumped-up rhetoric that verged on paranoia, challenging the "cunning enquirer, envenomed with resistance," to discover his sub-

---

* Even the biographer has to admit that some facts are of little value—interesting, perhaps, but not necessarily illuminating. Does it matter who Geoffrey Aspern is "based on," if anyone? I didn't think so until I came across a person in Richard Holmes's *Shelley* named George Silsbee, described as "a young Harvard graduate" who had made his way to Florence in search of Shelley's love letters. "He tried ineffectually to charm them from the dark-eyed lady"—Claire Clairmont, Byron's lover and the mother of his illegitimate daughter, Allegra—"by parading his youthful zeal and enthusiastic knowledge of Shelley. His performance inspired James's cutting story *The Aspern Papers* (1888), which is the final damnation of all biographers." Suddenly Aspern has taken on flesh and blood; he's a scoundrel with a story of his own. Why pretend these connections between characters and their real-life models make no difference? They don't cancel out the writer's capacity for invention; they call attention to it. The art is in what's made up.

ject's traces: "The pale, forewarned victim, with every track covered, every paper burnt and every letter unanswered, will, in the tower of art, the invulnerable granite, stand, without a sally, the siege of all the years." This is James at his word-swaddled worst—defensive, grandiose, beleaguered by the world and its demands. The fact is, he could have incinerated enough letters to burn down Lamb House and still not got his hands on the ones that really mattered—the ones he wrote himself, safely in the hands of his recipients.

I grew weary of reading about these backyard autos-da-fé. Dickens burned his correspondence with his mistress, Ellen Ternan. Flaubert once spent eight hours incinerating a lifetime's worth of letters. Thomas Hardy was always setting fires in the backyard of Max Gate, his gloomy Dorset manse. ("I have not been doing much—mainly destroying papers of the last thirty years," he wrote a friend with maddening insouciance.) At the age of twenty-nine, Freud kindled his first conflagration. "As for the biographers, let them worry," he wrote his wife, Martha Bernays: "I am already looking forward to seeing them go astray." Why not just throw your correspondence in the trash? Because you could end up like Wilfred Barclay, the novelist in William Golding's novel *The Paper Men*, who catches his biographer rooting about in the garbage for his letters—"the badger in the bin," as he's henceforth known.

But as with journals, intention can be equivocal. T. S. Eliot and W. H. Auden urged their correspondents to "destroy" their letters—an even more violent directive than "burn," which didn't make it more sincere. If they felt so strongly about the matter, why didn't they do more about it while they still could? When Kafka directed his friend and executor, Max Brod, to burn his papers—including, by implication, their correspondence—surely he knew, or at least suspected, that Brod would decline. Which Brod did, on the grounds that he knew Kafka didn't *really* want them destroyed and was just bluffing.

This ambivalence was not uncommon. Thomas Carlyle left instructions for his heirs regarding the love letters between him and his wife, Jane: "My strict command now is 'Burn them if ever found. Let no third party read them; let no printing of them or any part of them be thought of by those who love me.'" And yet here they are, still with us—thirty-eight volumes in all. Philip Larkin was always threatening to set his papers on fire. "When I see the Grim Reaper coming up the path to my front door I'm going to the bottom of the garden, like

Thomas Hardy, and I'll have a bonfire of all the things I don't want anyone to see," he wrote Andrew Motion. (Again with the fire.)

This couldn't have been what Motion, who was then planning to write Larkin's biography, wanted to hear. Fortunately for him, the instructions Larkin gave the trustees of his estate were so complicated and contradictory that any decision in regard to the disposition of his papers could be justified. The trustees were given permission to publish "all manuscripts and letters," yet those same papers were to be "destroyed unread." Then in still another clause, Larkin stipulated that the trustees were to consult the literary executors "in all matters concerned with the publication of my unpublished manuscripts." As a journalist wrote in *The Independent:* "In three breaths Larkin gave his trustees the power to publish his unpublished work, instructed them to destroy it, and told them to discuss the matter with the literary executors." Is that clear?

Holed up in the Beinecke Library one day reading the verse journals that Delmore typed on yellow paper, I came across a deft couplet about the afterlife of letters: "These pieces of the self are with my friends / They show me as myself, which never ends." *Never ends* is right. Gathering Delmore's correspondence was turning out to be a big job. For one thing, the letters weren't all in research libraries, filed in the card catalog, and ready to be brought out by silent librarians gliding across carpeted floors in the hush of a reading room. They were scattered across the country, in their recipients' desk drawers—or in the memorable case of a literary critic with a hook for a hand, in a box under the bed, which he dragged out with his piratical prosthesis.° Still, I depended on these letters and not only as primary sources, territory—in my case virgin—that mapped out the all-crucial chronol-

---

° I thought of calling this book *Sundays at Kinko's:* when I was writing my biography of Saul Bellow, I had a full-time job for a period of years that meant I often had only weekends and the occasional vacation day to do my research. I had to work fast to pry letters out of his relatives and friends (and sometimes enemies); I would go to their homes in my rented car, explain why handing over Bellow's letters was good for American literature, and then, booty in hand, hurry to Kinko's to copy them. In Hyde Park, Evanston, Los Angeles, and San Francisco, I stood before the copying machine, shielding my eyes from its atomic flash as the precious documents were duplicated for my eager scrutiny. I worried about going blind, but that didn't slow me down: someone could always read me the letters or translate them into Braille. What mattered was that I had them in my possession.

ogy of who, what, and where (the *why* was up to me). They were also artifacts on paper. The stationery itself was a text studded with valuable information: the logo of a hotel, accompanied by a little drawing—the Roosevelt, Manhattan; the Palmer House, Chicago (where Delmore's father lived for a time); the blotted letters issued from a faulty pen; the addenda in the margins, scrawled in haste. What the biographer is inspecting is so much more than a written communication: it's a document from a remote period in history, miraculously spared the random attrition of moving house or the impulsive purge, on a rainy afternoon, of a chaotic archive because papers annoyingly cascade out whenever you open the cabinet door.

Often my interlocutors had no memory themselves of what treasures were in their possession.° It wasn't until a third interview that one of Delmore's friends suddenly recalled a cache of letters in his garage—a revelation he delivered while sitting across from me at the Carnegie Deli and contemplating the corned beef sandwich before him. "How could you not remember?" I admonished the forgetful correspondent. "Don't you realize how important this is?" "For who?" he said. "For literature! For posterity!" I replied in a state of agitation. "What's that got to do with me?" he said calmly, gnawing on a pickle. In other words: *I'm* not the one this book is about.

Then there was the psychodynamic factor. My access to the letters was often the subject of heated negotiation, in which I had to prove my worthiness as a biographer and struggle against the resistance of the letters' owners. There would come a suspenseful moment, a point at which the recipient would visibly hesitate, wrestling with his conscience. Was it ethical to share private correspondence with a young man, still in his mid-twenties, who had never written a book before? Meanwhile I would sit quietly with an air of studied detachment—early on I learned to maintain a psychiatric silence—awaiting its surrender. Confronted with the competing claims of privacy and an impulse to share their treasures with a biographer whose eventual use of them is

---

° As I grow older, I have a better understanding of these once-incomprehensible lacunae of memory. Going through my own correspondence, I was startled to find letters from Anaïs Nin—a now-somewhat-faded name but not so long ago a writer who qualified for a major biography by Deirdre Bair—written in longhand on stationery bedecked with colorful drawings of flowers. ("Like my hippy paper?") I had invited Nin to give a benefit reading for my college literary magazine, prompting a brief flurry of correspondence. I'd forgotten all about it.

beyond the owner's control, my interlocutors had several choices, all of them ambiguous in both motive and outcome: to hand over the letters on the grounds that they ought to be shared for the sake of literary history; to hand them over in order to embarrass or "get even with" their author out of envy, spite, competitiveness, some mischievous impulse, or sheer malice (often unconscious); to *not* hand them over, driven by a wish to appear principled or by in fact *being* principled; finally, to prevaricate or stall, requiring the biographer to return again and devote to the recipient more energy, more attention, and more supplicating expressions of need. In virtually every instance, I managed to wrest them loose in the end. Why? It might have been in part the owners' vanity. After all, having such important documents in their possession meant they were part of the story. Or perhaps it was simply out of a disinterested commitment to the preservation of literary history: these weren't just anyone's letters. They belonged to the canon.

Letters often came into my hands, I felt, out of a kind of pity elicited by my doggedness. When I arrived at slip number forty-nine in the Isle of Pines Mobile Home Court in Gautier, Mississippi, to see Delmore's brother, Kenneth, he greeted me with a quiet kindness, reminiscing about their childhood as he cut up a chicken and handed over to me Delmore's letters to their parents without hesitation, the arduousness of my pilgrimage having apparently convinced him of the urgency of my claims.

Kenneth was so different from his poet-brother that I could hardly believe they were related. He was an engineer, divorced and working at an industrial site on the Gulf. He was clearly not a reader—there were no books in his trailer that I could see—and he apparently knew almost nothing about Delmore's career. But it was clear that he cared about his dead brother. In his blue jeans and faded denim shirt, he seemed right out of Flannery O'Connor's novella, "A Good Man Is Hard to Find."

Sometimes I just lucked out. I take down from my shelf a slender volume that I purchased at the Gotham Book Mart on my first visit in the fall of 1971.° The Gotham—long since out of business—was on

° The book I acquired on that initial foray and that, forty years later, I now hold in my hand was *Marcel Proust: An English Tribute,* published in New York in 1923 by a

West 47th Street in the Diamond District; for several decades, it was one of the great bookstores of New York. It had a wooden sign over the door in the shape of a boat; on its hull was carved the motto WISE MEN FISH HERE. The proprietor, Andreas Brown, was an irascible presence; whenever you entered the shop, you'd hear him yelling over the phone in his tiny, book-crammed office. I could never quite understand the intensity of his wrath. They were only books, and most of them old out-of-print books. What was there to yell about?

The Gotham was a bibliophile's dream: floor-to-ceiling bookcases crammed with first editions; a table in the back room piled high with every literary magazine in the English-speaking world; photographs of famous writers on the walls. My favorite was a group portrait of Randall Jarrell, Sir Osbert and Dame Edith Sitwell, Marianne Moore, Gore Vidal, and seven or eight others, including W. H. Auden, perched on a ladder, and Delmore, cigarette in hand, gazing dolefully at the camera. It is 1948, and he is thirty-five, already teetering on the cliff of his decline. They're all dead now. When I began visiting the shop in my twenties, Frances Steloff, the founder and original owner, then in her nineties, still drifted up and down the aisles, spectral, white-haired, a ghost out of another time.

"Andy" (as I was allowed to call him a few years into regular patronage of the shop) was also a rare-book-and-manuscript dealer who seemed able to find anything. Over the years, he sold me at a very reasonable price or gave me outright a first edition (sadly, there would be no second) of *Genesis;* an early poem in Delmore's own hand;* and a signed first edition of *Herzog.*†

---

firm called Thomas Seltzer. The dust jacket, if there ever was one, is gone; the cardboard is a pattern of faded gold fleurs-de-lis against a brown background that reminds me of the dilapidated wallpaper in a nineteenth-century hotel across the street from Paddington Station. The contributors include Arnold Bennett, Compton Mackenzie, George Saintsbury, and Arthur Symons, among once-illustrious others, remembered now only by a few dedicated students of early twentieth-century literature. But they were famous then, in the middle of it all—the Kazins, Edmund Wilsons, and Lionel Trillings of their day.

* I sold it to the rare book dealer Glenn Horowitz, who has a great knack for extracting huge sums from research libraries for the archives of famous writers, and purchased with the proceeds my first computer, a model the size of an old Philco TV that saved data on pliable "floppy disks."

† Actually, it was a gift from Annie. A generous friend, Ilyas Khan, gave me another, so I now own two, one of which is inscribed to "Aileen"—Aileen Ward, who wrote a fine

One day when I was already well into my biography, I came into the store and found Andy in a state of great excitement. He had something to show me. He grabbed a folder off his desk and pulled out a sheaf of typed letters from Delmore. "These came into my hands," he said—the book dealer's cagy phrase for a provenance he didn't wish to reveal. Even now I know only—and this from a selection I edited for Daniel Halpern's literary journal *Antaeus* in 1976—that "they are the property of Mr. Andreas Brown of the Gotham Book Mart, who was kind enough to let me print them here."

They were letters from Delmore to Julian Sawyer, a classmate at the University of Wisconsin and "a strange, haunted figure," as I wrote, with a fanatical devotion to Gertrude Stein. ("When she arrived in New York in 1934 he met her and fell to his knees on the pier.") Little more is known of him; according to my prefatory notes in *Antaeus*, "he committed suicide in the 1950s." And there the story ends. Where are Sawyer's heirs? He was gay and had no children.

What remain are the letters, ghostly imprints—"fossils of feeling," in Janet Malcolm's marvelous phrase—of a relationship that, for a brief moment, consumed both parties. They vibrate with adolescent urgency; they're dispatches from—the seventeen-year-old Delmore unashamedly claims, with only a tinge of irony—"the most important being in the world of time":

> It is fifteen minutes after three o'clock, Central Standard Time. It is the last Monday morning of October. The trees near my window have become bare of leaves during the past week. The trees stand against the night of blueness, like tall flowers. As for flowers, (resuming two cadences) the small flowers of the night burn steadily and purely, like the clear eyes of my burning mind, when I am asleep. The sweet stars make me say my prayer in the time that is past, or my new thing which would have been a prayer at the time that is past: The Time is past.

I imagine Sawyer waiting for this letter in his apartment in Washington Heights, reading the fervent words with eager attention. They

---

biography of Keats and was Delmore's girlfriend for a while. (Richard Ellmann also had a crush on her.) The inscription was by Saul Bellow.

form not "another piece of the puzzle"—the pieces are infinite and in any case can't be put together—but a glimpse into a consciousness, an imagination, taking shape. That's all we know. The two parties to the correspondence—writer and recipient—are long dead; there is only the letter, published in a literary journal that no longer exists.

Reading Delmore's letters to Sawyer was exhilarating—here was my subject in the full bloom of adolescence, the most unguarded time of life—but it also felt transgressive. The journals, I had convinced myself, were a deliberate if unacknowledged communion between subject and biographer. Writing journals could seem like talking to yourself—the act of a desperate mind, compelled to utterance by loneliness or an extremity of mental pain. But it was also an act driven by the longing to communicate. Journals are the message in the bottle, discovered by the biographer months or years later. Letters—at least the kind that writers write—are journals addressed to someone else. However self-conscious, however contrived in tone, they are addressed to a recipient—an Other. The monologue becomes a dialogue. Even in his silence, the addressee influences the tone of the letter's author. As the eavesdropper, I was less confident about my rights. I couldn't convince myself that Delmore was writing for his biographer, even though there was considerable evidence that he was.

"It was pleasant to learn that you expected our correspondence to be read in the international salons and boudoirs of the future," he wrote to James Laughlin in 1951. Now a third party is involved: the biographer. In this epistolary triangle, the writer is addressing both his subject and the future curator of their correspondence. Delmore understood this:

> Do you think they will be able to distinguish between the obfuscations, mystifications, efforts at humor, and plain statements of fact? Will they recognize my primary feelings as a correspondent— the catacomb from which I write to you, seeking some compassion? Or will they just think that I am nasty, an over-eager clown, gauche, awkward, and bookish? Will they understand that I am always direct, open, friendly, simple and candid to the point of naivete until the ways of the fiendish world infuriate me and I am forced to be devious, suspicious, calculating, not that it does me any good anyway?

Delmore is clearly playing to the gallery here, keeping an eye on the future. He's self-conscious, sacrificing for the sake of literary effect the candid impulsivity of a letter meant to be read at the time it was written. ("Never send an angry letter at night, only in the morning," Delmore once instructed himself in his journal—a sensible injunction that he violated often and with predictable results.) At the same time, his confidence that posterity will take an interest in him is at war with his insecurities and self-doubt. He's trying to figure himself out, using the occasion of a letter to engage in self-therapy.

In a way, Delmore's barrage of questions got me off the hook: if he couldn't answer them, why should his biographer be expected to? But I also found the fact that my subject was, in a sense, acknowledging my presence unsettling. I felt used—a mere secretary, a go-between, an archivist working to preserve Delmore's correspondence for generations to come. Not that there weren't letters meant to be read the moment they were written. "I don't see why you need to bring a ham to Cambridge," he writes on January 20th, 1946, to the novelist Jean Stafford, who shared an apartment with him and her then-husband Robert Lowell. It's not a sentence I'll quote in my biography: who cares about the ham? It plays no role in any story. But it brings him before me with startling vivacity. Delmore isn't thinking about poetry or his career or sex at this moment; he's thinking about a ham.

"Call me at CH 2-3615* if you can when in N.Y.," he writes to Robie Macauley, then the editor of *Kenyon Review*, on October 7th, 1961. I'm tempted, in a fit of madness, to dial the number in the hope that Delmore himself will answer, enabling me to ask the million questions that force their way into my consciousness as I sit at my desk day after day, writing his life. ("Life-writing," biography is sometimes called—a compound that conveys both the stolid former corporeality of the subject and the biographer's act of imaginative re-creation.) *What made you decide to become a poet? Who were your literary influences?*

It could have been the *Paris Review* interview that Delmore never had, since by the time of the magazine's founding in 1953, he was incapable of giving a straight answer about anything—certainly not

---

* The exchange—"CH"—recalls, as John Cheever famously wrote, "a long-lost world when the city of New York was still filled with a river light, when you heard the Benny Goodman quartets from the radio in the corner stationery store and when almost everybody wore a hat"—a time when you could title a novel, as John O'Hara did, B*Utterfield* 8.

the "craft" questions posed by George Plimpton, the inventor of this famous literary institution. *Do you use a typewriter or a pen?* I also had questions of a more intimate nature—questions he wouldn't have answered and I probably wouldn't have had the nerve to ask, even if he had picked up the phone. Questions about his parents' marriage; his relationship with his brother; his divorce from his first wife, Gertrude Buckman . . . Holden Caulfield said there were times when you liked a book so much you wanted to call up the author. I guess he didn't mean dead authors.

VI

Have you read Richard Holmes's *Shelley*?" Dwight Macdonald wrote me not long after it came out. "I feel like a bee drowning in honey." I could imagine him sitting in his gloomy apartment on East 86th Street on a steamy summer day, the air conditioner blasting, cigarette holder in hand, a glass of Scotch positioned by his side, lost in this prodigious book. It was Holmes's first biography, an eight-hundred-page tour de force. He was only twenty-eight.

I hurried over to the Pangloss Book Shop in Harvard Square, which specialized in recondite titles—the books on display in its window tended toward members of the Frankfurt School, Structuralists, and Continental philosophers like E. M. Cioran and Roland Barthes. Mr. Hillman, the shy, slight, bespectacled proprietor, didn't have a copy of the *Shelley* on hand (he had once dropped into our desultory conversations the information that he didn't "believe in" biography); but he ordered one with an ostentatious show of reluctance, muttering to himself as he filled out the invoice, and a few days later the prize arrived.

I instantly saw what Macdonald meant. Here's how it starts:

His bedroom looked west, toward the setting sun. There was a wide lawn, with a shallow bank to roll down, and then a cluster of enormous trees, elms with rooks in, cedars, American redwoods brought back to England by his grandfather, and further and darker, rhododendrons and fir trees. Through the trees was the lake.

Was this a biography? The intensely visualized opening, with its unnamed subject ("grandfather" didn't have a name, either), read like a novel. And it was written—this was perhaps the most remarkable thing—from a child's point of view. When Shelley's nurse tells the boy

Richard Holmes

tales of the Great Snake that lurked in a nearby pond, Holmes employs interior monologue ("She said it lived in St Leonard's Forest and was at least three hundred years old"), and his simple declarative sentences, often beginning with a pronoun, have the repetitive sound of a primer. It's no surprise to learn on the second page that "Bysshe," as the poet was called by his family, is six years old as the book opens.

A few pages later, however, Holmes radically disrupts the chronology, jumping forward to foreshadow the poet's premature end ("The visions and sleepwalking recorded by Mary Shelley in the last weeks of Shelley's life—he was then aged 29") and placing him firmly within a historical context: "Shelley had been born in 1792. It was the year in which Tom Paine published his *Rights of Man*, and the year in which the French revolutionary forces declared war on Europe." There follows a brief sketch of developments in art, science, and political philosophy, summing up in a few brusque sentences the works and deeds of the painter Joshua Reynolds and "the young Turner," Thomas Malthus and William Pitt—the key figures of the age. It's not until page nine that Holmes get around to the genealogy ("Shelley's great-grandfather, Timothy Shelley, the third of five sons") that most biographers, bored and boring, hurry through at the beginning.

Holmes had subtitled his biography *The Pursuit*—he was out not only to depict his subject but to *find* him, to conjure up an actual person who had once lived in the world and fix his image, his reality, his essence on the page. Like Ellmann's *Joyce*, Holmes's *Shelley* was an act of virtual resuscitation. Here was the poet rendered animate: falling asleep on the hearth rug in the Oxford rooms of his friend (and future biographer) Thomas Hogg and waking abruptly after a few hours, "rubbing his hair wildly and launching without pause into a rapid and highly involved discussion of some abstruse problem"; waiting anxiously for a chaise on a London street at four a.m. as he prepared to elope with "two girls," Mary Wollstonecraft and Jane Clairmont ("One has the impression that the air round [*sic*] Shelley was heavy with what can only be described as sexual static"); wandering in the Italian Apennines, where he spent long hours "gazing upwards at the changing skyscapes, and the shifting light values in the trees, and the blue-green transformations of the air in the Lima valley."

I was struck by Holmes's capacity to intuit his subject's interior life. When he claimed to know how Shelley *felt* ("He felt his friendship with Hogg was one more example of an intimate emotional relationship that had failed him"), I believed him, though he had violated a fundamental rule of biography: You can't know what your subject felt. But you can get close. Going deeper into his subject through the artful deployment of his materials, the biographer inhabits his subject's life as if he had been there—as if the events he's relating hadn't occurred in the distant past but had just happened. So when Shelley, having relocated from London to the Lake District, goes exploring in his new neighborhood, Holmes writes: "He walked out alone over the cold and beautiful upland pastures, gazing down on the ruffled waters and brooding on mutability." Many books and letters and other documents have been marshaled in support of this scene, but no amount of citation can prove that Shelley was "brooding on mutability"—even if Shelley himself said he was. He could have been brooding on a great many things: Was he having second thoughts about moving to Keswick? Was he worried about ruining his shoes in the wet field? Nevertheless the reader goes along with Holmes's assumption because the biographer has internalized Shelley's unconscious. The evidence isn't empirical, but it's based on a decade of investigation. Holmes had earned my trust.

"Ah, did you once see Shelley plain?" asked Robert Browning. I did. In Holmes's book.

Among Delmore's papers at the Beinecke Library were typed drafts of his late poems, written in the 1950s—late in the tragic chronology of his own life. He was only in his forties then but already in deep trouble. Invited to give the prestigious Christian Gauss lectures at Princeton, he rambled on about the anti-Semitism of T. S. Eliot and was clearly unprepared. He didn't look well; deep pools of fatigue had formed under his eyes.

The unpublished poems were depressing—just as I had remembered them from my first encounter in the Bodleian. Drafts are, in a literal sense, essays: the writer is trying out, in the privacy of his own room, a new subject, a new method, a new voice, a new style. Why not leave him alone to make his mistakes, stumble into false beginnings, get it wrong? These drafts constitute the writer's private lab: they're none of your business. In the end, he got it right: isn't that what matters?

Not to the biographer. For the obsessive diggers drawn to this odd profession, *everything* matters. And that's why every electric bill, every grocery list, every torn envelope must be scrutinized in case it yields the genesis of a poem. And if it doesn't, there is still the aura of the writer's long-vanished presence; you are holding in your hand a document, however pedestrian, once held in your subject's hand. It emanates the reality of that lost moment when it was part of another's life, before it became part of yours. And in that transfer of emotional energy, that current running between subject and biographer, lies the significance of the draft. Its literary errors, lapses in taste, misjudgments, and stumbles offer a clue to what the writer was thinking before he'd even formulated the thought. When all you know is the finished product, it's illuminating to come across its origins: how did those scrawled words become this burnished work of art?

It pained me to read the early, often inchoate versions of Delmore's poems. Encountering a disastrous (and in fairness to the author, often discarded) draft, I felt the mingling of disgust and voyeuristic thrill that a child might feel catching a glimpse of his mother in a girdle as she's getting dressed.

Not that I had any choice. I reminded myself of a pupil sitting beside his teacher as he points out the flaws in a poem—repetitions, flawed diction, grammatical infelicities, the embarrassing catachresis, the botched metaphor, the lapse in taste—that can wreck it. Only in this instance it was Delmore's composition that was under scrutiny, not mine, and I would be the one giving the grade. Being in charge— deciding what to share with the reader and what to suppress—was a big responsibility. It gave you power over your subject. You wanted to show the genesis of his best work, the missteps and wrong turns, but you didn't want to embarrass him.

Manuscripts and journals and letters—the written record—form only a part of the biographer's evidence. There is also the writer's—for lack of a better word—*stuff*. In his account of the death of Shelley's dissolute friend Scrope Davies, Richard Holmes provides an inventory of the objects found in a battered leather chest Davies had left behind, locked, until 1976, when it was discovered in a vault at Barclays Bank: "white kid evening-gloves; a lock of hair from the head of the society beauty Lady Frances Webster; tailor's bills for tennis shoes and red lounge slippers; collections of aphorisms; 20 letters from Byron; and two previously unpublished poems by Shelley." Some of these time-faded items are poignantly valueless, the detritus of a lifetime—"everything that Scrope valued, and much that he did not," as Holmes describes it. Davies fled England in the dead of night, having incurred a gambling debt he could never hope to repay, and ended what must have been, given his circumstances, an excruciatingly long life; he died in 1852, at the age of 69, an exile in Paris, holding court on a bench in the Tuileries. His chest survives as an artifact that brings before us the physical world he inhabited in a state of uncanny preservation—"a sort of miniature Pompeii of the late Regency period."*

Delmore, too, had left behind a time capsule. Housed in the Special Collections Research Center at Syracuse University is a cache of bank statements, canceled checks, old photographs, letters from tradesmen to whom he had owed money,† finds—to continue Holmes's metaphor—as thrilling to the biographer as the sudden glimpse of a shard of clay in the sand must be to an archaeologist. There, at last, is the buried figurine.

When the library closed, I would trudge back to the Mohawk Lodge, where Delmore had once wrecked his room—perhaps the very room where I lay on my bed watching reruns of *The Twilight Zone*. In the Orange Bar, Delmore's hangout on the Syracuse campus, I sat in the corner eating a grinder and mourning the shabby poet in a black raincoat who had sat there a decade before.

On occasion, though, I would come across something that had real value. One of the most fascinating objects in my possession (a gift from Macdonald) was a report card from Delmore's three years at New York University, where he had been a student from 1932 to 1935, salvaged, along with the porn mags, canceled checks and unpaid bills, torn-up letters and other junk, from his last hotel room. I studied it often,

---

* Holmes is eloquent on the talismanic aura of such artifacts: "Anything a hand has touched is for some reason peculiarly charged with personality—Thomas Hardy's simple steel-tipped pens, each carved with a novel's name; Shelley's guitar, presented to Jane Williams; Balzac's blue china coffee-pot, with its spirit-heater, used through the long nights of *Le Père Goriot* and *Les Illusions Perdues*. . . . It is as if the act of repeated touching, especially in the process of daily work or creation, imparts a personal 'virtue' to an inanimate object, gives it a fetichistic power in the anthropological sense, which is peculiarly impervious to the passage of time."

† Why do we save old bills and bank statements, scribbled thank-you notes, and invitations to long-forgotten parties? Is it that to throw them away is to admit the transience of it all?

always finding fresh details to ponder on this single yellow page. For instance, the address:

Mrs. Rose Schwartz
2157 Ocean Avenue
Brooklyn, N.Y.

Ocean Avenue? For a biographer, finding a previously unknown address is as electrifying as it must have been for an astronomer to find an uncharted star in the sky: where there had once been nothing but black inky darkness, a giant blot of uncharted universe, there now came into focus a pinpoint of light that had never been glimpsed before. *Brooklyn.* What was she doing there? I thought she would still have been living in Washington Heights. And so, retracing my chronological steps like a hiker lost in the woods, I had to return to familiar terrain—Eastern Parkway, Ocean Parkway, 179th Street in Washington Heights—in order to figure out where I'd gone off course. I gradually pieced together the story: money was tight with Harry gone, and Rose had been forced to move back to Brooklyn, where the rent was cheaper. Delmore's report card was gold. And this was all before I even got to his grades.

Which were, for the most part, good. He'd received As in all the courses he cared about—History of Philosophy, 17th Century Literature, Aquinas and Dante—and struggled where I would have expected him to struggle. (His D in Algebra comforts me; I barely scraped by myself.) As always, there were enigmas: Why the C in Music? Cs and Ds in Elementary Greek? But he got an A in Metaphysical Analysis. He liked to spin out theories; philosophy entertained him because it challenged the illogic of the world. Music and Greek were too learning-intensive: you had to sit down and memorize. He could do this with poetry—he knew a great deal of it by heart—but not with information presented in unfamiliar signs. The report card was a graph chart of Delmore's mind, a map of the way it was laid out. It gave me pleasure to think about him in this way. The grades anchored speculation to fact.

And yet, examining this document now, four decades after it came into my hands, I feel sad. Like the faded blue uniform of a Union soldier pinned to burlap in a glass case of the New-York Historical Society, it feels lifeless, empty, devoid of the person who once inhabited it and for whom it had been no museum remnant but the very clothes he wore. I remember the excitement that coursed through me when I first held it in my hand and saw the evidence of Delmore's academic rigor, as proud as if he had been my son. All those As! And in such difficult courses, too. The report card is folded and creased; on the back, someone—Rose?—has written in pencil, with a childish script, *Delmore Marks.*

As I recount the pleasures and ordeals of archival research, it occurs to me that I might as well be describing the way a monk dips his feather into a bottle of ink as he copies a medieval manuscript. What reader under the age of fifty will ever know the experience of putting a spool of microfilm tape on a machine with a handle as archaic as the crank of a Model-T Ford, sliding it under a square of magnifying glass, and squinting through a viewer as some ancient issue of *The Nation* or *The New Republic* flashed by until you found the date you were looking for, then inserting a nickel (or was it a dime?) into a slot as if it were a jukebox and waiting for the desired page to unfurl from the tray, the black type smeared on sheets of coated paper? And you didn't just read the article. You could handle the magazine itself, in a bound volume with the year stamped on the spine. Like a jewel set in a bracelet, its brilliance enhanced by the stones that surround it, a book review or literary essay was hedged about by advertisements for books and conferences and luxury goods—the objects that give a historical period its look and feel.

Robert Lowell, in a poem from *Life Studies*, invoked "the tranquilized fifties," the Eisenhower era, the country in a stupor of self-satisfaction and repressed sexuality; in the pages of *The Saturday Review*, where Delmore's film reviews sometimes appeared, you could actually *see* this texture. Beside the text were ads for Buicks and other long-extinct makes of automobile; Westinghouse refrigerators curved at the top beside a red-lipsticked, curl-coiffed woman in a long-sleeved blouse and a calf-length skirt; unfiltered Camels, "prescribed by nine out of ten doctors" for "nerves," with little cartoon devils shooting arrows of anxiety into some jittery midlevel executive in a suit. Looking up an article online—again I fail in my determination not to sound a wistful note about the old days—simply isn't the same as holding in your hand an original copy of *Partisan Review* and losing yourself for hours in the ancillary data that crowd its pages: the masthead, the table of contents, the letters column with its once-fiery debates grown as cold as the fireplace of a summer home after a long winter, its burned-charcoal odor still lingering in the dead air. Old magazines were museums; encountering a famous essay in the course of thumbing through back issues was like coming across an old photograph by Steichen on the wall of a deserted gallery. Here in the very lettering—*Partisan Review*'s square typeface, the squiggly fonts of *The New Yorker*, the gothic curlicues of *The New York Times*—was the city of an earlier time, still visible in the outlines.

I wondered what it must have been like to pick up an issue with one of these world-altering pieces in the table of contents at the local newsstand and read it the way I'd read the latest issue of *Granta* or . . . or . . . there *is* no equivalent.° What for me was a keystone of American literary history had once been contemporary, of the moment, news. *Did you see Clem's piece on Pollock?*—"Clem" being the art critic Clement Greenberg, who had made Jackson Pollock's reputation. Lionel Trilling's "The Meaning of a Literary Idea," Philip Rahv's "American Intellectuals in the Postwar Situation"—these essays defined an era.

A friend familiar with my strange emotional involvement in *Partisan Review* taste gave me a copy of the spring 1949 issue that she had found in her late father's library, and I read it through with avidity. The table of contents is itself a terse museum catalog of the period, announcing an excerpt from *The Adventures of Augie March*, a novel-in-progress by Saul Bellow ("who lives in Paris," according to his contributor's note); a book review by Robert Warshow (a brilliant critic, dead of a heart attack at thirty-seven); a contrarian reevaluation of the British novelist Elizabeth Bowen by Elizabeth Hardwick ("Her sunny reputation invites the cheerful, impressionistic remark; disinclination is rude; the air here is mild, polite, congratulatory"); and a brooding story by Albert Camus, one of the *PR* gang's literary heroes.

° But of course there is: *The Believer, Tin House, Salmagundi,* and *N + 1*—to name only the "print journals," as they're now called, that I read on a regular basis; and yes, I know there now exist online journals—*Slate, Salon, The New Inquiry,* in whose pages (rather, on whose sites) one can still find references to Walter Benjamin and other esoteric icons of the intellectual Old World—as sophisticated, and as influential, as the great "little magazines" of my day, if not more so, given the number of "eyeballs" they claim. I'm not naïve: that I am approaching the end of my time in this world doesn't mean the world is approaching its end. Forgive me for indulging in this common—no, universal—preconception: how many of us have the fortitude to see things as they really are?

There was a subscription card stuck in the pages of the issue:

Partisan Review
1545 Broadway
New York 19, N.Y.

I was tempted to send it in. At $5.00 a year, it would have been a bargain.

Reading Holmes's *Shelley*—"drowning" in it, to borrow Macdonald's aquatic image—I began to understand what motivated me to loiter in front of the townhouse at 8 West 105th Street where Delmore and Gertrude had lived after their Vermont sojourn. It was a freezing afternoon in winter, and I had forgotten gloves. I stood with my hands shoved deep in the pockets of my overcoat (like Delmore on Ellery Street, it occurs to me now), waiting for a revelation that never came. It was an ordinary Manhattan brownstone, and since I didn't know what floor Delmore had lived on, I couldn't imagine him peering woefully out of it, but perhaps that *was* the revelation—that the place contained only the husk of the subject's life, the self it had once contained scattered like the soft white stalks of a dandelion. Eluded again!

Yet one persists: *Delmore lived here.* On another day I took a taxi out to Brooklyn and maintained a solitary vigil in front of the nondescript apartment house on Eastern Parkway where Delmore had been born. I'm studying a photograph I took of it now—it's by no means dreary; pillars frame the doorway, and the ground floor is limestone. But again, it gave off no vibration.[*] My prayers for insight went unanswered.[†]

---

[*] "Pausing on the metal doors of a sidewalk elevator, Moses received the raised pattern of the steel through his thin shoe soles; like Braille. But he did not interpret a message." Saul Bellow, *Herzog.*

[†] I'm struck by one ancillary detail in the photograph that has nothing to do with Delmore but was rather part of my own life, the particular historical epoch in which it was taken: the cars parked in front of the house. They are cars—no surprise—from the 1960s and '70s, and they have the dated look you see in old movies of that era: fins and boxy squarish tops and ornaments on the hood, "makes" now classified as "antique" that gather in the parking lots of upstate Dairy Queens on weekends. The cars in photographs from earlier periods in Delmore's life are of an even older vintage—the black, round-roofed automobiles you see in gangster movies, rented from prop companies or stored in Hollywood back lots. Yet to Delmore they were just cars.

Illusory or not, the confrontation with the actual—the café, the motel room, the country cottage—makes the elusive figure real. Something about the standing desk in the attic of Dr. Johnson's house at Gough Square, where he wrote his dictionary, gives off a distinct emanation of the man that is available from no book. Though only the desk is left, I recall a description in Walter Jackson Bate's biography of the furniture—"a very large deal writing-desk, an old walnut-tree table, and five ragged chairs of four different sets"—that conveys the squalor of the tall, narrow house where Johnson lived with his unruly ménage in "three very dirty rooms."°

Johnson was noticeably unclean himself, according to the painter Ozias Humphrey, who described him in *London Town: Past and Present* as "dressed in a dirty brown coat and waistcoat, with breeches that were brown also (though they had been crimson)" and "a little old shriveled, unpowdered wig." As I gazed out the top-floor window of his house on a visit to London, listening to the roar of buses on fume-heavy Fleet Street—still a metonym for the newspaper industry, though the papers have dispersed—the rhythmic clangor of police sirens vibrating in the grit-thick air, Johnson was both there and not there. Mostly not, so you had to make an effort to recover the part that was.

We take it as a vocational obligation to engage in what Lady Antonia Fraser, the distinguished English biographer of royalty, has described as "optical research," a hike down "the geographical trail." We feel compelled to absorb the physical ambience. Jonathan Bate, Ted Hughes's biographer, rented the poet's childhood house in Aspinall Street, conveniently available as a "holiday let." Robert Skidelsky went him one better and bought John Maynard Keynes's house, which he lived in while he was writing his three-volume biography of Keynes. Norman Sherry, the fanatical biographer of Graham Greene—his triple-decker is both a feat of research and an act of near-madness—followed Greene's shade to Mexico, where he "contracted dysentery in exactly the same mountain village, staying in the same boarding house as [Greene] had done." For Sherry, getting inside Greene's skin is not a metaphor. "I had to experience, as far as possible, what my subject

---

° Oddly, when I look it up online to refresh my memory, a crisp photograph shows the place freshly painted, the baseboards white, the walls a smart lime green, the wide-board floors polished to a high sheen. It must have been renovated, but for whom? Johnson's house was supposed to look the way it had looked in his day: that was the whole point.

experienced.''* It's part of the job. "Traveling to the birthplace of their subjects is something that biographers do," wrote James Breslin in the preface to his biography of Mark Rothko: "Going was a professional duty, to 'soak up the atmosphere,' even across the distance of 80 years." Thus did Breslin journey to Daugavpils, Latvia—where Marcus Rothkovitch was born.

Surely, though, there's a limit to the fetish of proximity. Frederick Karl didn't don a pith helmet and light out for the Congo in search of Joseph Conrad. Dostoyevsky's biographer, Joseph Frank, didn't put himself in front of a firing squad. Sometimes, out on the trail, you could go too far—like the night I got lost in the wilds of rural New Jersey during a snowstorm. I was searching for the ramshackle farmhouse where Delmore and Elizabeth Pollet had lived when he was teaching at Princeton in the 1950s. At twenty-four, I was too young to rent a car and had boarded a Trailways bus, alighted in some town I'd never heard of, and persuaded a taxi driver to take me to a house that turned out not to be Delmore's; I had a photograph of it. Meanwhile it snowed and snowed. I thought I would need a team of huskies to get home. At such moments I was overcome by the inanity of the task I had set myself. Was I really "in pursuit" of Delmore, or was I in flight from him—from the harder work of understanding who he was?

Geoff Dyer, in *Out of Sheer Rage*, his riotous burlesque of the "quest" genre, sets out to write a biography of D. H. Lawrence, only to find that he's not really interested in the project at all. In search of what he calls "the Lawrence experience," Dyer drives from London to the dreary Midlands in a rainstorm (he calls it "the Motorway Experience") and ends up having tea in the White Peacock Café at the D. H. Lawrence Birthplace Museum and Giftshop. "I am behaving exactly like someone who has come to visit the D. H. Lawrence Birthplace Museum. Impossible to pass oneself off as anything else. Why else would I be drinking tea in the White Peacock café?"

For all of Dyer's irony, the subtitle of his book, *In the Shadow of*

---

* Robert Graves describes this process, not entirely approvingly, in his poem about biographers, "To Bring the Dead to Life":

> Limp as he limped,
> Swear by the oaths he swore;
> If he wore black, affect the same;
> If he had gouty fingers
> Be yours gouty too.

D. H. Lawrence, hints at the lonely ardor, at once futile and consuming, of the biographer's quest, the determination—the will—to track down every scrap of paper, visit every place, and interview every living witness, or if there are none, read their memoirs and journals and letters and postcards dashed off from some Greek island, in the hope of catching a glimpse of one's subject, as fleeting as a familiar face spotted and then swallowed up in a crowd, before all testimony has vanished forever and it's too late.

For Richard Holmes, biography was more than the gathering and organizing of facts. "Somehow you had to produce the living effect," he would write in *Footsteps*, his classic—*the* classic—account of what it means to be a biographer. You had, in essence, to live your subjects' lives, "tracking their physical trail through the past." Even so, they would evade us in the way that memory itself evades us, surviving as a blurred shadow of the original event. "You would never catch them," Holmes lamented in his touchingly elegiac way: "No, you would never quite catch them. But maybe, if you were lucky, you might write about the pursuit of that fleeting figure in such a way as to bring it alive in the present." Biography was like "a handshake, across time, but also across cultures, across beliefs, across disciplines, across genders, and across ways of life."

That was one way to see it. I admired Holmes's benignity; he was always reaching out to his subjects like God extending a hand to Adam in Michelangelo's painting. But their fingers didn't touch, and that was how I saw it. I was a biographical pessimist who wrote biography, an apostate who believed.

In my possession is a manila envelope with the return address of *The New Yorker* in that distinctive typeface, when its offices were at 25 West 43rd Street and there were no zip codes. I stare at Delmore's baby picture: generic for its day, it's in black and white and shows the infant Delmore in booties and a biblike pajama top against a milky backdrop, the photographer's name signed with a flourish in the lower right-hand corner. He's smiling at the camera, his tiny hands clenched. It yields nothing, no hint of what is to come. But what baby photograph does? Every Jewish household in America—or is it nondenominational?—contains a pile of these in a drawer: my father's baby picture, once on the glass-topped coffee table in the living room of my grandmother's apartment in Chicago, beside the silver nut bowl and the felt-bottomed coasters and the heavy glass ashtray, sits on our mantel in a pewter frame. The two photos were probably taken only a few months apart.

More disturbing is a photograph of Delmore at Rondax summer camp in the Adirondacks, also generic, sepia-tinted now, the boys on the deck of their cabin in the woods, dressed in kneesocks and lace-up shoes. On the back, in pencil, is the date: *Rondax 1924.* But a corner is torn off, and the photo is cracked and bent, as if someone had crumpled it up in a rage.

The photographs that turned up over the course of my researches form an eerie procession from cradle to grave. Here are Delmore's parents in Brooklyn two years before his birth. They're a handsome couple: Harry Schwartz's strong features and deep-set eyes will soon make their appearance in his son's face, perpetuating the visible existence of his DNA in this world for at least another half century. Rose wears a veil and a pricey fur coat; Harry sports a fedora. I recognize them from "In Dreams Begin Responsibilities"—confident, in love, unafraid of death. They're looking forward, not back.

Three years later the curly-haired son has appeared on the scene, seated on his father's lap in a carnival motorcar with the name *Rock-aways* on the hood. Then he's in Lakewood, New Jersey, with his mother's arm around him and another recent arrival, his younger brother Kenneth: am I imagining it, or does she look troubled now, her mouth turned down, her eyes alarmingly inexpressive? And where is Harry? If not gone, then on the way out. The doomed marriage is over.

We leap to Delmore in 1938, just after the publication of his first book. He is twenty-five, and *Vogue* has photographed him for a feature. What a gorgeous man! He gazes into a mirror, thick hair styled in a wave, and in another, his hand draped limply over a pile of books, at the torsoless head of a classic statue: the poet as Greek god. And here he is, holding hands with his pretty young wife, Gertrude; and at twenty-six, with the writer James Agee, a hunk in a short-sleeved shirt, unlit cigarette in hand, at an outdoor table in summer. You can almost hear the birdsong, the chirr of crickets, the drowsy buzz of bees in the background.

Leafing through my book, I encounter a photograph of the second wife, Elizabeth Pollet, a novelist and, in her day, a fabled blond beauty, crouching beside an equally stunning Irish setter. She looks as if she had leapt from the pages of a ladies' fashion magazine. On the facing page is Delmore in 1949, shirt open at the neck to show off his manly chest hair, but his eyes are haunted, even doomed. He's only thirty-six yet is already launched on his steep downward slide. The poet is urgent, scared, still hopeful that he can fulfill his promise even as he knows—*knows*—that it will never happen. The whole story— devastating, unbearable, too late to alter—is in this photograph.

It must have been about this time, or perhaps a few years later, that he wrote "During December's Death," one of the last poems included in his collection *Summer Knowledge:*

The afternoon turned dark early;
The light suddenly faded;
The dusk was black although, elsewhere, the first star in the cold
    sky suddenly whistled,
And I thought I heard the fresh scraping of the flying steel of boys
    on roller skates
Rollicking over the asphalt in 1926,
And I thought I heard the dusk and silence raided
By a calm voice commanding consciousness:
Wait: wait: wait as if you had always waited
And as if it had always been dark
And as if the world had been from the beginning
A lost and drunken ark in which the only light
Was the dread and white of the terrified animals' eyes.
And then, turning on the light, I took a book
That I might gaze upon another's vision of the abyss of conscious-
    ness—
The hope, and the pain of hope, and the patience of hope, and its
    torment, its astonishment, its endlessness.

The dread and white of the terrified animals' eyes . . . The photo- graph brought me closer than ever to Delmore—to his reality, to the fact that he had once lived. In the poem I heard him; in the photograph I saw him. But in the end, it was only an image. It didn't bring him back.

Philip Rahv

VII

L ike "the heavy bear who goes with me" in Delmore's poem, he was always "breathing at my side." My days were of stupefying length. I rose at dawn, drove Annie to the hospital, and settled down at my desk. By nine o'clock, when my next-door neighbor was pulling out of his driveway and heading off for work, I would have written three or four pages. I did the dishes, called up my editor, dawdled over *The New York Times*. I stood in front of the bamboo cage in which a pair of finches I had gotten to keep me company hopped from perch to perch, and draped bits of string over the bars for them to add to the nest they were building, which grew bigger as the pages of my biography mounted up. On warm days, I took the cage out to the yard— "walking the finches," as Annie called this practice—and removed the balsa-wood floor tray so they could forage in the grass. *Did Leon Edel do this?* I wondered as I sat cross-legged on the damp lawn beside the bamboo cage.

Delmore and I were like two quarrelsome shut-ins—except that his quarrel had been with life, and mine, unrequited, was with him. Why did he publish his awful translation of Rimbaud's *A Season in Hell* without even consulting a French dictionary? He should have known the critics would slam it. Why did he waste so much time on that hopeless epic poem *Genesis*, when he should have been working on his stories? And why did he have to drink so much? *I sacrifice for you*, I berated him. *I try to make a decent character of you, and what do I get? Bad judgment, neurotic behavior, poems that get worse and worse* . . . As Annie and I sat over dinner at the kitchen table in our apartment, my mind would turn involuntarily to this strange figure to whom I had attached myself. *Dude* (as we might address him now), *was it really necessary for you to read aloud the whole of "The*

Love Song of J. Alfred Prufrock" *over the vociferous protests of your high school English class? Did it ever occur to you that it was per-haps unwise to accuse your publisher of cheating you out of royalties when your books had yet to make a dime?* These were the questions I wished to discuss over the Hungarian cherry soup I'd fussed with for hours. (Cooking elaborate dinners had become a way of escaping from my desk.) Annie, meanwhile, could barely keep her eyes open after a thirty-six-hour shift; what to her the tribulations of my crazy subject? She just wanted to go to bed.

When he got too lonely in Cambridge, Delmore would flee to New York. When *I* got too lonely—oppressed by the monotonous chirp of the finches, the meals of gobbled Cheerios, the long days at the library—I followed in his shadow. In Grand Central Station, I headed toward the bank of phones in the waiting room. Delmore had spent most of his life in New York, and by searching through the phone book, I could generally find names I had come across in his papers. "Delmore?" said Joseph Lotterman, his counselor at the Pocono Camp Club in 1923. "He was a good boy and a lot tougher than you'd think." There was no surprise in his voice: it was as if he had been waiting for the call. While I sat in the phone booth, sweating in my winter overcoat, he launched into a long story about a fistfight in which Del-more had decked a camper named Herman Hochberg—unlisted in the Manhattan directory, so I never got his side of it. Nor did I have much luck with Leonard Nudelman, one of Delmore's teachers at P.S. 69. "I'm sick on account I just ate a TV dinner," said a feeble voice that I assumed belonged to Mrs. Nudelman. "Mr. Nudelman ain't here no more." But I did find Julie Solomon, who remembered Delmore's bar mitzvah, and Hannah Ehrlich, whose late husband had been Del-more's mother's dentist.

My archival interest in the period encouraged candor. I seemed objective, scholarly; and besides, how often did people get to talk about themselves? They could blab unfettered by social convention, ignore the annoying requirement of having to listen. My sources confided in me: "I wanted to be a writer then"; "That was when my second wife and I were living on Bedford Street"; "Delmore was going out with a girl I had been in love with when I first came to the Village."

These interviews often lasted for hours. For every anecdote about Delmore, I had to listen to the story of someone's life. The informa-tion yield was low. And every name suggested another, a classmate or a neighbor summoned up out of the inexhaustible procession of the living and the dead. I jotted down new sources: "Have you spoken to Norman Jacobs? He was at NYU with Delmore." "There was a girl named Emily Sweetser who worked in the New Directions office." "What about Arthur Berger? He was a graduate student at Harvard when Delmore studied philosophy there in the 1930s." "He doesn't live anymore," said the poet Louis Simpson when I mentioned a friend of Delmore's—a locution that has haunted me ever since, the present tense canceling out the past.

I usually stayed at the Earle Hotel just off Washington Square. The seedy room with its worn brown carpet, wobbly end table, and stained window shade depressed me, but it was all I could afford; and besides, Delmore used to stay there, so I could osmotically absorb his ghostly presence.°

I interviewed professors of Delmore's, distinguished men like the art critic Meyer Schapiro (portrayed in "The World as a Wedding" as the famously erudite teacher Israel Brown, "who knew about everything in the world"); Upper West Side European émigrés right out of *Mr. Sammler's Planet*, thick-accented and still wary of America, like the widow of Delmore's psychiatrist, Lola Gruenthal; and his frail, ancient aunt Clara Colle, a wisp in a long white dress who lived with her retarded son in a nearly furnitureless apartment adjacent to the George Washington Bridge. But there was also a harder crowd, drinking companions from Delmore's later—and last—days who loitered at the 55 in Sheridan Square, where, a decade after his death, I found dedicated barflies who remembered him and forced me to linger in that smoke-stinging grotto for hours in order to extract a single anecdote.

I visited Seymour Krim in his one-room apartment on East Tenth Street, a cheerless first-floor box crammed with books and papers. Krim was a prominent character on the Village cultural scene—or had been. *Shake It for the World, Smartass,* a collection of his essays from *The Village Voice,* had come out in 1970 and created a mild sensation; he'd gone after Norman Mailer and Norman Podhoretz and other noisy commentators a rung above him on the hipster totem pole. But he was a figure of pathos now, peering at me through Trotsky spectacles with lenses as thick as the bottom of a Coke bottle. Though only

° It's since been renamed the Washington Square Hotel and has a "fitness center" and "Internet access." Hard to imagine Delmore on the treadmill.

in his early fifties, he was already a relic out of another time, the Village of basement jazz clubs like the Blue Note; of "reefer" and "pads" furnished with mattresses where nonmarital sex was practiced; of early Ginsberg chanting his anticapitalist litanies. Krim belonged to history. For me, a twenty-five-year-old from the Ivy League, this history was unimaginably exotic; perched on a metal chair in his smoky room, I took down Krim's testimony.*

Some years later he committed suicide.

There were others, forgotten then, more forgotten now, who had joined Delmore at the 55 or the Lion's Den, drinking away their lives; and various *Luftmenschen* who seemed to have limitless amounts of time to spend with me and were always around in the middle of the afternoon. I remember a man in a well-furnished loft with a skylight, lounging in a Herman Miller chair and smoking a cigarette; he, too, was "a writer"—all of Delmore's friends were "writers," though there was often no evidence that they had written at all—but a writer who clearly had a trust fund. How else could he have afforded to live in such opulent digs? He had often loaned Delmore money. He seemed forlorn. I sat with my notebook open on my lap like a cub reporter at a murder scene. (Only what was the crime, and who had committed it? All I knew was that someone had died.)

Milton Klonsky, the editor of a respected Blake anthology—his name still occasionally turns up in accounts of the period—whiled away hours in a coffee shop on Sixth Avenue patiently explaining to me that I was too young to understand Delmore. And maybe I was. They meant well, these not-so-Ancient Mariners of dissolution, but I was unnerved by the stories they told. One of Delmore's friends gave me a chilling account of running into Delmore at the Minetta Tavern† one afternoon not long after his collection of stories, *The World Is a Wedding*, had been published to great acclaim. He found Delmore alone at the bar,

---

* It turned out to be of more than casual importance: in the 1940s and '50s, Delmore had carried on a serious affair with Krim's first wife, a dancer named Eleanor Goff. And there was more to the story, as I would learn.

† The Minetta Tavern in those days was a dingy Greenwich Village bar with wooden booths and grimy windows—unrecognizable as the restaurant, which still retains its name and location, described in the Zagat Guide, where the hip "restaurateur" (a word unknown in Delmore's day) Keith McNally has "got it goin' on," having created a "sceney" redo of an "old Village favorite" where "'you'll eat like a star' and probably see a few." They won't be the stars in my firmament.

sobbing. Sometime later I came across a passage in his journals: "If I could accept defeat, then I might once more be able to see. If I can be patient: humility is the way and patience is the way—none other. Or will I die broken-hearted, or is this the way to failure, such as most endure who had lofty hopes?" He was thirty-four years old.

L ike a scientist who focuses his microscope and discovers on the slide a whole unseen realm, I found Delmore and his friends becoming known to me in a way I could never know my own contemporaries; I could see their lives from beginning to end, discern in these gray-haired men the boys I had read about in Delmore's stories, loitering in cafeterias, hanging around their parents' living-room parlors, going off to Greenwich Village parties. As they talked, their faces acquired a rapt, distracted look. And when they came out of their reveries, they saw before them, in the guise of Delmore's biographer, their vanished youth. My presence couldn't have been more unsettling if I'd worn a hooded cloak and carried a scythe.

This image isn't entirely fanciful. Even then his contemporaries were beginning to drop off. Not long after I moved back to Cambridge, I learned that Philip Rahv was living there and teaching at Brandeis. At some point in the late 1960s, he had "broken with" William Phillips, the cofounder with Rahv of *Partisan Review*. The origins of their quarrel have long since vanished into—Thomas Carlyle's great phrase— "the extinct cockpit" of old literary feuds; but Rahv, exiled from the red-hot center of New York, couldn't live without the harsh polemical culture of *Partisan Review*, the infighting of book reviews, the solemn symposia, the turf battles over Henry James. He needed his own forum and put together enough money, probably from one of his rich wives, to launch a "little magazine" called *Modern Occasions*.

Rahv had played a significant role in Delmore's narrative.* He was among the first to read "In Dreams Begin Responsibilities" when it came into the offices of *Partisan Review* as its editors were assembling its inaugural issue, and to recognize its genius. When I called

---

* My first encounter with his name clarified a hitherto puzzling reference in a Lowell poem to a boiling summer afternoon when he and his wife, the writer Elizabeth Hardwick, "drank with the Rahvs in Greenwich Village." I had thought the Rahvs were some kind of Arabian tribe.

up and introduced myself as Delmore's biographer—a brazen method of contact that would be unthinkable in the age of e-mail—he invited me over to his apartment in a modern white-brick apartment building on a side street near Radcliffe. A bulky figure in a seedy, somewhat rumpled black suit, Rahv resembled a member of Stalin's secret police, the NKVD. The Russian analogy is deliberate: his eyes were hooded, his features coarse; Delmore called him Philip Slav.°

Rahv was as eager to talk about his new project as to reminisce about Delmore, and after I put away my notebook, he began to fill me in about the magazine's "mandate." He had published only two issues so far, but it was clear that *Partisan Review* was his model. There was the same mix of essays, short stories, poems, and book reviews, and the same familiar names. The most notable was that of Saul Bellow, who had contributed to the first number of *Modern Occasions* a long excerpt from what was described as a work-in-progress called "Zetland: By a Character Witness," which I discovered at the Out of Town newsstand in Harvard Square one steamy summer night. To have landed this piece was something of a coup, and it showed that Rahv still had clout in the literary world.

A few weeks after our meeting, he called me up and asked if I would be interested in helping him find promising new "voices" he could publish in the magazine, writers who had a grasp of "the situation of the intellectual." And that's how I became a "consultant" to *Modern Occasions*.

I could see that Rahv was lonely. I hadn't mastered his complex marital history, but his apartment had the bare furnishings of the newly divorced, and he must have felt marginalized in the intellectual Siberia of Cambridge—Harvard professors, however distinguished, were "academics" rather than intellectuals, a crucial and invidious distinction. In need of company, he took to calling me, with a frequency that I found flattering, to discuss some new essay that had "come in" by a writer he'd never heard of. Did I know the work of . . . and he would mention a byline I might have come across in *The Nation* or *The New Republic,* some young critic trying to break in by tackling tough subjects like Russian Formalism or the Frankfurt School. I couldn't always

---

° He reminded the philosopher William Barrett of "a diamond merchant in Antwerp or a mysterious agent on the Orient Express."

make out the name. Rahv's croaky, Chesterfield-coarsened voice° over the phone sounded as if it were traveling through the transatlantic wire from his childhood village in Byelorussia instead of a few blocks away on Craigie Street.

As an undergraduate at Kenyon, Robert Lowell pitched a tent on Allen Tate's lawn for a whole summer; I pitched mine in Rahv's sparsely furnished living room, transfixed by the reality—the *fact*—of his existence. Yes, the author of *The Sixth Sense*, a collection of essays I had studied as a model of how to write literary criticism, lived and breathed and smoked and talked and, I assumed (he had been married four times), engaged in other activities that were none of my business.

It couldn't have been more than a few months since that first visit that I picked up *The New York Times Book Review* one morning, and there was a photograph of my puffy-faced mentor with his lidded eyes, alongside an obituary by Mary McCarthy. (A former lover of Rahv's, she had famously left him for Edmund Wilson.)

I had known Rahv only briefly and wasn't sure what I felt. Surprise? *He didn't seem sick, or not* that *sick.* Remorse? *I owed him a phone call about a manuscript he wanted to discuss.* Bafflement? *So people really die.* All of these, perhaps, along with an acute sense of loss that was almost physical: I would never again hear that voice, a low growl as if from some wounded animal, grousing about the idiocies of his Brandeis colleagues or recounting his latest feud with the editors of *Partisan Review*.

In *The Truants*, his fascinating memoir of that period,[†] William Barrett described his wonderment at the prominence of McCarthy's piece on Rahv: "But who was Philip Rahv, I imagine an impatient reader asking at this point. And why is he worth remembering at all?" The news

° More than forty years on, I could tell you the brand of cigarette that my intellectual heroes smoked: Clement Greenberg, unfiltered Camels; Harold Rosenberg, Pall Malls; Lowell, the short-lived Trues. It's hard to recall now, as cigarettes are being phased out of American life—some brands no longer exist—and smoking is often seen as a marker of mental illness, that in those days almost everyone smoked.
† The title referred, in Barrett's explanation, to "literary aspirants"—its subtitle was *Adventures Among the Intellectuals*—who "were escaping for a few years into bohemia, playing truant from the ordinary ways of life, hoping to spread their wings and soar for a while." But it also had, as Barrett recognized, a larger meaning: he and his *Partisan Review* compatriots saw themselves as intellectual exiles, determined not to be taken in by the various ideologies that competed for their allegiance. They were playing hooky from history.

of his death made me sad, but the attention paid him gave me hope. These people were worth writing about. They were important to the culture. They mattered.

I fretted about Delmore's obscurity. No one outside the literary world had ever heard of him, and his inadvertently comic name was enough to incite derisive remarks. And how could I explain the nature of my work? When people asked my mother-in-law what I "did," she described me as "unemployed." There was a bizarre moment when Annie and I were planning our wedding in the summer of 1975, and I had to go over the details of our marriage announcement with an editor on the "weddings desk" at *The New York Times:* I had supplied the information that I was writing a book about an American poet, and the editor had quite reasonably inquired as to who that might be. "Um, you wouldn't have heard of him," I dilated; but she finally dragged it out of me. "He's one of my daughter's favorite poets!" she exclaimed. And yet I remained impervious to her efforts to get me to mention Delmore's name—which is how the somewhat mystifying information appeared in our wedding announcement of *The New York Times* for August 3, 1975, that the groom was "at work on a biography."*

I sought reassurance in biographies of—and by—unknown writers. In a secondhand bookshop on Charing Cross Road in London, I came across an old book I knew nothing about: Alexander Gilchrist's biography of William Blake, published in 1863. When Blake died in 1837, he was "a forgotten man," according to Richard Holmes. His now-classic *Songs of Innocence and Experience* had sold fewer than twenty copies. The poet Robert Southey described him as "a man of great, but undoubtedly insane genius."

When Gilchrist signed a contract to write his biography of Blake, he was a twenty-six-year-old freelance critic and the author of a massive biography of the now-forgotten painter William Etty that had earned the admiration of Thomas Carlyle, the most famous biographer of his day—some would say, apart from Boswell, of any day—and gotten

---

* I have since come across another instance of Delmore suppression: the contributor's note to a review that I wrote for *The New York Times Book Review* in 1975, in which I was identified as "a literary critic with a special interest in literary biography." At that point I had been at work on my book for at least a year.

him a contract with Macmillan. Over the next five years, Gilchrist followed Blake's footsteps through Soho and the Lake District, haunted antiquarian bookshops, interviewed his subject's contemporaries, and searched museums for undiscovered manuscripts—the biographer's grail. He even sought out Blake's grave in the cemetery where he was buried, though none of the "five thousand head-stones" in Bunhill Fields bore his name. Undiscouraged, Gilchrist consulted an old register and closely interrogated the "ex-sexton" on the premises until the plot, mistakenly identified as "80," was found to be "a spot somewhere about the middle of that division of the ground lying to the right as you enter." These graveyard pilgrimages are as much a part of the biographer's ritual as the journey to the subject's birthplace—*rites de passage* that mark the literal beginning and the end.*

One might ask why such exhaustive sleuthwork is necessary, what it adds to our understanding of the poet's life and work; but that's how the biographer works. Sooner ask a dog why it chases after a tennis ball. Once embarked on his biographical quest, Gilchrist did what biographers do: he sought the physical remnants of Blake's existence out of a determination to unearth all the evidence he could that his subject had once lived.

I noticed the way he colored in the background of Blake's daily life. Passing the poet's former residence, Fountain Court, on his way to work, the scrupulous biographer stopped to take notes: "Blake's two rooms on the first floor were approached by a wainscoted staircase, with handsome balustrades, such as we find in a house of Queen Anne's date, and lit by a window to the left, looking out on the well-like back yard below." And he gave us a dramatic sense of the period: in one vivid scene, Blake is caught up in a mob headed for Newgate Prison during the No-Popery Riots and forced "to go along in the very front rank, and witness the storm and burning of the fortress-like prison, and release of its three hundred inmates."

Gilchrist's book is a sustained elegy—not only to the poet but to the transience of life. "Alas! for tenure of mortal fame!" he laments of Harriet Mathew, a legendary bluestocking "once known to half the

---

* Forster, in his biography of his great-aunt Marianne Thornton, recounts a similarly futile quest: "I have hunted in the tangled churchyard of Milton for her grave but have failed to find it." It's heartening that Forster, too, went the distance, as eminent as he was: I can imagine him, slight, stooped, bespectacled, his brushy mustache neatly trimmed, picking his way among the tombstones.

Town" who entertained in her grand house at 27, Rathbone Place such luminaries as the memoirist and correspondent Lady Mary Wortley Montagu, much admired by Dr. Johnson (and still read by his acolytes). "As no lettered contemporary has handed down her portrait, she has disappeared from us." Fretting over the loss of some books by a friend of Blake's that were translated into German, he bursts out: "O time! Eater of men and books, what has become of these translations?" They had gone the way of all things.

One of the most moving aspects of this now-forgotten gem is Gilchrist's deep empathy for his subject: his life of Blake is a work of advocacy. To the charge that the poet was just an eccentric who sat nude in his garden with his similarly unarrayed wife, suffered from hallucinations, and wrote unintelligible poetry—in short, that he was "mad"—Gilchrist gave an eloquent reply. Having quoted the approbative words of several friends, among them the poet William Cowper, "that fine-witted, heaven-stricken man,"* he invites the reader to suspend judgment:

> He must go out of himself for a moment, if he would take such eccentricities for what they are worth, and not draw false conclusions. If he or I—close-tethered as we are to the matter-of-fact world—were on a sudden to wander in so bizarre a fashion from the prescriptive proprieties of life, it would be time for our friends to call in a doctor, or apply for a commission *de lunatico*. But Blake lived in a world of Ideas; Ideas were to him more real than the actual external world.

What Gilchrist is asking us to do is exercise what Keats famously called Negative Capability, "that is, when a man is capable of being in uncertainties, mysteries, without any irritable reaching after fact and reason"—to allow for and condone the infinite mystery of human behavior, its refusal to be explained.

Gilchrist's own story turned out to be even darker than his subject's. At the age of thirty-three, having to contend with a sick child and money woes, he came down with scarlet fever and died within a week, a tragedy his wife attributed to his labors on the book: "The brain was tired with stress of work." It was published posthumously, after a great deal of additional labor on her part, and greatly acclaimed.

° *Heaven-stricken*: as fine a compound adjective as Yeats's "gong-tormented sea."

So biography could be fatal. I wasn't willing to go that far, but Gilchrist's book inspired me. I wanted to write a biography that some young writer would come across a hundred years hence in a second-hand bookstore, if such a thing still existed—or at least track down on AbeBooks and have delivered via drone. *Delmore Schwartz: What a strange name. Who was he?*

It wasn't long before I had amassed a modest shelf of books on people who would have been long forgotten had it not been for their exhumation by celebrated writers. In one of his Rambler essays, Dr. Johnson wrote: "I have often thought that there rarely passed a life of which a judicious and faithful narrative would not be possible." Thomas Carlyle's biography of John Sterling, a poet of negligible gifts, dead at thirty-eight, tested this proposition.

It's not a work of diligent scholarship. "Who John's express tutors were, at Passy, I never heard," Carlyle writes with arrogant insouciance; "nor indeed, in his case, was it much worth inquiring." A few facts the biographer deigned to supply. Born of middle-class Irish parents on the Isle of Bute, Sterling was an erratic student, directionless at Cambridge, one of a multitude of youthful London literati during what Carlyle refers to, without explanation, as the Talking Era; his father was a powerful columnist at the *Times*, swanning about the clubs of Pall Mall, and had a bustling house in Knightsbridge. He was, to use Carlyle's faintly denigrating term, "locomotive." The son, too, was ambitious. He cultivated friendships with Wordsworth and Coleridge and wrote a "stiff" autobiographical novel; he knew "religious, witty, and other distinguished ladies, and [was] admiringly known by them." Ruddy-cheeked, "singularly beautiful and attractive," dark blond and nearly six feet tall, he talked in a loud voice as he strode the crowded city streets. He was characterized by "impetuous velocity, all-hoping headlong alacrity, what we must call rashness and impatience"—or in another arresting phrase, "quick feeling." (My first thought, of course, was that he was bipolar.) In his thirties, he began to suffer from what Carlyle called "downbreaks."*

Sterling's life was even more unremittingly dolorous than Del-

---

* I wonder when, between Carlyle's time and our own, these syllables came to be reversed.

more's. (My subject, after all, had some ups along with his downs.) He couldn't get his poems published and had to resort to paying for printed editions—what would now be called self-publishing. Peripatetic to no purpose, he engaged in "swift jerkings" from a plantation in the West Indies to France and Italy and finally to a "pathetic" house in Bristol, piled high with unopened boxes of books. His last years consisted of "poor and ever-interrupted literary labors." He was beset by intolerable tragedies: his mother and his wife died within two hours of each other, the latter, as was common in those days, during childbirth. To top off these misfortunes, he wasn't even a good poet—perhaps the worst misfortune of them all. His work, according to Carlyle, was "crude"—a pitiless verdict that liberal quotations from it confirm.

Nor was Sterling particularly vivid. "His character was not supremely original," writes Carlyle:

> neither was his fate in the world wonderful. What he did was inconsiderable enough; and as to what lay in him to have done, this was but a problem, now beyond possibility of settlement. Why had a Biography been inflicted on this man; why had not No-biography, and the privilege of all the weary, been his lot?

The answer Carlyle offers is that his subject was "a representative man," one whose personal history was, "beyond others, emblematic of that of his Time"—and, it tacitly followed, of all men in all times. Sterling's life was tragic, "as all men's are." To bring him before us in his now-vanished corporeality was the biographer's job.

One of the most touching moments in this curious book is Carlyle's description of an evening spent together in London, at Sterling's Hotel, "some ancient comfortable quaint-looking place in the Strand, near Hungerford Market":

> We took leave under the dim skies; and alas, little as I then dreamt of it, this, so far as I can calculate, must have been the last time I saw him in the world. Softly as a common evening, the last of the evenings had passed away, and no other would come for me forever more.

So far as I can calculate: would it have killed the biographer to nail down this fact? But you could also look at it another way: Sterling was lucky to have as his biographer one of the towering figures of his age, the great defender of biography ("The History of the World is but the Biography of Great Men"), someone who could memorialize him simply because he had passed through the world.

The most curious volume in the small library of biographies about the obscure that I had by now accumulated was *The Quest for Corvo* by A. J. A. Symons, published in 1934. As its title suggests, Symons's book was a life written in the form of a narrative that described how it came to be written—"an experiment in Biography," as Symons himself described it, capitalizing the genre to lend it added gravity—about a character whose eccentricity was so flamboyant that he was said to have "brought amazement, fear, and repulsion" to everyone he met.

A novelist who signed his books Fr. Rolfe to create the impression that he was a priest—his fanciful title was a gift, he maintained, from the "former" Duchess of Cesarini-Sforza—Rolfe had been expelled from a Catholic college in Rome and carried out to the street on his bed; supported himself in a remote Welsh village by painting religious banners; been confined to a workhouse for debt; and composed pornographic letters to a prospective benefactor in medieval script. He once painted a mural consisting of 149 self-portraits shown bearing the corpse of Saint William of Norwich—who was made to resemble the portraitist as well. He was a master of invective.* He ended his life as a gondolier in Venice, floating about in the lagoons in a boat with hand-painted sails said to resemble "the barge of Cleopatra."

Symons was not above inventing scenarios to suit his purposes, but his intention was to create a narrative drama, unveiling his subject by means of sudden discoveries rather than a gradual accretion of detail. Having been introduced to Corvo's work by a mysterious acquaintance who turns over to him an article on the writer that appeared in a London journal and the letters it prompted, Symons initiates that process familiar to every biographer: the keyed-up missives to possible sources of information ("At once I began to write letters in all directions");

---

* To this day, I can quote his threat to make one of his enemies "smart and wince and squirm," and I have written down for possible future use, should I ever need to insult such a person, his description of an offending publisher as "a broad-nosed dough-faced dwarf with thin woolly hair scattered over his big head."

the being-gently-and-sometimes-not-so-gently fended off ("I wish very much that I could help you, but I'm afraid I can't do so"; "I fear I cannot spare much time"; "I know very little of Corvo"); the correspondence pried from unwilling hands ("I left his chambers with the packet of letters burning under my arm"); the confessions made and information suppressed over the course of interviews; the unpublished books and manuscripts discovered; the "pedantic masterpiece" retrieved; the dates nailed down only to be contradicted; the precise sums of money disclosed ("He wrote for fifty pounds, fifty pounds again, then again for more still"); the addresses learned ("Rolfe became an observed figure at Hotel Belle Vue"); the fugitive ancillary characters introduced and forgotten ("Dr. and Mrs. van Someren found his company a continual source of pleasure"); the telegrams dispatched; the doorsteps darkened; and finally, the thrilling payoffs: "My pertinacity was richly rewarded."

As intrigued by the author as by his subject, I was glad to find that there existed a full-length biography of Symons by his brother Julian.° *A. J. A. Symons: His Life and Expectations* turned out to be no less absorbing than *The Quest for Corvo*. It emerged that "Alphonse"—the trio of initials was designed to cover up his easily mocked name—had been a figure of modest renown in the London literary world between the wars. A collector of rare books, a frequenter of clubs, and a flamboyant dandy, Symons was not a "writer" as such—*Corvo* would be his only published book; his great contribution to English culture was the founding of the Food and Wine Society. (He also possessed a large collection of antique music boxes.)

Neurotic, high-strung, and hypersensitive (like Corvo; here was an "overt" match between subject and biographer), Symons possessed, according to his brother, "an angry knowledge of the life that might have been his if all had gone well." His arrogance and deliberately cultivated hauteur masked a crippling vulnerability: "There can be few men—certainly few so little prepared to tolerate adverse criticism—who have been so eager to submit their work to other eyes for approval." Yet when it *was* approved, the praise felt insufficient. (It always does.)

Symons died, at forty-one, of a "vascular abnormality" that led to a

---

° I now find myself in the position of wanting to read a biography of *him*. The image that comes to mind is of Russian nesting dolls, the kind that unscrew to reveal ever-smaller dolls.

hemorrhage of the brain—an exceedingly rare disease that was some-how appropriate to the strangeness of the whole story.[*]

How could such a rarefied, exotic biography have been of interest to me, a person from Illinois who had never entered a London club and couldn't distinguish Bordeaux from Beaujolais? "He wore extravagant shirts and ties and hand-made shoes," observed Julian Symons; the cut of his suits was "extravagantly individual." I bought my shoes at the Harvard Coop and didn't own a suit until I got married. But the struggles Symons endured—the doomed love affairs and marital discontents; the money troubles; the health issues, both physical and mental; the family clashes; the wrestling with self-doubt—were universal. Toward the end of his life, he wrote a friend: "Behold me now, struggling to escape from my own toils, and hasten to help me from myself."

As if one can.

---

[*] I noted Symons's early demise with mild trepidation. Biographers often seemed to die young: was there some corollary?

Alfred Kazin

VIII

I'm so glad you are going to do a biography of Delmore, but I don't envy you some of the interviews you are going to have," Alfred Kazin had warned me in a postcard I kept pinned above my desk. What was he talking about? The chance to interview Schwartz's contemporaries was one of the things that had drawn me to this unlikely project in the first place, and Kazin was at the top of my list. I wanted to be like him—to write essays and reviews and books about literature. I can't remember what waspish, too-often-stung novelist said that no one grows up wanting to be a literary critic, but I actually did. And if Schwartz was "*the* genius, *the* writer of the old Partisan gang," as Kazin had scrawled on his postcard, Kazin was *the* critic.

He had invited me to visit him when I was in New York, and now here I was, in a wooden phone booth° with tin-stamped walls in a drugstore on Columbus Avenue, as nervous and damp-palmed as if I were calling up a date.

"Where are you?" he said. Aggressive, rude, peremptory: over the years I would get used to these traits, but now they still rattled me. I was twenty-five years old. I glanced around the store, a dingy grotto with a wall of girlie magazines, and blurted: "The New York Public Library."

Kazin snorted. "You culture types. All you care about is books." Still, he seemed glad to hear from me and invited me down to his office. Emerging from the subway at Fourteenth Street and Eighth Avenue,

---

° An enclosed box the size of a large coffin with a "landline" affixed to the wall and a slot for coins. You had to fumble for change and "dial" the number. Phone booths were dramatic: you stepped in, closed the accordion-folding doors, fed quarters into the slot—and presto, Clark Kent was Superman.

I was elated; it was like putting down the Goncourt brothers' *Journals* and setting out to interview Sainte-Beuve.

Only was I on the right street? I studied the numbers on the transoms of cheap clothing stores and luncheonettes. Racks of dresses and leather jackets crowded the sidewalk; men in overcoats were hawking gloves and lingerie out of cardboard boxes. Salsa blared from a loudspeaker above a record shop. The address Kazin had given me was next to a Spanish-language auto-driving school. There were no names on the mailboxes in the hall, but the door was open, and I groped my way up the steel-treaded stairs. On the first landing, I heard the faint clack of a typewriter and knocked on the metal door.

The room I stepped into could have been Delmore's last residence. The walls had a dark cafeteria look, and the chicken-wire windows were coated in grime. In the corner stood a tiny porcelain sink. There were books everywhere: on the floor, the couch, the wood-chipped windowsill.

Kazin, in a dark suit and tie, seemed out of place in this office. He was professorial, as if he were about to lecture on the Transcendentalists to a hall of undergraduates. His high cheekbones and pouchy, slitted eyes bore traces of the same exotic Asian ancestry Delmore had boasted of. (He called it "Tartar blood.") "So you're writing about Delmore," Kazin said. "A dear, tormented man. Who else have you seen?"

"You're one of the first, actually. I've wanted to meet you ever since I read *A Walker in the City*."

"Okay, okay." Flattery was a waste of time. He draped a hand over his face and kneaded it like dough. "But who's on your list?"

I mentioned a critic who had known Delmore at Harvard. "A self-promoter," Kazin muttered. "I don't know how he got as far as he did." I mentioned another name, a poet. "He hasn't written anything in years."

Like any smart, competitive family, the New York intellectuals got on each other's nerves. To me, they were published authors—names—and no matter how many issues of *Partisan Review* I read, I could never figure out who had insulted whom at some Greenwich Village party three decades before, whose contemptuous dismissal of whose book had gotten back to the author, whose politics had changed to accommodate what fashion. To Kazin, they were the old *Partisan* gang, as familiar as the kids he'd played stickball with on the streets of Brooklyn.

Kazin was then at work on his memoir *New York Jew* and offered to read me some passages about Delmore. He spread a bulky notebook open on his lap, and suddenly the bristling critic gave way to the rhapsodist of *A Walker in the City*. Reading in a rapid, eager voice, he conjured up Delmore in his youth, "a pillar of agony" with "a stone-white, sweaty brow, knotted with intellectual indignation," his face radiant with "the fine distraction, the obstinate love behind the familiarly Jewish-frantic manner." And when he described their last meeting, Kazin faltered as he told of the tortured poet "accusing, erupting, plotting, demanding, suffering," in his "squalid box of a room."

"Why don't you show me some of your book?" Kazin said when he was finished. "Did you bring any of it with you?"

I had, I admitted, flattered by his interest. Only then did I remember that the chapter I had in my briefcase included a few typical instances of Delmore's malice—and that Kazin was among his victims. "It's not very good," I said, stalling. "I mean, it's just a first draft."

"That's okay," Kazin said affably. "We all have to write first drafts." He held out his hand. Clutching my briefcase, I said, "The thing is that Delmore . . . He's very nervous in this chapter, because he's about to publish *Genesis* and he's worried about the reviews and . . ." He was that way with everyone, I explained (as if this were news to Kazin), and it was even worse when he had a book coming out; and besides, it was just a way of blowing off steam.

"What did he say about me?" Kazin demanded, giving me—as my grandma Rae would have said—"such a look."

I blurted out the offending phrase: Delmore had called him "a serious menace to criticism"—only a few months after Kazin had praised him in *On Native Grounds*, his compendious survey of American literature, as one of the most promising critics of their generation. "How could he say that?" Kazin lamented, rubbing his eyes. "We never quarreled." I could see him brooding over their various encounters in his mind. What forgotten slight could have prompted such a remark? "Believe me, it was nothing personal," I assured him. "You should hear what he said about other people."

"Like what?" Kazin eyed me dubiously. I had arrived on the scene and awakened painful memories, then spoiled his elegiac mood by delivering bad news. Still, he was curious despite himself. "Look, what are you doing for dinner? There's a nice Italian restaurant around the corner."

Sliding into a booth at Il Grand Ticino, a restaurant on Thompson Street once frequented by Delmore, I considered myself lucky; in ancient Greece they murdered the bearers of bad news. Kazin was in a talkative mood; after all, this was his life we were discussing, his social history. Every name evoked memories. Reminiscing about a party in Greenwich Village in the 1930s, he could recite the whole guest list: Max Eastman, V. F. Calverton, Josephine Herbst—

"Who?"

Kazin was stunned. "God, Atlas, where have you been? She was one of the greatest novelists of my generation. How can you pretend to know about the period if you've never heard of Josephine Herbst?"

I stared at the candle dripping down a Chianti bottle.

"You know what I don't get about you?" Kazin studied me intently. "You don't stand up for yourself. I've read your reviews. You say whatever you like in print, you take on this big book, and then you sit here like a schoolboy in the principal's office."

"It's hard," I said. "You bully me." Cowed by his intensity, I was afraid to open my mouth. My way was to creep through the underbrush, as stealthy as a Vietcong, toss a grenade—"Delmore said you were a serious menace to criticism"—then melt away before he could get off a shot.

But Kazin liked to argue; it was a way of working off grievances, improving one's mental circulation. For him, rudeness was to conversation what polemic was to journalism—a style, a genre, an expressive mode.

Kazin paid for dinner—I didn't even know enough at that age to murmur about splitting the check—and we shared a cab uptown; I was meeting a friend at the West End, a Columbia hangout once frequented by Allen Ginsberg and Jack Kerouac. "Thank you very much for dinner," I said as we pulled up to the bar. "I really enjoyed myself."

Kazin shook his head: when would this kid get it? "I like you, Atlas," he said as I slammed the door, "but cut the crap."

The stock market of American literary success can be as unpredictable as Wall Street," William Barrett observed in an appreciation of Delmore that appeared in *Commentary* in the spring of 1974—itself the sign of a modest revival of interest in my subject. By then John Berryman had devoted a sequence of wrenching "Dream Songs" to his "pal" ("I imagine you heard the terrible news, / that Delmore Schwartz is dead, miserably & alone"); and Philip Rahv had reviewed a collection of his essays in *The New York Review of Books,* accompanied by a David Levine drawing of the poet with a tormented look on his face. Given the marginal role of literature in our nation's life, these two prominent *homages* seemed enough to constitute a spike in Delmore's stock.

Barrett's own stock was already high, in my estimate. *Irrational Man,* his book on existentialism, had been a canonical text when I was a teenager, and I hadn't read it only for show. He wrote about ideas in a cosmic, "totalizing" way that seems quaint now but that in the Cold War 1950s had an aura of genuine urgency about it. When he insisted that "the phenomena of mass society and the collectivization of man are facts so decisive for our age that all conflicts among political forms and among leaders take place upon and within this basis," it didn't sound like jargon. Remember, *Irrational Man* was written in "The Age of Anxiety," "The Atomic Age." We could be blown up at any minute.

I had written Barrett after reading his article in *Commentary,* and he had suggested lunch at Il Grand Ticino, apparently the canteen of New York intellectuals.

It was hardly a relaxed meal. As would emerge, Barrett's emotional investment in Delmore was even more intense than Kazin's: for a long period in their lives—all throughout the late 1930s and '40s—he had been Delmore's closest friend. (In the derangement of the poet's last years, when he picked quarrels with everyone he cared about or who cared about him, Barrett hung on almost to the end.) They had met when they were both twenty at the "salon" of Florence Wolfson, the daughter of a wealthy doctor who allowed her to entertain her literary friends in their large apartment on the Upper West Side. Barrett was then a graduate student in philosophy at Columbia, and Delmore was at CCNY.

From the beginning, they were—Saul Bellow's word—"soulmates." They read the same books, nourished the same ambitions, and had the same conception of themselves as intellectuals. To say they were friends doesn't begin to convey the emotional intensity of their connection. And when they had a violent falling-out, Barrett described it as a "break-up," almost as if he were talking about a love affair.

"The ending of a personal relationship is rarely a grand exit in the style of opera," Barrett wrote in *The Truants,* his memoir of those years:

Usually it's a squalid anticlimax disfiguring everything that may have been splendid in the friendship. This one took place under the implacable heat of a New York summer, Dostoevski unspoken but in the air, and madness lurking in ambush. Delmore's self-destructiveness could not help being destructive of me. I remember his eyes, always so expressive, gloating now in self-recrimination for his own evil, as he called it, and sucking me into it with him. I couldn't take it any more, and walked out. And so walked away from a relationship that had been a good part of my life.

And now here I was, a total stranger, right in the middle of it.

I was never prepared for the way Delmore's friends would pour their hearts out to me. One of the stranger aspects of writing a biography is the candor it elicits. You become a confidant of your subject's friends and enemies and lovers; they have no compunction about confiding to you the most personal matters without knowing the least thing about who you are. I couldn't understand why my interviewees were so unguarded. Why were they willing to make these profligate confessions? The answer, I think, is that I was their one remaining bond to our mutual obsession, a medium—in the literal sense—through whom they could reach their friends or parents or lovers beyond the grave.

Stuffing his pipe and ordering more wine, Barrett dwelled with brilliant, obsessive concentration on the smallest details of Delmore's life: what he read in the bathroom (Boileau); what he wrote in the margins of his books; what he said to Paul Goodman in 1934 and I. A. Richards in 1937. Wine-dazed in the restaurant gloom, I listened with flagging attention. There was much relevant lore in these monologues, but also much else—meandering anecdotes about how Barrett and his friend Apostle, a young Greek translator, would sit around in their underwear on hot summer afternoons poring over Aristotle's *Metaphysics* in the original; recitals of the menu at the Foltis-Fischer cafeteria; detailed descriptions of Jackson Pollock's rudeness to bartenders at the Cedar Tavern.

I could have slid out of the booth and stolen off through the empty restaurant: Barrett wouldn't have noticed. His mind was on the past. In the dim restaurant, the little shaded lamp in the booth giving off a reddish glow, he reminisced with a doleful, droning ardor. When Joyce died, Delmore had summoned Barrett up to Cambridge "to keen for their dead brother"; when Delmore got married, he had invited Barrett to join the newlyweds on their honeymoon; when Delmore got back to New York, he had expected Barrett to show up for dinner every night; in the 1950s, Delmore's psychiatrist had requested an interview with Barrett, and Delmore had paid for their session. Even a decade after his death, he still had Barrett powerfully in his grip.

Lunch was long over. The waiters had stripped the tables and were setting places for dinner. But now I had a new question: if their friendship had been so special, why had Delmore and Barrett not been able to patch things up after their final, galvanic argument? What was the "squalid anticlimax" mentioned in his *Commentary* piece? I had heard enough about their splendid youth: what happened later?

"It was nothing important," Barrett murmured, pulling on his pipe. This was his closest friend we were talking about, and here he was, sitting across from Delmore's biographer instead of dear Delmore himself, so promising, so beautiful, so once *alive,* who had died and was never coming back.

"Why are you so obsessed with him?" I asked.

Barrett gave me a bewildered look. "I don't know." He peered at me as if he were trying to remember who I was. Delmore was dead: that was the message I had unwittingly delivered. I was like that Stoic philosopher invoked in Barrett's memoir who berates the father of a dead child, demanding, "Why do you weep? It is irrational. Your weeping will not bring him back." "That is why I weep," the father answers. "Because it cannot bring him back."

Robert Lowell and the novelist Jean Stafford, who was then his wife, had spent a few months at Delmore's apartment on Ellery Street, but I gathered from a note in Delmore's journal that things had ended badly; there had been a falling-out.

I dreaded interviewing Lowell. I wasn't sure how much I wanted to know about this period, which I suspected wouldn't reflect well on either of them; also, I worried that it might seem both intrusive and somehow oddly formal to show up with my tape recorder. But I didn't really have any excuse for avoiding him. He was living in Brookline with his third wife, the novelist and Guinness heiress Lady Caroline Blackwood, and their two-year-old son, Sheridan. When I finally worked up the nerve to call him, he was friendly. We made a date for the following week.

I was nervous as I drove through the leafy suburban streets looking for the house: I had been in his poetry seminar at Harvard, but would he remember me? Would it matter if he did? The subject was Delmore.

He came to the door, a stooped figure in bedroom slippers, and led me into the kitchen, where Lady Caroline sat peeling vegetables, a cigarette in a tin ashtray by her side. In her riding boots and denim shirt open at the neck, her coppery hair fanning down her back, she was both slovenly and beautiful, very much the mermaid with *"bel occhi grandi"* celebrated in Lowell's Dolphin poems.

"This is Mr. Atlas," he said in his tentative drawl, "and this is Sheridan." It was a dark winter's day, and there were no lights on in the house. I could scarcely see the small boy who stood in the doorway until Lowell reached down and picked him up. "Say hello, Sheridan," Lowell prompted, but Sheridan eyed me silently. He was named after the general—another instance of Lowell's obsession with the Civil War.

The house had an unoccupied feel to it. The rooms on the first floor were empty, and I soon realized why Lowell had chosen his upstairs bedroom for our interview: it had a chair. I pulled it up to the bed, where he sprawled out amid books and manuscripts, and opened my notebook like a doctor taking a history.

It was an ordeal to remember Delmore. "He was grieved about Eliot, thought him anti-Semitic but wanted his approval." "He persuaded us to boycott a faculty picnic at Kenyon because our wives hadn't been invited, saying it was homosexual to go without them." "He showed up drunk at a party in New York, was abusive to Hannah Arendt, and flaunted his ripped trousers."

Lowell smoked morosely. Hadn't there been some disastrous argument in Cambridge? I asked. He stared out the curtainless window. "I sat on his overcoat on the train up to Bangor, and he made a lot of mad accusations, complained I'd treated Jean badly." Lowell fixed me with a melancholy eye. "People say Delmore slept with Jean," he murmured. "Someone said he could tell by the way he lit her cigarette."

I closed my notebook.

"Have you seen Jean yet?" Lowell said as I was putting on my coat.

I hadn't, but the following summer I called on her in East Hampton, where she lived in a weathered old clapboard house with a view through the pines to Long Island Sound. A hand-lettered sign on the screen door warned, "Use of the word 'hopefully' not permitted on these premises." She was then nearly sixty (not so old from my current over-sixty vantage), but she seemed like the girl Lowell must have had in mind when he spoke of "Jean"—the girl he married when they were both still under thirty. She had a co-ed's bony shoulders and skinny waist, wore her straw-covered hair in a pageboy, and padded around in a red pullover and saddle shoes. Only the wrinkled skin around her eyes and her blue-veined hands betrayed her age. "I was just making some eggnog," she said in a raspy voice. "That way I don't have to eat."

She led me into the parlor, a comfortable, old-fashioned room with oval throw rugs and a fireplace, and curled up in a wing chair. I opened my notebook and glanced over my questions: When did she meet Delmore? What was he working on then? How did she and Lowell end up on Ellery Street?

But she had questions of her own. Had I seen Cal° yet? Had I met his new wife? How did he seem? Was he happy? On our third eggnog, I finally brought the conversation around, feeling as rude as if I were talking about myself. "Didn't Lowell and Delmore have a quarrel?"

"They sure did." She peered at me over the glass cupped in her hands. "I shouldn't tell you this, but if I do—" She lit a cigarette. "It's yours."

I said nothing. "Cal was a terrible anti-Semite. He once told me he could never have a close friend who was a Jew."

She waited for that revelation to sink in, studying its effect with a clinical eye. "We all had dinner at the Lowells' one night—and Cal kept going on about this ancient relative of his who was Jewish, and how that made Cal himself one-eighth Jewish, until Delmore was just livid. When we got back to Ellery Street that night, they slugged it out, and we left the next morning for Maine."

She regarded me with satisfaction. I knew a little bit about her unhappy marriage to Lowell—though it wasn't until I read Ian Hamilton's biography that I learned he had left her for Delmore's estranged wife, Gertrude Buckman—and I could see that she was glad to even

---

° "Cal," short for the ruthless Roman emperor Caligula, was Lowell's nickname, bestowed on him at the upper-crust private school St. Mark's by his classmates, who noticed his own ruthlessness—his willingness, in the words of one, "to take on everybody."

the score. I was an emissary shuttling between old flames, a conductor of the passions that still flowed between them.

It was dusk when I got up to leave. Jean followed me into the kitchen and kissed me on the cheek as I stood by the screen door. I left her opening a can of Chef Boyardee ravioli.

In Los Angeles to consult an archive of Delmore's papers at UCLA, I made an appointment to see Maurice Zolotow, a friend of Delmore's from his University of Wisconsin days who had written biographies of John Wayne and Marilyn Monroe.

He lived in a stucco apartment building on the fringes of Hollywood. "So you're writing a book about Delmore," he said in a gravelly smoker's voice. He pushed aside a pile of magazines to make room for me on the couch. "What a wonderful idea. I wrote a book about him myself, a novel called *O Careless Love*."° Zolotow's fluffy gray hair stood out on his head. "God, I hardly know where to begin," he said wearily, leaning back in his chair and closing his eyes. "I knew him for so many years."

They had met at the University of Wisconsin in 1931, when a drunken Zolotow was reciting Hart Crane's "The Wine Menagerie" and Delmore knocked on the door in his pajamas: "He knew the poem by heart." He looked at me with the wistful eyes I would come to see so often in my interviews: *How long ago that was. And now I'm old and he is dead.* "We used to go to a speakeasy called Paratore's," he said. "The Paratores were lovely people; Papa Paratore looked a little like Vanzetti. He'd been an anarchist in Naples during his youth." He lit a cigarette, thinking. "They had a daughter at the university. What was her name?" Zolotow tried to remember the name of the daughter of the owner of the speakeasy he and Delmore had frequented in 1931. I waited. "Angelica!"

He could recall which magazines Delmore had read at seventeen (*transition* and *Hound & Horn*); the make of the car Delmore's father had bought him in Chicago (a white Packard); Delmore's professors in 1933 (James Burnham, Philip Wheelwright). Below his window, the rush-hour traffic swished past, and the sky grew purple through the

---

° When I got back to Cambridge, I checked it out of the library—the first person ever to do so. The Delmore character was named Algernon Stein, "a noisy and lecherous and brilliant fake."

sliding-glass doors, but Zolotow was in Madison forty-five years before, exulting in the time he had been arrested for singing "The Internationale" and Delmore had bailed him out.

The later years were a different story. The farmhouse where Delmore had lived in New Jersey was littered with empty gin bottles; there were no chairs to sit on, just packing crates. A psychiatrist at Bellevue told Zolotow that Delmore's "brain was rotting" from alcohol and amphetamines. He ground out his cigarette in a seashell and lit another. "The waste of it," he said. "His last years were crazy, demonic, right out of Dostoyevsky." More troubling memories emerged: Delmore boasting about how much money his father made; belittling "Hollywood journalism"; storming off in a rage at some imagined slight. "He was self-absorbed," Zolotow said. "He took, but he never gave." Zolotow had testified at his divorce trial; Zolotow had visited him in Bellevue; Zolotow had lent him money. "And for what? That he should tell me I was a sellout?" He buried his head in his hands, wrestling with the two Delmores, then looked up, as if startled by a new insight. "Delmore was a bad person."

Sometimes as I went about my work, I thought about what it would be like to be on the other side—to have someone writing *your* biography. So you're the one who told a precocious writer friend how much you loved his debut novel even as you were putting it down all over campus? Who gave a collection of poems by his own creative writing teacher a bad review in *Poetry*? Such a person—someone I thought I knew—would be unrecognizable to me. Except it *was* me. So was the person who, unwitnessed by anyone, pressed a dollar into the hand of a beggar in the subway; chose not to share a piece of good news with a friend going through a hard time; consoled a bartender grieving for his dead son, killed in Vietnam, in the club car of a train out of Boston late one night. Being the subject of a biography would be like looking at yourself in a funhouse mirror, now stumpy as a dwarf, now elongated like a ghost, now quivering with fat, now thin as a Giacometti. And these revelations of character are innocent compared to the things you've done that no one knows about or ever will, betrayals and lies buried so deep they can never be exhumed, along with acts of goodness so instinctual, so embedded in your nature, that you're not even aware of them. Zolotow's contention that Delmore was "a bad person" didn't feel fair to me. He *was* a bad person—a bad person who was also a good person. Like everyone.

Saul Bellow

IX

In the winter of 1974, I came across an issue of *Playboy* with an excerpt from Saul Bellow's new novel and discovered that it was about a character named Von Humboldt Fleisher, a "grand, erratic, handsome" poet whose first book had made him famous in the 1930s, a "Mozart of conversation" who went insane and "died in a flophouse near Times Square." Not even the Playmate of the Month could distract my eye from the specifics: the three a.m. heart attack in the corridor of a seedy hotel, the triumph of Humboldt's first book. "Nineteen thirty-eight was his big year," I read. Conrad Aiken and T. S. Eliot praised him; the book got fabulous reviews. "Humboldt was made." It was widely known that Bellow based his characters on real-life models. People would be curious: who was this Humboldt?

I dashed off a letter to Bellow requesting an interview and got back a cordial reply: he would be glad to tell me what he knew about Delmore. He also confirmed a surmise of mine: "You're right, that was Isaac in the M.O. piece."

"Isaac" was Isaac Rosenfeld, and "M.O." was *Modern Occasions*, where I had come across "Zetland: A Character Witness" two years earlier. Written in the form of a biographical portrait, it told the story of a Jewish intellectual growing up in Chicago. Bellow described him as "a junior Immanuel Kant" familiar with the whole of Western literature and thought, from Hume to Nietzsche, Heinrich Heine to the Surrealists, Russian novels to Yiddish poets. He played the violin, could explain Lenin's concept of "democratic centralism," and had Plato down cold. "He was a clever kid," wrote the unnamed narrator: "His bookishness pleased everyone."

Bellow's fiction was highly autobiographical, as he himself acknowledged: Augie March was Bellow, Moses Herzog was Bellow, Dr. Sammler was Bellow. Each had his own characteristic traits but also traits one could readily identify as Bellovian: a hunger for books combined with an irrepressible need to display their erudition; a penchant for metaphysics; and a profound grasp of what it meant to be Jewish. But his other characters were closely based on people in his life.° Just as Humboldt was Delmore, so Zetland was Rosenfeld, Bellow's closest friend at Tuley High School in Chicago—a tragic figure who had never fulfilled his great promise and died of a heart attack in a rented room on the city's North Side at the age of thirty-eight.

How did I know this? I had been obsessed with Isaac Rosenfeld ever since I was a teenager. My best friend, Josh, a slight, moody boy with jet-black curls and sensuous, mournful eyes that made him attractive to girls, had pressed on me a worn paperback copy of *Passage from Home*, Rosenfeld's one published novel. It was about "someone like us," he told me. The bookshelf in my Evanston bedroom contained the high school canon: *Howl, The Naked and the Dead, Tropic of Cancer, On the Road, Naked Lunch, The Beat Generation, No Exit, Waiting for Godot, The Duino Elegies*. But no one had written about the specific, actual life I led: its geography, its cast of Russian-Jewish grandparents, its histrionic family dramas. I took the book home and read it overnight.

It wasn't an eventful story: Bernard Miller, a book-besotted boy, "sensitive as a burn," growing up in an emotionally stifling household on the North Side of Chicago with his father and stepmother, runs away from home and goes off to live with his progressive, free-thinking aunt and her unemployed hillbilly lover. A few weeks later, put off by their sordid bohemian ménage, Bernard returns home to a tentative reconciliation with his father.

What made the novel resonate so deeply with me was its depiction of adolescent vulnerability and excess of feeling. Trapped in his parents' unhappy marriage, afflicted with longings he finds it hard to

---

° To claim that Bellow's characters had real-life models doesn't begin to suggest their proximity. Even Martin Amis, one of his most passionate defenders, acknowledges the claims against his mentor: "When we say that this or that character is 'based on' or 'inspired by' this or that real-life original, we indulge in evasion. The characters are their originals, as we see from the family *froideurs*, the threatened lawsuits, the scandalized friends, and the embittered ex-wives."

articulate, Bernard at fourteen has a precocious sense of "the universal sadness of life." He suffers from "a certain homelessness in the world." He's Jewish without knowing what it means. To read a book that so closely mirrored my own "predicament"—one of Rosenfeld's favorite words—was a revelation.

Josh's preoccupation with the book was more than literary, it turned out. His mother, Freda, had dated Rosenfeld when they were high school students at Tuley; they had necked in Humboldt Park. And toward the end of his life, when Rosenfeld was living in his last apartment, they had taken up again; Josh had a blurred memory of Rosenfeld, puffy-faced, pasty-complexioned, overweight, in a car with Freda, driving his brother to summer camp.

Sitting in the kitchen of their Evanston bungalow, cigarette and drink in hand, Freda seemed worn-out but exotic. As I look back now, I realize that she was only in her forties then, but to me at that age she seemed old. It was hard to imagine, as it always is, that she'd ever been a girl at all. She talked obsessively about "Isaac"—her use of Rosenfeld's first name struck me as improperly familiar. This was a writer who had published books. To Josh's mother, he was a dead boyfriend.

Once she found out that I knew who Saul Bellow was, Freda latched onto me; whenever I came to the house after school, she would motion me to sit down in the kitchen and told me "Isaac stories." Bellow was writing something about Isaac, she said. He had come to visit her— Saul Bellow, dapper in a three-piece suit and fedora.

As if these memories weren't sufficient proof that Rosenfeld was the model for Zetland, I had the evidence of a foreword Bellow had written to a collection of Rosenfeld's posthumous essays and reviews entitled *An Age of Enormity*. "Isaac had a round face and yellowish-brown hair which he combed straight back," Bellow's foreword began. "He was near-sighted, his eyes pale blue, and he wore round glasses." With a few strokes, he evoked his subject, "gesturing like a Russian-Jewish intellectual, a cigarette between two fingers"; playing the clown ("He imitated steam irons, clocks, airplanes, tugboats, big-game hunters, Russian commissars, Village poets and their girlfriends"); dwelling in Hogarthian squalor on West 76th Street during his New York years, "cockroaches springing from the toaster with the slices of bread." The piece closed on an elegiac note stunning in its simplicity: "During the last years of his life he was solitary, and on Walton Place* in one of his furnished rooms, he died alone."

Now Bellow was writing about Rosenfeld and Delmore at the same time. My touchstones. My icons. My obsessions. It couldn't have been chance that had brought us all together.

Emboldened by the welcoming tone of Bellow's letter, I called up to make an appointment. Miraculously, I was put through by the switchboard of the University of Chicago just by uttering the man's name. His secretary urged me not to come out to Chicago as Bellow was very busy, but it was too late; my bags were packed.[†]

Bellow found time for me when I phoned again from O'Hare, and I took a cab over to his office in one of those stony neo-Gothic buildings on the University of Chicago campus. His secretary showed me into a linoleum-floored room with a metal desk and a filing cabinet. A coat rack stood in the corner, bare except for a herringbone fedora— Bellow's hat.

I pretended to study my notes, glancing up whenever I heard footsteps in the hall. At last he came in, a small man with sad, liquid eyes and a head of silky white hair. I had read somewhere that Bellow was an elegant dresser, and I wasn't disappointed; his raincoat had a Burberry look, and his gray-plaid three-piece suit gave off a high-thread-count sheen. He sank down into a chair by the window, shielding his

---

* Actually, it was on East Huron Street, according to Rosenfeld's biographer, Stephen Zipperstein. "Isaac Rosenfeld did not die in the room described by Bellow," Zipperstein reports without censure. "Nor did he die on Walton Place [where Bellow had last visited him]. His new, airy, two-room apartment . . . was on Huron," and he had just bought himself "a sporty car." He had "nice clothes," he had written Freda. "I have lots of friends." I cite this instance of wrongness not as an excuse to bang on about the uncertainty of fact but to show how the *shading* of fact can have a significant effect on the coloration of a whole life. For me, with my attachment to the narrative of squalor in Rosenfeld's last days (and hence of the self-sacrifice required to be a writer), Bellow's "furnished room" is preferable to the "sporty car" version (a red convertible yet). Just the facts, please: the facts that suit us.

† "People doing articles, academic theses, wrote to me or flew in to discuss Humboldt with me," recalls Charlie Citrine, the wiseguy narrator of *Humboldt's Gift*, pluralizing the singular biographer in his sardonic fashion.

brow from the overhead light as if he had a migraine. No small talk here. I opened my notebook and began.

"I gather you're writing a novel about Delmore."

He raised his hand from his forehead like a visor. "Where did you get that idea?"

"Well, that story in *Playboy* . . ."

"It's not about Delmore," he said, a resentful note in his voice. "It's a composite portrait of a few poets I knew: Berryman, Jarrell, Delmore. I'm writing a novel, not a biography." He leaned back in his chair, waiting for the next question as if it were a dentist's drill.

I retreated to safer territory. When had he first met Delmore? "I met him in Greenwich Village. That's where the cultural action was in those days, and Delmore was the man to know. But it was when we were teaching at Princeton that we really got to be friends." Bellow launched into a complicated tale about Delmore's efforts to land a job there in the 1950s, his tireless maneuvering in the English department, his elaborate scheme for getting the Ford Foundation to underwrite a chair in poetry.

"But then he went nuts," Bellow said in his Augie March idiom. He threatened the art critic Hilton Kramer, who happened to be living next door to him at the Chelsea, claiming that Kramer was having an affair with Delmore's wife, and ended up at Bellevue. Bellow collected money for his treatment, but Delmore used it to hire a private eye, who tailed Bellow and made his life hell. "This Stanzioni was making a good profit off Delmore. All the money I raised ended up in his pocket." Stanzioni: another name to look up in the Manhattan phone book.

Bellow looked pale in the weak winter sunlight streaming through the window. Delmore had tormented his friends with recriminations during his terrible last years and bequeathed them a legacy of unresolved emotions. The lawsuits and private eyes and phone calls in the middle of the night had taken a toll.

"What a maniac," I commented, eager to show where my sympathies lay. Bellow nodded. He was tired of Delmore and his biographer. But I had a message to deliver. "My mother was very grateful for your note to Evelyn Stone," I said. Evelyn, my mother's closest friend, was dying of Alzheimer's. Bellow, who'd had a crush on her when they were both at Northwestern, had written her a note. "She wanted me to tell you how

much it meant to Evelyn."* Bellow eyed me warily. "She was a beautiful girl," he remembered. I waited for more, but he just stared out the
window, and I was overcome with that empty feeling one gets when the
houselights go up at the end of a movie. The interview was over.

Back home, I wrote Bellow to clear up a minor point. He had read
In Dreams Begin Responsibilities at the University of Wisconsin, where
Charlie Citrine had read Humboldt's *Harlequin Ballads;* he had gone
to New York on a Greyhound bus, just like Citrine. From this I could
deduce that Bellow had written Delmore a fan letter, right? Citrine
had written Humboldt a fan letter. Wrong. I was confusing fact with
fiction, Bellow tersely replied. He wrote no such letter.

Confusing fact with fiction . . . the Biographical Fallacy.

W hen Bellow's novel began to circulate in galleys, I managed to
wheedle a copy out of his publisher. From the first sentence—
"The book of ballads published by Von Humboldt Fleisher in the
Thirties was an immediate hit"—to the last scene in a cemetery in
"Deathsville, New Jersey," Delmore's whole story was there, told
through artful flashbacks and twists and turns of the plot.

There was another plot, too, about the narrator's own frenetic life—
women troubles, literary fame, aggravation from an Italian gangster
who seemed to have been imported from some other novel (not necessarily by Bellow). To say that Humboldt was Delmore doesn't begin
to convey Bellow's uncanny act of biographical—and yet fictional—
re-creation. I was stunned as I hurried through the fat yellow galley and encountered the very episodes that Bellow had recounted in
our interview: Humboldt drinking gin out of a jar in the ramshackle
New Jersey farmhouse he rented in the 1950s; hiring a seedy private
eye—now named Scaccia—to follow Citrine around; making trouble at
Princeton; being hauled off to Bellevue in a paddy wagon. And finally
the tragic end in a "decayed" Times Square hotel. On his last night on
earth, around three in the morning—"he wasn't sleeping much toward
the end"—Humboldt decided to take his garbage down and suffered a
heart attack in the elevator: this was just how it had happened.

° Evelyn had often noticed Bellow staring at her on the El, the elevated train he rode
to campus from Chicago when he lived at home on the South Side. "She didn't think
he was so cute," my mother recalled.

Bellow's ability to capture the speech rhythms of his characters was phenomenal. Humboldt's manic soliloquys spill over from page to page, arias° of angst, rants about the deleterious effects of capitalism on poetry, erudite commentaries on philosophy and popular culture, free associative reflections on the whole of Western literature, "cadenzas"—in Delmore's vernacular—on "Poetry, Beauty, Love, Waste Land, Alienation, Politics, History, the Unconscious. And of course, Manic and Depressive, always capitalized."[†]

There were moments when I wearied of Bellow's prose; it felt glib, and it obscured the tragedy of Delmore's story. "I thought about Humboldt with more seriousness and sorrow than may be apparent in this account," says Charlie Citrine, apologizing for his comedic soliloquys at the expense of his old friend. If you thought about him with seriousness and sorrow, why not put some of that in?

I was alarmed when I encountered a passage about young scholars "fabricating cultural rainbow textiles" out of the 1940s. "Young people, what do you aim to do with the facts about Humboldt," asks Charlie Citrine. "Publish articles and further your careers?" It was a relief when he moved on to a rumination about Humboldt. A satirical aside was one thing; a whole portrait I didn't need. Still, as Citrine remarks of his old friend, for whom malice was a literary exercise, a verbal limbering up: "To be loused up by Humboldt was really a kind of privilege. It was like being the subject of a two-nosed portrait by Picasso, or an eviscerated chicken by Soutine." The same could be said of Bellow. If I was going to be made fun of, at least it should be done by a pro.

It was strange to see the figure I'd been living with night and day for two years brought to life by a—the—master of the English language. I felt like an apprentice in Giotto's *scuola*, watching as he applied chiaroscuro to some gaunt-faced prince. What incredible luck! The great novelist lighting the way: this would put Delmore on the map.

° Bellow had a fondness for this word and would use it as the title for the section of comic anonymous soliloquys (most by Bellow himself) at the front of *The Noble Savage,* the short-lived but valiant literary journal he edited in the 1960s.
† I loaned the galley to Bernard Malamud, a friend of Annie's family, and he called back at eight o'clock the next morning, his voice sounding rueful: "Saul has three words for every one of mine." As I stood in my underwear clutching the phone and looking blurrily out the window—I hadn't even had time to put on my glasses—I felt a great sense of privilege in hearing one of America's greatest novelists compare his prose style to that of a rival. This kind of stuff had never happened in my college course on The Post-War Jewish Novel.

Which it did. When *Humboldt's Gift* was published in the summer of 1975, the critic Richard Gilman, in a front-page review in *The New York Times Book Review*, pointed out the figure of Delmore lurking within Bellow's portrait of the tormented genius Von Humboldt Fleisher; in the daily *Times* review, Anatole Broyard, a friend of Delmore's from his Village days, declared the protagonist to be "too plainly modeled after the late Delmore Schwartz not to be acknowledged." *The New York Times Magazine* published an article by the poet Louis Simpson titled "The Ghost of Delmore Schwartz," about the Delmore/ Von Humboldt connection. And there was my subject's photograph in *Newsweek*, which featured Bellow on its cover.

I wished I had listened to that lady on the *Times*'s weddings desk.

X

No species of writing seems more worthy of cultivation," wrote Dr. Johnson, who liked "the biographical part" of literature the most: "I esteem biography, as giving us what comes near to ourselves, what we can use."

By now I'd come to share this view. I had on my shelf three or four of those compact Loeb Classical Library Classics with pallid green covers that I enjoyed in part for their brevity: the lefthand pages were in Latin or Greek, so the books were half as long as they seemed. They had a forbidding academic look about them, but they were fun to read and I learned a lot. That Socrates had been sentenced to death by drinking hemlock did not come as news to me, nor that he was "formidable in public speaking." But I hadn't known until I read Diogenes' biography that he also had a reputation as a courageous soldier who saved Xenophon's life when he fell off his horse in the midst of a battle. And I loved Plutarch's *Lives*, written ca. A.D. 100. They were so vivid, so real, that I might as well have been reading about Cambridge or New York ca. A.D. 1975. Plutarch had it on good authority that Caesar was "effeminate in his dress and would walk through the market place trailing his long purple robes." He actually had a comb-over, just like Louis Calhern in the movie: "He regretted most bitterly the loss of his looks through baldness and was often the butt of jokes on the subject by his detractors. For this reason he was in the habit of combing his thinning hair upwards from its crown." (It explained, too, the omnipresent laurel wreath.) Then there was the Greek soldier Lamachus, who was so poor that "whenever he sent in his accounts for a campaign, he was in the habit of claiming expenses for his clothes and shoes."

I envied Plutarch his insouciance toward the "facts." In his world, hearsay was considered evidence. The Cimmerians, he wrote, "lived at the end of the world by the outer ocean in a land of shade and forests

Plutarch

so thick that the sun is never visible because of the size and thickness of the trees which extend inland as far as the Hercynii"—a range of mountains whose whereabouts were unknown. For Plutarch, a sufficient citation was "They say." In his life of Marcellus, he reported that "an ox had uttered human speech, and a boy had been born with an elephant's head." (I wished I could get away with that: *They say Delmore encountered a tiger outside the White Horse Tavern and spoke to it in a secret tongue.*)

I was beginning to get a sense of how the biographers of the classical period worked. "The educated man of the Hellenistic world was curious about the lives of famous people," noted Arnaldo Momigliano, whose great work, *The Development of Greek Biography*, was my guide: "He wanted to know what a king or a poet or a philosopher was like and how he behaved in his off-duty moments."

Plutarch was aware of this interest, which encouraged him to depict his subjects as what we would now call "individuals"—human types with special characteristics. "My design is not to write Histories, but lives," he stressed:

> And the most glorious exploits do not always furnish us with the clearest discoveries of virtue or vice in men; sometimes a matter of less moment, an expression or a jest, informs us better of their characters and inclinations, than the most famous sieges, the greatest armaments, or the holiest battles whatsoever. Therefore as portrait-painters are more exact in the lines and features of the face, in which the character is seen, than in the other parts of the body, so I must be allowed to give my more particular attention to the marks and indications of the souls of men, and while I endeavor by these to portray their lives, may be free to leave more weighty matters and great battles to be treated by others.

With Plutarch, "the souls of men" are, for the first time, the object of the biographer's focus. Suetonius, whose *Lives of the Caesars* could be considered the second biography—he was "some years younger than" Plutarch, according to one classical scholar as casual as her subject about the "no-chronology rule"—introduces the concept of moral character. Nero, Suetonius tells us, was guilty of "insolence, lust, luxury, greed, and cruelty"—though why he was that way, we don't know: it was simply his "disposition," his "nature." Of Nero's father, we learn only that he died when Nero was three, and of his mother, that she was power hungry. Raised without rules, Plutarch's Nero is boundaryless—he puts on a wig and wanders the streets at night, picking fights and pillaging taverns; he hits on senators' wives; he allows a rich friend to spend four million sesterces° on a dinner where all the guests wear turbans (which doesn't sound so bad after all the other stuff he did).

Still missing is the concept of motive. This would come later.

Einhard's life of Charlemagne, written around 830, was one of the first biographies by a writer who knew his subject personally. Not that there was any hidden agenda; right at the outset, the biographer disclosed that the emperor was his friend and patron, and made it clear that his biography would be sympathetic. It would give us Charlemagne as his biographer knew him: "strong and well-built," "tall in stature," with "a fine head of white hair," a "mettlesome spirit," and an air of "imperturbability." Charlemagne ate and drank in moderation, according to his biographer, and was so fluent in Latin that "he spoke it as well as his own tongue [Frankish]." He was a good father and, whenever he was home, dined with his children. His only failing, it appeared, was that he wouldn't keep to a healthy diet and ate too much meat. (I sympathize.)

No one could possess all the virtues Einhard attributes to Charlemagne, yet we're tempted to believe his account of events, "for I was present when they took place and, as they say, I saw them with my own eyes."† Einhard was there, a witness to history: "The many events which are happening in our own lifetime should not be held unworthy of record and permitted to sink into silence and oblivion." The biographer's credo, then and now.

Einhard brought his subject closer to us, but it wasn't until the

° I spent half an hour on the Internet trying to figure out how much this would be if you went to Cook's and tried to exchange sesterces for dollars, but all I got were contradictory answers; let's just say it was a huge amount, well into the millions.

† Another contemporary biographer of Charlemagne, the memorably named Notker the Stammerer, was almost defiantly insouciant about his editorial methods: "Since the occasion has offered itself, although they have nothing to do with my subject matter, it does not seem to be a bad idea to add these two stories to my official narrative, together with a few more which happened at the same time and are worthy of being recorded." Note to Notker: Don't try this at *The New Yorker*.

Renaissance that biographers began to focus attention on their subjects' physical features as a way of making us see who they were. Machiavelli, in his biography of the warlord Castruccio Castracani, noted: "His hair had a red sheen, and he wore it cut short above his ears, and always, whatever the weather, even if it was raining or snowing, he went about with his head bare." Boccaccio, in his entertaining biography of Dante, made much of the poet's handsome looks: "His face was long, his nose aquiline, his eyes rather big, his jaw large, and his lower lip protruded beyond the upper. His complexion was dark, his hair and beard thick, black, and curly, and his expression was melancholy° and thoughtful." Studying the exterior became a way of peering into the interior.

By the time we get to the painter/biographer Vasari, you can make out the lineaments of human character as we understand it; in *Lives of the Artists,* he used the words "personality" and "temperament" the same way we would use them five centuries later. I noticed the way he considered the motives (a word he *didn't* use) that drove his subjects to behave the way they did. "History is the mirror of human life," Vasari wrote, "not merely the dry narration of events which occur during the rule of a prince or of a republic, but a means of pointing out the judgments, counsels, decisions, and plans of human beings, as well as the reason for their successful or unsuccessful actions." He also knew a great deal about how human nature works and could generalize persuasively: "Since it rarely happens that talent is not persecuted by envy, it is necessary to do one's utmost to overcome envy through absolute pre-eminence or to become vigorous and powerful in order to endure under such envious attacks."

Vasari had an eye for his subjects' idiosyncrasies. Luca della Robbia, when he was sketching at night and it was cold, would warm his feet "by placing them in a basket of wood shavings." Or the generous Donatello, who "never placed much importance on money and kept his in a basket suspended on a cord attached to the ceiling from which all his workers and friends could take what they needed without saying anything to him." Uccello lived alone in his house "with few conveniences, as if in the wild, for weeks and months without allowing himself to be seen." Was he paranoid, I wondered, always on the lookout for diagnostic symptoms? Or did he just like to be alone?

° The biographer Giannozzo Manetti, writing a century later, also referred to this trait in Dante, noting that he was "often sad and absorbed in his thoughts."

As I worked my way through the biographical canon, I gradually became aware of another theme: self-consciousness. *Know thyself.* Juvenal and Plato, among others, had suggested this might be a good idea if one were to live effectively in the world, but when it began to crop up in Renaissance biographies, it resonated with a kind of pre-psychoanalytic insistence. Boccaccio, in his book on Dante, remarked, almost as an aside: "In this world it is of great importance to know yourself." And Vasari said of Brunelleschi: "He knew himself." Why did these cautionary words so affect me? They suggested that insight into one's own motives and character was the key to self-autonomy—that in knowing yourself, you could control your fate, if such a thing is possible.° It was out of that struggle that all the interesting dramas in life emerged—and out of those dramas came biography.

I worried that my biography was getting too long—two years in, I had accumulated more than four hundred typed pages, and Delmore was still in his thirties. John Aubrey's *Brief Lives* offered an example of how to make it short. A seventeenth-century writer, scholar, and archaeologist, Aubrey had assembled an eccentric compendium of letters, odd documents, hearsay, manuscripts, and interviews with contemporaries, the longest three or four pages, the shortest just a sentence or two.†

It was amazing how much you could say in so few words. Mrs. Abigail Sloper was dispatched with extreme brevity: "borne at Broad Chalke, near Salisbury, A.D. 1648. Pride; lechery; ungratefull to her father; maried; runne distracted; recovered." Thomas Fuller, we're informed, had "a very working head, in so much that, walking and meditating before dinner, he would eate-up a penny loafe, not knowing that he did it." Critics are always haranguing biographers that their books are too long: surely Aubrey would have escaped this censure.

Perhaps the most interesting character in *Brief Lives* was its author, a victim of relentless misfortune. His education at Oxford was interrupted by the civil wars; he lost most of his property in lawsuits; much of the biographical material he compiled was either destroyed or appro-

---

° It's not. See world literature.

† His two-page portrait of Shakespeare didn't add much to the record, though it was strange to think of Aubrey interviewing Shakespeare's contemporaries, like Sir William Davenant, who testified that the playwright had "a most prodigious Witt."

priated by other scholars. And he had an extremely poor self-image: his own biography, he suggested, should be "interposed as a sheet of waste paper only in the binding of a book." He had Oedipal issues. "He was, one suspects, made unsure of himself by an obtuse and obstructive father," Edmund Wilson wrote in an informative introduction to the edition I owned, "and his life became a series of projects that almost invariably ended unsatisfactorily."

Yes, it's true: Aubrey was a flop at most of the things he tried, but he did write the incomparable *Lives*. (Anthony Powell called him "England's first serious biographer.") Some of the portraits are clearly based on third-hand gossip or the impaired memories of someone who woke up on many mornings with a hangover: it's hard to believe that Isaac Selfe, "a cloathier of Milsham," when he died at the age of ninety-two, left behind eighty-three children, some of whom were born without various limbs or even heads; or that a "Fellow from North-Wales," having been killed by a fallen tree limb, rose out of his coffin, still alive. Imagine that!

Dubious, even absurd as these fugitive portraits are, there is something haunting about them. They testify to the power of the impulse that motivates all biographers:

> to raise the dead, so that the retriving of these forgotten Things from Oblivion in some sort resembles the Art of a Conjuror, who makes those appeare that hae layen in their graves many hundreds of years: and to represent as it were to the eie, the places, Customs and Fashions, that were of old Times.

If we peer behind the veil of orthological and grammatical oddities that obscures Aubrey's curious dialect, we can make out one of the most eloquent manifestos ever written about the purpose of biography.

That the brevity of life should become a dominant theme in the seventeenth century makes sense. It was a death-haunted period. Life was short, mortality real, the grave close by. Izaak Walton, remembered as the author of *The Compleat Angler,* wrote far darker books. I cherished his biography of the poet and clergyman John Donne for its brooding account of the death of Donne's wife:

> In this retiredness, which was often from the sight of his dearest friends, he became crucified to the world, and all those vanities,

those imaginary pleasures, that are daily acted on that restless stage; and they were as perfectly crucified to him. Nor is it hard to think—being, passions may be both changed and heightened by accidents—but that *that* abundant affection which once was betwixt him and her, who had long been the delight of his eyes and the companion of his youth; her, with whom he had divided so many pleasant sorrows and contented fears, as common people are not capable of;—not hard but to think that she being now removed by death, a commensurable grief took as full a possession of him as joy had done; and so indeed it did, for now his very soul was elemented of nothing but sadness; now grief took so full a possession of his heart, as to leave no place for joy: if it did, it was a joy to be alone, where, like a pelican in the wilderness, he might bemoan himself without witness or restraint, and pour forth his passions like Job in the days of his affliction: "Oh that I might have the desire of my heart! Oh that God would grant the thing that I long for! For then, as the grave is become her house, so I would hasten to make it mine also; that we two might there make our beds together in the dark."

The writing has such incantatory power that it overwhelms our natural hunger for the truth. Walton writes in the conditional: "might bemoan," "not hard to think," "would hasten." However vivid the prose, you couldn't be sure if the scene it described was a hallucination.

Not that it mattered. Maintaining the pretext of accuracy had yet to become an important part of the biographer's job. Even James Boswell, the most scrupulous of biographers, admitted to the occasional fabrication—as did his impeccably moral subject. "When the information was not directly available it had to be supplied by guesswork," Macaulay admitted in the preface to his brief biography of Dr. Johnson, still the best apart from Boswell's: "The unscrupulous biographers added invention to their ingredients." Invention was frowned upon but tolerated.*

---

* The academic world has little tolerance for this kind of guesswork: it should come as no surprise that the exact number of days Boswell spent in Johnson's company remains the subject of much lively dispute. The distinguished scholar Donald Greene argues for 327, while Professor A. W. Collins, taking into account undated entries, comes up with 425—a significant discrepancy. "This must pose a problem for those scholars who extol the 'artistry' of Boswell's composition," Greene notes with scorn. There *is* no artistry, in his view; the shape of the *Life* was dictated by when the biographer was on the

At the end of Dr. Johnson's biography of the Delmorean poet and vagabond Richard Savage, he put forward the possibility that Savage, on his deathbed in debtors' prison, was on the verge of confessing to his jailer that he was an imposter, then forgot what he was about to say ("'Tis gone!"). Did this scene happen the way Johnson reported it? How could anyone know what Savage had been on the verge of saying, since he didn't say it? As Boswell noted: "The world must vibrate in uncertainty as to what was the truth."

The assumption that a biography would be accurate didn't establish itself until the Victorian era. As I made my ponderous way through the triple- and quadruple-volumed biographies of people I'd never heard of written by biographers I'd also never heard of, like Samuel Smiles, author of *The Lives of the Engineers;* Wilfrid Ward, the biographer of Cardinal Newman; and Viscount Morley of Blackburn, author of a then-definitive biography of Gladstone, I noted how formal and reserved they were—the biographers of a rationalist age.

Here is the deathbed scene in Lockhart's biography of Sir Walter Scott:

About half-past one P.M. on the 21st of September, Sir Walter breathed his last, in the presence of all his children. It was a beautiful day—so warm, that every window was wide open—and so perfectly still, that the sound of all others most delicious to his ear, the gentle ripple of the Tweed over its pebbles, was distinctly audible as we knelt around the bed, and his eldest son kissed and closed his eyes.

It's crisply told, without any of the eccentricity that lurks in the testaments of Walton on Donne or Johnson on Savage; the facts ("half-past one P.M. on the 21st of September") are laid out with a reassuring specificity; the scene is recounted with placid eloquence. What it lacks is the dark atmosphere of Aubrey and Walton, the levity of Boswell and Johnson; we have arrived at the age of normalization, when biography is domesticated, death has lost much of its terror, and what we read could well be true.

---

scene. When he was there, it expanded; when he wasn't, it shrank. Greene, a Johnson partisan, wants to keep the number down in order to reduce Boswell's importance. (We might call this "day-suppression.")

Afflicted with a serious case of book collector's zeal, I had acquired one of the stubby volumes in Morley's English Men of Letters series—brief biographies packaged in threes by writers who were then distinguished and are now forgotten.° My trio consisted of James Anthony Froude (most famous for his controversial biography of Carlyle) on John Bunyan, now known[†] only for his quaint and strange religious parable *The Pilgrim's Progress;* R. W. Church, whom I'd never heard of, on Francis Bacon; and Leslie Stephen, the father of Virginia Woolf, on *Johnson and His Friends.*

Stephen's book was a revelation. I knew hardly anything about Dr. Johnson at that time—not even why he was called "Dr."—but Stephen brought him instantly to life, offering a vigorous sketch of his subject's physical oddities: he was pockmarked; he had a compulsion to touch every lamppost when he walked down a street; he was so agitated that he once twisted off the shoe of a woman sitting beside him. He was afflicted with a variety of tics: "Once he collected a laughing mob in Twickenham meadows by his antics; his hands imitating the motion of a jockey riding at full speed and his feet twisting in and out to make heels touch alternately." He had uncouth table manners: his friend Tom Davies the bookseller said that he ate like a wolf, "savagely, silently, and with undiscriminating fury."[‡] He was of strange appearance: he wore

---

° The scholarly rigor of these volumes varied widely. Anthony Trollope's on Thackeray is one of the more egregious; hedged about with "probablys," it hustles through the facts, few of which seem to be known—at least to the biographer—and devotes a stingy paragraph to his subject's family, alluding to "a skeleton in his cupboard" that he declines to explain. But if you want to know what it feels like to try to become a writer, read this book. In three eloquent pages, Trollope enumerates the perils that lie in wait for the literary aspirant. No one can teach you how to write; no one cares if you do it or not; nor can you support yourself. "It is an idea that comes to very many men and women, old as well as young—to many thousands who at last are crushed by it, of whom the world knows nothing." (This from the author of forty-seven novels.) I wish someone had told me that.

† If known at all. Let's be honest about the radical shrinkage of what was once thought of as the core curriculum, which required at least a cursory knowledge of the corpus of English literature. No one—except perhaps a few Ph.D. candidates in the field, and in many cases, I suspect, not even those—is expected any longer to have read systematically in the literature of our own language, much less others. But why complain about it? The world changes. Few tweet about Bunyan.

‡ Boswell: "When at table, he was totally absorbed in the business of the moment; his looks seemed rivetted to his plate; nor would he, when unless in very high company,

a "shriveled" wig and worn slippers; his breeches hung loose about his knees. But he was powerful, too; he could box and wrestle: "Once he is said to have taken up a chair at the theatre upon which a man had seated himself during his temporary absence, and to have tossed it and its occupant bodily into the pit."

This was my introduction to anecdotes I would encounter over and over in the years to come, as I proceeded through the substantial shelf of Johnson biographies (finally figuring out that it was Boswell I wanted to read about). Thus it was that I heard for the first time about Johnson as a young man refusing to help out his father in his bookstall and returning years later to stand bareheaded in the rain as atonement for that ancient dereliction; being outraged by the anonymous loan of a pair of shoes when he was an undergraduate at Oxford; his importuning letter to Edward Cave, publisher of *The Gentleman's Magazine*, asking for work; the eloquent kiss-off epistle to Lord Chesterfield, who had turned him away when he came, hat in hand, to plead for Chesterfield's support; the Club (the painter Sir Joshua Reynolds, the actor David Garrick, and the playwright Oliver Goldsmith were its most prominent members) that met at the Turk's Head in Gerrard Street once a week at seven o'clock; the motley tenants in the house on Gough Square (his Jamaican servant, Francis Barber; the taciturn apothecary Mr. Levet; his boarder Mrs. Williams); the hoary proverbs ("No man but a blockhead ever wrote for anything but money") and the famous ripostes, so familiar that it was hard to imagine Johnson ever actually said them, as when Boswell reported that he had heard a Quaker woman preach and Johnson replied: "A woman's preaching is like a dog's walking on his hind legs. It is not done well; but you are surprised to find it done at all."

Such anecdotes would become part of what academics called Johnsoniana—the accretion of folkloric stories that made up the mythic, as opposed to the real, Dr. Johnson, who would appear in his full majesty in the greatest biography in the English language, *The Life of Samuel Johnson, LL.D.*, by that drunken, depressive, philandering,

---

say one word, or even pay the least attention to what was said by others, till he had satisfied his appetite, which was so fierce, and indulged with such intenseness, that while in the act of eating, the veins of his forehead swelled, and generally a strong perspiration was visible."

whoring, obsequious, comic, effusive, and compulsively indiscreet genius James Boswell.[*]

There were also many interesting facts in Stephen's brief biography, such as how much money writers of that era made: the philosopher David Hume got 700 pounds for each volume of his *History of England;* Laurence Sterne got 650 pounds for *Tristram Shandy.* What did such pecuniary details have to do with the books these writers produced? They filled out the sociological picture, gave us an idea of how much literature was valued, in the literal sense, during the eighteenth century.

And the work? Wasn't this supposed to be all about the work? Yet it's not until *after* the deathbed scene that Stephen gets around to the books the man wrote, in a chapter—the *last* chapter—entitled

---

[*] Had it not been for a series of serendipitous events, we would possess only a skimpy selection of the letters and journals—in effect, we would have almost no Boswell at all. Ian Hamilton recounts this story in his neglected book, *Keepers of the Flame: The Making and Unmaking of Literary Reputations from John Donne to Sylvia Plath.* I've decided to quote from it at inordinate length: why struggle over some lame paraphrase with a writer as good as Hamilton?

> One of Boswell's heirs had married an Irish peer and moved a huge trove of the biographer's papers from Auchinlech, his family seat, where they had been languishing, despite occasional sieges by scholars, for a musty interval in their long sojourn through this world, to a castle in Ireland, where they reposed until a later heir woke up to the possible monetary value of the papers and, short of cash ("like all Boswells and sub-Boswells"), responded to a query letter in the *Times Literary Supplement* from the eminent Boswell scholar Professor Chauncey Brewster Tinker. It was Tinker, on a foray to Malahide Castle, who first glimpsed the cache that would become the foundation of Boswell's posthumous fame. "I felt like Sinbad in the valley of rubies," he recalled of the moment when the ebony cabinet that contained them was opened and revealed its treasure: thousands of letters and Boswell's 8,000-page journal. It remained for an avid American collector, Lieutenant Colonel Ralph Isham, to acquire the papers after years of tortuous negotiation involving greedy heirs and Scottish courts of law, going broke in the process. Isham eventually sold his collection to Yale, even as more Boswell papers turned up in a croquet box, a hayloft, and the attic of a house in Scotland. These, too, were transferred to Yale, where they repose today.

> Think of it: no Boswell at a public execution, clambering up on the scaffold for a better view; no Boswell consorting with the Queen "in a suit of imperial blue, lined with rose-coloured silk, and ornamented with rich gold-wrought buttons"; no Boswell and friends in a Covent Garden theatre, "oaken cudgels in our hands," shouting down a bad play. A close call: it would be as if Columbus had floated around the ocean and failed to find America.

"Johnson's Writings." ("It remains to speak of Johnson's position in literature.") Acknowledging "the inferiority of Johnson's written to his spoken utterances," he trots through the monumental *Dictionary*, impressive but a stunt; the translations of Juvenal; the essays published in *The Rambler; Irene,*˙ a play about some Turkish sultan "which can be read by men in whom a sense of duty has been abnormally developed" (funny!); and *Lives of the Poets*, his still enchanting collection of brief biographies. Stephen's biography wasn't about his work—What did he even write besides the *Lives?*—but about his character: It was written as all great literature is written: with style, wit, elegance, and verve. Who wouldn't prefer it to the pedantic essays in *The Idler.*

One of Dwight Macdonald's favorite biographies was Lytton Strachey's *Eminent Victorians.* It consists of four brief portraits of Victorian figures significant in their own day—and, as is so often the case, forgotten in ours. What did I care about Cardinal Manning, Florence Nightingale, Thomas Arnold, and General Gordon? But as Virginia Woolf, herself a shrewd commentator on biography, noted: "There are some people who without being themselves famous seem to sum up the qualities of an age and to represent it at its best." This had clearly been Strachey's criterion in choosing his subjects, and I marveled at his capacity for expanding the particular trait into the general rule. He wasn't interested in doing original research or even pretending to do it; he ransacked others' biographies and generalized from his borrowings.

Strachey lost me sometimes in the thickets of Victorian culture. It was hard to follow the religious disputes of Cardinal Manning, and I could never remember what the Oxford Movement was or who the Tractarians were. But half of the chapter about Manning, it seemed, was about Cardinal Newman and his dramatic apostasy from the Church of England, which he renounced for the Roman Catholic Church. What seized my imagination was less this spiritual agonizing than the problems of Newman as a writer wrestling with the limitations of his mind and the ravages of time: "Newman was now an old man—he was sixty-three years of age.† What had he to look forward to? A few last years of insignificance and silence. What had he to look back upon? A long

---

˙ Pronounced *Ear N A*, should you have a need to say this name aloud.
† I write this at the age of sixty-seven (no longer in my "mid-sixties") and hardly think of myself as an "old man." But I guess in 1840 it was considered old. In a Chekhov story, a man of fifty-eight is identified as old.

chronicle of wasted efforts, disappointed hopes, unappreciated pow-ers." (How powerfully I could identify, even in my twenties, with this compressed summation of another man's life.)

A year later Newman writes his *Apologia pro vita sua,* still one of the great autobiographies in the English language; "and he does it in seven weeks," writes Strachey,

> sometimes working twenty-two hours at a stretch, constantly in tears, and constantly crying out with distress. The success of the book, with its transparent candor, its controversial brilliance, the sweep and passion of its rhetoric, the depth of its personal feel-ing, was immediate and overwhelming; it was recognised at once as a classic, not only by Catholics, but by the whole English world.

This is Newman at the height of his career, the great work done; but it's not long before, life being life, he is brought low and becomes again an ordinary, anonymous man:

> At about this time, the Curate of Littlemore had a singular expe-rience. As he was passing by the Church he noticed an old man, very poorly dressed in an old grey coat with the collar turned up, leaning over the lych gate, in floods of tears. He was apparently in great trouble, and his hat was pulled down over his eyes as if he wished to hide his features. For a moment, however, he turned towards the Curate, who was suddenly struck by something famil-iar in the face. Could it be?

The question is written in the biographer's voice, rather than as a quote. But it dramatizes the scene without violating the facts. The unstated answer to "Could it be?" is "It was."

That exchange, so portentous with omission, liberated Strachey from the most oppressive stricture of biography: he could make it up with-out making it up. A biographer isn't a novelist, Leon Edel was always reminding us: "Novelists have omniscience. Biographers never do. The personages exist; the documents exist; they are the 'givens' to a writer of lives." Okay, so we don't have omniscience; what I'd learned from Lytton Strachey was that we have permission to write as if we did—not to invent but to imagine.

XI

I read biographies with the absorption of a car mechanic, repair manual in hand, peering under the hood at a steaming engine: *What's gone wrong here? And how do I fix it?* In order to write a biography, I had to know how the thing was done.°

I read without system the massive multivolume biographies: Leslie Marchand's *Byron*, Joseph Blotner's *Faulkner*, Richard Sewall's *Emily Dickinson*. P. N. Furbank's two volumes on Forster occupied me for weeks. I snailed through them pen in hand, scribbling notes in the margins. I had the British edition, published by Secker & Warburg,† with a painted portrait of Forster as a young man on the cover in a crisp gray suit, seated in a willfully casual pose that somehow managed to intimate his timidity, and a quote from Pindar on the back that was a favorite of Forster's: "Man's life is a day. What is he, what is he not? Man is the dream of a shadow. But when the god-given brightness comes a bright light is among men, and an age that is gentle come to birth."

The most compelling details, I began to notice, were the ones that instantly made you want to flip to the citations at the back in order

---

° I also read biographies by novelists, of which there were a surprising number: Graham Greene on the Earl of Rochester, Virginia Woolf on Roger Fry, Evelyn Waugh on Edmund Campion, Anthony Powell on John Aubrey. They were all great books—sturdy additions to the writer's oeuvre rather than eccentric departures from it. They were writing nonfiction as if it were fiction, in their own distinctive styles, but adapted to the conventions of biography. After a while you forgot it *was* nonfiction.

† By now, I could distinguish British from American editions of books at a glance, the way it's possible to identify an Italian or a Spaniard or a Frenchman on the street with the briefest of glimpses; one isn't even able to put the variation between these outwardly identical European types into words. In books, to start with, there was the typeface, the British dark and formal compared to the lighter American type; also the minuscule type of the index in the British editions. Maybe, in the end, it was simply an aura, a distinction that over the years had become unconscious.

Lytton Strachey

to find out where they came from. At lunch with the historian G. M. Trevelyan, who talked a great deal but ate nothing, Forster brooded about the food: "On his own plate, in the middle of a very warm helping of lukewarm mince, mashed potatoes and brussels sprouts, was one sprout which was quite raw, and he kept wondering, as the inspiring torrent poured over him, 'What a very curious thing. How could it have got in? And how impossible to interest my host in the subject.'" Where could the biographer have possibly dug up this odd tidbit? I flipped eagerly to the notes in the back, only to find . . . no note! The meditation on the raw sprout was on page 70, but there was a barren tundra of notelessness that stretched all the way from page 44 to 77. I clucked in frustration. Why was it so often the most salient bits that went unsourced? And always without apology—no explanation of why the very citation you had interrupted your reading to look up had gone missing. Why did biographers, so conscientious that their notes often took up fifty or even a hundred pages of text, feel they had the right to blithely omit the origins of some obscure and tantalizing—tantalizing *because* obscure—detail? The sprout that arrested Forster's attention, for instance: had Furbank gleaned it from someone's journal? A letter? A report on the lunch to a friend, who put it in *his* journal? And why did it matter? In part, I suppose, because it was a feat of research: how could the biographer possibly know this?

Furbank is especially good on his subject's physical features, which he registered with unpitying specificity. That Forster had "a queer pedantic tic of speech" was the least of it. The most damaging descriptions were supplied by the subject himself. An entry from Forster's journal, written when he was forty-six: "red nose enormous, round patch in middle of scalp . . . Face is toad-like . . . The anus clotted with hairs." (And how was this proctological detail obtained? One doesn't want to know.)

Then there was the milieu—the social world, the ancillary characters, the manner of dress and traits of speech. The rector of Stevenage, Mr. Jowitt, "a genial, out-of-doors style of parson, who rode to hounds"; Forster's tutor, Oscar Browning, who napped while Forster read his weekly essays, a red handkerchief draped over his face; R. C. Trevelyan, the brother of G. M., who fancied himself a poet and "lived his chosen part wholeheartedly, striding about the country with a knapsack, his hair flying, or writing poems in a furrow": it's E. M. Forster and His World that Furbank wants to evoke, a particular stratum of English society that he depicts with anthropological exactitude. He shows us the house in Abinger where Forster waited out World War II, "an intensely old-fashioned household" with no electricity or phone or baths; Agnes, the "parlourmaid," who lugged hot water up to the bedrooms in heavy brass cans; a church fund-raising pageant that contained "ancient Britons in skins gathering fuel in the Abinger woods"—a scene as alien to the American reader as a Nambikwara burial rite.

I also had to consider how to start the book. In-the-beginning chronology was the safest course, especially after the reader had been forced to scrutinize one of those eye-glazing family trees that preface so many biographies. The standard method would go something like . . . let me pull a book down from the shelf: "Ann (b. 1747) was the daughter of William Cookson, a successful linen draper in Penrith, and of Dorothy, sister and heiress of James Crackenthorpe of Newbiggin Hall." This dry and unrewardingly informative sentence occurs on the first page of *William Wordsworth: A Life*, by Stephen Gill. No throat-clearing here, just a clipped let's-get-on-with-it.

Or you could start, as Walter Jackson Bate did, with a general observation: "Samuel Johnson has fascinated more people than any other writer except Shakespeare." Bate's purpose here is to make it clear that, despite Johnson's great and universal fame, there is still much to say about him that is new (which, in this instance, there emphatically was). But I was looking for a more dramatic way into the narrative. I wanted, above all, to tell a story.

"A writer of lives is allowed the imagination of form but not of fact," Leon Edel pronounced in *Principia Biographica*, his useful if somewhat humorless edict on the limits of biography. The "fact" part I got (though I would come to question the whole notion that there *was* such a thing as fact). It had never occurred to me that the "form" could be so elastic—that, in effect, you could construct a biography however you liked. Richard Holmes had a useful term for this method: "nonfiction story-telling," biography that has "a protagonist, a time-sequence, a plot, and a dramatic pattern of human cause and effect." *Nonfiction story-telling*: that's what I was after.

Edel himself had gone about as far as you could in this direction. I couldn't stop reading his biography of James—two thousand pages, five volumes in all. It went down easily; I ceased work on Delmore for two weeks while I gobbled it up. They were handsomely designed, handsomely made books, with comfortably large type and interleaved folios of photographs. I also liked the way Edel broke up the chapters

into manageable size, then broke them up into still smaller bits separated by roman numerals; it didn't make you feel, as so many biographies did, that you were traversing an arid desert of type. The narrative
was well paced; clearly a lot of thought had gone into the beginnings
and endings of sections. Most often he would start with a scene, as in
the chapter on James's friendship with the minor writer Hugh Walpole:
"They faced each other for the first time in February 1909 when James
came up to London to attend a matinee of *The High Bid* [a play by Wal-
pole]. He gave the young Hugh dinner at the Reform Club." This terse
stage-setting is followed up with an entry from Walpole's diary; then a
letter from James to Walpole. On their first weekend together at Lamb
House, the power of James's presence renders Hugh mute—normally
a problem for a biographer but not in the case of the energetic Edel,
who conjectures that "if he did not speak in his diary," we can turn to
a tale of Walpole's called "Mr. Oddy," in which "the emotion of their
meeting" is represented. Here the obese novelist, "his large Johnsonian body set on his short legs," is evoked both in his physical form and
in his speech, inflected with "the reverberation of the late style." Note
Edel's agility in giving Walpole the space to invent—to write fiction—
while at the same time making the connection between James and
Walpole's fictive protagonist unambiguous. This is how James spoke,
he's informing us; it "rings true."

Collecting the data wasn't even the hardest part. As Boswell noted,
it was putting the thing together that really took it out of you. The
biographies on my shelves were finished products, printed and bound:
there were no facsimiles of biography like the facsimile of *The Waste
Land*, with its cross-outs and additions, whole stanzas revised word by
word. I would pick up a handsome finished book—say, volume three
of Marchand's *Byron*—and marvel at its beauty as a physical object.
The elegant cover with its drawing of the poet, the glossy paper of the
illustrations insert, the sewn binding, the rough-cut pages: it was a joy
to hold in the hand. But it yielded no directives as to how the contents
had been made. That I would have to learn for myself.

As with any trauma, the emotional and physical pain caused by the
composition of a biography fades over time. The letter misfiled, the
tape recorder that failed to record (this was one reason I took notes),
the quote you'd forgotten to write down and now couldn't find: these
lapses a biographer could weather. But what happened when you sat
down to write?

I was drowning in documentation. Manuscripts, clippings, transcriptions of interviews, and Xeroxed articles lay strewn about the floor. I crawled around amid the notecards laid out as if for some immense game of Solitaire until I developed rug burns on my knees. "Omission, generalization, intensification: that's your clue," Macdonald had advised me—advice I chanted to myself like a mantra as I faced my chaotic archive every morning. Delmore had never thrown anything out, and my original fear that I wouldn't have enough documentation soon gave way to despair about how I would get it all in.* My study looked as if it had been ransacked. Papers were strewn about; five-by-seven notecards were arranged in little piles; books were scattered everywhere. Of manila folders there were many: some contained xeroxes of Delmore's typed journals, others his handwritten letters, still others articles from old literary journals yellowed by time.† The biographer's task, said Lytton Strachey, was to collect every scrap of data he could and then "row out over that great ocean of material and lower down into it, here and there, a little bucket, which will bring up to the light of day some characteristic specimen from those far depths, to be examined with a careful curiosity." The challenge was to keep from falling overboard myself.

---

* Years later I came across this sentence from E. M. Forster's biography of Goldsworthy Lowes Dickinson: "His other university activities are not important." Now there's a basic lesson for biographers! If it's not important, leave it out. The trouble is that to the biographer everything *seems* important.

† Reviewing Philip Davis's fine life of Bernard Malamud, Joyce Carol Oates described biography as a literary edifice "constructed out of a small infinity of letters, drafts, notes, manuscripts, printed texts, interview transcripts, etc." How tidy she makes it sound. My own experience conformed more to Virginia Woolf's evocation of biographical chaos: "How can one make a life out of six cardboard boxes [the exact number I faced on my first encounter with Delmore's papers] full of tailors' bills, love letters, and old picture postcards?" And what do you do with gems that you just can't find a place for, like this quote from a review of John Haffenden's two-volume biography of the British critic William Empson that I came across in *The Independent*:

> To register Empson's weirdness of character, a touch of hysterical laughter is surely called for. There was, for a start, the grotesquerie of his beard, a star-shaped fan below his chin, or his demure request to a young colleague that he be allowed to kiss his member, or a typical menu for guests in 'The Burrow,' his filthy basement: hard-boiled egg in bottled curry sauce followed by a doughnut soused in condensed milk, plus a tumbler of Japanese whiskey.

Thank god for footnotes.

You couldn't just stuff all this crap anywhere, and if you got the order wrong, you had to type the whole page over. This was before computers; you couldn't move paragraphs around, cutting and pasting at will. Or rather, you could: but "cutting and pasting" in those days meant snipping out a paragraph and literally pasting it onto a separate page with Elmer's glue. "You cannot imagine," Boswell complained to a friend, "what labour, what perplexity, what vexation I have endured in arranging a prodigious multiplicity of materials, in supplying omissions, in searching for papers, buried in different masses, and all this besides the exertion of composing and polishing; many a time have I thought of giving it up."

Who could blame him? I'd thought about it, too.

It was through Michael Holroyd's gigantic° biography of Lytton Strachey—even the compressed single-volume Penguin edition ran to 1,134 pages—that I fell in love with what might be called the apparatus of biography, the scaffolding or latticework that surrounds the main text.

If I can recall little of its contents now, I have a very clear memory of the effect it had on me when I first held it in my hands. The "Preface to the Revised Edition" was one of those how-I-wrote-my-book sagas that biographers love to read. Having discovered, in the course of researching his first biography—of the now-forgotten biographer and literary critic Hugh Kingsmill—that no biography of Strachey existed, Holroyd embarked on the usual tortuous biographer's journey toward authorization or at least access. The executor of the estate was Strachey's brother, James, the translator of Freud's collected works—and rumored to be difficult. (What executor isn't? That's why they're apppointed.) "It was therefore with deep qualms," writes Holroyd forebodingly, that he set out for his first meeting with Strachey at his "red-brick Edwardian house" deep in the Buckinghamshire countryside:

° I'm aware that I have a tic about the physical *size* of biographies, on several occasions describing them as "plump" or "thick" and, less charitably, "fat," as if bulk were somehow a determinant of their value rather than, as is too often the case, a flaw. But why single out these notecard-profligate offenders? They know who they are. Anyway, great biographies that are sometimes taxingly long can still be written: I place in evidence Blake Bailey's *Cheever* and John Unterecker's *Hart Crane;* there are plenty of others.

I arrived at mid-day by a complicated system of trains and taxis, prepared for practically anything—but not for what I actually came across. Though it was cold and frosty outside, the temperature within the house seemed set at a steady eighty degrees Fahrenheit. No windows were open, and to prevent the suspicion of a draught cellophane curtains were drawn against them. There was an odour of disinfectant about the rooms. I felt I had entered a specially treated capsule where some rare variety of *homo sapiens* was exquisitely preserved.

After a lunch of "spam, a cold potato each, and lettuce leaves," James leads the future biographer of his brother to an outbuilding housing the trove whose contents would come to occupy Holroyd for a good part of his life: "In the middle of the building were two great wooden tables piled high with boxes and files, and on the floor were littered innumerable trunks and cases, all full of letters, diaries and miscellaneous papers. Cobwebs and a pall of dust covered everything."

Confronted with this chaotic mass of documents, Holroyd experiences the first wild surge of elation known to every biographer who stumbles, at long last, upon the elusive archive that will instantly transform his inchoate dream into a viable project, quickly succeeded by a sense of dread as the magnitude of the chore before him begins to sink in: "I left the house late that afternoon in a profound depression." He has tracked down "one of the major caches of literary papers in modern times"—to cite Holroyd's own synecdoche, "a miniature Pompeii." Now he must dig.

And dig he did. For the reader curious about Bloomsbury, which Holroyd himself did so much to turn into a humming literary industry, his book is brimming with gossip, often mildly* salacious, about the overly refined, overprivileged and overeducated, witty (though perhaps less so than they thought), polymorphously perverse, annoyingly mannered behavior of this infinitely fascinating "set." Everything about their world, from the quaint country house names (Ham Spray, Lord's Wood, Chilling) to the minor characters who pass through the nar-

---

* An account of Strachey's obsession with sodomy leads (not inevitably) to a cochlear fetish. "Among his post-Cambridge writings," Holroyd dutifully reports, "can be traced the development of more sophisticated sexual deviations, and the suggestion that he could become erotically aroused by other parts of the body, especially the ears."

rative (one party included among its guests "a cosmopolitan Jewess"; "a couple of American Negroes, crude, amiable, and inconceivably rich," one of whom played the banjo; and the mother of the celebrated cellist Madame Suggia, "unable to speak a single word of any known language"); from their coy upper-class nicknames ("Dadie" Rylands, "Pippa" Strachey) to what they talked about ("Henry James and Cymbeline and the essence of Architecture"), seemed bafflingly intricate, as did the interlocking love affairs—the unrequited passions of Ralph Partridge for Dora Carrington, Carrington for Lytton, Lytton for Mark Gertler; the elegance and refinement of their lives, the cleverness of their correspondence, the books they wrote . . . and, unspoken but ever present, the gossamer evanescence of it all.

Over the course of more than a thousand tightly packed pages, Holroyd assembled these elements with consummate skill, combining the features of character, daily life, and history just as a novelist would, the authorial voice always in the background, paraphrasing the subject's thoughts without claiming to know them ("Beauty, truth, intelligence—these were mere trifles, he reflected, dimly expressive of the single inner truth of love"); and then how the world looked and felt and was, as in the great deathbed scene on the penultimate page:

> Early that morning, Stephen Tomlin* was urgently called to the house. Other friends and relatives arrived, their cars crunching backwards and forwards on the gravel. The fine frosty weather that had gone on without a break since Christmas still lasted. It was intensely still—the sort of weather Lytton had always loved. A soft golden mist lay over the green meadows and enfolded the elm trees. The sunlight, sprinkling through their branches, seemed to delay and delay, before touching the walls of the house, and streaming through the windows. It was impossible for those who waited not to contrast this beauty with Lytton dying, or to wonder what result might follow for the three [Carrington, Ralph Partridge, and Gerald Brenan], bound together in precarious balance, whom he left behind.

---

* "A brilliant and erratic sculptor, bisexual and deeply melancholic at times, yet perhaps the most acutely intellectual of all Lytton's younger friends."

And not a single quote from a book or letter or diary or interview in the whole paragraph, I noted: it was all in the biographer's own voice.

Perhaps the most intricate component of this biographical apparatus was the genre known as acknowledgments, a hypnotic litany of family members who had "provided assistance" or "offered shelter"—editors, publishers, librarians, and research assistants—that often ran to several pages, behind each of which, one knew, was a story involving sleuthwork, courtship, perhaps arduous travel, protracted acts of letter extraction, enduring friendship or enmity (or both, in the way of things, one leading to the other) and eventually, a new cohort to mourn, as acknowledgees died off (earning them the dreaded adjective "the late"), so that by the second or third edition, if one were fortunate to *have* a second or third edition, the drumbeat of those listed who were "late" reached a crescendo, the survivors dwindling to a dozen or two, in the same way that one's classmates dwindle from one reunion to the next.* I made my way through this litany of names as if it were simply another page of text.† Holroyd's acknowledgments read like a group portrait of the British aristocracy and intelligentsia in the mid-twentieth century: the Dowager Lady Abercomway, Lord David Cecil (a biographer of distinction, he qualified as both), the late Aldous Huxley, Lady Mosley, the late Lord Russell, the late Leonard Woolf . . . They all go into the dark.

Maybe that was it: the disproportion between the extremity of effort and the inexorable denouement. Everything in life taught you, if you paid close enough attention, that no matter how sturdy an edifice you built, it would eventually tumble down around you. A biography was a tombstone. And who was content with an empty slab? You wanted to put everything into it that you could, make it sturdy and beautiful, built to last. It wouldn't, any more than the mosaic walls of Pompeii or the slender-columned Temple of Artemis. But did the ceramicist afflicted with this thought under the hot Aegean sun pack up his tiles and go home?

---

* The acknowledgments page in *The New Strachey* is in fact less than a page. It's been whittled down to three terse paragraphs, prefaced by a melancholy sentence that explains its brevity: "The list of people who helped me with the preparation of this biography in the 1960s has become a necrology."
† The incomparable Richard Holmes, unsurprisingly, has a flair for the form. Having praised his "visionary" typist, he really turns it up: "Finally I would like to greet the unknown student of Calderon who bought me a glass of brandy one stormy night in a crumbling bar overlooking the Arno at Pisa." I hope the "unknown student" saw this.

XII

ne day in the mid-1970s, while browsing in the Harvard Bookstore—usually the last stop on my procrastinatory rounds of Harvard Square, after Out of Town News, Bartley's Burger Cottage, and the Grolier Book Shop—I came across a new edition of James Joyce's letters, compiled by Richard Ellmann. "He and Nora exchanged letters much more open than Bloom's and Martha's," Ellmann had written of Joyce's correspondence with his wife in early editions of his biography. Now he was publishing these letters "in the hope," he explained in a preface, "that readers will countenance [their] value as an extreme of Joyce's and perhaps of human, utterance."

Extreme they were. I had read Molly Bloom's soliloquy as an exemplar of inspired prurience but also as a major breakthrough in the rise of Modernism. Joyce's letters to Nora belonged to another realm entirely: they took you not only into the bedroom, not only under the sheets, but into the cavities of the human body, with all its effluences and smells, a realm so taboo that most of us didn't even go there in private, much less in letters intended for another to read. Yet Joyce *had* gone there, and reported back to us on his journey into the sexual interior:

> *. . . a little brown stain on the seat of your white drawers . . .*
> *. . . to come on your face and squirt it over your hot cheeks . . .*
> *. . . fat dirty farts came spluttering out of your backside . . .*

In one scatological passage, so dirty that I feared a clerk was going to come over and ask me to leave the store just for having it in my hands, Joyce describes Nora "squatting in the closet, with your clothes up, grunting like a young sow doing her dung, and a big fat dirty snaking thing coming slowly out of your backside." As I read this account— beautiful in its own way—of a woman defecating in front of her hus-

James and Nora Joyce

band, I thought of the moment in *Ulysses* where Bloom admires Gerty MacDowell on the Sandymount shore: "Her hands were of finely veined alabaster with tapering fingers and as white as juice and queen of ointments could make them."

It didn't seem strange to me that these sentences were by the same author. Who else could have written such exquisite prose? Each bore the Joycean imprint: lyrical cadences, vivid images, powerful but suppressed emotions. The sex stuff was exciting to read, but even more exciting was to see how the two passages showed the elasticity of Joyce's mind. He could write about anything and still be Joyce. No: he could write about anything and not *not* be Joyce.

Why had Ellmann waited until now to make these letters available?* His explanation was evasive: "At the time when my Volume II appeared, there were several obstacles to publication in its entirety of Joyce's correspondence with his wife, and of the total of 64 letters, I was permitted to give the complete text of 54, a partial text of 8, and no text at all of the remaining 2. Publication of the missing correspondence has now been authorized." Behind this bland litany of mathematical precision and passive syntax must have lain some story involving executors, family members, prudish publishers; we wouldn't learn it here.

Had Joyce expected these letters to be published? I doubted it, but after I got over my shock, I was glad they had been. To be able to write openly about this shit, as it were, requires an exceptional degree of trust. Joyce's cloacal riffs were meant to test just how much smut Nora could tolerate—to explore the limits of their intimacy. "Are you too, then, like me," he asks hopefully, "one moment high as the star, the next lower than the lowest wretches?"

I wasn't sure about the "high" part, and Nora's letters don't survive, but there are hints that she could keep up her side of the correspondence. "Write more and dirtier," Joyce instructs her: "Tickle your little cockey while you write to make you say worse and worse." I could never read these prods without laughing: their lustful exuberance revealed a side of Joyce—proud, lustful, devious, *gross*—that had been hidden until now. "Goodnight, my little farting Nora, my dirty little fuckbird!" Haha.

---

* It was hard to believe that, even as we talked about Joyce in Ellmann's cold but cozy New College office until the room began to darken in the short Oxford afternoon, the tables around us piled high with books, he had been sitting on these fiery letters.

Joyce was one of the few writers whose work I knew in an immersive way. I had read him—except for *Finnegans Wake!*—with the sharp attention Ellmann demanded; for all his affability, he was an exacting tutor and expected me to be able to trace the connections between *Ulysses* and *The Odyssey* as if I'd read them twenty times, as he had. But I was reading in a different way now: it was the creator of Bloom who interested me—not just the figure in the carpet but the figure who walked on it.

Like every art form, biography is bound by the conventions of the moment—not only the subject's moment but the biographer's as well. We forget that sexual behavior we now acknowledge and discuss openly was once hidden beneath the surface of daily life; biographers couldn't write about it, not only because they didn't know about it but because it would have disgraced both their subjects and themselves. "The whole truth is not always to be exposed," warned Boswell. That was the general rule in eighteenth-century England. Boswell himself was so prudish° that he once crossed out a line from a letter of Johnson's to David Garrick: "I'll no more come behind your scenes, David; for the silk stockings and white bubbies of your actresses excite my genitals."

Johnson's sexual relations with his bibulous wife, Tetty, were the subject of much mirth among his circle, but we get only a peek of it in Boswell's *Life.*† Twenty years Johnson's senior, she had "cheeks coloured both by paint and cordials," according to Garrick, who entertained company by mimicking scenes of their "connubial felicity." When Garrick and Johnson had taught together at a boarding school, Boswell recounted, "the young rogues used to listen at the door of his bed-chamber, and peep through the key-hole, that they might turn into ridicule his tumultuous and awkward fondness for Mrs. Johnson."

Further evidence of Johnson's sexual feistiness turned up in a five-

---

° He was more open about his own sexual adventures. In his journal, Boswell kept a meticulous record of every STD he contracted: "Too, too plain was Senor Gonorrhea."
† Boswell does acknowledge that the (apparently) abstinent Johnson wrestled with temptation: "It was well-known, that his amorous inclinations were uncommonly strong and impetuous. He owned to many of his friends, that he used to take women of the town to taverns, and hear them relate their history." For Johnson, sex was more of an aural than oral experience.

page document found among Boswell's notes and headed "Extraordinary Johnsoniana-Tacenda" ("to be kept silent"). The transcription of an exchange between Boswell, a painter friend of Johnson's named Mauritius Lowe, and Elizabeth Desmoulins, a boarder in Johnson's home, it addressed the matter of whether Johnson was sexually "capable." Mrs. Desmoulins reported to the gossip-hungry pair that she used to sit by Johnson's bed while Tetty slept in another room and let him fondle her until he was visibly aroused, at which point "he'd push me from him and cry, 'Get you gone!'"

A more controversial, even explosive issue looms: was Johnson into sadomasochism? Nothing seems more unlikely: he bestrode the drawing rooms of eighteenth-century London with magisterial authority; his essays in *The Rambler* were unassailable; he was enveloped in a penumbra of dignity. But there was the inconvenient matter of his relationship with Hester Thrale, long debated by Johnson biographers. Thrale, the wife of a wealthy brewer, made Streatham Park, her elegant country house, a refuge for Johnson from the rigors of city life and served as his confessor. Had she added to her duties as a loyal friend shackling him in handcuffs and whipping him? The main evidence is a letter from Johnson to Thrale in which he refers to "that bondage which you know so well how to render agreeable" and a one-line entry in his diary, *"de pedicis et manicis insana cogitatio"* ("from the fetters and handcuffs of crazy thoughts"). Thrale confirmed his preoccupation: "the Fetters and Padlocks will tell posterity the Truth," she wrote in her journal. Among the possessions left behind after her death was an item labeled "Johnson's padlock."

And yet it wasn't until 1949, when the eminent Johnson scholar Katharine Balderston published an article entitled "Johnson's Vile Melancholy," that the subject was raised in public. Balderston posited that Johnson's fantasy "assumed a masochistic form, in which the impulse to self-abasement and pain predominated." The "mind-forg'd manacles"—Blake's phrase—weren't just in the mind.

Most biographers have rejected this theory, often violently. In the view of Walter Jackson Bate, Johnson had fears of insanity; the padlock was there to restrain him and maintain his self-control in the event that he was seized with a fit of madness (which he sometimes was). "With touching historical naivete, our minds leap to sex," Bate adds condescendingly, "in biographies if not in sober histories—at the mere mention of anything connected with either 'secrecy' or 'guilt' in any human being from the ancient Greeks to the end of the eighteenth century."* John Wain concurred: "If one thing can be taken absolutely for granted, it is that Hester did *not* engage in any degrading sexual activity with Johnson."† But of course nothing can be taken for granted. All biographers know this—or should.

The gap between what is known and what it's permissible to say narrows as we approach the Age of Candor. Johnson's practices, real or alleged, seem innocent compared to the sinister rituals described by George Painter in his biography of Proust. Apparently the novelist got off on sticking hatpins into rats at brothels or having a chicken killed while he cowered under the protection of a young man dressed as a policeman. Here again it's not the sex act (if that's even what it is) that grabs our attention but the outlandishness of the desire. He *what*? "No doubt his victims represented many things," Painter writes helpfully, "for rats are among the most powerful, universal, and complex symbols in the inferno of the unconscious, and are regarded with special libido and dread by homosexuals as emblems of aggression and anal birth." About the chicken, he leaves us in the dark.

R. W. B. Lewis's biography of Edith Wharton, published in 1975, describes a florid sex scene from an unpublished short story, "Beatrice Palmato." ("She flung herself upon the swelling member, and began to caress it insinuatingly with her tongue.") But the impact of this titillating episode is muffled by the author's decision to stick it in an appendix, as if to suggest that it was just a fragment of erotica and not part of the story. Wharton was a prim fin de siècle aristocrat—not Linda Lovelace, fellatio doyenne of a later era. How could she have written about that kind of thing?

Why Lewis felt he had to relegate the sex scene to the appendix is unclear, since he discusses it at length in the narrative. There he relates the story's plot, which hints at an incestuous affair between Beatrice and her father that is revealed only after his death in a confrontation with her husband. As they stare at each other in revulsion, the hus-

---

* The suspiciously prolific Jeffrey Meyers, author of nearly forty biographies, is one of the few pro-flagellants: "Despite the overwhelming evidence of Johnson's dark secret, his modern biographers have not been able to reconcile his obsession with their exalted image of the great moralist." But his "overwhelming evidence" is no more persuasive than the non-evidence of Bate and Martin.

† I once stood next to Wain at a urinal in an Oxford pub but was too shy to address him. Anyway, what would I have said? *How do you explain the handcuffs, Mr. Wain?*

band becomes aware of "some profound moral perversion of which he had always been afraid to face the thought"—and about which he says nothing.

"The little fragment is, of course, pure and utter fantasy," Lewis assures us, and as a story about incest, in all likelihood it is. But it suggests a great deal about Wharton's avidity for sex—enough, perhaps, that Lewis might have felt he didn't need to go into the details himself. Her long affair with the American journalist Morton Fullerton introduced her to "an intensity and variety of sexual experience that Edith Wharton never dreamed of," writes Lewis; there's no need to spell it out. The "Beatrice Palmato" fragment "suggests that Edith Wharton was indeed, of a sudden, an uninhibited woman, eager to experiment—with a kind of generous and innovative energy—in all the modes of sexual enjoyment." That is all you know and all you need to know. And if it isn't, you can always turn to the appendix.

Some biographers relish taking on their subjects' sex lives; others are content to let this cup pass. Leon Edel handled the debate over the well-known matter of Henry James's "obscure hurt"—a mysterious affliction that may have prevented him from consummating the act of sex—in a gingerly fashion, attributing the "hurt" to a strained back incurred while putting out a fire in a stable in his role as a volunteer fireman. (He also quoted one of James's physicians, who described James as having "a low amatory coefficient.") But Edel, despite his own protracted bout of psychotherapy, was no Freudian. "The physical habits of the creative personality, his 'sex life' or his bowel movements, belong to the 'functioning' being and do not reliably distinguish him from his fellow humans," he wrote.

Three decades later, in a revised one-volume edition of what had come to be regarded as a classic but prudish biography, Edel tried to overcome his *pudeur* in order to stay relevant. It was a halfhearted effort. "I am not trying to suggest that I have, in my revisions, gone in quest of a 'sex life' or even a 'love life' for Henry James," he insisted: "My data remains the same." Sometimes a celibate is just a celibate.°

° And sometimes not. In the late 1990s, an acrimonious dispute broke out in the online journal *Slate* prompted by the publication of Sheldon Novick's massive two-volume biography of James; Novick alleged that, contrary to Edel's belief that the novelist was "celibate and sexually diffident," a "querulous old maid," he was in fact "a passionate, engaged man" who was "actively gay." He had extrapolated from a phrase of James's own, at the age of twenty-two, in a journal entry describing his "*initiation*

It was hard enough to look at the photographs of nude women from the cache of porn mags with anachronistic names like *Whisper* and *Stare* that I found among Delmore's "papers" at Syracuse University. Porn was less raw in those days, just breasts and a glimpse of ass—"rotundity of buttock."

Still, Delmore's stash was unsettling: what bad luck for both of us that it had ended up among the belongings salvaged from his last hotel room. It was like rummaging in your father's closet and discovering a stack of *Playboy*s. It destroyed his authority. I wanted to know Delmore, to understand him, to find out as much as I could about his life, but only up to a point. "Human kind cannot bear very much reality," wrote Eliot in *Four Quartets*. Neither can the biographer.

---

premiere"—a "divine, unique" encounter with Oliver Wendell Holmes, Jr. According to Novick, "James had his sexual initiation in Cambridge and Atherton Place," the James family's residence in Boston. As for the physician Edel had cited, it was "a bizarre, homophobic pronouncement by a doctor who examined James once he was ill and away from home, then announced to a breathless world that the famous novelist was badly hung."

For Edel, by then a near-nonagenarian, such terms as "badly hung" might have been pushing at the borders of acceptable idiom. But Fred Kaplan, another James biographer, ratcheted up the terms of the debate by suggesting that James might have "jacked off" Holmes. "I'd like James to have had sex (mutual masturbation? belly rub? anal intercourse? Even hot kissing—that kind of thing) with someone else, male *or* female, that he wanted to," Kaplan stated with magnanimity, introducing the idea that the repressed if not virginal novelist was drawn to the polymorphous perverse. "I'm baffled as to why you [Novick] think that James would be somehow *lesser*, even diminished, if he hadn't fucked or sucked or whatever with someone." Their bad language had an adolescent swagger that annoyed me. They weren't just biographers: they were men speaking to men. But their gross locker room talk made me nostalgic for the days when Edgar Johnson, one of Dickens's biographers, could refer to his subject's "nocturnal adventures" and leave it at that.

XIII

Dwight's* hesitation about my project had vanished once I got it under way, and he had even agreed to edit my work-in-progress. The chapters I sent him came back marked up like freshman themes. His challenges, objurgations, rebukes—and occasional praise—defaced every page. Phrase after phrase was judged "pretentious, cliché," "verbose." "Oh, God!" he expostulated, denouncing a failed rhetorical flourish: "You have a great vocabulary of vague and dull terms." "Why summarize what the letter will tell the reader in twenty-five seconds?" he exploded over some lame paraphrase. "You're like a museum guide who talks too much." When I glossed over a religious crisis in Delmore's life, he noted simply: "weasel." And when I skirted the reason for Delmore's fistfight with Robert Lowell, he scribbled: "Can't you explain? For once!"

If I said too little on that occasion, I generally said too much. "Leave the reader alone!" Macdonald protested; I was always "reader-nudging." Quoting a journal entry in which Delmore confided his anxieties, I summed up: "No more succinct or thorough evaluation of Delmore's malady is to be found in all his work"—to which Macdonald retorted: "And no more vague recapitulation of the main aspects of D's malady that have been described a dozen times. You keep wandering back to the old boneyard like a dog that's forgotten just where he buried that bone." And when, only a page later, I returned to the subject

---

* At what point did "Macdonald" become "Dwight" for me? Perhaps about the same time that "Schwartz" became "Delmore." I spent more hours in his company than I did anyone else's during these years, and there must have come a moment when, even in my own mind, I began to refer to him by his first name. Certainly the days of addressing him as "Mr. Macdonald" came to an end early in our relationship: Dwight didn't encourage formality and would probably have given one of his neighing laughs if I had addressed him this way after our first or second meeting.

Dwight Macdonald

yet again, he exclaimed: "MY GOD, you're back sniffing around again for that lost bone already!?"

I subsisted on crumbs of praise. "Trust you realize that I, unlike the sundial, only record the cloudy hours," he wrote at the bottom of one heavily scored page. There was an occasional "good" or "brilliant" or "masterful" (amended to the correct "masterly") to keep me going— and once, a terse but eloquent "Ah!" He got in the habit of annotating pages with stars "a la Mimi Sheraton," but he doled them out even more sparingly than the famous food critic and was so scrupulous that he once crossed out "very fine" and replaced it with "fine." The manuscript had a battle-scarred look; there were singed holes where smoldering cigarette ash had been scattered over the page, and one chapter, edited from the hospital bed where Dwight was recovering from an operation, arrived in the mail wrapped in gauze, the pages smeared with blood—visible evidence of the surgery he was performing on my sickly prose.

What prompted this editorial zeal? He continued to write the occasional essay, but he was "blocked," according to his wife, Gloria, and generally had a glass of Cutty Sark in his hand after four in the afternoon. Then there was his loyalty to the memory of his friend, and his love of editing: he had a lot of time on his hands. But I think what drove him was mainly literary enthusiasm. He often complained that he was having trouble writing and spoke wistfully of the memoirs he couldn't seem to get started on. My manuscript gave him the opportunity to roll up his sleeves and go to work. I was cautious in the early drafts, in the grip of a priggish restraint attributable to my youth and lack of confidence, and Dwight had little patience for this infirmity. "Can't you spur your pegasus into a livelier gait?" he exhorted me:

> At times he canters, sometimes even gallops (when you give your own personal ideas their head) but too often he ambles along at an academic jog trot. You seem to back away from or edge up to what you want to say, putting everything into indirect (and impersonal) discourse, using passive, circumlocutory syntax as if you were looking over your shoulder at a PhD committee and were afraid they'd catch you with your feelings and ideas too nakedly exposed. The nervously qualifying adverbs, the doubled adjectives (a belt AND a suspender) and the defensive—and needless—summings up of what you have established or what you are going to establish,

mostly at the start or the end of a paragraph—these academic tics are part of the same stylistic disease. You're a writer, with your own peculiar viewpoint on D, not a Congressional Investigating Committee, and you should only record what gives you pleasure. Enjoy yourself as a stylist, simplify and generalize acc. to YOUR taste & pleasure & fun, kick those Facts around, ignore them if they don't strike you as important to YOUR view of D. In short, be a (literary) man, not a (research) mouse.

I quailed whenever I saw a letter from Dwight in the mailbox, instantly recognizable by the rubber-stamped return address in the corner, framed by a boldly drawn box in red or purple Magic Marker. But he was good cop as well as bad cop. "You've got the makings of a superb and definitive biography of Delmore," concluded a harsh critique of my "clotted and verbose," "long-winded, heavy-breathing" prose. "Only why not write in your own personal voice, addressing, directly and informally, friends, acquaintances, and in general people like you, as bright as you, not academic bonzes who have to be elaborately briefed in woolly prose because they're so much dumber than you (or me)?"

Dwight responded to literature with Orwellian directness, undeterred from judgment by an author's reputation, and was effortlessly well read in what now seems an old-fashioned way, as familiar with Byron and Sir Walter Scott as with the latest Updike novel. In his letters he ranged back and forth from Delmore to Shelley, Jane Austen to Evelyn Waugh, with a chattily brisk authority. "Just read your excellent wrecking job on that academic bonze-ass* Bruccoli's hagiography of O'Hara," he wrote me about a review of mine:

> You make just the right points re. O'Hara (fair but strict—one negative you MIGHT have noted is his lack of love/feeling, w. is why he's so inferior to Scott [Fitzgerald], whose snobbishness like Proust's came from a romantic love, while O'Hara's came from Thersites envy: his catalogues of social hierarchy are cold,

---

* I'm not quite sure what Dwight meant by this word, which recurs in his correspondence: its dictionary definition (minus the "ass") is "spiritual person" or "Buddhist," but Dwight gave it a perplexing negative spin. Maybe such types were anathema to his practical mind.

boring, repulsive and Madame-Tussaud-wax-museum-like, while Scott's—as in the Homeric catalogue of the people who came to Gatsby's parties—were alive and moving bec. he wrote about the milieu as a guilty and so "involved" participant and not as an "objective"/Zolaesque "social scientist" cum snarling outsider.

There was nothing labored about these flights of literary criticism; they were utterly spontaneous, dashed off to make a point. He dismissed Edith Wharton as "middlebrow," compared Delmore to Wilde and Poe ("ALLAN, for Christ's sake!" he scolded me when I misspelled Poe's middle name: "Youth is no excuse—or maybe it is—in the wake of the post-fifties Zeitgeist.") When I complained that I was bogged down in the boring details of chronology, he noted that Poe had wrestled with the same problem in *The Narrative of A. Gordon Pym*: "He can't manage the kitchen-work of making his fantastic tale plausible except by throwing in huge sections of undigested factual stuff from voyages and natural histories that don't work (Defoe could do it because he wasn't at all imaginative)."

I tried to loosen up, but my authorial voice was still hopelessly solemn. "The students would enter the classroom in Sever Hall to find him sitting behind his desk, and when they left he would remain motionless, as if to discourage conversation," I wrote of Delmore at Harvard—prompting Macdonald to object, "Any professor in any class would be thus 'found' by his students unless he had a trampoline or a trapeze installed in Sever 106." A stiff remark about the "terrible irony" of Delmore languishing in a down-at-the-heels hotel while a lead article in *The New York Times Book Review* celebrated him as a major poet was likewise hooted down: "You sound like a Victorian moralist on the perils of drink." And when I offered a morose interpretation of some Delmorean quip, Macdonald circled it in red and wrote underneath, in purple block letters, "JOKE: Signed, D.M."

He was so impatient that I often mistook for anger what was only high-spiritedness. "What?" he would cry in amazement when I insisted that Ford Madox Ford was a better novelist than Conrad; that Martin Green (long forgotten now) was a good critic; that *A Farewell to Arms* was Hemingway's masterpiece. "How can you say that?" And he would embark on a vehement refutation, willing to hear me out but determined to get to the heart of the matter. "Do you really believe that Delmore didn't write any good poetry in the 1950s?" he said once, challenging a claim I'd made in an early version of the manuscript. He took out a soiled handkerchief and mopped his brow, as if convincing me that I was wrong required physical exertion. "What about all those poems in *Summer Knowledge*?" He rubbed his stubbly beard. "And even if it's true, which I doubt, why say so, for God's sake, this early in the book?" Gesturing with his cigarette, he reasoned, "But if you don't say so, you're holding back from the reader, who will find out your opinion later and wonder why you didn't say so then."

Baffled by this dilemma, invigorated by its moral ambiguity, he got up and strode around the room. In the end, we both gave ground: I came to admire a handful of the late poems, and Dwight conceded that he was partial to Delmore's work just because it was Delmore's. "You make me out in my usual role of a stubborn Scotch argufier, I see," he complained about my portrait of him in the book, but it was an image he cultivated. Once, after a long afternoon spent going over a new chapter at his house in East Hampton, he hurried me off to a cocktail party, only to arrive an hour early. We got back in the car, drove to the beach, and trudged up and down in the sand. Our subject that day was Edmund Wilson, whom I persisted in overpraising. "Wilson was a classic middlebrow," Dwight declared, halting in his tracks to make a point. "Look at *To the Finland Station*," he said, indignant at the thought of how wrong Wilson was about so many things. "Don't tell me you liked that book!" Obscurely ashamed of myself, I admitted that I did. He looked at me as if I had just said I believed in reincarnation. Ignoring the waves that swirled about his ankles, he made me explain what I could possibly admire about such a badly written, shoddily organized, poorly researched book, a book that was written only to popularize ideas Wilson never really understood in the first place and that, furthermore, Dwight didn't believe he was even interested in, except for the purpose of showing off how much he'd read—"which is what he always does," Dwight argued, his voice cracking in dismay. "He doesn't know a thing about politics; there's hardly a word about Stalin. It's just another subject he's read up on."

Back at the party, I could hear Dwight's braying voice across the room as he explained to a surly Vassar girl why David Riesman's *The Lonely Crowd* wasn't "an American classic." But he hadn't finished with the Edmund Wilson question, and driving me back to the train station that night, he crept along the road at five miles an hour, afraid we would arrive before he'd gotten his main points across. (I, meanwhile, was afraid I'd miss my train.)

Yet for all his sharpness in debate, Dwight could be willfully naïve, and his literary acumen deserted him at the most improbable moments. Not long after *Humboldt's Gift* came out, we were gloating companionably over the various characters Bellow had made fun of: the manic Delmore, the blandly genial Carlos Baker, the bibulous R. P. Blackmur. "What did you think of Orlando Huggins?" I said—"one of those ever-youthful lightweight high-spirited American intellectuals," as Bellow described Humboldt's "argumentative" literary executor, a blustering, "rosy-faced" character with a "tall man's belly," a "neighing stammer," and a "white billy-goat beard." There was a stunned silence. "Was that me!?"

Vigilant about prose, he was utterly indifferent to possessions. His apartment on East 87th Street, noisily patrolled by a yapping terrier that skidded up and down the hall, ignoring Dwight's exasperated cries, was dowdily comfortable: ceiling-high bookshelves, a plump-cushioned sofa, threadbare Persian rugs. His bungalow in East Hampton reminded me of a cottage in Devon or Cornwall—leaded windows, stucco walls, a flagstone terrace decorated with a curious assortment of relics. Terra-cotta statues of animals and saints were scattered about on the lawn. The walls of the gazebo that Dwight had made into a study were festooned with magazine ads of women in kilts and pullovers. Dwight had spent a good deal of his modest inheritance on *politics,* the magazine he published and edited during the 1940s, and he was always short of money. He and Gloria had to rent the East Hampton cottage for the lucrative summer months and sweat it out in New York. But there was no pose in his simplicity. The only thing Dwight cared about was the subject at hand—whatever it was. I once saw him get so caught up at a dinner party trying to explain to the table why Hemingway "couldn't write" that he spilled a steady stream of bouillabaisse on the carpet, oblivious to its splattering cascade.

One afternoon I called on him at the John Jay College of Criminal Justice, a gloomy building on West 56th Street, beyond Ninth Avenue, where he was teaching a course on American film. His office was a bare room with a metal desk, a grimy window that looked out on an air shaft, and a flickering fluorescent light—a fitting backdrop for the cross-examination that was about to occur. Dwight wasn't in a genial mood. Fierce, irascible, antagonistic, he paced about the room—Dostoyevsky's Inspector Porfiry interrogating Raskolnikov. Only whom had I murdered? The memory of Delmore. "You're turning him into a nutty paranoiac," he complained.

Had I been unfair to Delmore? It was certainly possible. I was charmed by his letters, amused by his journals, moved by his work, but I found his self-destructiveness oppressive. There were many Delmores: shambling, disheveled, self-deprecating, ironic, endearingly funny, brooding, depressed, remorseful, bitter, nail-bitten, wistful, anxious. But the sad story of his later years—the squandered talent, the mental suffering, the chaos of his life—weighed on me, and perhaps I judged him the way we tend to judge those closest to us: harshly.

If I was impatient with Delmore, Dwight was curiously obtuse. "He always made sense to me," he said when I described one of Delmore's paranoid soliloquies, and when he came to the scene in my book where Delmore insulted him over the phone, then tore it from the wall, he noted mildly: "Don't remember." Loyal to the very end, he simply couldn't—or wouldn't—grasp that his old friend had gone insane.

I left Dwight's office that afternoon in a rebellious mood. I was tired of his objections, his lectures, his jocular editorial asides. In fact, I was sick of Delmore and his whole generation. Diatribes in restaurants, boring accounts of life in the 1930s, drab offices in neighborhoods that made my heart pound: was this what the literary life was about? It wasn't until some months later that my thwarted pride sought redress—and then it was unconscious. In the last chapter of the manuscript, I told of a scene that had been reported to me by an editor who had accompanied Dwight to the hotel where he went to collect Delmore's belongings after he died. "Standing amidst a sea of papers, magazines, notebooks, and clothes, Dwight tried on a jacket of Delmore's," I wrote. "After all, it would have been a small reward for his loyalty and generosity over a decade." "Ye Gods, No!! What's the matter with you?" Dwight fulminated in the margin, underscoring the words with a purple pen. "Not my feeling at all. Not a dime-store ghoul. I liked the idea of wearing a jacket to remember D by—not 'getting a small reward.' Minuscule indeed! If I'm to be made a burlesque ghoul, at least record that I paid D's last hotel bill, $25—and have not yet collected."

Chortling over this comic outcry, I turned the page—only to find that he had just been warming up. "Really, Atlas, it's as if you weren't there half the time and were just wordily going through the motions," he scrawled on the last page. "I think you should put the ms away for six months or a year and then you'll see how dead and tedious large parts of it are." I was stunned. He had been hard on me before, but no matter how unsparing his annotations, they had invariably been witty, specific, suffused with irrepressible enthusiasm. And for once I thought he was wrong. The book was good now; it was finished. I just knew it.

I called him up. "I really wonder about you," he shouted over the phone. "After all these years, and all the time I spent on your manuscript, you don't even mention me in your acknowledgments!"

Apparently that business about Delmore's jacket hadn't been revenge enough for the mockery I'd endured. I had managed to thank every minor character I interviewed, every librarian who had given me access to Delmore's letters, every friend and relative who had put me up for a night, yet failed to include even a single reference to the man who had authorized my biography, made available to me Delmore's archive, spent hundreds of hours poring over my work-in-progress— the man who had taught me how to write. As Dwight commented in the margin about some Delmorean misdeed: "What a guy!" Still, hadn't I been good-natured about Macdonald's brutal annotations? It had been a great education, but a hard one, and I was still smarting from the welts raised by his red-felt-tip birch. Guiltily, I held the phone away from my ear. "If I'd thanked you the way you deserve," I joked (sort of), "you couldn't have written the blurb you promised me."

But Dwight had been doing some calculations of his own. "What are you going to do with the manuscript when you're done?" he said.

"Publish it, I guess."

"No, I mean the one I've edited."

"I don't know. I hadn't thought about it."

"Why don't you deposit it at Yale, among my papers?" So that his editorial genius—and my ineptitude—would be known to posterity. How could I not? The man had changed my life.

A week later we met in my publisher's office—neutral turf. Dwight had just gotten out of the hospital, and he hobbled in with a cane, his lips trembling through his ivory beard. But he revived when we sat down over the manuscript, his pencil hovering like a harpoon ready to spear offending phrases. Once more we made our way through my disheveled pages, only this time I stood up for myself. I had been working on this biography for three years now and knew Delmore better than those who had known him. After all, they couldn't see him as I did, day by day, through what he divulged in his journals, his letters, his conversation, even the margins of his books. It's said that no one knows what goes on inside a marriage; no one knows what goes on inside a biography either.

Dwight appeared to enjoy my new militancy. Hunched over the desk, dropping cigarette ash on his turtleneck, he beamed like a violin teacher with a blossoming pupil whenever I refuted an objection. "Our last session was vivifying for me bec. you so readily accepted my revisory suggestions when you were convinced," he wrote me later that summer, "and so clearly explained why you rejected them when you weren't."

It was vivifying for me, too, but also sad. This would be our last editorial skirmish. When we got to the end, Dwight stood up and patted me on the back—just as he had the day I first met him. Then he shuffled off down the hall. The elevator was slow to come, and when I walked by a few minutes later, he was still there, leaning on his cane.

Back in Cambridge, I rewrote my acknowledgments page, giving a full account of Dwight's role in the book: "His brilliant, copious annotations had a profound influence on my style and ideas." Meanwhile he was laboring over a blurb. "Took me well over a week, off and on (mostly off, guiltily fretting) in my present dilapidated period to get down a page and a half," he reported—and he wouldn't have relinquished it then if my editor's assistant hadn't shown up at his door like the boy who fetched Dr. Johnson's copy for *The Rambler*.

It was a generous blurb, and I responded with a grateful letter. "No reason for you to be 'overwhelmed' by my statement," Dwight replied— less than a month after he had urged me to put the manuscript away for a year. "Didn't you know how good it all finally came out?"

XIV

The book appeared in November 1977 to appreciative reviews and more attention than I could ever have expected. It was featured on the front page of *The New York Times Book Review*, which named it one of the Ten Best Books of 1977, and my normally stingy publisher* paid for a full-page ad: I even got nominated for a National Book Award. I was twenty-eight years old.[†]

One of the greatest pleasures was hearing from readers. In the months that followed, I got many letters from Delmore's friends and teachers and students and mistresses. Most were friendly; some were eager to point out errors: one correspondent informed me that the reviewer of Delmore's verse play *Shenandoah* wasn't Edna Lou Walton but Eda Lou Walton. Another scolded me for leaving the *e* off Montague Street in Brooklyn.

The most chastening corrections were contained in a long letter—to be followed up a year later by an article in the *Michigan Quarterly Review*—from Maurice Zolotow, Delmore's classmate at the University

---

* Its title, settled on after much discussion, was *Delmore Schwartz: The Life of an American Poet*. Roger Straus had wanted to call it *Delmore*.

† I also received a letter from Philip Roth, his name and Connecticut address neatly typed in the upper-left-hand corner of the envelope. He had just finished my book, he wrote, and was still "under its spell." I spent a whole day drafting a reply with mounting hysteria as I described the joy of reading *Portnoy's Complaint* when I was a sophomore in college; praised *Letting Go* for its "Jamesian amplitude"; and ostentatiously displayed my knowledge of Roth's entire oeuvre (a word I actually used). When I showed it to Annie, she suggested cutting it down. "Why not just say that you're a great fan of his work and were deeply honored by his praise?" I did as I was told—in general, a good idea when she gives advice. (She also persuaded me to cut my opening sentence: "When I received your letter, I felt like K. in Kafka's *The Castle*, only I had been waiting for it not months but for my entire life.")

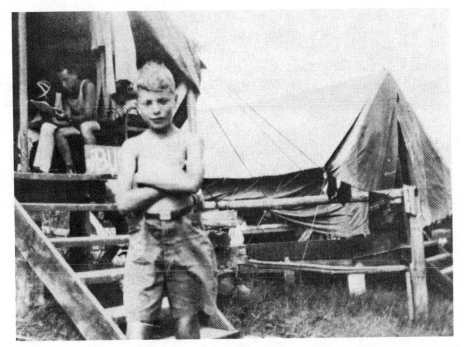

Delmore at the Pocono Camp Club

of Wisconsin. The letters to Julian Sawyer that I'd acquired from Andy Brown at the Gotham Book Mart were, according to Zolotow, "largely fabrications, fantasies." Delmore had written them to impress Sawyer, "with whom"—and here he dropped his bombshell—"Delmore was deeply in love." It wasn't just a youthful infatuation, either: "For Delmore was a homosexual who never came out of the closet. That was one of the frustrations of his tragic life."

Zolotow claimed that he wasn't alone in this supposition: "It was clear to the wives and lovers of Delmore's male friends (including my wife, Charlotte) that there was a powerful homosexual component in the feelings we had for Delmore and of course vice versa."

This wasn't entirely news to me. I had dealt extensively in my book with the possibility that Delmore had homosexual impulses, at the very least, and may have acted upon them; I had even placed in evidence a Rorschach test administered by a psychiatrist that supported this thesis. But it was still shocking to have it laid out in such raw form, as a factual statement.

It was also true that I didn't have to believe everything Zolotow said. Not because he'd been a failure: he had written celebrity biographies that made money and got mostly favorable reviews. But he had struggled with alcoholism, eventually vanquishing it through AA; and he hadn't achieved what he would have wished to as a writer.° So maybe he was bitter. On the other hand, as he noted in his *Michigan Quarterly Review* article, I was an innocent, untested by the disappointments of life, its disorder and ambiguity; it had been hard for me to reconcile "these confused and wandering old men and women with the gods and goddesses of the 1930s and 1940s." It's only now that I can observe them from the vantage of my own sixties—the same age as Delmore's contemporaries when I interviewed them—and see how clueless I was at the time, scribbling in my oblong reporter's notebook.

I also heard from people who had somehow eluded my gumshoe efforts over the years to track down anyone who had ever known my subject, however tangentially. A childhood classmate by the name of William Golub supplied one of those nuggets of gold the biographer sifts for with such irrational fervor: an address. "I had a close relation-

---

° Who does?

ship with Delmore for a year or so when I was about seven years old,"* Golub informed me: "When I knew him, he lived at 575 West 172nd Street, which was at the corner of St. Nicholas Avenue. I believe this was the first place he lived in Washington Heights." He, too, had a correction to make, though he slipped it in so casually that it hardly seemed like a rebuke: "The elementary school he went to was P.S. 169, not 69."†

One of the most poignant letters I received was from Mrs. Ethel Travis, who had been the neighbor of Delmore's mother at 34 Hillside Avenue. (Wait! When did she live there?) "She was a most attractive woman," wrote Mrs. Travis, now resident in Panorama City, California, "a chronic complainer about her arthritis and her neglectful children." This I already knew or at least wasn't surprised to learn. Delmore was always going on about his annoying mother, a whiner, a nag, a collector of grievances. But that she sat outside her building, disheveled in a wheelchair, "with her blouse usually half buttoned"—now there was one of those "small details" that Boswell was always looking for as a way to show character.

There were others. For instance, that Rose had gone out to California to visit Delmore's brother and returned with two avocados: "I was thrilled that avocados were so easily available in California, for in New York they were a great delicacy and I could rarely afford them," recalled Mrs. Travis. But say I had managed to track her down, and suppose she had told me about the avocados. What could I have done with this detail, how worked it into the narrative? Would I have even written it down? *Brought back avocados from California . . .* Even so, I was haunted by the image of Delmore's mother returning home, avocados in hand, and showing them off to her neighbor: were they soft by then, after their long journey, or were they still hard and shiny, waiting to ripen?

Irving Lowe of Mill Valley, California, also had a story about Rose:

When Delmore returned to N.Y. after his first (and only) year at Wisconsin, I met him one day on the Coney Island Boardwalk and

---

* I smiled at this idea of a "close relationship" between seven-year-olds: it made it sound as if they were business colleagues rather than two small Jewish boys growing up on the streets of New York and trading baseball cards.

† Included in Golub's letter was an entry on Delmore from the yearbook for Public School 115: "In writing he can take a hand / And as an actor takes his stand." That would have been nice to put in my book—along with a thousand other things.

at his urging went home with him to meet his mother—"She'd be glad to see you," he said. I wondered at that. Our conversation had been dry, and I was uneasy and wanted to get away. He introduced me to his mother, who seemed harried; went unceremoniously to his room and didn't come out until a couple of hours later, when she knocked at his door to say I was leaving. She had given me some tea, and we talked and talked, and it was clear that she was troubled about her wild, tender, unkind, gifted son. Before she went to call Delmore, she whispered to me, "Be Delmore's friend, Irving."

I nearly wept when I read this letter. How Delmore had needed such a friend; how hard it had been for him, given his stormy temperament, to *be* a friend. Irving, like so many others, had tried and failed.

Now and then a correspondent would supply an anecdote that I could have used as counter-evidence to the somewhat glum portrait of Delmore I had drawn, such as a description of how he appeared on the tennis court from F. Scott Fitzgerald's biographer, Arthur Mizener. They were together at a summer writing workshop at Kenyon College, and Mizener would wander over to Delmore's house after lunch and find the poet hard at work annotating *Finnegans Wake*: "He almost always beat me; he had a serve that would knock the racquet right out of your hand." *Right out of your hand* . . . Who knew? And this would have been the summer of 1950, when Delmore, then thirty-six, was already deteriorating. I had quoted the novelist George Lanning, who described Delmore that same summer as "shambling, sweaty, untidy."* Where was "the happy Delmore," Mizener wanted to know, the Delmore who was "easy, gay, and great fun"? I have no idea, professor. Why didn't you tell me about this side of Delmore—especially the detail about his big serve—when I interviewed you?

Sometimes it felt as if the letters I got were excuses for the writers to reminisce about their own lives: "I went to the same camp as Delmore, Pocono Camp Club"—and Isaac Bashevis Singer's nephew was in his bunk! "I was in Gertrude's geology class [in] Washington Square College . . ." Or to find out if I had come across information that might

---

* Lanning recalled that Mizener, "with his big convertible and striped polo shirts, looked like an ad for the best Scotch whiskey"—and he probably wore spotless tennis whites, too.

prove useful for the books *they* were writing. "I was intrigued by your account of his Harlem nightclub crawl with Louis MacNeice," wrote a scholar from England at work on a book about MacNeice, a passing presence in my own. I wasn't omniscient; I could contribute no more details about Delmore's night out in Harlem with a British poet of whose life I knew nothing other than what I'd reported. One notecard = one sentence. And what about Delmore's relationships with Berryman, Auden, Lowell, Paul Goodman, R. P. Blackmur? their biographers queried me. For them, Delmore was a transient figure in their subject's life, a name in the index. As Janet Malcolm shrewdly notes in *Two Lives,* her biography of Gertrude Stein and Alice B. Toklas, the major characters in one book are minor characters in another; sometimes they play a walk-on part, at others a supporting role:

> The biographer is writing a life, not lives, and to keep himself on course, must cultivate a kind of narcissism on behalf of his subject that blinds him to the full humanity of everyone else. As he turns the bracing storylessness of human life into the flaccid narrativity of biography, he cannot worry about the people who never asked to be dragged into his shaky enterprise.

We are all, to ourselves, the center of the universe: why should biography be any different? It, too, has a star—or, to stay with the celestial motif, a sun, around which the lesser planets orbit.

Reading these letters made me miss Delmore. Termination—as I thought of it, the term implied both the end of therapy and the . . . end—was in this case less painful for the analysand, who was dead (and had been throughout the entire term of treatment) than for the analyst. One letter in particular, from Delmore's dear friend William Barrett, indicated that I wasn't alone in my bereavement. "I put off reading your book for so long because I knew it would be painful to me," he wrote a few months after it came out. "I wanted to approach it when my mind would be clear of other things. Well, it was painful to me. My friendship with Delmore was the closest I've ever had, and it is still very painful to think of him in his decline."

It was a moving letter, drenched with loss; a decade after Delmore's death, Barrett was still struggling to come to terms with it: "One of the things I need to do for myself is to retrieve in my memory what was good and fine in that friendship, as well as to retrieve the image of

what, with all his conflicts, was beautiful and wonderful about Delmore
before he began slowly to come to pieces." To reconcile the Delmore
of *In Dreams Begin Responsibilities,* the handsome, charismatic, self-
dramatizing, comic, and passionate figure who had mesmerized the
best writers of his generation with the shouting, abusive, drunken and
decrepit figure of his last years had been a challenge for me, too.

Perhaps the most provocative letter was from a man named Milton
Schafer who lived on Riverside Drive. It was long and carefully considered. Among the issues Mr. Schafer wrestled with was the difference between my portrait of Delmore and Bellow's. My biography "put
[him] in mind of" *Humboldt's Gift,*

> which for some reason I never finished. Bellow's Schwartz as
> Humboldt is merely ludicrous. I found no possible basis to feel
> him empathically and after reading your book it became much
> clearer why I felt as I did. Then it occurred to me, once being
> drawn into his orbit and made to feel his uncomprehending rage,
> power, and irreversible atrophy or decomposition with such an
> accompanying howling and lamentable sadness about it, that Bel-
> low actually does him a huge disservice. Not that character dis-
> tortions in the literary world are by themselves all that shocking
> anymore, mind you. It's just especially in the case of Schwartz,
> when Bellow must have known to a large extent how much he
> was going through continually, it seems shamefully heartless and
> self-serving of him to so insensitively strip him of his humanity—
> and so totally.

What struck my correspondent, who didn't seem to have known Delmore, was the evident sympathy I had for my subject—"his demons,
his quirks, his essential solitariness." He found the intensity of my
identification eerie: "In a way, it seemed at times that you were as literally obsessed with him as he was with himself."

Milton, thou shouldst be living at this hour.* Too late! Which didn't
prevent me from looking him up in the Manhattan phone book.

He wasn't listed.

---

* Forty years later, it turns out that he *is* living, but is in a nursing home and in no
shape to discuss *Humboldt's Gift* or anything else.

Edmund Wilson

XV

I still had to earn a living; being a literary biographer isn't a highly remunerative occupation. (The advance for *Delmore* had been three thousand dollars, which came out to a thousand dollars a year.)

After much strenuous lobbying of the human resources department of Time Inc., I had gotten a job as a staff writer for the magazine, which, despite what Dwight would have deplored as its "middlebrow" reputation, had at one time or another employed Alfred Kazin, Irving Howe, James Agee, and Dwight himself as book reviewers.[*]

I arrived in New York on July 14, 1977, just a few weeks before my book was published, leaving Annie behind to finish her last semester at medical school. It was the day after the blackout that sparked arson and rioting throughout the city, and as I came up the steps from the subway at 79th and Broadway, the air was acrid with stale smoke. Garbage littered the street. So this was Manhattan, where Hershey Green, the hero ("O New York boy") of *Genesis,* had celebrated the city's energizing pulse; where the *Partisan Review* crowd had carried out its backstabbing work; and where Annie and I were to spend the next year in a one-bedroom apartment, with black iron garden furniture in the kitchen, that I had sublet from an ad in *The New York Review of Books.*

My tenure at *Time* was ignominious. I was a "floater," assigned each week to whatever section of the magazine was short-handed. Often it was Milestones, the page that recorded the deaths of famous people or significant—usually malign—events in their lives, such as divorces or

---

[*] Their names are fading now; a recent article in *The New York Review of Books* footnoted a reference to Howe, identifying him as "an influential critic in the 1950s and 60s." To an intellectual of my generation, this is like saying that Frank Sinatra was "a popular singer in postwar America."

prison convictions or spectacular financial crashes. In the next cubicle sat Michiko Kakutani, chain-smoking unfiltered Camels as she turned out fast-breaking stories with a machine-gun clack of typewriter keys. Who could have predicted that within a decade she would land the job of daily book reviewer for *The New York Times* and become the most feared critic in America?

After fifteen months, I was released from this benign journalistic bondage when Harvey Shapiro, the editor of *The New York Times Book Review*, called me up and offered me a job as an editor. It was a lucky break. A few years before, I had interviewed Harvey, then an editor at the *Times Magazine* and a poet of considerable distinction, about Delmore, whom he'd known in his later Greenwich Village days. Not long afterward he was made editor of the *Book Review* and responded to my bold request for assignments by sending me books to review. I used to lie rigid in bed on Saturday mornings, praying the phone would ring; usually the call came in around eight o'clock (if it came at all), and an operator would read a telegram: WOULD YOU REVIEW H. MONT-GOMERY HYDE'S BIOGRAPHY OF OSCAR WILDE STOP NEED 800 WORDS DUE NOVEMBER 17 STOP.

A few hours later, the telegram itself would arrive at the door in a yellow envelope, the words pasted on white strips of paper. The way everything, including the period, was spelled out in CAPS made the message seem urgent—which, to me, it was.

What I loved about reviewing biographies—apart from the thrill of seeing my byline in *The New York Times Book Review*—was that I didn't have to know much of anything about the subject under review. Harvey trusted me. I would "work up"—to use Edmund Wilson's phrase—Melville or T. E. Lawrence or Ford Madox Ford, speed-reading their books and previous biographies in marathon sessions at the New York Public Library; after a week or so of late nights, I usually knew enough to write a passably well-informed review. The brevity of the form required ruthless selectivity, and you needed to keep in mind that you were writing for a newspaper, not for *Partisan Review*. Only a few reviewers had mastered this skill. Cyril Connolly, editor of the important literary journal *Horizon*, was one, and I kept a volume of the weekly reviews he'd written for the London *Times* in the 1940s and '50s close at hand. Another was Wilfrid Sheed, himself a regular reviewer for the *Book Review* who had left the paper to become a "full-time writer"—an exalted vocation that I hoped someday to emulate.

Wilson was my model. On my shelf were the successive volumes of his book reviews for *The Nation, The New Republic,* and later on, *The New Yorker,* collected decade by decade: *The Shores of Light* (the 1920s and '30s), *Classics and Commercials* (the '40s), and *The Bit Between My Teeth* (1950–65). He had a knack for distilling the essence of the book before him, the author's career, and his place in the cultural history of his time, all in the space of a thousand words. I read these collections straight through, as if they were brief chapters in a novel with a hundred plots.

I owned all of Wilson's books: not just the review collections but plays, poetry, novels, and as they accumulated over the years, the letters and journals, also in decadal form. They took up, literally, a whole shelf and included the late works of reportage, *Israel and the Dead Sea Scrolls* and *Red, Black, Blond, and Olive: Studies in Four Civilizations: Zuñi, Haiti, Soviet Russia, and Israel,* written at a point when Wilson had read virtually the whole of the Western canon; *Night Thoughts,* an eccentric miscellany of poems; even *O Canada,* a collection of essays about writers no one had read or, based on his droning plot summaries, would ever feel compelled to read. I was one of the few fans of the novels, *Memoirs of Hecate County* and *I Thought of Daisy,* noble failures that were nonetheless compelling as portraits of the sexual manners and morals of the 1930s. (The first was briefly banned.) The plays, I had to admit, were pretty lame; *This Room and This Gin and These Sandwiches,* about some guy who wants to marry a girl who refuses to marry him, was as bad as its title and never got produced. It was hard to picture the word *sandwiches* on a Broadway marquee.

What I admired most about Wilson was the no-nonsense way he treated the job of critic. His prose was workmanlike, almost aggressively unliterary. He was a great popularizer (a quality that gave some critics an excuse to condescend to him), capable of covering a vast amount of ground without breaking a sweat. He wrote in a voice that spoke directly to the reader, and he went about his work with a sleeves-rolled-up, elbows-planted-on-desk enthusiasm, sharing his discoveries with a muted passion that gained power from its restraint. And he got the job done. I admired his dogged determination to read a writer's entire oeuvre: who else could have persevered at the self-assigned and unrewarding task of plowing through George Saintsbury's three-volume *History of English Prosody from the 12th Century to the Present Day*?

Wilson's vivacity of style reflected the excitement of discovery; he always spoke in plain language, never showing off his vast erudition. That literature excited Wilson—sometimes in the literal sense—was evident: he derived "a pleasure almost sensual" from learning languages;* as an undergraduate at Princeton, he claimed to have once had an orgasm while reading a book. (He didn't specify its title, but I assume it didn't come in a brown wrapper.) He was "exhilarated" by Waugh, "stimulated" by Voltaire, "thrilled" by the eighteenth-century critic Hippolyte Taine, whose *History of English Literature* became his model: "He had created the creators themselves as characters in a larger drama of cultural and social history, and literature, for me, has always meant narrative and drama as well as the discussion of comparative value." *Narrative and drama*: those were the engines that drove Wilson's most ambitious books, among which I count *Axel's Castle*, his primer on the Modernists, whose work was then still new enough to require a level-headed guide; the eight-hundred-page *Patriotic Gore*, his stoically comprehensive survey of the literature of the American Civil War (the one book of Wilson's, I confess, that I could never finish);† and *To the Finland Station*, subtitled, in a deliberate effort to heighten the drama, *A Study in the Writing and Acting of History*.‡

Many of the figures Wilson wrote about are long forgotten now, and others already were by the time I encountered these reviews. Who reads—who has even heard of?—Glenway Wescott, Paul Rosenfeld, or Max Eastman? Still others (Katherine Anne Porter, William Saroyan) will go in their turn, as the present recedes mercilessly into the past, and the past recedes further into the deep reaches of obscurity. It didn't matter. I read Wilson to read Wilson.

He had his weaknesses. He could be naïve; the timing of *To the Finland Station*, an excitable defense of the Russia Revolution, hap-

---

° He was conversant with the classical and major Romance languages; had mastered Hebrew in order to write about the Dead Sea Scrolls; learned Russian, primarily, it sometimes seemed, for the purpose of showing up Vladimir Nabokov, with whom he had a public and foolhardy skirmish over Nabokov's translation of *Eugene Onegin*; and undertook, toward the end of his life, to learn Hungarian.

† Wilson admitted that he himself "got bored and depressed" by the end.

‡ This was the book Dwight and I had argued about on the beach at East Hampton.

pened to coincide with Stalin's consolidation of power, preparing the way for the Terror. He had a tin ear for poetry, tending to overpraise mediocrities like Phelps Putnam, and opportunistic enthusiasms; he crassly praised the work of Anaïs Nin in order to get her into bed. And he had blind spots: "Must we really, as his admirers pretend, accept the plight of Kafka's abject heroes as parables of the human condition?" he asked in a somewhat bellicose essay entitled "A Dissenting Opinion on Kafka." (Yes, Edmund, we must.)

His great strength, or originality, was not as a formal critic—he lacked the sensitivity to literary style the job requires—but as what might be called a biographical journalist. Among my favorite books of Wilson's was *A Piece of My Mind*, essays on diverse themes ("War," "Sex," "Religion") that displayed his unique hybrid, a form that combined personal essay, formidable scholarship, and closely observed reportage. I was especially taken with the last essay, "The Author at Sixty,"* a meditation on his relationship with his father that seemed to me, then and now, Wilson at his best—a memoirist whose conversational, forthright manner conveyed a kind of brusque self-knowledge. There was something melancholic and fusty about this essay that I found appealing: Wilson wrote as if he were winding down his career, though he would live another seventeen years and add seven more titles to his imposing bibliography.[†]

Looking back now, I wonder if it might have been the hybrid of biographical and autobiographical portraiture—the fugitive presence of the writer in the writing—that I admired. Wilson's sketch of his depressive father, a lawyer who willfully thwarted his own career and suffered a nervous breakdown, had a quality of empathic observation that I sensed, even before I began to write biography myself, was a key to the whole enterprise. Knocking about the old stone house in Talcottville, New York, that had been in the family for generations—it would serve as the stage for his book *Upstate*—he conjured up his father's visits there in long-ago summers, recalling how "he would occupy himself

---

* This seemed an inconceivably old age when I first read it in my early twenties, as remote in time as the "sixty-year-old smiling public man" of Yeats's "Among School Children."
† *Israel and the Dead Sea Scrolls, A Window on Russia, The Devils and Canon Barham, The Cold War and the Income Tax,* and three posthumous volumes: *Letters on Literature and Politics, The Sixties,* and *Dear Bunny, Dear Volodya: The Nabokov-Wilson Letters.*

with the inspection of his fishing tackle or whittle sticks into slender canes." The antiquity of the house, with its fireplaces and small-paned windows and wideboard floors, prompted Wilson to brood on his own self-chosen obsolescence: "Am I, then, in a pocket of the past? I do not necessarily believe it. I may find myself here at the center of things—since the center can be only in one's head—and my feelings and thoughts may be shared by many."

They were—at least by one. On a hot August day in 1975, when I was in the middle of my Delmore book, driving to a friend's wedding in a small town on the shore of Lake Ontario, we made a detour to go by the house in Talcottville. I recognized it instantly as the one pictured on the cover of *Upstate*. I went up on the porch and peered into a first-floor window. The heavy wooden furniture was still in place. I could imagine Wilson at his desk, reading a volume of Tennyson's poems (as he did in his final days, according to one of the last notations in his journal). His presence—he had only been dead three years—seemed almost palpable, a ghost risen from the pages of all the books I had read over the years with such rapt absorption.

On the essay's last page, the thought occurs to Wilson that he might be "stranded," out of touch with his own life and times.

Even at twenty-five, I felt this way.

One day in the spring of 1980, while I was sitting at my metal desk in the *Book Review*'s office, a dusty open space with chicken-wire windows, fluorescent lights, and linoleum floors—these were the pre-cubicle days—my black rotary phone rang.° It was Roger Straus, with a proposal: was I interested in writing Edmund Wilson's biography? I agreed without hesitation. Why would I not?

Wilson had lived a fascinating life and known everyone worth know-

---

° What actually happened—to clarify the moment for the sake of giving an accurate picture of life in that long-ago time—was that I was in conversation with a colleague when I heard my phone ring across the room (after a while one grew adept at picking out the ring of one's phone, even though it was just like the ring of every other phone in the office, in the way that a veteran bird-watcher learns to distinguish a particular bird whistle from what, to an uninitiated ear, sounds identical to other bird whistles) and sprinted to get it, nearly tripping over a pile of galleys in the process. There were no answering machines in those days; you either got to the phone in time or it stopped ringing, leaving you to wonder who the caller might have been.

ing: John Dos Passos ("Dos"); F. Scott Fitzgerald ("Fitz"); Ernest Hemingway ("Hem"). He had been everywhere: he drove an ambulance in France during World War I; lived in Greenwich Village during the Roaring Twenties; traveled around America, notebook in hand, during the Depression; filed dispatches from a ruined Europe in the aftermath of World War II. He had dined with Kennedy in the White House and Santayana in Rome. He offered a large canvas on which you could draw a map of the twentieth century—the ideal subject for a big, "definitive" biography.

Wilson's personal life was also—I put the word out there with some embarrassment—juicy. He was married four times—most notably to Mary McCarthy—had a massive problem with alcohol, and struggled with depression: the failure of his first novel, *I Thought of Daisy*, precipitated a full-scale nervous breakdown. There were chronic money problems: he was in a state of near-permanent penury. His advance for *To the Finland Station* was $1,700—less than $300 for each year he worked on it. A regular writing job at *The New Yorker*, where he signed on as a staff writer when he was forty-eight, provided some measure of stability, but his finances were precarious up until the end.* That he had survived as "a man of letters"—perhaps the last one—was a tribute not only to his remarkable breadth as a critic and scholar but also to his sheer endurance.

Why, then, did years go by while I procrastinated? I never even made it up to Yale to look at his papers. After a while, whenever I passed my Wilson shelf, I averted my eyes, hurrying past as if it were a friend I'd dropped. Part of the problem was the sheer surfeit of available documentation: after *Upstate* and his autobiographical essays, the volumes of letters and journals—*The Twenties, The Thirties, The Forties*—there wasn't much left for a biographer to discover. I knew all about the wives: the actress Mary Blair; the hard-drinking Margaret Canby, a wealthy California socialite who fell down the stairs drunk and died; and Wilson's last wife, the stylishly cosmopolitan Elena Thornton, an heir to the Mumm champagne fortune, who managed to keep the marriage together by spending several months of each year

---

* He spent a good part of his sixties sitting in the office of the Internal Revenue Service in Utica, New York, negotiating a settlement of the tax bill he had failed to pay out of some combination of principle, neglect, and megalomania. (*The Cold War and the Income Tax* is a dyspeptic account of his long skirmish with the IRS.)

in their cottage on Cape Cod while Wilson sequestered himself in the stone house upstate. As for Mary McCarthy, the story of their combative relationship—the drunken fights that once resulted in Wilson slugging her after an argument over who should take out the garbage; the sexual misfires; the dramatic public displays of marital animosity—had already been told in a number of books, most notably McCarthy's own.° And then there was the parade of girlfriends: Dawn Powell, Edna Saint Vincent Millay, and others less renowned, such as "a little Roumanian Jewess" and a woman named Bernice Dewey whose only identifying trait was "the smell of her light dress washed with Lux." I would have been a mere literary custodian, collating and organizing the published data into a tidy narrative. Wilson had done the job himself.

It wasn't only the number of women Wilson "bedded" that got on my nerves. It was his insistence on recording the mechanics—what Richard Ellmann called "the precise anatomical convolutions"—at great and annoying length in his journals. Wilson's cold clinical accounts of sex made Kinsey seem like Henry Miller. I was startled not only by his profligacy but by his potency: at the age of seventy-four, he seduced the bibulous *New Yorker* film critic Penelope Gilliatt on a couch at the Princeton Club and also managed to work in a hot affair with his dentist's wife. He seemed to have no taboos, even dabbling in bondage and discipline. (He briefly owned a whip). He was a prodigious engine; women marveled at what one described as his "bull-like physical stamina." He was so insatiable that I sometimes wondered how he could have slept with so many women while reading as many books as he did. And it didn't even sound like fun. Cyril Connolly, reviewing *Memoirs of Hecate County,* complained of the "insect monotony" of its couplings. It's not enough to say that Wilson was clinical; he could be downright creepy. He described his penis as "meaty" and compared his mistress's feet to "moist little cream cheeses."[†]

° Wilson showed up as a character in her first *five* novels, most witheringly in *The Groves of Academe* as the Irish writer Henry Mulcahy, "a soft-bellied, lisping man with a tense, mushroom-white face . . . bad teeth, and occasional morning halitosis."
† Yielding to the insidious ease of Google, I type in the words "Edmund Wilson penis" and .27 of a second later, up comes an essay by Gore Vidal in *The New York Review of Books.* With his usual bracing acerbity, Vidal writes: "Wilson is proud of his 'large pink prong.' (Surely, Anaïs Nin said it was 'short and puce'—or was that Henry Miller's thumb?)"

But the biggest obstacle was Wilson himself. He was hard to like: one of his wives described him as "a cold fishy leprous person." Could I spend years of my life with a subject who, even in the company of his wife and daughter, read at the dinner table? He was anti-Semitic; he was rude to waiters. He found no merit in Anthony Powell. It finally dawned on me: what I felt was more complex than "distaste" or "dislike"—it was a question of compatibility. Was Edmund Wilson someone through whose eyes I would come to see life in a new and different way? Did he possess qualities of temperament or character that would remain fresh throughout the many years it takes to write a major biography? In short, did he *interest* me?

The voice of the unborn son in Delmore's story "In Dreams Begin Responsibilities" rang out: "Don't do it!"

I returned the advance.

There would be other opportunities. Once you've published a biography, you're a biographer. I would get calls from editors: Did I want to write the biography of Tennessee Williams? Dashiell Hammett? Invariably, I was excited at first. Invariably, after a few days of remembering what it was like to sit in the Syracuse library for ten hours at a stretch and then have dinner alone in the gloomy Orange Bar; to pore through old telephone books and call up nine people on the Upper West Side named Sheldon Horowitz, hoping to find the one who shared a cabin with Delmore at the Pocono Camp Club in 1924; to crawl around on the floor day after day, pawing through files and notecard boxes and disorderly piles of manuscripts . . . I would turn down the project. Why go through that ordeal again?

Meanwhile I had left the *Times* and was supporting myself as a contract writer for magazines. But I was still obsessed with Chicago, which I had now tried twice to write about—first in a strange, abandoned novel about a circle of Chicago intellectuals that I had struggled with for most of my twenties, and then in my one published novel, *The Great Pretender*, the story of a boy from the North Shore of Chicago in quest of "authenticity." I felt more attached to my own past than to the New York literary world I uneasily inhabited. "I had unfinished business in Chicago," says Bellow's Charlie Citrine. So did I, even if I was from the suburbs.

Bellow had obsessed me ever since I read his first novel, *Dangling Man,* in a Penguin paperback edition, at the age of fourteen. I had been transfixed by the Hyde Park intellectuals lost in their deep thoughts, braving the "unmitigated wintriness" of the city to ponder "what we are and what we are for, to know our purpose, to seek grace"—the European sensibility of Rilke's *The Notebooks of Malte Laurids Brigge* imported to the snowbound streets of Chicago. The rattling El on its dark iron girders hadn't been depicted in literature yet, as far as I knew, though I had read James T. Farrell's *Studs Lonigan* trilogy about Irish Chicago with excitement; the industrial wasteland, the "Christmas blaze" of garishly lighted shops on Devon Avenue over the dusk-darkening holidays, the hulking warehouses—none of this had made its way into any book I had read. It was Bellow who saw it and wrote it down.

Chicago was more than a backdrop: it was a character in itself. "I am an American, Chicago-born," opens *The Adventures of Augie March;* never mind that Bellow was born in Montreal. It is Chicago, in all its raw vigor, that forms his mental life, forms life itself: "The heat of June grew until the shady yards gave up the smell of the damp soil, of underground, and the city-Pluto kingdom of sewers and drains, and the mortar and roaring tar pots of roofers, the geraniums, lilies-of-the-valley, climbing roses, and sometimes the fiery devastation of the stockyards stink when the wind was strong."

My favorite of Bellow's novels, the one I read over and over, was *Herzog.* Published in 1964, when he was forty-nine, it was the book that brought him wealth and fame. Written partly in the third person, partly in the form of letters from Moses Herzog, an untenured professor who teaches the history of ideas in a New York night school "to everyone under the sun," both living and dead, it was a comic tour de force. The trope of Herzog's one-way correspondence—with Heidegger ("Dear Doktor Professor Heidegger, I should like to know what you mean by 'the fall into the quotidian'") and Nietzsche ("Der Herr Nietzsche, You speak of the power of the Dionysian to endure the sight of the Terrible"), with his psychiatrist and his lawyer and the department store Marshall Field, where his harrassing, haughty, cuckolding wife Madeleine has been running up bills—was liberating. It enabled Bellow to say whatever he wanted to say to anyone, unfettered by self-censorship or the demands of narrative order. He could just free-associate (an illusion, of course; this was Bellow's most tautly controlled novel) and marvelous utterances would spill forth: "Awareness was his work; extended consciousness was his line, his business." "His duty was to live."*

As with all of Bellow's fiction, the novel is lightly plotted: Herzog has been left by his castrating wife, who, it emerges, is having an affair with his best friend; he calls upon and has sex with various girlfriends; he reminisces, in passages of great beauty, about his childhood in the slums of Montreal as the son of Russian Jewish immigrants; he retreats to the Berkshires and sets about the quixotic renovation of a dilapidated Victorian mansion with "a twenty-thousand-dollar legacy from Father Herzog." After great labor, mostly cerebral but some of the handyman variety, he lies down on his "Recamier couch"† and assesses his situation, which turns out to be not so bad after all. His last letter is to himself. What does his "intensity," his "idiot joy," add up to? Herzog asks. (The question was often on Bellow's mind: he titled a late book of essays *It All Adds Up*.) What good has it done the world? What good has it done him? What does he want? "But that's just it—not a solitary thing. I am pretty well satisfied to be, to be just as it is willed, and for as long as I may remain in occupancy."

And talk about experience-near. Bellow had been born in a year equidistant from the years of my parents' births (Donald Atlas, 1913; Saul Bellow, 1915; Nora Atlas, 1917); had grown up and gone to high school in a Jewish-immigrant Northwest Side neighborhood not far from my father's (Bellow, Tuley; Atlas, Senn); and shared a weird geographical affinity. (Herzog's father lives on Mozart—pronounced *Moh-zart* in Chicago—around the corner from where my grandfather, Herman Atlas, had a drugstore.) There was even an intertwined personal history: the family of my mother's best friend, the Teitelbaums,‡ had sold their bakery to Bellow's uncle, Louis Dworkin.

But it wasn't just the convergence of biographical and autobiographical facts—the overt element—that moved me. It was the way Herzog exists in the world, immerses himself in its essence. He is a sentient being, a consciousness, and this capacity for special insight brings life itself before us in all its stunning radiance. Waiting for the ferry at

---

* This is not as easy as it sounds.

† An eighteenth-century divan made fashionable by . . . oh, just look it up if you're interested. The Internet has spoiled the pleasure to be found in displaying recondite erudition as if you just happened to know it.

‡ The maiden name of Evelyn Stone. Remember, my mother's friend who had Alzheimer's?

Woods Hole, he stares down at the clear water and reflects: "He loved to think about the power of the sun, about life, about the ocean. The purity of the air moved him." *Soul, human, heart,* and—alas—*death*: these were Bellow's touchstones, the words that animated and defined his experience of being in the world. I read *Herzog* the way a Victorian family in its Cornwall cottage might have read the worn Psalter that had been handed down from generation to generation: for comfort, spiritual insight, moral instruction, and the most important thing—not available from anyone else—a sense of what it felt like to be alive.

In the spring of 1986, a few months after my novel came out, I was assigned to write a profile of Bellow for *Vanity Fair,* "pegged to" a PBS version of the novella *Seize the Day,* featuring Robin Williams as Tommy Wilhelm. I hadn't seen him since our brief meeting more than a decade before, when I was writing my biography of Delmore, and I was excited, as always, by the prospect of spending time in his company. I wrote and requested an interview.

Seize the Day was Bellow's darkest book—the only one, apart from the penumbral *Dangling Man,* devoid of high-spiritedness. *Augie, Henderson the Rain King,* and *Humboldt's Gift* all had antic heroes, large-hearted, life-loving, and loaded with verve. Even Sammler, in *Mr. Sammler's Planet,* a tough-minded Holocaust survivor, had a resilience that defied the tragic. Only Tommy Wilhelm, the protagonist of *Seize the Day,* was a failure—divorced, unemployed, rejected by his own father—whose downward spiral culminates in his losing, over a single day, the last of his money through foolish speculations in the stock market. In the harrowing last scene, Tommy stumbles into a stranger's funeral and, as he contemplates the inert figure in the coffin, begins to weep: "The source of all tears had suddenly sprung open within him, black, deep, and hot, and they were pouring out and convulsed his body, bending his stubborn head, bowing his shoulders, twisting his face, crippling the very hands with which he held his handkerchief." The world eludes his grasp; by the end, he is a man with nothing.

Eventually a letter from Bellow arrived in the mail. I felt a tremor of joy: the University of Chicago return address was a Pavlovian trigger. "It used to be that 'commitment' meant locking up a mad relative," he wrote in his best self-satirizing manner. "Now I myself appear to be the mad relative in need of protective custody." But he would be happy to take me on a tour of his old Chicago neighborhoods. We would have fun, he promised.

Bellow's apartment was on the fourth floor of a concrete high-rise in Hyde Park, surrounded by a moatlike wall. When I rang the buzzer, I noted the names of three other Nobel laureates: the economists Milton Friedman and George Stigler, and the physicist Subrahmanyan Chandrasekhar, his first name shortened to "S." so that it would fit in the slot under the doorbell.

When I came out of the elevator, Bellow was waiting at the door. I felt underdressed: he had on a dark-brown suit with a matching vest, black loafers, and a pink shirt with a white collar. There were deep pouches under his eyes.

His living room overlooked the Museum of Science and Industry, with its Greek pillars and rotunda. I had gone there in a yellow bus on field trips to stand in the giant replica of a human heart, listening to the swish of blood in its slow-beating chambers (*lub-dub, lub-dub*). The apartment was simply furnished: two leather chairs, a couch, an antique desk, and everywhere, books: *The Brothers Karamazov; The Orphic Vision: Seer Poets from Novalis to Rimbaud.*

Rain was streaming down the windows, but we decided to go out anyway. Bellow opened his closet: inside were several shelves of hats. He invited me to choose.° I picked out a small one, of black felt.

His car, a Cadillac Cimmaron, was parked out front. We headed north on Lake Shore Drive and got on the Eisenhower Expressway, turning off at West Division Street, a neighborhood of ramshackle houses, vacant storefronts, and trash-strewn empty lots. Bellow had grown up here. He pointed out a dilapidated apartment building and told me that his violin teacher, "Mr. Grisha Borushek," had once lived there: "He trained his pupils by whipping them on the buttocks with his bow when he got sore at them."

He slowed down before a Wendy's. This was where the Crown Theatre had been, Bellow informed me. It was here that he had seen *The Mysterious Dr. Fu Manchu*—"Lon Chaney threw knives with his feet." I thought of the passage in *Humboldt's Gift*—it seemed as if every moment I spent in Bellow's presence brought to mind an analogous

---

° Herzog "put on his fedora, as if he hoped to derive some authority from it."

scene in his work—where Citrine hails a taxi° and goes on a tour of the old neighborhood: "The sausages in the *carnicería* were Caribbean, purple and wrinkled. The old shop signs were gone. The new ones said HOY. MUDANZAS. IGLESIA."

On our way back to Hyde Park, Bellow pulled in at Burhop's, on the corner of Chicago and LaSalle, to buy "a piece of fish." One piece. He would be dining alone. In the fish store, he took a number and, when his turn came, asked for a half pound of sturgeon. No one recognized him. No one came up and exclaimed, *Why, you're Saul Bellow!* The man behind the counter wrapped the fish in flesh-colored paper. Bellow took it to the cash register and paid. I wondered if he had a vegetable in the refrigerator at home, or at least some frozen Green Giant peas.

Back in his apartment, I brought up the matter of the fishmonger's cluelessness. "People aren't aware of my presence," Bellow said with apparently unfeigned equanimity. "What am I compared to the Cubs, the Bears?" I asked if he was lonely, and he replied firmly: "No, not a bit."

Not that he was so alone. "I had tea with a lady," he announced with a trace of pride, emerging from the small kitchen with two floral-patterned cups and saucers on a tray. "She brought the fancy dishes."

His fourth wife, Alexandra Tulcea, a renowned mathematician and said to be a great beauty—Minna, her counterpart in *The Dean's December,* is described as "handsome"—had left him only months before. "Emanations from my convulsed self were hard to take," Bellow said when I worked up the nerve to ask him about this most recent breakup. He had been working for ten hours a day on *The Dean's December.* "Nothing else mattered. I turned into a beast. I was soaring, but to Alexandra it was offensive. I couldn't make too many concessions on this score. She wouldn't live with a writer anymore." *Nothing else mattered.* You couldn't write a great novel without breaking up your marriage? Apparently not; for Bellow, marriage was pugilistic: "It was like fighting with one hand tied behind my back."

When it was time to go, Bellow put on his hat and coat and walked me to the corner of 57th and Dorchester to wait for the shuttle bus to O'Hare. As we stood on the corner in the rain, he put his hand on my

---

° "The driver was wild-looking with an immense Afro like a shrub from the gardens at Versailles." No one would dare write a sentence like that now.

shoulder. Had we brought along an umbrella? Had he given me the hat again?

I can't remember.

In the spring of 1987, I went to Oxford to write a profile of Iris Murdoch, whose donnish oddball husband had once declined to tutor me. When I arrived, I learned that my revered tutor Richard Ellmann had just died of ALS and that his funeral would be on one of the days I was there. I hadn't brought along the one suit I owned, but I had an old tweed jacket, and I went into Ede & Ravenscroft on High Street (est. 1689), an intimidating establishment whose salesmen, in their fine suits, were always lurking by the door, where I found a thick wool tie.

Seated in a pew at the back of the New College Chapel, I watched as the coffin was carried down the aisle, borne by six strapping men, one of whom I imagined must be Ellmann's son Stephen, a lawyer in New York. I didn't see the two girls, Maud* and Lucy, now young women launched on writing careers of their own; I often saw their bylines in the London papers. But there was Mary in her wheelchair, an invalid who had outlived her husband.

Ellmann was only sixty-nine and had been nearing the end of a biography of Oscar Wilde; now it would be published posthumously. "During the last weeks of his life," wrote Walter Goodman in a *Times* obit, he completed his book "with the help of small machines on which he typed out messages that were then printed on a screen or on paper." I knew Walter Goodman (now dead, naturally), a slight, fastidious, elegant man who clearly had no idea what he was talking about when it came to technology. What the fuck were "small machines"? And how did you print on a screen? Let's give Goodman a pass; he was trying to be complimentary, calling attention to Ellmann's diligence, and I was moved by the thought of my tutor laboring to make his final deadline; his *Wilde* came in at over eight hundred pages.

It is natural for biographers' subjects to die, which they invariably do in the closing pages, muttering some portentous last-minute observation (Henry James, "So it has come at last—the Distinguished Thing,"[†]

---

* Probably named after Maud Gonne, the great love of Yeats's life.
† In fact, these *weren't* the last words James uttered; the Distinguished Thing came for him two months later, but they're the ones we remember. James's actual last words

Thomas Hardy, to his sister-in-law: "Eva, what is this?").* But it is also natural for biographers to die, I thought, as I walked out into a warm spring rain. And while their passing is less important than their subjects' passing, it still matters to a small circle of people who love them and sometimes to a wider audience; biographers who wrote a good book or two can usually count on a fairly extensive obit. We like to think we matter, too (if anyone does): we have done the necessary work of preservation.

I had been in touch with Ellmann only once since I left Oxford—he had written me a nice note about *Delmore*—but I had thought of him often. He was the one who had set me on my life's path, who had shown me that the work and the life, literature *as* life, were intertwined. When he read Joyce or Yeats, his touchstones, he saw how each illuminated the other. *Yeats: The Man and the Masks* he'd called one of his books— the masks were the poems that concealed the poet's true identity, but they were also what revealed him. This was the purpose of biography.

H ow does the biographer choose his subject? *Does* the biographer choose his subject? Sooner ask how each of us became the person we are and how we spend our lives. Isn't it just random? A matter of genes and family background and historical circumstance? Of fortuity? We come across a book, a manuscript, a letter; someone who knew the subject; the subject himself. But why this one instead of that one? It's impossible to know. The decision to write Delmore's biography was made after a forty-five-minute lunch at Benihana; settling on my next would take a lot longer.

In the summer of 1987, I wrote Saul Bellow a terse letter asking if I could be his biographer. I laid out my credentials: the biography of Delmore, my Chicago background, my deep knowledge of his work. Without being pushy about it, I made a strong case: I was the one.

I waited three weeks and then, my patience (never highly developed to begin with) at an end, called him up. He was cordial: "Oh, how are you, Mr. Atlas?"

I was nervous, but he was friendly and seemed glad to hear from

---

were addressed to his sister-in-law, William James's wife (not to be confused with their sister): "Stay with me, Alice, stay with me."
° A good question.

me. He switched to Jim, then, perhaps deciding that was too informal, proposed to call me James. Either was fine, I assured him: "I'm still having an identity crisis."

"It's something you never get over," he said.

I came right to the point: "I wonder if you've given any thought to my letter."

"Oh, yes," he said. "I've been meaning to write you, but you know, it's summer . . ." He trailed off and after a moment resumed: "I've been turning it over in my mind, and I'm very flattered that you should think me a worthy subject. I liked your book on Delmore Schwartz."

All the same, he put me off. He might consider this "a future project." For the moment he intended to write a memoir of his own, and he didn't feel he could both reminisce and write. But he "would be glad to have a talk" at some point. He was friendly and reminded me that we had "crossed paths" when he was writing *Humboldt's Gift*—"about Delmore from another point of view"—and I was writing my biography.

"You put Delmore on the map," I said—an ingratiating remark but true. I wasn't the one responsible for "the Delmore revival." Had it not been for Bellow's novel, I suspect, my own biography might not have aroused so much interest.

There was no hurry, I continued; it wasn't as if he had to decide now. But once again I pointed out how well suited I was to write about him: I was from Chicago, people in my family knew people in his family, my father had grown up in the same Jewish neighborhood on the West Side of Chicago. I reminded him that relatives of the Stones, my parents' closest friends, had bought Bellow's uncle's bakery many years ago . . . a familiar litany by now.

I asked if anyone else was working on his biography. Only a woman his "own age" who'd known him for many years, he replied. Her name was Ruth Miller.

When I suggested that I might write my book "later on," he said: "After my departure."

"No!" I protested. "After you've finished your memoir."

Our conversation was winding down. Bellow wished me "a good summer."

"Good-bye."

"Good-bye."

After we hung up, I stared out the window for a long time. I felt that

Bellow had left the possibility open of my becoming his biographer—had even encouraged it. I would let the idea marinate and write again in a few months.

Ruth Miller wasn't Bellow's first biographer. She had been preceded, a decade earlier, by Mark Harris, a vaguely well-known journalist and novelist whose self-respect had been eaten away by a perception of neglect: the only book of his that had risen above the tide of forgotten novels was *Bang the Drum Slowly*, about a baseball player dying of Hodgkin's disease, which got made into a movie starring Robert De Niro. It gnawed at Harris that he wasn't better known. He had approached Bellow in a spirit of homage, or so he thought, claiming the novelist had "enriched" his life, and presented himself as a self-abnegating acolyte: "In this book I come off the worst," he says on the first page of his curious memoir/biography. But he emanates resentment. Charlie Citrine in *Humboldt's Gift* coins a term—"contrast-gainer," someone with flaws who nevertheless stands out in comparison with someone who has more flaws. Harris is a contrast-loser, fretting that he's "a man of a different and lower class" than Bellow—which he probably was. His book was called *Drumlin Woodchuck*, from a poem by Robert Frost about a wily species with many escape tunnels "who shrewdly pretends / That he and the world are friends."

Bellow never made his position on Harris's aspirant biography clear. He let Harris tag along to lectures and dinner parties in Hyde Park but never directly acknowledged that he was sitting for his portrait. He was still "groping," he explained; he was not yet "*fini*." He didn't want to get involved: "There are enough people with their thumbprint on my windpipe." Yet there he was, dragging Harris to Imported Motors in Lafayette, Indiana, to get his Mercedes repaired.

The actual work of a biographer held no interest for Harris. "For specific facts you must go to a certified public accountant," he declares with disdain. He "believes" that Bellow is associated with the Committee on Social Thought; introduced to one of Bellow's friends in a restaurant, he fails to catch the name: "Stat or Staps or Stat or Stap."[*]

---

[*] Maggie Staats, later Simmons, a lively and beautiful young woman with whom Bellow fell in love and depicted as Demmie Vonghel, one of Charlie Citrine's girlfriends, in *Humboldt's Gift*.

After a decade of purported research, he writes Bellow: "I date this letter your birthday. It is one of the *hard* facts I have about you." But even that's wrong: it turns out that Bellow's birthday wasn't July 10 but June 10.°

Yet despite his self-absorption, his need to occupy center stage, Harris does in the end manage to capture some essence of Bellow. Driving past a travel agency, Bellow refers to it as a "travail agency"; greeting a neighbor walking his dogs, he calls out, "You appear to be meditating." No, the neighbor replies; he's only waiting for the dogs "to go." I don't know why I love this anecdote so much, or what it says about Bellow, but it resonates with the strangeness of life. And Harris is funny. Annoyed by Bellow's then-considerable wealth, he boasts over dinner that he has $60,000 invested in a lucrative mutual fund (this is 1970s money), then worries—his paranoia hovers over the book like a dank cloud—that Bellow will hit him up for a loan. When he calls the novelist's home, Bellow's three-year-old son picks up the phone and, mistaking Harris for his often absent father—Bellow is in the midst of one of his divorces—announces that he loves him: "I could not but tell him that I loved him, in turn, and I think that I fooled him with my voice." He reminds me of Boswell imitating Dr. Johnson's stammer.

Always willing to deceive himself, Harris thought he had produced a book his subject would like. He wrote Bellow (a letter that of course went unanswered): "This book is going to be interesting, reliable, unique, kind, loving, appreciative, sound, intelligent, and artistic." And so it was.

Bellow didn't think so. After an excerpt appeared in *The Georgia Review*, Harris called Bellow to find out what he thought of it, a call that, insanely, he recorded—who did he think he was, Richard

---

° Or was it? On Bellow's birth certificate, the date of birth is listed as July 10, but subsequent biographical and reference works list his birthdate as June 10. . . . It is also possible that Bellow's mother could have been going by the Jewish calendar . . . Yet on his application for a Guggenheim Fellowship . . . And so on and so forth. In my biography of Bellow I would spend several hundred words on the subject. In the end, did it matter when he was born? And yet the facts are often significant in themselves, *are* the story. That Bellow's mother might have been calibrating her son's birthdate by the Jewish calendar (immigrants were habitually negligent about such details) tells you a lot about the culture she came from; the accretion of such facts and near-facts and pseudo-facts builds up a richly detailed portrait of a time and a milieu that is one of the essential features of biography. Facts matter.

Nixon?—later depositing the tape among his own papers at the University of Maryland. "I thought I looked like a turd," Bellow said. "Bad-tempered. Nasty. Snappish. I don't see myself that way."

It had been a mistake to let a biographer into his life—not that he would learn from it.

XVI

The freelance life wasn't for me; it was too uncertain, and I didn't have the versatility required to produce articles on culture and politics month after month. Literature was my beat, but you couldn't make a living writing about the Belknap twelve-volume edition of Byron's *Journals*. Also, we had a four-year-old daughter, and Annie was pregnant again. Soon we would be struggling to support two young children in Manhattan. It was time to look for a job.

After many wheedling letters and phone calls, I managed to claw my way back to the *Times*, as an editor at the Sunday *Magazine*. In my absence, the old metal desks had been replaced by burlap-lined cubicles. The phones were now equipped with answering machines.

I started work in the fall of 1987. One afternoon I was wandering the streets a few blocks from the *Times* offices on West 43rd Street when I found myself driven inexorably toward the New York Public Library, that lordly edifice whose grandeur Alfred Kazin had celebrated so rhapsodically in *New York Jew*, recalling "exultant hours in the long sun-filled reading room" where he wrote his first book, *On Native Grounds*. For Kazin, the library was more than a great civic institution: it was the shrine at whose altar he had learned to worship what would come to be known, in a later, more contentious decade, as "the canon"—the Great Works of Western civilization. I, too, had spent many hours in the library during my Delmore days, climbing the steps of "exhilaratingly smooth marble," hurrying past "the great catalogue room lined wall to wall with trays of endlessly thumbed cards" to arrive, winded, at my ultimate destination, one of "those great golden tables" shining in the sun.

There was nothing exhilarating about my situation now. Stone-hearted in a dark suit, I was as lost as I had ever been. My novel, *The*

Allan Bloom

Great Pretender, had annoyed the critics; the protagonist, Ben Janis, turned out to be a pretentious jerk.*

"You took a wrong turn," Roger Straus had said to me that summer, when I was sitting in his office talking about possible subjects. Four floors below us, on Union Square—this was in the pre-gentrification years, before Barnes & Noble, chic restaurants, and the farmers' market, with its attendant crepes and preserves and gelato stands, arrived on the scene—drug dealers were peddling their wares, muttering "smoke, smoke" beneath the drooping elms. Roger wasn't angry, just concerned about what "his" author—he thought of us as family—should do next. I remember thinking, *How many wrong turns do you get in this life? Is there a fixed number—two? three? ten?—after which you're so deep in Dante's "dark wood" that you can never find your way out?*

Longing to escape the deadness and desolation that clung to me like Delmore's heavy bear, I ducked in the door of a wood-paneled room on the first floor of the library that housed the Dorot Jewish Collection—floor-to-ceiling shelves packed tight with books devoted to the history of My People. As I was browsing, a massive tome, bigger than the Manhattan phone book, caught my eye: it was entitled *A History of the Jews of Chicago,* by H. L. Meites. I lugged it over to the table and, for the next two hours, sat bent over its time-faded pages like one of my forebears in some Polish shtetl poring over the Talmud in a wooden synagogue.

Published in 1924, Meites's book was a compilation of brief portraits of prominent "Chicago Jewry" combined with articles, letters, pamphlets, and miscellaneous other documents chronicling the history of the Jewish community in what I considered—allowing myself some latitude—my hometown. The book was seven hundred pages long, but over that afternoon and on several subsequent visits, I read it nearly cover to cover, beginning with the account of the first Jewish community in Chicago around the turn of the nineteenth century, when the Jewish Burial Ground Society was formed; the growing population of Jews as more immigrants arrived from Eastern Europe; the formation of the Standard Club (in my parents' and grandparents' day, only German Jews were admitted); the founding of the Chicago Hebrew

---

* The novel contains a riff on Bellow's hat, and the shadow of Isaac Rosenfeld lies heavily over its pages. Haberdashery and failed Jewish American writers from Chicago: two dominant themes in my work.

Institute, created to supply "comfort kits" to soldiers during World War I ("The splendid showing of the Jews of the West Side in these and other activities gained the respect and admiration of the city"); the construction of Michael Reese Hospital, where my father once practiced; and—this excited me most of all—the contribution of Jews to Chicago culture, the violinists and conductors and opera singers whose heirs I had often heard perform at the Chicago Symphony Orchestra Hall and the Lyric Opera, towed there by my music-mad parents. Interspersed throughout this lively narrative were brief, dictionary-entry-size biographies of prominent Chicagoans—not least among them the author himself, who, I learned from the introduction written by his grandsons, was born in Odessa and immigrated to Chicago with his family when he was twelve years old; one of his major achievements was the establishment of the Jewish Historical Society.

I would come to know it well.

O n an impulse, I called up Adam Bellow and invited him to lunch. Adam was the son—there were three in all—of Bellow's second marriage, to Sondra Tschacbasov, a union depicted with great anger and verve in *Herzog*.

We agreed to meet at a restaurant in Midtown. When I walked in, the maître d' motioned me toward a table in the corner, and there he was: the dreamy wide eyes, the handsome aquiline nose . . . the photograph on the dust jacket of *Dangling Man*.

Our conversation was constrained at first. Adam was thirty-one— eight years younger than me. He was an editor at the Free Press, but it quickly became clear that his father was the emotional center of his life. It had been hard to grow up as Saul Bellow's son. "You didn't have the freedom to be no one," Bellow had once said to him.

Over lunch, Adam told me about Bellow's brothers, Morry and Sam, who got caught up in the nursing home scandal that I remembered reading about in the *Chicago Sun-Times* when I was in high school. They both went to jail. "Just like the books," I said, recalling the tough, unsentimental *machers* who populate Bellow's work.

"Nothing is made up in my father's life," Adam said. "If you want to know about his life, all you have to do is read his books."

He asked me what I was working on, and I told him that I was considering several projects: a biography of Cyril Connolly, a book about the New York intellectuals, a history of Chicago. "Anyone who writes my father's biography—and someone inevitably will—has to be literary in his bones," he said. But I hadn't said anything about writing his father's biography; I had come with no declared agenda, even if I had one. It was Adam who brought it up. I wondered if he was sounding me out.

The *Times*'s executive editor, Max Frankel, had gotten it into his head that I should write a profile of Allan Bloom, the University of Chicago professor whose crackpot but eloquent polemic, *The Closing of the American Mind*, had been at the top of the best-seller list for months. A distinguished philosopher who left Cornell after armed black militants took over a campus building, Bloom had found a home at the Committee on Social Thought, a catchall department for intellectuals who didn't belong anywhere else. Its faculty was distinguished: the classicist David Grene, the social theorist Hannah Arendt, the Romanian philosopher Mircea Eliade—and Bellow, a major character in Bloom's story. It was he who had encouraged Bloom to write the book and helped get it published; he had even written an introduction.

The "culture wars," as they were called—a term now as remote in time as the Wars of the Roses—were being hotly fought in those days between a band of conservatives who believed that the Great Books of Western civilization, Arnold's "best that has been thought and known," were under assault by Marxist radicals who controlled the English departments of universities across the land and were lobbying to make the curriculum more "inclusive." Against the threat of black studies, deconstruction, and most insidious of all, "cultural relativism"—the notion that all societies, all cultures, all values are equal—Bloom had made an eloquent case that only the classics could save us.

It was bracing to read this theoretical call to arms, with its obscure references and tangy rhetoric, even if you had to sit there clutching your head in your hands as if you were back at the college library bent over Kant's *Critique of Pure Reason*. For Bloom, philosophy was a priestly calling; the decadence of modern civilization had corrupted the soul of man; egalitarianism, soft-pedaled by the classical philosophers, was the enemy of the true and the good: "The real community of man is the community of those who seek the truth, of the potential knowers, that is, of all men to the extent they desire to know."

Bloom and Bellow were close friends; they taught a course on the Great Books together, garbed alike in their bespoke suits, and Bellow spent long evenings in Bloom's apartment, next door to his own, listening to Bloom rant far into the night about the pending end of civilization. The two men were so inextricably bound up in the public mind that a review of the book in the scholarly journal *Academe* facetiously attributed its authorship to Bellow, who, the reviewer suggested, had written "an entire coruscatingly funny novel in the form of a pettish, bookish, grumpy, reactionary complaint against the last two decades."

Two months after I started at the *Times,* I flew out to Chicago on a freezing day in December—the kind of day, Bellow had written, when you half-expected to see a polar bear floating on an ice floe in Lake Michigan. I enjoyed trotting after Bloom while he held forth excitedly on the campus protests around the country that were proving his point. "Look what's happening at Stanford," he said, showing me a clip from *The Maroon* about the latest uproar over the curriculum. "We're really getting to them."

We, of course, included Bellow, his virtual collaborator; and you couldn't discuss Bloom without discussing Bellow.

I showed up at his cramped office on the fifth floor of the Social Science Research Building—the same office where I had visited him twelve years before, only this time I had an appointment. It was a wintry Chicago afternoon, and the office was cast in gloom; I recalled from my previous visit that Bellow liked to sit in the dark. He had no wish to illuminate—not for the benefit of a reporter, anyway. He looked fit and dapper in a nubbly brown suit, pale-green shirt, and bow tie. We talked about Bloom's book for a while; about the perils of fame ("It's like going through the *Inferno* without Virgil as a guide"); and about the furor Bloom had created with his incendiary book. Bellow was sardonic on the subject. "Who is the Tolstoy of the Zulus, the Proust of the Papuans?"° he said. "I'd be glad to read them." He laughed, and I joined in. I could see that he enjoyed his bon mot, with its consonantal

---

° Alas, I have come across the notebook in which I scrawled this now-famous (or infamous) line, and it turns out that the word Bellow used was "Polynesians," unless I mistranscribed it—which is quite possible, given the splutter of the two *p*'s that, I distinctly recall, induced such merriment in the novelist and his interlocutor. If it turns out that "Papuans" is a later embellishment (we'll never know), apologies to the untold number of journalists who have misquoted Bellow's comic and wildly offensive remark over the years.

fillip. It *was* funny, despite its flagrant violation of the code of political correctness.

Still, the controversy was no laughing matter. Bellow's comment, spoken in levity, would provide ammunition to those inclined to see him as a racist, an elitist, and a reactionary—a large constituency. He got into these public scrapes in part out of a wish to provoke, I sensed, to stir things up, but also out of principle. If Bellow was guilty of the charges leveled so stridently by the Left, he had his reasons—some of them unconscious, others the product of his own experience; it disturbed him to see the neighborhood he'd grown up in transformed by a new generation of immigrants with different values (to put it delicately), or to watch student radicals occupy universities where his own books were taught.

I left Bellow's office elated. He was wry, acerbic, funny, mournful, bitter, shrewd—sometimes all in a single sentence. Boswell tells us that when he was in Dr. Johnson's presence, the marvelous talk he heard "was not a particular selection from Dr. Johnson's general conversation, but was merely occasional talk at such times as I had the good fortune to be in his company; and, without doubt, if his discourse at other periods had been collected with the same attention, the whole tenor of what he uttered would have been found equally excellent." This was also true of Bellow.

Two days after I got back to the office, Harriet Wasserman, Bellow's agent, called my boss at the magazine, Jimmy Greenfield, to request an interview on her client's behalf. It was urgent, she said. That afternoon she bustled into his office; I was called in soon afterward.

Bellow was concerned that there would be too much about him in the piece, Wasserman had been explaining to Greenfield, a genial *Times* man who had spent a good part of his life at the paper. Dapper in his tailored pin-striped suit, he couldn't see what the fuss was about, but Wasserman was beside herself. Zaftig, voluble, and as fussily intense as a Jewish auntie, she had been Bellow's agent for virtually his entire career; he was her most important client. (Of course, he would have been any agent's most important client.) As she faced the good-natured editor, she was literally on the edge of her seat. She also admitted that Bellow was worried about his photograph: the *Book Review* had used one a few years back that he claimed made him "look like a herring that's been left out in the rain too long." But he didn't want a new one taken. Was he annoyed the piece *wasn't* about him? I had no evidence for this uncharitable thought. Maybe he just didn't want to divert attention from Bloom.

The next day I got a call from Adam Bellow. He'd had dinner with his father the night before, and Bellow was "sore" at me. "He's very irascible right now," Adam said. "He's paranoid about being identified with Bloom." Ah! So that was it. *The Closing of the American Mind* had caused much controversy around Hyde Park; Bloom was "taking a lot of heat." Bellow wanted to keep his distance. "If you want to write more about my father someday, maybe you should hold off writing about him now," Adam advised.

I defended myself as best I could. "I'm going to write what I write," I said firmly. Nevertheless, I dashed off a letter to Bellow assuring him that there was nothing to worry about. My piece was intended to be about Bloom, and it was; Bellow played only a minor role. They were close friends and colleagues; Bloom's book had been Bellow's idea. But the piece was about the whole intellectual world of the Committee on Social Thought, a great subject in itself. In the end, it was illustrated by a full-page color photograph of the entire committee on a staircase in the wood-paneled Faculty Club. There was nothing piscine about Bellow's visage, and I thought it was gracious of him to agree to a photo shoot with his colleagues, all distinguished figures but none remotely of his stature.

A week after it came out, I heard from Adam. He said his father had received my letter and all was forgiven; I was back in his "good graces." "You won't hear from him," Adam warned me, and he wasn't sure if Bellow would even read the piece. But the word of mouth was apparently good.

For the moment, all was well.

One day I was sitting in my cubicle working on a piece about nuclear throw weights by McGeorge Bundy when a book crossed my desk that was also a bomb—less shattering in its potential impact on society, but momentous all the same. It was a thick paperback, published by Wayne State University Press and entitled *Preserving the Hunger: An Isaac Rosenfeld Reader.* Within was a generous selection of Rosenfeld's work: book reviews, literary essays, commentaries on Jewish culture, short stories, journals. There was also a reprint of Bellow's preface to *An Age of Enormity.*

I put aside Bundy's piece and immersed myself in Rosenfeld's essays, reading in my fevered way until the only people left in the office were the cleaning staff. The literary pieces were exemplary: He could write about Orwell, Stendhal, or Kafka, writers as remote from his own sensibility as they were from one another's, with a confident ease that showed deep familiarity with their work. His voice as a critic was natural and aphoristic. He raised an eyebrow without (quite) being cruel. The British novelist Henry Green, he wrote, intended "to have you admire his prose." And of Gandhi's ostentatious acts of renunciation, he pointed out that failure can be "a kind of egotism." His elegy to the great Yiddish writer Sholem Aleichem was more than an exercise in nostalgia; it was a lament for the catastrophic disappearance of a whole culture:

> He defined a peculiar intellectual and spiritual province of the Jews, revealing the hidden vitality of their religion and the historical viability of their culture. It is a province which is lost to the majority of us today, who know nothing of such blessings, even as that which was once our world, with Kasrilevke° its Jerusalem, was lost to the world that engulfed and destroyed it.

Rosenfeld's voice was direct, without pretension, engaged; nothing could deflect him from the critic's job of assessing a writer's work. But it was also a voice that spoke to *me*—the same one I'd heard in his novel *Passage from Home* when I'd first read it so many years before.

I was leafing through catalogs one day when I noticed that a small publisher named Markus Wiener had issued a reprint of Rosenfeld's novel. I ordered it instantly: what a perfect occasion to write about him. Graced—or perhaps afflicted—with a limitless and unearned self-confidence, I wrote to Robert Silvers, the fabled editor of *The New York Review of Books*, alerting him to the existence of the two books and boldly suggesting that I review them. To me, as to everyone else in the literary world, Silvers was a distant, exalted figure—refined, impossibly erudite, genial but forbidding, not just an editor but a person of enormous importance in our culture. He referred to the *New*

° The fictional town in Sholem Aleichem's stories.

York Review as "the paper," which was like calling Piranesi's Temple of Neptune a "sketch."

A few weeks later, long after I had given up hope, the phone rang. It was Silvers, speaking in his elegant voice, faintly inflected with an English accent. He was "keen" on a review. "Is this part of some longer work?" he asked.

On a scorching summer afternoon in 1988, on a sudden impulse, I went to visit the Berg Collection at the New York Public Library. The streets were empty; molten seams of black tar oozed through the asphalt. Housed in a suite of hushed, carpeted rooms on the third floor, the Berg was a literary researcher's dream: the walls were lined with hand-tooled leather-bound editions of Dickens and Thackeray; on the long wooden tables were green-shaded lamps. I had spent a few happy afternoons there when I was writing *Delmore;* the Berg had extensive holdings in modern American literature, including letters from Delmore to Alfred Kazin and other treasures. I remembered that you needed a special card to enter and applied at the desk downstairs, hesitating when asked what it was I had come to see. Finally I wrote down *Bellow.*

I pushed open the double glass doors and introduced myself to the librarian, a petite, elegantly coiffed woman in her sixties whom I identified as Lola Szladits, the curator of the Berg Collection; I had read a profile of her in *The New Yorker* a few years before and recognized her from a drawing that accompanied the article. She had strong features, high cheekbones, and close-cropped gray hair. "May I help you?" she said in a European accent. I remembered from the piece that she was Hungarian, a refugee from Hitler who had come to New York after the war, the only member of her privileged *haute bourgeois* family to have gotten out. "You're Mrs. Szladits," I said. "I've read about you."

"I've read you," she said when I gave my name. "That's very different."

She invited me to sit down at one of the long tables in the oak-paneled room. "I have something to show you." She disappeared through a wood-paneled door and returned a few minutes later with a gray cardboard box* in her hand. Silently, she placed it before me on

---

* Unpublished books, typed on white paper, were circulated in this way before the advent of "attachments."

the table, like a waiter with some exotic dish the kitchen has slaved over all day and is at last preparing, with great pride and fanfare, to serve the hungry diner.

Mrs. Szladits lifted the top off with elegant tapered fingers, and I peered inside. It was a manuscript, perhaps two inches thick; typed on the first page in caps was the title THE FUTURE OF THE MOON. And beneath it: *by Saul Bellow.* "The Library bought it for $66,000," she said. "We've just had it on display."

I turned to the first page and read the opening sentence: "Shortly after dawn, or what would have been dawn in a normal sky, Mr. Artur Sammler with his bushy eye took in the books and papers of his West Side bedroom." I glanced away as if someone had shone a flashlight in my eyes.

I had read *Mr. Sammler's Planet,* as the manuscript had come to be called, the instant it was published, as I read all of Bellow's novels. I still owned the paperback, a Fawcett edition somewhat the worse for wear—the front cover was missing, and sometimes when I picked it up, loose pages fluttered to the floor. I had torn through it in a fit of excitement, intoxicated by the deep thoughts of Artur Sammler, the "Polish-Oxonian" Holocaust survivor, uneasily transplanted to the Upper West Side, whose meditations on history, murder, death, religion, metaphysics, and other big ideas unspool in page-long paragraphs. Now I had the original manuscript before me. I leafed through it with shaking hands. There was no one else in the reading room. Every few pages I came across a handwritten annotation in green ink. Who was this?

I put the lid back on the box and got up to leave. As I was gathering up my things, Mrs. Szladits came over and said: "Atlas on Bellow. We've been waiting for you. Come back. This is a good place for you to hang your hat."

Isaac Rosenfeld

XVII

L ike a birder spotting a rare painted bunting in Central Park, I grew flushed with excitement when I saw in the 92nd Street Y catalog that Bellow would be giving a reading that fall. I sent in for tickets so early that the ones I received in the mail were numbered three and four. (I wondered what zealot got there first. And was it a zealot who had invited along a friend, lover, relative? Or were there two *separate* zealots?) I had invited my friend Judith Thurman, the biographer of Isak Dinesen and another literature-mad soul, to go with me. We met in the lobby just before eight to find the place jammed. A thousand people must have shown up. An usher led us out onto the stage, where folding chairs had been set up to accommodate the overflow. Those, too, were filling up fast, but I told an usher that Judith was five months pregnant—not the kind of thing you can make up—and he gave us two seats in the front row. My chair was two feet from the edge of the stage, in full view of the audience.

My new friend Lola Szladits gave the introduction.

Then Bellow walked onstage. The applause was loud and seemed to last for five minutes. He was wearing a gray suit and looked older than a year ago, when I'd seen him in Chicago. He was frail and white-haired but elegant as always. "A greeting like this makes me wonder why I didn't run for president," he said wryly.

He read a passage from *Humboldt's Gift*, the one in which Humboldt is living in the rural wilds of New Jersey and his friend Charlie Citrine goes to spend the night—and read it beautifully. In his voice was all the pathos and humor of manic, eloquent, amphetamine-fueled Delmore rattling off references to

jewboys, goyboys, chorus girls, prostitution, and religion, old money, new money, gentlemen's clubs, Back Bay, Newport,

Washington Square, Henry Adams, Henry James, Henry Ford, Saint John of the Cross, Dante, Ezra Pound, Dostoevski, Marilyn Monroe and Joe DiMaggio, Gertrude Stein and Alice, Freud and Ferenczi.*

Then he read the closing of *Henderson the Rain King*—less good, flawed as it is by his penchant for jokiness (riding a roller coaster with a bear named Smolak?), but full of energy all the same, as when Henderson is bunking in a stable in Ontario: "There the rats jumped back and forth over my legs at night, and fed on oats, and the watering of the horses began at daybreak, in the blue light that occurs at the end of darkness in the high latitudes." It was thrilling to hear that long, run-on, rhythmic sentence, the *ands* piling up, the adjectiveless nouns,† read in its author's dry voice with such precise enunciation.

He read for about an hour, followed by a question-and-answer period. The Y's procedure was always the same: members of the audience would write down their questions on file cards that had been included with their programs and hand them to the ushers going through the aisles. While he was waiting to receive them, Bellow spotted me and, shielding his brow like a seafaring captain, gave me a warm smile.

When the stack of cards arrived, Bellow leafed through it and picked out the ones that interested him, muttering aloud, to great laughter from the audience, the best of the rejects ("What are you doing tonight after the reading?").

The first question was about what had made him want to become a writer. His answer was right out of *Herzog*, but he told it well. Stricken with TB at the age of eight, he had been quarantined in a Montreal hospital, where he was visited by a volunteer from the Bible Society

---

* I feel a little rueful typing out this quotation from my edition of *Humboldt's Gift*, an old Avon paperback, its pages parchment-colored and brittle with age: will there be a next generation of readers patient enough to make their way through a book of this length (471 pages in small type) and density, the prose packed with literary references incomprehensible to all but graduate students writing dissertations on "American Intellectuals and *Partisan Review* in the Postwar Era"? (Exam question: of these five writers referenced in a Citrine monologue—Schapiro, Hook, Rahv, Huggins, and Gumbein—which two are invented, and who do they represent?)

† Or nearly so; and when there *was* an adjective, it was one syllable (*blue, high*), so that the effect was to make the sentence gallop along at a terrific clop, imitating the motion of the horses.

who read to him from the New Testament. "I was moved by the Gospels," he said: "His words and deeds—'Suffer the little children to come unto me'—were a revelation."

By the time he was eleven or twelve, he knew he would become a writer: "There was nothing else to do." He was so proficient—and here Bellow somehow deflected what could have sounded like boastfulness, telling the story in a bemused tone of voice—that a teacher had accused him of plagiarism and demanded that his parents show up at school. "But they had a hard enough time feeding me and weren't going to see the principal on my behalf." Much laughter.

How did he support himself when he was starting out? He went to New York, where it was rumored that you could live on a thousand dollars a year, and reviewed books for *The New Republic* and *The New York Times Book Review,* where there was "a very kind editor" who would allow reviewers to take review copies off the shelf and sell them to a used-book dealer on East 58th Street. "Plus you got the five dollars for a brief review."

There was a question in the form of a declarative sentence: "Congratulations, killer bee." The reference was to an article in the *Times* that had linked Bellow to Allan Bloom and the secretary of education, William Bennett, a blustering reactionary prone to harangues about the importance of reading the classics of Western civilization (I wondered if Bennett had read them himself), identifying the three men, in a lame pun, as "killer B's." "I'm glad to be a killer bee in that sense," Bellow said. "I believe in honoring the old books. I'm not trying to kill off the third world. For all I know, I may be from the third world myself. But I'm soon going to be a Dead White Male," he said with a laugh. "I believe in being kind to them."

Afterward there was a reception, and I talked with Bellow's agent, Harriet Wasserman. She was very friendly. "It was interesting watching you up there onstage," she said. I said something about how wonderful it was to hear Bellow read from *Humboldt's Gift.* "I could see your lips move," she said. Rachel, Adam's wife, came over as the party was thinning out and Bellow was getting ready to leave. "Should I go over and say hello?" I asked her.

"You should."

I followed her out through a back door where Bellow was about to step into a waiting limousine. A photographer was snapping pictures. I approached him tentatively and put out my hand. "That was great, Mr.

Bellow," I murmured. He seemed glad to see me. "How are you, Jim?" Jim. A good sign: when things weren't going well, I was Mr. Atlas. "I meant to write and tell you how much I enjoyed your article on Bloom, but I've been tumbling around in the dryer." How easily metaphors came to this man. "I told Allan to tell you that I liked it."

I mumbled that I hoped to see him soon and floated off into the night.

A few months later, making my literary rounds, I entered the Gotham Book Mart to find Andy Brown in his office, poring over a thick manuscript bound in black cardboard. "I have something to show you," he said in a breathless voice: "The catalog of Bellow's papers that have gone"—again, the passive syntax of the book dealer—"to the University of Chicago." The circumstances surrounding this transfer were left unclear, but Andy intimated that Bellow had sold them for a lot of money.

He made a copy, and I took it across the street to the Diamond Deli. The Gotham was in the heart of the Diamond District; walking down West 47th Street jostled by black-hatted Hasidim in their long black frocks, I might as well have been in seventeenth-century Antwerp.

I studied the contents as I gulped down a corned beef on rye and a can of black cherry soda.

It was about a hundred pages long and listed the holdings by folder, sorted into manuscripts, published articles, diplomas, transcripts, drafts of lectures, report cards, photographs. The correspondence was of special interest: there were letters from people named Nathan Tarcov, Abel Swirsky, Hyman Slate, Louis Sidran, and—him again!— Isaac Rosenfeld. So Bellow must have replied to these letters. I would find them and, if they were still alive, interview their authors. There was also a collection of taped interviews with friends of Bellow, mostly deceased, conducted by a local scholar. I could sit in the library, put on earphones, and listen to the voices of the living and the dead.

The next day I was on a plane to Chicago. I had phoned ahead and spoken to the librarian in Special Collections at the Regenstein Library, and she had assured me that there were no restrictions on Bellow's papers; I could see them whenever I wanted.

The taxi ride into the city was so familiar—both from Bellow's descriptions of it and from my own returns home over the years—that I felt as if I were inhabiting one of his books. I experienced Chicago double: through what Bellow had written and through what I saw. (Or were they now the same?) It was bleak, so my mind* went to "the big winter-gray Chicago scene" described in *To Jerusalem and Back,* in which Bellow finds evidence of "a grim power whose materials are streets, bungalows, tenements, naked ironwork, grit, wind." In Hyde Park, we drove through the University of Chicago neighborhood, home of professors, freelance scholars, graduate students who dawdle for a decade over their dissertations, colleagues like Marshall Hodgson—"a vegetarian, a pacifist, and a Quaker," as Bellow described him, author of a three-volume work entitled *The Venture of Islam*—and the sociologist Morris Janowitz, a fervent neighborhood preservationist who saved the bookstores on East 57th Street: the intellectual heart of what is known out there as Chicagoland.

In the Special Collections Reading Room, I stowed my researcher's toolkit—pen, notebook, laptop—in a locker and filled out a slip for a manuscript titled "Charm and Death." I'd seen it listed in the catalog, and it sounded promising.

A silent librarian glided over and set before me a gray cardboard box.

"CHARM AND DEATH"—as it was labeled—was a typed, double-spaced manuscript of ninety-seven pages; at the top right-hand corner of the first page was the author's signature: *Saul Bellow.* I was always glad to see it.

The font was old-fashioned: it reminded me of the little portable Smith-Corona I had used in high school. There were revisions, black-ink scrawls, cross-outs in the form of typed *x*'s, and, on one page, a sentence blacked out. I tried to read it by holding it up to the light, but the black felt-tip pen had done its job. When was it from? Dating a manuscript is to a biographer what carbon-dating a mummy is to an archaeologist: it involves a lot of guesswork. I was stumped until a handwritten date leaped from a margin: 1951.

I read the first sentence: "Flashing through short light, running through long darkness, externally fast, internally all delay, electrical passages bound by slurs of gritting steel: it was the E Train in its tun-

---

* Not "*and* my mind": these associations were predictable and involuntary.

nels." So we were in New York, not Chicago. And here was the second sentence: "Within these sets of chambers, cars, stations, tubes, fixed and sliding, lighted and dark, Elias Zetland read French poems."

Zetland. This must be the work-in-progress that had been excerpted in *Modern Occasions*. There, too, was the autodidact, immersing himself in the works of Bentham, Kant, Rousseau, de Tocqueville; reciting Keats in a rowboat on the Humboldt Park lagoon; theorizing about the eighteenth-century Enlightenment.

The Zetland = Rosenfeld equation was never in doubt: of this I'd had confirmation from Bellow himself. But the portrait had been filled out in these nearly hundred pages. The chaotic household, with its neglected children, adulterous wife, deadbeat friends babbling on about metaphysics in a cloud of cigarette smoke: it was all new (except, perhaps, for the incontinent dog, Smokey, whom I had encountered in Alfred Kazin's memoir). And in the midst of it all, surrounded by dusty plants and Salvation Army furniture, grubbing out articles for the highbrow journals in order to support this supposedly bohemian but in reality squalid Greenwich Village ménage, was "clever young Zet, not so young, nor so clever at thirty, no longer the prodigy his father had expected."

Charm and Death was dark but funny. In the opening pages, Zetland is on the couch in the basement bunker of Dr. Sapir,[*] a Reichian analyst, pounding his fists and screaming at the top of his lungs in an effort to break through the crust of repression that is stifling his life. "'Hit it, Zetland!'" the doctor urges him: "'Strike it out. Kill it.'"

Sexual blockage was no small matter: it indicated a larger, more consequential impediment, a blockage of the self. For all his great intelligence, Zetland lacked a clear sense of his own identity. In the margin, Bellow had written "Nothing there."

I noted with surprise the fleeting appearance of a character named Von Humboldt Fleisher, a precocious poet, "the successor to T. S. Eliot and Wallace Stevens." Delmore!

The conviction hit me with great force: I would write Bellow's biography—with or without his permission. I thought back to my epiphany at the Yale Library on that Christmas Eve in 1974 when I had

---

[*] Edward Sapir was a distinguished anthropologist at the University of Chicago whose work Bellow would have known. He was in the habit of appropriating the names of real people in his life and attaching them to his characters.

my first glimpse of Delmore's papers in their bulky cardboard boxes. Randall Jarrell once described a poet as someone who manages, in a lifetime of standing out in thunderstorms, to be struck by lightning five or six times. For a biographer, that's a big number: I had now been struck twice and considered myself lucky.

Not long after my life-changing discovery, I got a call from a man who identified himself as George Sarant. This, I knew, was Isaac Rosenfeld's son. I had been trying to track him down for my *New York Review of Books* piece, but had no luck until learning—from Bellow—that he had changed his name to a shorter version of his mother's maiden name: Sarantakis.[*]

I invited my caller to lunch, and we agreed to meet at a coffee shop around the corner from my apartment. I recognized him at once, I'm not sure why—perhaps it was simply that a limited number of people who might have been Isaac Rosenfeld's son were in the coffee shop at that moment. He was in his early forties, I guessed, plump and soft like an over-aged baby, with thick glasses.

We talked for a long time. George was shy and sweet-natured and clearly still obsessed with his father. He had grown up in a state of domestic anarchy: his parents, Isaac and Vasiliki, a sensuous Greek beauty, had an "open" marriage, and there were many tumultuous confrontations in their pet- and intellectual-filled apartment on Barrow Street in Greenwich Village. "My mother used to sleep on the couch." They got divorced when George was six.

Much of what George told me about his father I already knew from Alfred Kazin's memoir and Bellow's Zetland novel. His description of the orgone box, a device the size of a telephone booth, made of tin and wood, that Wilhelm Reich had invented to "accumulate" the universal life force known as orgone, belonged to Rosenfeld lore: so why should I have been surprised to learn that his father would sit naked in such a box right in the middle of their living room? This confluence of fiction and reality fascinated me: Bellow made up some things, it turned out, but not that many.

George remembered his father's death: "We flew into Chicago for

---

[*] A psychiatrist affiliated with Einstein Medical School, he practiced in the Bronx and was, like his father, a Reichian.

the funeral and went to Sam's house." Sam was Rosenfeld's father. "Isaac's family wanted the kids to go. My mother's family didn't."* He related minor details that tell you everything and nothing at once—the kind that biographers file away but never get to use because they serve no purpose in bringing the story forward, such as the fact that when Rosenfeld's aunts "kissed you hello, they'd suck your cheek." (This is what Jewish aunts in Chicago, and probably elsewhere, do.)

I told George about the Zetland manuscript. He listened with keen attention, gripping his coffee cup in a stranglehold. It was all there, I told him: the apartment on Barrow Street, the poets and intellectuals and children and pets swirling through the cluttered parlor; the screaming sessions with the Reichian therapist; the high-minded babble about Kant and Rimbaud and the philosopher Morris Cohen, who taught at City College. This was George's childhood I was describing—the novel as life. And no one on the planet cared about it as much as I did, except for George himself.

A week later the doorman handed me a package. It was big and messily wrapped in brown paper. It bore George's name and a return address in Queens.

I hurried upstairs and unwrapped it on the dining room table. Out spilled a jumble of worn black leather notebooks, yellow legal pads, typed manuscripts, letters, and other literary miscellania—the archive, such as it was, of Isaac Rosenfeld. For days I immersed myself in this new treasure, leafing through time-faded typescripts and reading articles he'd written for *Commentary, The New Leader, Partisan Review*—those touchstones of the intellectual vocation in the 1940s. But I couldn't keep all these precious documents on the dining room table indefinitely: they had to go somewhere. And that's how it came about that Isaac Rosenfeld's private papers ended up in my hall closet.

From time to time, when I tired of exploring my ever-enlarging trove of Belloviana, I would go over to the closet and paw through Rosenfeld's papers, lodged amid a jumble of tennis rackets, hockey sticks, ice skates, soccer balls, and baseball gloves. Always I found something

---

* Steven Zipperstein, in his biography of Rosenfeld, offers a poignant account of that sorrowful day that doesn't quite resolve the matter: "Vasiliki forbade the children to attend the funeral, but those in the procession related that as they drove through Chicago on the way to bury him, they happened to pass Eleni and George standing outside, staring at the cars; some in the procession called out their names."

new. Once it was a poem scrawled in a child's script on the back of an envelope:

> *Grandfather sits in his armchair*
> *Long is his beard*
> *white are his hair*
> *He is reading a book*
> *with much interest*
> *Please, don't disturb him*
> *He is taking a rest*

There was a letter to Rosenfeld's aunt Rae complaining about the meagerness of his literary output—three poems a week, all of them "vile." Later on, when he had moved to New York and joined the staff of *The New Republic*, there were letters to his aunt typed on the magazine's stationery; in one, he expressed—a touching immigrant locution applied to the literary life instead of the garment business—"hopes of making good." And on June 15, 1944, when he was twenty-six, he dispatched a telegram to his aunts on Wabansia Avenue: SOLD MY NOVEL DETAILS TO FOLLOW LOVE AND KISSES ISAAC.

The novel was well received: the sociologist Daniel Bell° called it "a parable of alienation"—high praise in the terminology of that era, when alienation was seen as a positive trait. But Rosenfeld soon ran into trouble—as I put the story together from his journals—struggling to support his family on the income of a freelance critic while negotiating the Greenwich Village bohemia of the postwar era.

After the modest triumph of *Passage from Home*, Rosenfeld made little headway with fiction, laboring over a novel called *The Enemy* that went nowhere. "*The Enemy* bores me," he admitted to himself. "How I've ruined it with this nonsense. I want in Pathfinder a person, not a case-history. A *character*, by God!" He filled his journals with notes on mystical gurus, characters with names like Jarman and Bramallah Gudoy, but he acknowledged that he would do better to find material in the daily dramas of his own life:

° Bell was a Harvard professor and author of *The End of Ideology*. He was also— though I'm not sure why this is relevant, I feel instinctively that it is—married to Alfred Kazin's sister Pearl.

I look at something I have published—say, most recently, the *Three Parables*. I understand that there is an external Isaac Rosenfeld, who exists in the reader's mind, a person and a character deduced from the writing, and which, even at the time of writing, I have helped to create. I see the great distance between myself as I am in publication, and myself as I actually am. When will I be able to write so truthfully that only I, as I actually am, will appear on the page?

In his journals, Rosenfeld wrote as who he was.° They were full of malicious gossip, catty observations about friends, and details of his marriage and the "libertinism" that he indulged in with such deep ambivalence. How could he reconcile the "bourgeois" pleasures of domesticity with the equally seductive pleasures of *la vie bohème* as he found it in the Village? "This is what generates the conflict," he noted: "the desire to keep the marriage intact and the desire for strong sensations." He had lots of girlfriends for hot sex ("strong orgasm with full bodily convulsions"), but only Vasiliki seemed to elicit feelings of genuine tenderness and love. In one entry, he recorded the "resurgence of family feeling" that accompanied their lovemaking in a cabin at Black Mountain College, the children in bed, a fire blazing. "And gradually, slowly, to sleep, as the fire burns out, the first blissful night in a long time."

Then there was this whole Reich business: Rosenfeld was much more caught up in it than Bellow, who saw Reichianism as a comic (or anyway, tragicomic) fad. Rosenfeld believed that if he could only pierce his own defenses—his "character armor," as Reich called it—and fight through to some more authentic self, his writing would somehow open up. But the more he got involved with Reich, the less he wrote. "You had so many ideas on literature," Vasiliki chided him: "Why don't you ever write about that? Why not Dostoyevsky's life, for instance?"

She was right. Rosenfeld was a first-rate literary critic, but he never could overcome the obstacles he put in his own way, and by the 1950s, his early promise had turned to ashes. In his journal, he wondered: "Maybe I have learned something? That I have been wrong for the last seven to nine years. One does not, must not live by or for passions alone: that life of such a kind is destructive?"

° Or who he thought he was.

Bellow, meanwhile, was "making it." *The Adventures of Augie March* appeared in 1953 to nearly universal praise. Delmore, writing in *Partisan Review,* ranked it above *The Adventures of Huckleberry Finn* and Dos Passos's *U.S.A.* Rosenfeld found Bellow's success hard to take:

> Ordinarily, I'm fairly modest. I try to be humble, to keep my tremendous ego under cover. When someone praises something I've written, I shrug it off. My greatest pleasure, when young kids talk about writers, is to pretend I'm no writer. "Oh, I've written a few things," I say. Or about Saul's book, I'll say, "I like this about it. I don't like that." While all along, what I really have in mind is: "That? Why my book's a million times better!" I'm terribly competitive.

Guilt was another big theme. What provoked Raskolnikov to murder, Rosenfeld theorized, was the need to "have a great guilt to expiate." Killing off the pawnbroker and her sister was a substitute for killing off "Mom and Sis," an act of revenge against his family. It was the same with Kafka's Joseph K, who longs for the court to execute him in the hope of provoking God's intervention: "Yet he feels it is precisely his effort to provoke God that deepens and reaffirms his guilt."

Early in 1956 Rosenfeld dreamed that he would soon be dead: "It is dreadful to look two weeks ahead and know one's life will be over." Thoughts of suicide alternated with memories of his Chicago childhood and summer days in Humboldt Park. Listening to Toscanini and the NBC orchestra perform the Beethoven Choral Symphony one afternoon, he was seized with nostalgia for his old Tuley gang. Why hadn't he written about them? "It is my task to know my own story, to recover my shame. What do I know? I have access to myself—but not the courage to go into it."

He had moved back to Chicago by then and was living in the cheerless apartment on East Huron Street* that Bellow had described in his preface to *An Age of Enormity.* The last entry in his journal read:

> This is what I have forgotten about the creative process, & and am only now beginning to remember—that time spent is time fixed. One creates a work to outlive one—only art does this—&

---

* Or not so cheerless. See footnote on p. 98.

the source of creativity is the desire to reach over one's own death. Maybe now, if I want to create again, I want once more to live; & before I wanted, I suppose, to die.

Two weeks later he was dead. It was Freda, my friend Josh's mom, who found him slumped over his desk.

George had gone to see Bellow at the Lotos Club in New York in the spring of 1987, and they'd had a long talk that left them both in tears. "There was a bond between us and a closeness," he wrote me some months later. "I really felt for him and was so deeply moved and touched. I felt how much he really did love my parents and also felt how terribly lonely he is."

XVIII

The moment had come. It was the early summer of 1989. My piece on Rosenfeld had been published in *The New York Review of Books;* I seemed to be in Bellow's good graces (to borrow Adam's phrase), and had gotten a book contract.

I wrote to Bellow and made it clear that I wasn't looking for authorization. I also called up Adam to share the news. He was cordial; he said his father would not "hinder" me but would never authorize a biography. Bellow wasn't wild about the prospect of a biography now: Adam thought it would be "the nail in his coffin." At the same time, he acknowledged, his father believed he was "the greatest writer of the 20th century" and would be "very unhappy" if he thought no one was going to write his biography. But the story wasn't over yet: "There will be a few twists and turns."

I was too idolatrous, he warned me. Bellow was adept at "concealing the warts." He cautioned me about the family: "He's the focus for a lot of passionate feelings. Many resentments still flourish." That said, he was pleased that I was doing the book, and he would help in any way he could.

Three months after my piece appeared in the *New York Review,* a letter from Bellow arrived. The piece was generous, he wrote, and he was "touched" by it. What a relief! It had never even occurred to me that I might hear from him. A few months later I wrote to ask if I could come and see him, but heard nothing back. I decided to go to Chicago anyway—I was eager to have another look at the papers, and there was a chance he would see me if I called.

I arrived on a Saturday night and checked in at the Quadrangle Club on East 57th Street, a gloomy place with stained-glass windows and gothic arches and faux-medieval stone floors. The room had a monkish simplicity—no TV set, no phone, just a bed and a dresser.

The Homestead

The next morning I called Bellow, who seemed neither happy nor unhappy to hear from me. He suggested I come over at two o'clock.

He greeted me rather stiffly; he was dressed in khakis and a sports shirt open at the neck. He seemed wary—it wasn't the greeting of someone I had met on several occasions and had profiled for a magazine. We chatted for a few minutes, but we were both ill at ease. I couldn't figure out if we were having the first of many interviews—was I there in my official capacity as the biographer?—or a preliminary, "exploratory" session, in which I was being sized up and my suitability as his biographer weighed.

I decided to get on with it.

"May I ask you a few questions?" I said.

Bellow looked away, gazing out the big picture window at Lake Michigan. "I'd like to discuss with you how I feel about this project," he said, an edge in his voice. "I was burned by Ruth Miller."*

Her book on him was about to come out, and Bellow was very unhappy with it; he had thought she was writing a study of his books. "I've known her for fifty years. She said she was interested in my work, and I gave her access to the papers in the Regenstein. She couldn't resist the gossip. I've lived a life like any other, and she made much of it. I haven't been a good caretaker of other people's letters. I'm concerned for them." He paused. "I'm not ready to be memorialized. I don't have all the answers. I'm still trying to figure things out."

He would see me from time to time, he said, but he didn't want to become too involved. I worked up my nerve by counting to seventeen[†] and asked about access to his papers. He had no objection to my reading manuscripts, but at least for the moment, letters were off-limits. "Maybe I'll simmer down."

He mentioned that Isaac Rosenfeld had destroyed their correspondence. I hesitated, then told him that George had turned his father's papers over to me when I was working on my piece about Rosenfeld for

---

* Miller had been a friend—perhaps girlfriend—of Bellow's for half a century and had been given permission to quote liberally from his correspondence. But he grew apprehensive about the book's contents as publication day neared and put a lawyer on the case. In the end, Miller had to paraphrase and barely averted a lawsuit.

† The talismanic number I counted to when I needed to gird myself for a difficult task, like jumping into the chilly Walloomsac River behind our house. I have no idea why I chose that number instead of, say, sixteen or eighteen.

The New York Review of Books. (I didn't say they were in my closet.) A mistake. It was clear that Bellow still had Rosenfeld on his mind. After all, he had written a whole novel about him—*Charm and Death*, the one I found in the Regenstein archives. Now he wanted to know what Isaac had said about him in the journal he kept. I promised to send him the relevant entries.˚

A young woman came into the room, and Bellow introduced me. It was his new wife, Janis—his fifth. They had met when she was a student in his modern literature class, writing her thesis on Dostoyevsky. She was twenty-nine, maybe thirty, I calculated, and very pretty, with ringlets of curly black hair. Her dark eyes shone. She smiled and put out her hand. Her gentle face invited trust.

I was hoping she would join us, but it was time to go—a "girl" was arriving to "take letters." As I was putting away my notebook, Bellow asked if I had a hat—it was starting to rain—and opened up a closet by the front door. It was full of hats—shelves and shelves of fedoras lined up in rows. "My dead brothers' hats are in here, too," he said. I reminded him of the time, several years earlier, when he had loaned me a hat. I had come to interview him for *Vanity Fair*, and it had also been raining then, I recalled. "It was three sizes too big." I declined the offer. My head is small to begin with; a too-big hat makes it seem even smaller. And did I really want to adopt Bellow's haberdashic idiosyncrasies? Also, how would I return it? Best to steer clear of the whole business.

We stood awkwardly by the door. I descended in the metal elevator with a pounding heart and sat in the car for a long time. Then I drove off and parked a few blocks away, afraid that Bellow would come out and see me writing in my notebook.

I had been twenty-four when I embarked on *Delmore;* I was forty when I began *Bellow*. The young biographer had been thrilled to interview the distinguished *Partisan Review* intellectuals Irving Howe and Clement Greenberg. But on my second tour of interviewing the

---

˚ Why did I make this ill-considered offer? To show Bellow that I had the goods? To please him by sharing information that I knew would be meaningful, even if it was upsetting? I never brought it up again, and to my relief, neither did he.

distinguished *Partisan Review* intellectuals Irving Howe and Clement Greenberg, I felt a little sheepish. *Not him again,* they must have thought. The slight, eager youth with his oblong reporter's notebook had metamorphosed into a weary middle-aged writer. *Not them again.*

Some were dead and thus no longer available for interrogation. Harold Rosenberg, with his eagle eyebrows and brushy mustache, had died not long after my book came out. I had interviewed him about Delmore at his apartment in Hyde Park, where he was on the faculty of the Committee on Social Thought. Rosenberg was fiercely intellectual, more European than American. Gimp-legged, he clutched his cane, a cigarette smoldering between his fingers.

It was odd to think of him in gritty Chicago; he belonged at the Café de Flore, seated at a marble-topped table with an espresso by his elbow. He would have been fascinating on Bellow. Death: the biographer's worst enemy.

Others were living in improved circumstances. Irving Howe had published *World of Our Fathers,* his best seller about the immigration of Eastern European Jews, in 1976, and could now afford to make his own migration, from the West Side to a spacious white-brick building on the East Side—not as strenuous, perhaps, as the first journey, but still hard to achieve. I remember leaving his apartment, where I had gone to interview him about Delmore, and emerging into the late afternoon light of Broadway still unable to believe that I had interviewed *Irving Howe,* long a hero of mine; I had read *Politics and the Novel* in high school, entranced by the idea that politics could even be associated with the novel. (Wasn't the novel all about art?) By this visit, however, our relationship had darkened: I had given Howe's memoir, *A Margin of Hope,* a disrespectful review in *The New York Times Book Review.* Oh reason not the why (though I have a few ideas). I was lucky to get an interview.

Clement Greenberg had deteriorated. In 1975, when I interviewed him about Delmore at an elegant townhouse on Beacon Hill where he was staying with some Mayflower art collector, he had announced upon my arrival that he had been up late the night before and was "hung over." For some reason, even forty years later I can hear the romantic association I had with that phrase at twenty-six. I was certainly no stranger to alcohol, but it connoted a decadence and sophistication that reminded me of those Peter Arno cartoons of starry-eyed drunks in

The New Yorker. We met in a bright sunroom filled with large plants. Greenberg was crisply dressed in a blazer, a white-collared shirt, and a dazzling azure-blue tie.

Twenty years later I was back to gather his testimony about Bellow. He lived in a nondescript but clearly expensive apartment in a modern building on Central Park West. I can't recall what art was on the walls, but neither could Mark Stevens, de Kooning's biographer, who said of his interview with Greenberg: "I think I don't remember much about the walls because *he* was so disturbingly vivid. He padded over to let me in wearing a sort of robe and in bare gnarly feet."

His work was done now. The name Clement Greenberg, once so powerful in literary and art circles, had faded like an old copy of *Partisan Review*. He would have talked all afternoon. He had agreed to see Stevens only on condition that the biographer match him drink for drink. I was allowed a more moderate ratio of one brimming glass of vodka to Greenberg's three. Even so, when I stumbled out into the summer street three hours later, I had to sit down on the curb until my head cleared.

I n early 1991, I went to Chicago to interview Bellow. I had decided to be his biographer, and this is what biographers of the living did: they conducted interviews with their subjects, going over the same ground again and again in an effort to get the story straight. I had taken Bellow's *not no*—or was it *maybe*—for *yes* and gone unchallenged. That was good enough for me.

I called him from the Quadrangle Club and explained that I was in town. He told me to come the next day from one-thirty to three p.m. He called me Jim.

I arrived promptly at one-thirty—I had learned that Bellow valued punctuality—took out my notebook, and began to go through my questions. After a while he said, "Why do you want to know all this?" *I'm not a census taker*, I felt like saying. *I'm your biographer.*

When I told him I had interviewed Ezra Davis, who lived in the Bellows' house on the Northwest Side of Chicago in 1926, he looked stunned and demanded to know where I dug him up. "You know more about me than I know about myself," he said. I told him the story: I had gone to Montreal to interview friends and relatives from Bellow's early childhood, and a writer, Ann Weinstein, a devoted Bellow maven, had taken me to a senior citizens' center, where I found Ezra Davis in the sun parlor. Bellow took me in with that keen, appraising look of his: *Who is this guy?* It was beginning to dawn on him: I was going to write his biography.

I had an alarming fantasy that he was going to rise up out of his chair and order me from his door, like the father in Kafka's story "The Judgment," who commands his son to jump off a bridge. But he wasn't in that kind of mood. He wanted to reminisce. He showed me his mother's passport: *épouse du bourgeois.* It was yellowed, with an ornate seal from the governor of St. Petersburg, just like the one described in *Herzog.* His father, Abraham, had traveled under a separate name. "I'm sure they were the best papers he could buy," Bellow said.

One of his mother's brothers had owned a restaurant in St. Petersburg; another had gone off to South Africa in search of diamonds and come back "with piles of money."* Growing up in Chicago, Bellow lived first at 2629 West Augusta Boulevard, then at two addresses on the 2200 block of Cortez, and finally at 3340 LeMoyne.† His chemistry teacher at Tuley, Mr. Olson, "held court down in the ancient part of the school, in the faculty toilet; he'd sit on the toilet with his pipe and his pants down around his knees and talk to the boys." Lovely. I scribbled Bellow's words in my notebook, hoping I had gotten them right. Should I ask him how to spell *Olson?* What if it was *Olsen?* Someone would write in to correct me.‡

That was the whole problem. What if Bellow had misremembered, and the teacher who'd held court on the can wasn't Mr. Olsen/Olson at all, but some other teacher? Or what if he had taught math instead of chemistry? What difference would it make? We yearn for things to be true: if they're true, the world will make sense. But this isn't how the novelist operates. Bellow's job, he maintained, was "to learn how long

---

* Just like Willy Loman's brother, Ben.
† Biographers love addresses for their facticity. You can pull up in front of an apartment building and see the numbers above the door. *Yes, here it is* (glancing at my notebook): *the same number that's on the letter. So he lived here. The very building I'm standing in front of now.* The absence of an exact address is frustrating. "We don't know the precise location of the Old World Drug Store and Ice Creamery that Yacov Rothkowitz managed in the last years of his life," writes Annie Cohen-Solal of Mark Rothko's father, describing the immigrant family's life in Portland, Oregon. How can you wring the obligatory geographic atmosphere out of a vacant lot? Urban renewal is a disaster for biography.
‡ Paratore's, not Perratoni's; Eda Lou Walton, not Edna . . .

clover flowers could hold their color in the dusk." And to that there was no answer.

At three o'clock, I got up to leave. That was our agreement. But it was clear I could have stayed longer. I asked Bellow about a rumor I'd heard that he was moving to Boston. "It's too far from here to Vermont," he said. "But a move at my time of life, even though I'm in fairly good shape . . ." He couldn't decide what to do. But it felt wrong to advise him: I was writing Bellow's life, not telling him how to live it.

He helped me on with my coat. "I can do this for you." Then: "It was nice to see you."

"I find this moving," I said.

"Next time I'll show you the family photographs."

A few months later, back in Chicago, I called Bellow from the Quadrangle Club. Today we were going on a field trip. A few weeks earlier, I had written him asking for permission to obtain his high school transcripts, and he'd replied with the offer of a "personal tour of the city." Why rummage through grammar school records from which I'd learn nothing* when we could drive around his old neighborhoods together? "What does your day look like?" he said.

"It's pretty clear. I've saved it for you—along with a lot of other days."

"Point taken," he said.

I had been on this tour before, when I profiled Bellow for *Vanity Fair,* but I was eager to go again. I had an expanded mandate now: I was writing a book, not just some ephemeral magazine article. Future biographers would depend on it. If they wanted to know what Bellow— the actual man—felt when he stood in front of the house where he'd lived when his family came to Chicago in 1924, they would have to go to my book. They could bury it in a footnote or omit attribution altogether. But I would be the one who had been with him—the only one. I was the biographer. I was there.

I was also hoping our tour might allow me to slip in a few questions about his psychiatric history, a touchy subject. Bellow saw four

---

* Any biographer would vigorously disagree with this assertion, knowing that grammar school records can yield nuggets of gold. Was the subject good at math? Was he often absent? Did he excel at phys ed? Report cards had a runic quality, as if the biographer were deciphering Mycenaean Greek on a scrap of papyrus. Linear Bellow.

psychiatrists during his lifetime: Dr. Chester Raphael, a Reichian who practiced in Queens and who was the model for Dr. Sapir in his unfinished novel about Rosenfeld; Paul Meehl, a psychologist in Minneapolis he had consulted during the disintegration of his second marriage, when he was teaching at the University of Minnesota; Albert Ellis, the famous "sexologist" whom Bellow saw for what he once described as "pool room work," or sexual technique; and Heinz Kohut. It was the last of this quartet of shrinks, I suspected, who held the key to my subject's psyche—insofar as there was such a thing as a "key" to anyone.*

I had interviewed the first three, all of whom were willing, no doubt out of vanity, to violate patient/doctor (or psychologist) confidentiality. Kohut was dead, but I suspect he alone would have honored the contract the others were so cavalier about. He took his vocation seriously; his books were all about how important it was for the analyst to establish his patient's trust through the "tool" of empathy. The subtlety and ethical gravitas Kohut displayed in his work made it unlikely that he would have consented to be interviewed by a biographer.

It was George Sarant who tipped me off that Bellow had been in treatment with Kohut, and it seemed plausible. They had lived in the same building in Hyde Park for a time during the 1970s. More important, Kohut's work explored in a sympathetic and nuanced way the origins and traits of the narcissistic personality—my layman's diagnosis of Bellow's condition. Kohut identified this type as "the crumbling, decomposing, fragmenting, enfeebled but also powerfully self-realizing self" who is driven to collect women "not by libidinal but narcissistic needs."

Reading this passage in the middle of the night during one of my insomniac spells—I can still remember the moment many years later—I rose off the living room couch in a state of high excitement. Here was one of the greatest psychoanalysts of the twentieth century, Chicago-based (always a plus), making a diagnosis that, whether or not it referred to Bellow in particular, described his type, and without censure.

Kohut's method focused on the chaos and psychic pain caused by a condition that was especially hard to treat because the patient didn't want to be treated. Herzog suggests that "people of powerful imagination, given to dreaming deeply and to raising up marvelous and self-

---

* "If I had as many mouths as Siva has arms and kept them going all the time I still would not do myself justice," says Bellow's Dangling Man.

sufficient fiction, turn to suffering sometimes to cut into their bliss, as people pinch themselves to feel awake." Yes, that was it: *to cut into their bliss.* Bellow experienced the joy of creativity, but it was sometimes so intense that it required a dose of masochism to contain it. And masochism hurt.

The problem was that I had no written evidence that Bellow had actually *seen* Kohut. How to nail it down? Annie had come up with a clever solution: "Why don't you just ask him what it was like seeing Kohut? Then he can either deny that he ever saw him or lie outright—a possibility you'll have to live with."

When I arrived at Bellow's apartment, we chatted for a while about the difficulties of living in New York. He asked me where I lived— one of the few times he'd ever asked me anything about myself—and noted that Philip Roth was my neighbor. This casual validation of *my* biography, attesting as it did to the fact that I had a life outside of his life, was gratifying: there were moments when I felt ghostly, a spectral presence shadowing my subject, notebook in hand, all but invisible even to myself.

We drove off in their forest-green Range Rover, Janis in back, and headed toward the Northwest Side on I-94. I noted that Bellow was a good but cautious driver; he was clearly proud that he knew his way around town.

Soon we were in his old neighborhood—again. We drove down Cortez, a tree-lined street with small grassy front yards, wrought-iron fences, and elaborately carved wooden doors with lozenge-shaped glass windows. Bellow had lived here from the ages of ten to fourteen, first in a ground-floor apartment, then down the street in a larger three-bedroom with a side yard that was the landlord's garden.

As we loitered on the sidewalk, Bellow fell silent. I thought of the apartment house where my grandparents had lived when I was a child, around the corner from their drugstore on Mozart: the tiny plot of grass out front, the cracked sidewalks, the dark vestibule . . . In writing this book, I was retrieving not just Bellow's past but my own.

"I'm not showing you where my girlfriends lived," he said suddenly. "Those are the memories I really treasure."

"You don't need to," I murmured.°

° I don't see how this exchange could fit here, even though it shows up in my notes of that day. Why would Bellow be talking about his girlfriends in the presence of Janis?

At the end of our tour—Division Street, Tuley School, Humboldt Park, stops as familiar to me by now as if I'd grown up there myself—we pulled into the parking lot of Jewel Food so Janis could pick up some things for dinner. Bellow and I sat in the car. He was in the front seat, and I was in the back. We talked for a while about the trio of known psychiatrists: Bellow played down his sessions with Dr. Raphael: "That wasn't psychology; that was zoology." We laughed. Bellow loved to laugh at his own jokes, and now he had company. I brought up Dr. Ellis: wasn't he Dr. Edvig in *Herzog*?

"No, that was Paul Meehl." *Come on, Atlas! You should know these elementary facts by now.*

Why did he go see Ellis? I pursued. Bellow looked at me narrowly: "You know why."

I did: Sasha (as Sondra was familiarly known), impotence, adultery . . . "Which I'm not going to talk about," he announced emphatically. A strange assertion, since the whole story was in *Herzog*.

Now was my chance. I counted to seventeen and said, "So what was Kohut like?"

Bellow sat in silence for a few seconds, weighing his options, then explained, with great deliberation, that he had seen Kohut only "a few times" during "a period of turmoil" in his life. *Yes!* It was clear that he didn't want to talk about this particular figure in his psychoanalytic history, but it didn't matter. I had what I needed.

The next day I called him up to find out how he had weathered our tour of the old neighborhoods. He said he'd had a good time, but it had left him "in a mood" (no adjective). He was "metaphysically bushed." He quoted a Berryman poem: "'Often he reckons, in the dawn, them up. / Nobody is ever missing.'" Then he said, "There are many missing."

D riving through Hyde Park, Herzog thinks of it as *his* Chicago:

> massive, clumsy, amorphous, smelling of mud and decay, dog turds; sooty facades, slabs of structural *nothing*, senselessly ornamented triple porches with huge cement urns for flowers that contained only rotting cigarette butts and other stained filth; sun

---

He had many strange attitudes toward women, but he wasn't a cad. False memory? True memory? No memory? That's more like it.

parlors under tiled gables, rank areaways, gray backstairs, seamed and ruptured concrete from which sprang grass; ponderous four-by-four fences that sheltered growing weeds.

This was Bellow's great gift: he had shown, neighborhood by neighborhood, sometimes block by block, what the city looked and smelled and felt like, from Hyde Park (see above) to the glittery high-rises of Lake Shore Drive to the West Side slums. He was a metaphysician of the ordinary. He gave meaning to what he saw by simply describing it.

For me, though, there was also *my* Chicago, less epic, less visually stunning, less immense (somewhere Bellow speaks of the "galactic number of bungalows"), not even, to be accurate, mine. Our house in Evanston was a block from the city line, which didn't hide the fact that it was in the suburbs.° Well, okay, so it was my *Evanston.* I harbored a deep attachment to my hometown. The 31 Flavors was still there, on the corner of Davis and Main Street. I used to go for a walk with Mom and Dad after dinner on summer nights more than thirty years ago for ice-cream cones: I always had cherry vanilla.

Sometimes I stayed at the Homestead, an old white-pillared residential home near Northwestern where my grandma Liz had lived as she made her downsizing journey from a burgundy-brick house by a golf course in Wilmette to her final home in California, an assisted-living residence called Chateau La Jolla. I adored the Homestead, with its reverberant associations of a safe haven, a place where you could seek refuge from the storms of life. The name had an Old West connotation, but Grandma Liz had arrived from the other direction: a town named Ekaterinoslav in Ukraine, site of bloody pogroms. She sat in her book-lined room, her wrists wreathed in bracelets, a batik kerchief wrapped around her head, Chagall prints on the wall, and recited Pushkin by heart to entertain me. I loved the Russian *shush*ing sounds.

One time I stayed with John Blades, a *Chicago Tribune* reporter who lived in Evanston and covered the "Bellow beat." His house was a few blocks from the Homestead. As I got out of the car on the dark tree-lined street, the scent of the fresh-cut grass was fragrant. He put me in his son's room, adorned with Cubs pennants and other adoles-

---

° When I read Bellow on Evanston—he had gone to Northwestern and had lived in the Orrington Hotel just a few blocks from my house while he was writing *Henderson*—it was with an ecstasy of recognition.

cent paraphernalia: a model airplane, a Bulls jersey, a guitar. A radio stood on the bedside table. I had an impulse to turn it on and find WLS, the rock music station I'd listened to late at night as a teenager. I wondered if the disk jockey Dick Biondi was still there; he called himself the Screamer. I remembered the number on the dial: 890. But I'd had a long day buried in the *Tribune* archives. I wanted to lie on the bed of John Blades's son and think about the strange set of events that had brought me here.

Pulling up the red flannel cover, I could have been in my own bedroom ten blocks away listening to the Lovin' Spoonfuls' "Summer in the City." It was a trivial youth compared to Bellow's in Humboldt Park, with its vivid family dramas and rich cultural life. The death of his mother; the brutal fights with his father; the sound of accordions and player pianos floating through the neighborhood on summer nights; the barrels of used books in front of Walgreens; the trips down to the Fine Arts Building across from the Art Intitute for violin lessons; the basement apartment, furnished with Salvation Army furniture, where Bellow took his girlfriends to make out. How could Saturday night dances at the Plant Room and solitary dinners at the Hut deli compete? But it was the only past I had.*

I marveled at my good luck that our little summerhouse in Vermont was only forty-five minutes away from Bellow's. The proximity wasn't just convenient. It seemed to me a sign of our mutual bond (bondage?). I had once asked him what had drawn him to Vermont; he was such a city boy. His explanation was that it reminded him of the rural countryside around Montreal, where he'd grown up and where the family went by train on summer outings.

We never talked about the fact that we were near-neighbors—or, as I've noted, about anything else that touched on my own life. All the same, I wondered if the fact that I, too, was drawn to Vermont had a positive reverberation for Bellow (if he thought about it at all). It was another affinity, along with my family's Chicago roots and my

---

* It occurs to me now that I, too, had access to a basement apartment for makeout sessions and took the El to the North Side for mandolin lessons at the Old Town School of Folk Music, but these things had always seemed too ordinary to write about. Bellow could make any world seem exotic because he was Bellow.

biography of Delmore, that had made me a logical choice to be his biographer—or so I hoped.

The first time I visited, Bellow instructed me to drive to his house in a tiny hamlet a few miles from Wilmington, over the mountains from Bennington, and asked me not to divulge its name.° I was to call him up from the general store. There was nothing cloak-and-dagger about this plan; Bellow's house was deep in the countryside, on a dirt road reached by other dirt roads, and I got lost more than once in the years that followed, even after I'd driven there several times.

The store was quintessential Vermont—sawdust sprinkled over the creaky floorboards, a taxidermy of stuffed wild and semi-wild animals affixed to the wall; old snowshoes and crossed wooden skis; cords of fatwood and tenting equipment stacked in the corner; fishing rods and vintage Vermont license plates; shelves crammed with maple syrup, lures, roll-your-own tobacco, camouflage hunting caps, sterno cans, pocket knives, compasses for if you get lost in the woods, cans of Dinty Moore beef stew. A scene out of Norman Rockwell.

On the porch was a pay phone that required a dime.

Bellow picked up after a few rings. He seemed glad to hear from me and said he would be right over: "Find a way to amuse yourself."

Fifteen minutes later he drove up in the Range Rover, Mozart drifting out the window from his tape deck. We were both constrained about shaking hands and finally didn't. I have no idea what went into this decision. Uncertainty about where things stood between us? Was I a literary colleague? A friend? Would shaking hands be too formal?

The plan was for me to follow him to the house. The narrow country roads wound among lily-coated ponds and white farmhouses and fields of goldenrod. Then we were on a dirt road through a forest before turning in at a driveway with a mailbox that had no name on it. The house was a two-story salmon-colored dwelling they had built a few years before. It was modest but handsome—the house of an affluent but not wealthy man. A new wing was being added on to accommodate Bellow's books—one large room, he explained as he gave me a tour, "big enough so that I can throw my weight around."

Janis showed me the garden, and we picked blueberries together while Bellow was on the phone, "taking a call from Chicago." She was

---

° I suppose it wouldn't matter if I did so now, but a promise is a promise. Let his next biographer tell the world where Saul Bellow lived.

proud of the spring-fed pond they had dredged themselves: "Saul swims in all weather, like a member of the Polar Bear Club." In a field behind the house they were growing sprouts and cucumbers, basil and a patch of corn.

When Bellow had finished his call, we sat in the garden, and I took out my notebook. I apologized for asking him the same questions over and over. "You could fix up some lights and give me the third degree," he said, "except I haven't done anything wrong." I raised my hand and waved away the idea. But there were times when he did seem to feel guilty, as if he were harboring some secret that he couldn't reveal even to himself.

We talked for a while, and I brought up the matter of access to his letters, this time taking a different tack. "It's one of the great literary correspondences of our time, probably the last one," I said—which it is.° Bellow wrote to his literary friends—Ralph Ellison, John Berryman, Bernard Malamud, Philip Roth—to his Tuley friends, to his girlfriends, to his family, with a Herzogian lack of inhibition. There were times when I was convinced he had one eye on posterity as he wrote them, but at other times I could see he was just dashing them off. They were about his life at that moment.

I was invited to stay for dinner. Soon afterward Walter Pozen, Bellow's friend and final lawyer—he had a house nearby—drove up in his pickup truck, and it was clear he was staying, too, which effectively ended our interview, though I continued to ask questions on the sly.

Janis served us salmon and corn, followed by blueberries with frozen yogurt and fudge sauce. They were going to watch a Wallace Beery movie, sent by their Chicago friend Eugene Kennedy, after dinner. They didn't ask me to stay for the movie, but I didn't mind. It was time to go home.

As I was about to leave, I laid out my wares on the table between us like a rug dealer displaying his Persian carpets. There were letters requesting transcripts from Northwestern and the University of Chicago, which Bellow signed; and a second request for grammar school transcripts. "Why do you want to see these?" he said, all at once suspi-

---

° The 484-page collection of letters edited by Benjamin Taylor is one of Bellow's best books. Laced with comic flourishes, rhetorical bombast, malice, tenderness, rage, self-justification, and a thousand other voices and postures and operatic notes, it belongs on the shelf of correspondence in the history of American literature with the letters of Emerson and Henry James.

cious. "I need facts," I answered. Then after thinking about whether he would find it funny: "Why? Did you get a bad grade in math?"

No, he had gotten good grades, but that was the end of the matter. He wouldn't sign.

On my way home, driving over the mountains in the mild summer evening, it suddenly occurred to me: *He doesn't want me to know that his name was Solomon*—the name he was given at birth. It was too Old World. "I am an American, Chicago born," proclaims Augie. An American, not just an immigrant Jew.

M y Chicago pilgrimages were acquiring a pattern. I generally flew in on Saturday nights, when fares were cheapest, and rented a car at the airport. Most of the time I stayed at the Quad. It was pretty empty on weekends, and I felt at home with its seedy decor, which I associated with Chicago.

I called Bellow on Monday morning; Sunday was a day of rest for biographer and subject.

He seemed pleased to hear from me: I, meanwhile, was ready to submerge myself in his life again, like a deep-sea diver poised to go under in search of tropical fish. I asked how he was, and he said, "Harassed." The phone had been busy. He seemed to be at the mercy of everyone who called up. He explained that he had to go to the dentist. "I'm sorry to bring you more pain," I said. I offered to drive him, an idea he dismissed as "silly"—which it was. I was the biographer, not the chauffeur.

The truth is, I didn't mind playing a servile role in Bellow's life. Normally a proud and stubborn person, easily wounded and short-tempered when "dissed," I was in Bellow's presence someone else entirely: meek, shy-eyed, muttering a Prufrockian "Do I dare and do I dare?" as I shuffled down the sidewalk by his side. Why this reversion to a second-grade self, afraid of girls, sports, Skate Nights? Hadn't that timid character been toughened up by life? Could it be that I feared my own aggression? That the chauffeur might inadvertently slam his passenger's fingers in the door?

Bellow asked me how much time I would need. I asked for an hour and a half; beyond that would have felt like pushing it. He said, as he always did, "What is it you want to talk about?" The 1930s and '40s, I replied. That was as far as I'd gotten in the narrative. We agreed to meet at five.

I showed up promptly at the appointed hour, having loitered on the sidewalk for a few minutes to make sure I would get there on the dot. Bellow came to the door in a red bow tie and a tweed jacket. He offered me tea but seemed relieved when I refused it: "I've been running around and want to sit down."

"First the dentist, then the biographer," I said. "What a day." He laughed.

I noticed a paperback edition of *The Brothers Karamazov* on the table. "How does it hold up?" I asked. A dumb question. If Dostoyevsky didn't hold up, who would?

"Very well," Bellow answered. "It's even older than I am."

"Do you reread it every year?"

"No, it's not like Yom Kippur." This time I was the one who laughed.

We got down to work. As usual, I had a list of questions. I heard about how he had met his first wife, Anita: it was during the summer of 1935, on the El at 51st Street (just like Daisy in *Herzog*): "We walked up to the university together. She was extraordinarily beautiful, with fair hair and green eyes. We were both socialists."

Bellow's mother had taken out a life insurance policy, and Bellow got the money—$500—after she died. (I scribbled in my notebook, fast, almost indecipherably: "mother—life ins policy—B got money after she died $500.") His father insisted the money belonged to him (why? I forgot to ask; this happened all the time), but Bellow kept it and went off to Mexico with Anita on a Greyhound bus. An edition of D. H. Lawrence's letters was the book that inspired them to go. In Mexico City he met up with Herb Passin, a friend from his Humboldt Park days, and they arranged to interview Trotsky at his fortified home in Coyoacán. When they arrived, they saw his corpse laid out on a table, a bloody bandage around his head. The assassin sent by Stalin had gotten there first.

Incredible.

Bellow started telling me about his mother's death when he was seventeen. I knew all about that catastrophic event from *Herzog*, but he was deep in his memories. I had already become aware that what I learned from our formal interviews was both random and rehearsed: the stories Bellow told me were the same ones he had told over and over to other interviewers. His talk was an anthology; he returned to its contents again and again because they moved him.

But I had to press on with my efforts to collect the correspondence:

this was my job. I asked him whether I could see the letters. After all, I'd been working on the project for three years. "I don't want my last tatters exposed," Bellow answered. "My poor porous fig leaf."

He sat silent in the gathering dusk. Finally he said, with feeling: "I don't give a damn. It's really for Janis's sake. It hurts her to read about all this. She doesn't think I should do it."

More silence. "What is it you want to see?"

I explained that I'd like to see as much as I could, in order to write a thorough account. "You're in a tough spot," I acknowledged. "I have no wish to violate your privacy, and I'm not going to press you. We can think about it later." I pointed out that he had known me for some time and that I had no more proof to offer of my good intentions. I simply wanted to write a book that was accurate and true. "I need to know everything."

"Everything?" he said doubtfully.

Dave Peltz, a Tuley classmate and one of Bellow's closest friends, had encouraged me to ask Bellow about "the women," perhaps as a way of reassuring him that he'd led a vigorous and varied life in that department. "He wants to talk about them." He did and he didn't. Or rather he did, but on his own terms. And I wanted to talk about them on *my* terms. This was the hazard of being biographed: you got all this attention devoted to your life, but you had no control over how it was depicted. Maybe it was better not to be famous.

Sometimes I wondered why Bellow was letting me write this book at all. Why was it my business—much less the world's—to peer behind his fig leaf? What was in it for him? After all, he had told the whole story himself—or enough of it to give his readers a pretty clear sense of his life from his Montreal childhood (*Herzog*) to the most recent episodes of marital discord (*Humboldt's Gift*) and social crisis (*The Dean's December*). Was he curious, hoping he would learn things he didn't know? Did he entangle himself in complicated situations from which he couldn't escape in order to gratify a need for victimhood?

Or was it for the attention? He seemed lonely, isolated by his fame. Peltz had said to me, "He doesn't feel he can just pick up the phone and call someone to say, 'What are you doing tonight?'"

As I prepared to leave, Bellow said, "I've really enjoyed this today. I don't always, but these were things I hadn't thought about for a long time. You'll probably learn as much from me as from the letters. I don't mind at all talking to you. I don't want to get too involved, but from time to time . . ."

We stood at the door, and he said, "At least I'm still here." While I was waiting for the elevator, he told me he was going to Italy and Israel. ("Without O'Hare / Sheer despair," says Charlie Citrine.) I said I hoped to see him in the spring, and he replied, "I'll be back in January," as if inviting me to return sooner. I left feeling that a deep connection had been established.

Early in their relationship—they had known each other less than a year—Dr. Johnson saw Boswell off as he embarked on his Holland sojourn:

> My revered friend walked down with me to the beach, where we embraced and parted with tenderness, and engaged to correspond by letters. I said, "I hope, sir, you will not forget me in my absence." JOHNSON: "Nay, Sir, it is more likely you should forget me, than that I should forget you." As the vessel put out to sea, I kept my eyes on him for a considerable time, while he remained rolling his majestic frame in his usual manner; and at last I perceived him walk back into the town, and he disappeared.

We embraced and parted with tenderness.
Yes, that's how it would be with Bellow and me.

Boswell and Johnson

XIX

I have on my wall a lithograph of Boswell and Johnson, obtained from the Princeton University Library after an online search that involved clicking on "Boswell and Johnson" and tapping the Images icon. Numerous drawings and paintings instantly came up, including a cartoon of the two writers in space suits on the moon; a photograph of a stocky white-bearded man in a skullcap purportedly reading a volume of Johnson's poetry; and the one I purchased, which depicts Bozzy (as Johnson called him) and the Great Cham (as Johnson was called) skipping arm in arm down the street.°

What appealed to me most about this drawing was its companionate rendering of subject and biographer. Johnson, the taller of the two (or is it his tricorn hat?), seems to be thumbing his nose at Boswell, but in a genial way. Or maybe he's caressing his own cheek with his thumb? Unclear. What's evident is that they're having a good time. They have on the vestments of their day (obviously): the frock coats, the buckle shoes, the wigs. Johnson grips his walking stick.

Johnson had been a preoccupation of Boswell's since his school-boy days, when he encountered some books by Johnson in his father's library; he read them† "with delight and instruction," he wrote in his journal, "and had the highest reverence for their author, which had grown up in my fancy into a kind of mysterious veneration."

Boswell's determination to lead what we now might call "a big life"

° For a long time, I thought this nickname had something to do with "champion," but it's actually an Anglicization of *khan,* someone who rules over a domain—in this case, literature.

† Which books? According to C. E. Vulliamy, an early biographer, "little is known"— that dolorous confession of ignorance that biographers should do everything to avoid—of Boswell's early life. Boswell is guilty of such lapses himself: "In 1761 Johnson appears to have done little." Or was Boswell just not there to record it?

was manifest from early on. He had grown up at Auchinleck, his family's estate in northern Scotland, and studied law in Edinburgh at the insistence of his father, a strict and humorless judge. But it was London, with its vibrant bustle, its busy literary life, and its easy women ("I fell into a heartless commerce with girls who belonged to any man who had money") that inexorably called him away from the boredom of Scotland. "When we came upon Highgate hill and had a view of London, I was all life and joy, and my soul bounded forth to a certain prospect of happy futurity," he wrote in his journal on November 18, 1762, the day of his arrival in a city that would bring him intellectual stimulation, riotous nights in the pit at Covent Garden, adventures with whores, vast quantities of alcohol, and close proximity over a period of twenty-one years to the man whose name would be yoked to his for all eternity.

Their first meeting was still six months off. On occasion, Boswell staked out the bookshop of Tom Davies on Russell Street, having been tipped off that Dr. Johnson was a frequent visitor. No luck. Then around seven o'clock on the evening of May 16, 1763, he happened to be in the parlor at the back of the store when the shadow of a large man darkened the glass door. Davies quoted Horatio's line to Hamlet as his father's ghost appears on the scene: "Look, my Lord, it comes."

It was an auspicious encounter. They talked for three hours, until Boswell had to go off to "Dr. Pringle's." A few days later, the future biographer paid a call on his future subject at Johnson's lodgings in the Inner Temple, tracking down "the Giant in his den." Three weeks later he was back again. "Come to me as often as you can," said Johnson, warmly taking him by the hand: "I shall be glad to see you."

They were an odd couple. Johnson was "scrofulous," Boswell "scorbutic"—eighteenth-century afflictions that manifested themselves in symptoms of a visually unpleasant nature: bleeding gums, loose teeth, welts on the neck. Neither was known for sophistication in sartorial matters. Boswell, according to Frederick Pottle, author of the definitive two-volume life, was "a tireless, if somewhat grubby, man of pleasure." Johnson, in the testimony of Joshua Reynolds's sister Frances, "literally dressed like a beggar."

In temperament, too, they were much alike. Both were severe depressives who suffered from what was then called "melancholy." One of Johnson's biographers describes him as beset by "foul beasts who watched him from the shadows." Another biographer, Christopher Hibbert, quotes a Dr. Adams who dropped in to find "the Great

Man"—as his friends referred to Johnson—"in a deplorable state, sighing, groaning, talking to himself . . . He looked miserable." He claimed that he would be willing to have one of his limbs amputated if it would relieve his mood.

Boswell was also subject to depression, but he was manic, too: when not sunk in gloom, he was seized by "grand ebullitions and bright sparkles." His journals over a lifetime are an exhausting record of mood swings: "Exceedingly high spirits"; "Your nerves were unhinged and your spirit very low"; "cheerful mind"; "I rose very disconsolate." Boswell had a name for his condition: *changefulness.* Today we would call him bipolar.

Among the characteristics of this disease are impulsivity,° alcoholism, and sexual excess—sometimes displayed all at once. He would start out the day determined to be calm and disciplined—*retenue,* restrained—to work on his biography or "brush up" on Greek, and finish it off "singing ballads with two women in red coats, probably prostitutes, in St. Paul's Churchyard," or "tupping" a compliant girl referred to him by a "harlot" named Nanny Cooms: "I sent for her and enjoyed her, and—a kind of licence I never had."[†]

He also had a thing for "safe and elegant intrigues with fine women," most notably the wealthy novelist and beauty Belle de Zuylen, a Dutchwoman Boswell courted during a year he spent in Holland as a young man.[‡] And he seduced Rousseau's mistress, Thérèse Le Vasseur, in a carriage on the way to London, claiming to have done it thirteen times.[§] But what he preferred, according to John Wain, was "frank and episodic grossness without responsibility."[¶] He was obsessed with

---

° Hugh M. Milne, editor of Boswell's *Edinburgh Journals,* remarked on his "fondness for publishing ill-advised newspaper articles, pamphlets and letters which cannot but have been injurious to his reputation"—a common manifestation of this trait.

† I wish some literary Alan Turing would come along to break the code of squiggles and dots in his journal that indicated the various sexual "experiments" (Boswell's word) in which he engaged.

‡ She herself was the subject of a classic biography, *The Portrait of Zélide,* by Geoffrey Scott.

§ Frederick Pottle, Boswell's most reliable biographer, questions this number but notes that "an eleven-day blackout imposed by family censorship" of his journal has made it impossible to pin down the facts. Whatever the case, he didn't get high marks for performance: Pottle characterizes the biographer's technique as "hasty, self-absorbed, and clumsy."

¶ If you want to hear more about it, get hold of Wain's edition of the *Journals* and go to the index, where you'll find such blunt entries as: "sex in the Park, 293; drunk, and

his fellow Scotsman David Hume, who faced the prospect of mortality with a calm that baffled Boswell. Four days before Hume's death, Boswell showed up at his door in Edinburgh "elevated with liquor" and was turned away. Slaking his disappointment in typical fashion, he "ranged awhile in the Old Town after strumpets." Six months later, as if in defiance of Hume's equanimity, he screwed a whore in a shed behind the late philosopher's house.

Fascinated by his own case, Boswell diagnosed himself as what he called a "Hypochondriack"—someone afflicted with feelings of emptiness and chronic discontent. John Wain, in his introduction to the *Journals*, offers a shrewd description of his subject's mind:

> In his bleaker moods of introspection, when he confronted his own shortcomings and wondered what failings of his own had stood in the way of the worldly success he so much wanted, Boswell could sometimes be appalled at the blankness of his own nature, how it was like a sheet of white paper ready to be written on by some decisive hand, and reverting to perfect emptiness when that hand had moved on: almost as if there were no *Boswellus ipsissimus* under the perpetually willing receptiveness. It was as if he couldn't establish a stable identity without the validation of another. On his own, he was nothing, a person without a self, an empty vessel waiting to be filled.

In other words, a biographer.

A sticker affixed to the back of my Johnson and Boswell print places them in Edinburgh, which would mean they were at the beginning of the famous journey memorialized in their dual (and dueling?) travelogues: Boswell's *Journal of a Tour to the Hebrides with Samuel Johnson, LL.D.* and Johnson's *Journey to the Western Islands of Scotland.*° The year would have been 1773, when Boswell was thirty-two and Johnson exactly twice his age.

---

sex with Jenny Taylor, 294; sex with Nanny Smith, 294; at Charing Cross bagnio, 295; sex at Duck Lane, 295-96."
° Note that Boswell included Johnson's name in his title, while Johnson's gave no indication that he'd had company along the way. As far as he was concerned, he was the main subject; his biographer was his amanuensis.

By this time their unacknowledged biographical collaboration was a decade old. Boswell confessed in his journal that he was having a hard time working up the nerve to let Johnson know that he intended—or aspired—to write his biography. "I have not told him yet, nor do I know if I should tell him. I said that if it was not troublesome and presuming too much, I would beg of him to tell me all the little circumstances of his life, what schools he attended, when he came to Oxford, when he came to London, etc. etc." Johnson was game: "He did not disapprove of my curiosity." But he first needed to assure himself that his potential biographer had done his homework: "I hope you shall know a great deal more of me before you write my life."

The trip was intended to be a trial run. Scotland was a lab in which to test out the younger man's suitability for the job and determine whether subject and biographer were compatible. Boswell was excited at the prospect of spending such a protracted interval in the proximity of Johnson; he felt, said one of his friends, "like a dog who has run away with a large piece of meat." But Johnson was compliant and claimed that he had "long desired to visit the Hebrides."

Boswell had a powerful need for discipleship. It wasn't enough for him to read the work of his literary heroes; he had to know them. On the trail of Voltaire and Rousseau, precursors to Johnson, he had longed for their approval and ingratiated himself to get it. "Enlightened mentor!" he addressed Rousseau, besieging him with importunate letters: could he just drop in at Neuchâtel for a visit? Incredibly, considering that Boswell was a young man of no reputation or credentials, Rousseau consented, if he would "make it short." Voltaire, too, found time for the obscure Scotsman, who refused to be shooed off by Voltaire's footmen and finally wangled an hour-and-a-half interview with the philosopher (who, claiming illness, showed up in a blue nightgown).

What quality was it that made Boswell able to command the attention of great men? A chameleon gift for adapting himself to their needs, he theorized in his journal—put less kindly, a genius for becoming someone else: "I can tune myself so to the tone of any bearable man I am with that he is as at freedom as with another self, and, till I am gone, cannot imagine me a stranger." It was this capacity for self-erasure—what his friend Edmund Malone called "ductility"—that defined Boswell's genius as a biographer.

Yet on the page, the personality of the biographer will inevitably reassert itself. We are all shadowy presences in our own books. We're there and not there, visible and invisible; our fingers leave faint but indelible prints. Our temperament, our character, our sensibility all become part of the story we're telling. We strive for objectivity, aware that it can't be achieved. "I profess to write, not his panegyric, but his Life," Boswell wrote of Johnson; "which, great and good as he was, must not be supposed to be entirely perfect. . . . There should be shade as well as light."

How much shade was there in the *Life*? On occasion Boswell showed his subject to disadvantage, but his criticisms tended to be mild and gently expressed. ("Notwithstanding the high veneration which I entertained for Dr. Johnson, I was sensible that he was sometimes a little actuated by the spirit of contradiction.") There was much light and little shade. And that is the Johnson we know today. But it's not Johnson. It's Boswell's Johnson.

They met up in sewage-drenched Edinburgh, where it was the habit of its citizens to empty their chamber pots onto the street. ("Sir, I smell you in the dark," said Dr. Johnson with good-natured annoyance.) Travel was rough in those days: rudimentary lodgings, poor roads, crummy food, and genuine hazards. At one point, they had a quarrel when Boswell rode ahead to secure lodgings, leaving Johnson out in the dusk on a wobbly horse. "I was thinking that I should have returned with you to Edinburgh and then parted, and never spoke to you no more," Johnson reproved him.

In consultation with a minister encountered on their way west, they had worked out a route from Inverness, by way of Fort Augustus, to the palindromic Glenelg, Skye, Mull, Lorn, and Inverary. Accompanied by Boswell's servant, Joseph, they set forth in mid-August, traveling by post chaise; when they got to Inverness, they switched horses, struggling over the muddy terrain in terrible weather.

Dr. Johnson dressed in Scotland as he did in England: "He wore a full suit of plain brown clothes with twisted-hair buttons of the same colour, a large bushy grey wig, a plain shirt, black worsted stockings, and silver buckles."* They found lodgings where they could: at the home of Sir Alexander Macdonald, a member of the ancient clan on the Isle

---

* Boswell likened biography to portraiture: "I draw him in the style of a Flemish painter . . . I must be exact as to every hair, or even every spot on his countenance."

of Skye, there were no teaspoons and they had to use their fingers; Sir Alexander stuck his fork into a pudding and hogged it all himself. Their next stop, a farmhouse not far away, at least had tongs for sugar, and they dined well: "We had for supper a large dish of minced beef collops,° a large dish of fricassee of fowl, a dish called fried chicken or something like it." And so on through many delectable-sounding courses, served on a white tablecloth, with napkins, china, and silver spoons. "It was really an agreeable meeting."

Scotland was a mixed experience. Sailing in a tippy boat to the island of Coll, they nearly drowned; in Eigg, they came upon "a very large cave in which all the inhabitants were smoked to death by the Macleods"; in Ulva, they were shown a room with nice beds but broken windows that let in rain to muddy the clay floor. But they enjoyed each other's company—Boswell in his role as verbal portraitist of Doctor Mor, the Big Doctor, as the Scots called him; Johnson as the Great Cham,† sounding off on everything from the derivation of words to the efficacy of different types of shovels, the taste of various game birds to "the nature of milk." Boswell recorded as much as he could get down in the thick notebooks he'd brought along "to glean Johnsoniana." He was practicing for the work ahead.

Subject and biographer were well suited, co-conspirators in an enterprise that required tacit collusion. "Each is a creation of the other," noted Adam Sisman in *Boswell's Presumptuous Task*, his fine account of the writing of the *Life*. While Boswell was transcribing Johnson's speech, Johnson was commenting on Boswell's project. "He read a great deal of my journal in the little book which I had from him, and was pleased; for he said, 'I wish the books were twice as big'"—in other words, had more about him. "He helped me to supply blanks which I had left in first writing it, when I was not quite sure of what he had said; and he corrected any mistakes that I had made." The future biographer was so assiduous in his labors that he sometimes got burned out and took the night off: "I did not exert myself to get Dr. Johnson to talk, that I might not have the trouble of writing down his conversation." But when he wasn't there, Dr. Johnson complained of missing his company.

° According to Merriam-Webster, "a small piece or slice especially of meat."
† There were times when, weary of Johnson's orotund proclamations, I thought of him as the Great Sham.

In effect, Boswell's masterwork was a collaboration. "Dr. Johnson told me there were two faults in my Journal: one was expatiating too much on the luxury of the little-house at Talisker." The other was about some clergyman they encountered: "'I did not say the man's hair could not be well dressed because he had not a clean shirt, but because he was bald.'" Here the subject is correcting the biographer: a dangerous precedent.

In this context, with his interlocutor setting the scene, Johnson could sound as if he were speaking for the ages: "If one was to think constantly of death, the business of life would stand still." "However bad any man's existence may be, every man would rather have it than not exist at all" ("all this delivered with manly eloquence in a boat on the sea," wrote Boswell, setting the scene, "upon a fine autumn Sunday morning"). There is a preening self-consciousness in these proclamations, but how could there not be, with Boswell hovering beside his pompous subject, even supplying the props? When Johnson drinks a rare dram of Scotch and leaves a drop, Boswell asks him to pour it into his glass "that I might say we have drunk whiskey together."

Johnson pretended to chafe at always having to be onstage. "You have but two subjects: yourself and me," he once complained. "I am sick of both." But he was more than willing to play his part. Prancing about his room in a blue bonnet, roaring Highland ballads, grousing about the crude table manners of the Scottish and the lack of privies, he was a character in search of an author. And he didn't have far to look.

Dr. Johnson published his account of their travels, *Journey to the Western Islands of Scotland*, two years after their return to London, and it has "the settled flavor of wisdom precipitated, conclusions pondered in tranquil recollection," wrote Israel Shenker, for many years *The New York Times*'s premonitory obit writer, in his charming travelogue, *In the Footsteps of Boswell and Johnson*. Boswell waited another decade to publish his *Journal of a Tour to the Hebrides with Samuel Johnson, LL.D.*, but his book was "livelier, chattier" than Johnson's, in Shenker's view, and had "the vividness of fresh reporting." Thus did the biographer, not for the first or last time, trump his subject.°°

° I note with satisfaction that the Yale edition of Johnson's *Complete Works* has been terminated for lack of funds, while Boswell's continue to emerge from the press, "so that we can count on being regaled indefinitely with the details of Boswell's claps and hangovers," as Donald Greene bitterly observed in the *TLS*.

It was the summer of 1992, and our children—now five and nine—were out of school for vacation. But we had no money. Somehow I managed to persuade my friend Muffin, who worked at a glossy travel magazine, to let me follow in the footsteps of Shenker. Thus it was that one day in August, our little crew flew to London, rented a navy blue Land Rover, and went bombing up the M-6 to Scotland.

We stayed in drafty castles and threadbare bed-and-breakfasts that would have made no Top Hundred Resorts list. I felt sorry for my nervous charges and their mother. While other families went camping in Yellowstone or rented a cabin on Cape Cod, we were headed for "a country where no wheel has rolled," as Johnson put it, the inns were "verminous," the people "savages," and the weather "dreary."

I had never been one for roughing it. Not for me the knapsack and walking stick of Richard Holmes on the path of Robert Louis Stevenson in the Cévennes, camping out in rough weather. But Tuscany and the Lake District were spoken for; it was the Hebrides or nothing.

I had brought along my primary copy of Boswell's *Life of Johnson*, a 1933 edition published by J. M. Dent that I had picked up in a secondhand shop for—according to the penciled-in price—$3.50. Such a handsome book, too: squarishly old-fashioned, its pages tissue thin. For me, the *Life* was more than a book; it was a guide to the practice of biography, as flexible from use as the thumbprint-smudged repair manual in the glove compartment of our rented Rover.

For our first night out of Glasgow, I had booked rooms at the Pheasant Inn, beside Lake Bassenthwaite, in the northern corner of the Lake District; Shelley had stayed in a nearby cottage in the autumn of 1810. Tucking into a plate of grouse in the oak-beamed dining room, I recalled Boswell's observation that "there is nothing which has yet been contrived by man by which so much happiness is produced as by a good tavern or inn."

The next day we crossed the border and headed for Auchinleck, the Boswell family seat (pronounced something like *Owthckh Leck*, according to the proprietor of the Pheasant Inn). Our destination was the Auchinleck Boswell Museum and Mausoleum, described in my guidebook as "the burial place of five generations of Boswells."

The border towns were grim; their treeless thoroughfares gave them a denuded look. I rolled down the window and asked a grizzled man on the street the whereabouts of the museum, and he answered in a language I had never heard before, a stream of gutturals and throat-clearing snorts; I surmised it was some Scottish dialect, or "Scots," if that was a language at all. The look of bewilderment on my face must have conveyed my incomprehension, for he beckoned us to follow and continued up the street as we crept along beside him. Some yards up, he pointed to a small windowless building made of ancient stone. Beside it was an empty car park and an outcropping of tilted tomb-stones on a weedy, overgrown patch of grass. Across the street stood a seedy pub—the Boswell.

We were greeted by Douglas Wilson, the curator. He was small and wiry and wore a crisp blue vest and a matching knitted tie. He gripped my hand tightly, as if he were afraid I'd wander off. I explained my mis-sion, such as it was, and he offered to show us around.

The museum's holdings were sparse, consisting largely of old books and crockery salvaged from the family home. Mr. Wilson suggested we have a look at Boswell's crypt. He pulled open a trapdoor in the rough-hewn wooden floor; the biographer lay below. I peered down into the crypt, declining an offer to descend a shaky-looking ladder. There was Boswell. Or what was left of him—a pile of bones in a coffin.°

That the ebullient, high-spirited figure who had stumbled drunk through the streets of London, learned Greek and Latin in some rented room, argued cases before the court in Edinburgh, studied chemistry "at stool," trotted after his corpulent prey from the George to the Cheshire Cheese, this complicated, unstable soul who outdid even Pepys in the number of whores and chambermaids he "tossed," who wavered between self-love and self-contempt, who was more vivid to me in his centuries-long absence than my own contemporaries, now lay in this dank tomb was impossible to grasp. But I was excited, too. For the first time—and perhaps the last—I experienced the sensation of being in the presence of a dead person who suddenly seemed alive, in his ale-stained vestments and ill-fitting wig, malodorous ("Sir, I smell you in the dark"), excitable, talkative, emanating colossal energy, "strut-ting about," as Fanny Burney's sister, Charlotte, memorably described him. . . . Maybe death wasn't the end after all.

As we were leaving, Mr. Wilson asked me to sign the register. There were only two names on the page, Japanese from the sound of them. "English literature students from Kyoto," he explained.

° Rich material for a "What I Did on My Summer Vacation" essay.

Mr. Wilson appeared to have a lot of time on his hands and now proposed a tour of the family estate. It was in the countryside, two miles from town.

Auchinleck, like everything old, had once been new. Boswell described it as "a house of hewn stone, very stately and durable." It had fallen into disrepair and the windows were boarded up, but the great blocks of quarried stone and the Georgian pediment attested to its former grandeur. The sun came out as we drove up, and all at once I could imagine the "very fine day"—November 4, 1773—when Boswell, "elated" to have his illustrious subject under his own (or rather, his father's) roof, had shown off the grounds to Dr. Johnson and strolled beneath "some venerable old trees, under the shade of which my ancestors had walked." They were still there, even older now, a canopy of ancient elms lining the road to the house. It was in this house that Johnson had complained about the "incommodiousness" of the weather, chewed out the local minister ("Sir, you know no more of our church than a Hottentot"), and had a violent quarrel with Boswell's father. "They are now in another, and higher state of existence," Boswell would observe in his *Life* of Johnson. "And as they were both worthy Christian men, I trust they have met in happiness." Boswell has since joined them, but with the recollection of his dank crypt still in mind, I doubt it was to a higher state of existence that any of them had gone.

It had been Boswell's ambition, he declared in his preface to the *Life*, to produce a portrait of a man who would be seen "more clearly than any man who has yet lived." The biographer's chief duty was to "lead the thoughts into domestick privacies . . . by interweaving what [his subject] privately wrote, and said and thought." And to achieve this goal—to see "the real Johnson," "Johnson as he really was"—you had to shadow your subject. "Nobody can write the life of a man, but those who have eat and drunk and lived in social intercourse with him," Johnson maintained. Thus did Boswell accompany Johnson to Lichfield, his childhood home; to Oxford, where Johnson had once been a student; and to London dinner parties, at which he would pull up his chair behind Johnson's, determined not to miss a *mot*. "When my mind was, as it were, *strongly penetrated with the Johnsonian ether*, I could, with much more facility and exactness, carry in my memory and commit to paper the exuberant variety of his wisdom and wit." Or when it wasn't too strongly penetrated with other kinds of ether.

Boswell had devised an ingenious method of transcription: having memorized as much as he could of a dialogue, he would scribble down rapid condensed notes, sometimes in Johnson's presence, abbreviating all but key words—"the heads," he called them, the ingredients of "portable soup," "a kind of stock cube from which I could make up a broth, when the time came to feed." It didn't always congeal. "I have the substance," he confided in his journal, "but the felicity of expression, the flavor, is not fully preserved unless taken instantly." And even that method was unreliable. Johnson once challenged his biographer to an experiment in which he slowly read a passage from William Robertson's *History of America*, while Boswell tried to transcribe it; when Boswell read the passage back, "It was found that I had it very imperfectly."°

Still, if he sometimes stumbled over the words, he was a brilliant mimic of Johnson's voice. "He had an odd, mock solemnity of tone and manner, that he had acquired imperceptibly from constantly thinking of and imitating Dr. Johnson," wrote the novelist Fanny Burney, who was often in their company. "Every look and movement displayed either intentional or involuntary imitation."†

Boswell's ability to capture Johnson's table talk was the natural outcome of an edict he had delivered to himself: "Be Johnson." It was a

---

° Imperfect or not, one must be grateful for the few instances of transcribed speech that have come down to us; however stilted—even fabricated—they sound, the occasional note of authenticity comes through. Coleridge's *Table Talk*, recorded by his son, is strange and electrifying. "Throughout a long-drawn summer's day would this man talk to you in low, equable, but clear and musical, tones," wrote his son Hartley in his introduction, "pouring withall such floods of light upon the mind, that you might, for a season, like Paul, become blind in the very act of conversion." (What he doesn't say is that his father was stoned out of his gourd on laudanum most of the time.) Coleridge wasn't as lively as Boswell, Hartley admitted, and he didn't have "the precise gladiatorial power" of Johnson, but he got off some good lines now and then: "Truth is a good dog; but beware of barking too close to the heels of an error, lest you get your brains kicked out." Or this rumination on July 10, 1834: "I am dying, dying," followed by an account of scenes from his early life that had stolen into his mind "like breezes blown from the spice-islands of Youth and Hope—those twin realities of this phantom world!" One feels that Coleridge *would have* spoken this way. And that, for the eighteenth-century biographer, was enough.

† Writers seem to be especially good at mimicry. In his biography of T. S. Eliot, Peter Ackroyd notes Eliot's "extraordinary ability to mimic Pound's verbal mannerisms, as if he were willingly immersing himself in his personality."

directive he took literally, imagining what it would be like to occupy Johnson's garret after his subject died: "I could not help indulging a scheme of taking it for myself many years hence, when its present great possessor will in all probability be gone to a more exalted situation." He was like a greedy heir, worshipping his benefactor but impatient to inherit his possessions.

In the meantime, he would simply be there, a witness to Johnson's vitality. To insinuate yourself into your subject's daily life, to experience it as it's being lived, was one of the advantages (I nervously told myself) of writing a biography of a living person. Boswell's account of a dinner at the home of his friend Bishop Percy has an uncanny verisimilitude. The two men—as recorded by Boswell—are having a heated argument about the landscaping of a castle in Scotland that both have visited. At issue is whether the grounds could be described as "trim." The bishop maintains that there is "a very large extent of fine turf and gravel walks." Johnson retorts that "there is no variety, no mind exerted in laying out the ground, no trees." Percy insists that there are in fact "an immense number of trees," but Johnson is too "short-sighted" to see them—a sally so provocative that the myopic Johnson can scarcely maintain his temper: "Inflammable particles were collecting for a cloud to burst."

Soon the two parties are accusing each other of incivility. The stage-managing biographer, meanwhile, is loath to intervene because he sees an opportunity to display his subject's "tender and benevolent heart" engaged in the act of forgiveness. Which is exactly what happens. By the end of the night, the two friends have made up: "Dr. Percy rose, ran up to [Johnson], and taking him by the hand, assured him affectionately that his meaning had been misunderstood, upon which a reconciliation instantly took place."

What fascinates me about this entry is how banal it is. There are no oracular pronouncements about God or Death or Education ("To learn is the proper business of youth"); no prefatory "Sir." Instead we have two men idly sitting around the dinner table squabbling over some pointless question. How many trees are there on the grounds of Alnwick Castle? They might as well have been two guys in a sports bar having a disagreement about how many years Ted Kluszewski had played for the Chicago White Sox.°

° Two.

B oswell's wasn't the first biography of Johnson to see print. The day after Johnson's death, his protegé received a letter from the bookseller-publisher Charles Dilly proposing an "instant" book: four hundred pages of Johnson's table talk.° But six other potential biographers were already on the case—Johnson was a huge deal in that day—among them John Hawkins (officially Sir John Hawkins, Knt.), one of Johnson's executors and a member of the Literary Club. He, too, had a personal acquaintance with the Great Cham.

Hawkins was first out of the gate, publishing his biography just three years after Johnson's death. (The world would have to wait another four years for Boswell's *Life*.) It was not well received, to put it mildly; reviewers "fell to their task," writes Bertram H. Davis, the editor of the 1961 edition, "with all the zest they would have given to a defense of London against an invading armada." The book was condemned as spiteful, rancorous, malevolent; Hawkins had been indiscreet about Johnson's marriage, revealing that he and his erratic wife, Tetty, had briefly separated on account of her husband's nocturnal perambulations with Richard Savage. As Davis put it: "Johnson's executor had become his executioner."

How fair was the accusation that Hawkins had dwelled excessively on the couple's marital discord? Johnson's affection "soon returned," he had noted, citing as evidence David Garrick's habit of imitating his subject's uxorious behavior. He was also generous, at least intermittently, in his depiction of Johnson's character. "With all that asperity of manners with which he has been charged," wrote Hawkins, "he possessed the affections of pity and compassion in a most eminent degree." Which he did, along with a lot of other traits that made him human, such as vanity, pride, and malice.

Boswell would have none of it. As far as he was concerned, Hawkins was out to get Johnson. "There is throughout the whole of it a dark uncharitable cast, by which the most unfavourable construction is put upon almost every circumstance in the character and conduct of my illustrious friend," he claimed in the preface to his own *Life*. Besides, Hawkins didn't really know Johnson, according to Boswell: "I never saw [Hawkins] in his company, I think, but once, and I am sure not

---

° Today it would be an ebook, followed by a print-on-demand edition.

above twice."* He even accused his rival of purloining a volume of Johnson's journal—though Boswell himself had copied out passages from the journals he found lying around Johnson's home when his subject wasn't there.

Read today, Hawkins's life of Johnson seems innocuous. Adam Sisman observes: "Many of the descriptions in Hawkins's book that dismayed readers—for example, of Johnson's disgusting eating habits or his slovenly style of dress—would find their equivalents in Boswell's biography. But by then their sting had been drawn." What had once been perceived as insult was now seen as candor.

Boswell found writing the book a torture. It had taken him six years just to organize his papers in preparation for the massive task that lay before him: "sorted till I was stupified," he noted in his journal.

Holed up in a half-furnished, rat-infested house in Great Queen Street, "struggling to stay sober by a regimen of bread and milk," he wrote to the accompaniment of his wife, Margaret, coughing in the next room; she was dying of consumption. Here begins a summary of Boswell's dire situation by Michael F. Suarez† that I came across in the *TLS*:

> Hopes of political preferment from Lord Lonsdale were dashed; his wife died in 1789, while Boswell was away on business for his unreliable patron. Beleaguered with seemingly insurmountable debts and suffering bouts of depression, he drank heavily,‡ contracted a venereal disease, was haunted by guilt, and struggled against the anarchy of his private life.

Had it not been for his close friend Edmund Malone, Boswell might never have gotten the book done at all. A bookish bachelor with a trust fund, Malone was the greatest authority on Shakespeare of his day. Night after night the two men sat side by side revising, editing, collat-

---

* But he did; they were often together at the Literary Club, once the "unclubbable" Hawkins had elbowed his way into becoming a member. In fact, Hawkins knew Johnson for twenty-four years longer than Boswell did.

† Identified as the author of *The Mock-Biblical: A Study in Satire from the Popish Plot to the Pretender Crisis*.

‡ He tried to limit himself to four glasses of wine at dinner, followed by a pint of ale afterward, but with only intermittent success.

ing, deleting, improving, questioning, scribbling in the margins; sometimes Malone wrote entire passages himself.

The most valuable service he performed was to mitigate Johnson's intemperate tone, which flared up unpredictably, as when he referred to the Reverend Kenneth Macaulay as "the most ignorant booby and grossest bastard." Malone persuaded Boswell to soften it to "a coarse man." It was all about tone. (It always is.) Frank Brady, author of the definitive two-volume biography of Boswell, called theirs "one of the most productive collaborations in literary history."

Not even Malone could stave off Boswell's dark moods. He worried that the book was too long, yet he kept discovering new letters that had to be included; desperate for money, he bought a lottery ticket; he was arrested for calling out the hour late at night in comic imitation of a watchman; he burst into tears on the street. He was, according to his journals of that time, "sadly ill," "dejected and miserable," "sore and fretful."

But he also knew that he had produced a classic. In its day, the *Life* was celebrated if not universally praised; its value as high entertainment was beyond dispute. "I have been amused at it," wrote one correspondent, "but should be very sorry either to have been the author or the hero of it." Boswell was banned from clubs out of fear that he would record private conversations in his notebook.

Publication proved anticlimactic. The labor that had consumed Boswell's days for over twenty years was done, and he had little to occupy himself; he was such a notoriously inept lawyer that few cases came his way, and he was reduced to practicing what he knew best, besides the art of biography: drinking and whoring. Finally, Frank Brady intones in *The Later Years,* "Death came to the rescue." In Boswell's case, the precipitating cause was a "swelling of the bladder,"° apparently exacerbated by alcohol. He was fifty-eight, even in those days a young age. Toward the end of his labors, he wrote: "I had now resolved the *Life* into my own feelings." He had written a book that, aspiring to immortalize its subject, would immortalize its author.

° Until the modern era, biographers were at a loss as to the exact cause of their subjects' deaths, which, given the limitations of medical knowledge in those days, they ascribed to various strange and often invented maladies, such as aigue or neurasthenia.

XX

I enjoyed being in Bellow's company, but I also enjoyed *not* being in Bellow's company. He could be "snappish," as he saw himself in Mark Harris's deeply ambivalent portrait, or so lost in his memories that he seemed to forget I was there (which was not such a terrible thing, as it allowed me to scribble notes without having to make conversation). I never felt that he was sick of me, though I'm sure he often was. I honored him by commemorating his life, but I also reminded him of its approaching end. On a good day, I would catch him in a playful mood, telling jokes and laughing at them, making fun of academics, pulverizing the many people he hated and satirizing his best friends for a worshipful audience of one. On a bad day, I was the robed prophet in *The New Yorker* cartoon, carrying aloft a banner that read: "The end is nigh." More to the point, *Bellow's* end was nigh. What else can having a biography written about you portend?

To me, Bellow was always a celebrity—always "Saul Bellow"—no matter how many times I interviewed him. Even after a decade, I experienced a nervous vibration whenever I was around him—a feeling that I suspect he would have understood. He had his own great men. These included the British philosopher Owen Barfield, whose work had made a great impression on him, and—for a time, until they quarreled—the distinguished sociologist Edward Shils. But even disciples can get tired of their role.

Affiliated with both Cambridge University and the University of Chicago, where he was a colleague of Bellow's in the Committee on Social Thought, Shils was perhaps best known as the eponymous hero of Bellow's controversial novel *Mr. Sammler's Planet*. Artur Sammler was a survivor of the Warsaw Ghetto who had managed to make his way, after the war, to the Upper West Side of Manhattan. Having witnessed horror, he felt nothing but contempt for the student revolution-

Saul Bellow and Janis Freedman Bellow

aries of the 1960s. He was imperious, intolerant, and—if you wished to read it that way—racist; he derided the rampant promiscuity of that era as "sexual niggerhood for everyone."

One afternoon I visited Shils in his apartment across from the Museum of Science and Industry. The building stood alone between vacant lots; it could have been Dresden in 1945. He reminded me of Richard Durnwald, a Shilsian figure in *Humboldt's Gift* described as "elderly but powerful, thickset and bald, a bachelor of cranky habits but kind." A Jewish boy from Philadelphia, Shils had turned himself into a Chicago Englishman. He carried a walking stick, said "shall" instead of "will," and offered me tea with elaborate ritual. His dark undertaker's suits looked as if they had been made on Savile Row. (They probably had.) But this was all for show. He was a formidable scholar who seemed to have read everything. His twelve-foot floor-to-ceiling bookcases were on the scale of a European intellectual's library: new hardcovers, old leather-bound books, complete sets of the great historians, and white-spined paperbacks in French. On the top shelf was a long row of the *Journal of American Sociology*.

Unlike Durnwald, Shils was not kind. He brutally disparaged his colleagues, both friends and enemies, as "idiots" and "worthless fellows." He had a sour view of life, thought human beings were corrupt, and showed contempt for the living and the dead alike. All the same, I enjoyed his company. He had one of the most penetrating minds I'd ever encountered, and there were times when I suspected his negativity was a pose. Intellectual challenges stimulated him; he was a natural pedagogue. As it turned out, I, too, would become a disciple of Shils.

Eventually I sat down to write. I had the biographer's tools ready to hand: the notecards, the manuscripts, the letters, the interviews, the books—what the awl and plane, the hammer and nails, the saw, the wrench, and the measuring tape are to the carpenter.

What I didn't have was a blueprint. Bellow's archive dwarfed Delmore's. He was a public figure, and he had written more books and letters, saved more press clips and articles, accumulated more manuscripts and drafts of lectures, legal documents and interviews—thank god there were no journals, or none that I knew of—than I could absorb as I sat at my desk in New York, shutting out the cacophony of sirens and yipping dogs below my window with Flent's Ear Stopples.

Biography is a lonely trade. It requires a capacity for sitting by your-self all day for years, sometimes decades, shuffling through yellowing manuscripts and letters. The Germans have a word for this: *Sitzfleisch* (literally "sitting down flesh," or the ability to keep your ass in a chair). It requires an ability to be egoless, to subjugate yourself to another. And it requires a curiosity about human nature, a need to find out why people are the way they are. But there is a deeper impulse, one born out of emotional hunger. It could be summed up in Forster's "only connect"—be empathic, establish enduring relationships, and try to understand others at the deepest level. This was the biographer's man-date, and every biographer I knew took it seriously. We were always preoccupied with our subjects in one way or another—sometimes to the exclusion of the life going on around us.*

When I wasn't writing, I was reading. This is one of the main things biographers do: they read their subject's books over and over, for all different kinds of reasons: sometimes they're hunting down a quote, sometimes they're reminding themselves about a plot, sometimes they're trying to fit the book at hand into the canon. Is it a masterpiece? An average book? A dog? Does it have great moments, even though it fails to cohere?

Rereading Bellow in my forties, I found that my opinion of his work had changed. *Dangling Man* and *The Victim* (Bellow called them his M.A. and his Ph.D.) now left me cold. But I was eager to return to his "breakthrough" novel, *The Adventures of Augie March*, five hundred pages of hectic goings-on that critics had hailed as a dramatic depar-ture—an escape, really—from the stiff and dutiful apprentice works. *Humboldt's Gift*, Bellow's "Delmore" novel, increasingly seemed a heavy-handed caricature of Delmore's craziness. And I was put off anew by his characters' self-regard. Harry Trellman, in *The Actual*, is "a world-class noticer." Charlie Citrine is besieged by women: "You

---

* The height of my growing manuscript was barely outpaced by the growth of my children, who measured the untidy pile of papers with wary eyes, wondering who this person was who could absorb so much of my time. About the man himself, they were largely incurious: as long as he didn't interfere with my ferrying them to hockey and tae kwon do, cello lessons and drama workshop, playdates and Science Club (I made that up; no child in our art-saturated household would go to Science Club), they never begrudged me what I had come to think of as Bellow Time. Not that he impinged on their needs: when faced with the option of typing up my interviews with Bellow's Tuley friends or watching my daughter play the Milkman in *Our Town*, it wasn't hard to choose.

some ladies' man," says Roland, the doorman of his Chicago apartment building, who talks like Rochester on *The Jack Benny Show*. "Literature can do with any amount of egotism," wrote John Updike, reviewing *The Dean's December*, "but the merest pinch of narcissism spoils the broth." This would become a problem for me. Only *Herzog* and *Seize the Day* survived scrutiny without being demoted. They were Bellow's Great Books.

As I got older, I found my feelings about his oeuvre beginning to change yet again. I had grown weary of *Augie March* (maybe because other critics were always raving about it) and took pleasure once more in the early novels, with their brooding European atmosphere. The melancholic air that I had once found mannered now seemed haunting; Joseph, who dangles on the South Side of Chicago, and Leventhal, who dolefully wanders the hot summer streets of Manhattan, were figures out of my own unconscious, never at home in the world, always on edge, untrusting. My view of life had grown darker. You can never read the same book twice.

It was August 1992, and I was back on twisty, mountainous Route 9—the road to Bellow. I was eager to ask him about a number of matters that had plagued me over the last Bellowless months.

Much as I cherished my freedom, I had missed him. He intensified my sense of life. And there was something about being in his presence that excited me. *Ecce homo.* In the years I knew him, he was still startlingly handsome, with silken white hair, a finely chiseled nose, and beautiful brown eyes. It was strange to think that he would soon be dead for all eternity, and not long after that inconceivable event, a few decades at most, no one who had ever known him would be alive. Mine would be one of the last records of what he had looked like in the flesh as he moved through the world.

When I arrived at the general store—I still couldn't find my way to the house on my own—he was standing by the meat counter. He was wearing a blue cap, a multipocketed denim jacket, khakis, and black leather lace-up shoes with—this I didn't get at all—pink tassels. His face was lined with age, and I noticed that he was a little hard of hearing.

Every time I saw him, Bellow was older; how could it be otherwise? It never occurred to me that I was growing older as well, and that my whitening hair and veinous hands would register with him as evidence of the obsession at the heart of his work: mortality. As Herzog says, noticing the crinkled neck of an old girlfriend, now in her forties: "Death, the artist, very slow, putting in his first touches."

When we got to the house, we sat down at the kitchen table over a cup of tea. Eager to bring him up to date, I asked if he had seen a famous critic's rave review of *The Bellarosa Connection*. No, he'd missed it: "My eyes are on eternity." I thought of Sammler's description of how he sees the world with "earth-departure objectivity" (though he was only fifty-seven).

The problem with biography is that the biographer's age inevitably affects the way he sees his subject. As that vantage changes, so does his viewpoint. A biography written by a forty-year-old will be more unforgiving, less sensitive to his subject's pain, than a biography written by a sixty-year-old. I'd been at work on my book for three years, and I was a different person from the person I'd been when I started, though still callow and arrogance-prone at times. Bellow was different, too, but I wasn't sure how. Maybe he was just sadder.

On this night we were going out for dinner. Bellow had made a reservation at Le Petit Chef, a French restaurant on Route 100, about a half hour away. We climbed into the Range Rover. Bellow wanted "company," he said. He didn't see why we should go in separate cars.

We talked in a desultory way as Bellow drove. I asked him if he'd had a good writing day. "I woke up at six because I was worried about Therese"—the housekeeper—"and had breakfast at eight. Then I started a fire. It was too damp to work in the house." The phone rang a lot, he complained. One caller was the writer Stanley Crouch, who spent a half hour filling him in on the latest news from literary New York. Then Allan Bloom called to tell him about a piece by Daniel Bell that had appeared on the op-ed page of *The New York Times* a few days earlier, mourning the end of his generation. Literature was no longer "central," Bellow said, a note of rancor in his voice. The novel wasn't important. *Yeah, yeah,* I thought to myself: *the problem is* your *novels aren't central.* Delillo, Pynchon, Gaddis had lots of readers (even if I wasn't one of them).

Bellow was a man for whom the world was becoming unfamiliar and confusing, overrun by a youth culture with beliefs and customs of its own—a man, in short, who was growing old. But his contention troubled me all the same: was it possible that even Saul Bellow's work would fade from the collective memory, that *Herzog* and *Humboldt's Gift* and *Henderson the Rain King* (the "three H's," he liked to call them) would one day molder on the shelf beside the works of Sinclair Lewis and Pearl Buck, their spines creased, the yellow pages crumbling; then recede even further back in time, like Stephen Crane and George Gissing, their hard-to-find volumes available only from Abe-Books; then become footnotes in some grad student's dissertation on twentieth-century American literature; and finally be forgotten altogether? Bellow's work had spoken powerfully to his generation and mine, but it was entirely possible—indeed, likely—that it wouldn't speak to the generation after that. Would I want to live in such a world?

Seated at an outdoor patio, Bellow ordered a bottle of wine. I was too wound up to notice the label and anyway was no oenophile; wine was wine. But I was struck by the fact that it was a whole bottle instead of "by the glass." Bellow wasn't a big drinker; it wasn't that. But didn't ordering a bottle of wine mean that our dinner was a social occasion? Was I allowed to ask questions—to "interview" him and use the answers in my book?

When the waitress poured the wine, we hesitated, about to toast—but what? My book? His book? Was he even writing one? Finally he said: "To your book."

He seemed more relaxed now that we were dining *en plein air*. He derided his contemporaries with such vigor and palpable enjoyment that it didn't even seem malicious. He was having fun. A famous writer who had never got over the "Trotsky worship" of the 1930s he dismissed as "a grade-school radical." A well-known Oxford academic was "a twit." Of a literary critic who had made a career out of the Transcendentalists: "He thinks mystique is a perfume."

I marveled at this unguardedness, at once so calculated and so naïve. Bellow never said, "Don't quote me" or "This is off the record." But then, did Johnson ever turn to Boswell and say, "Sir, this is a private conversation, not to be put in your book"? Boswell came and went as he pleased, was given the run of his subject's life and even of his mind; he was often known to set up situations to "incite"—Boswell's word—Johnson to speech.

The subject of Isaac Rosenfeld came up, and Bellow remarked that perhaps Rosenfeld had been jealous because Bellow got a Guggenheim first. But he didn't. He got his Guggenheim a year *after* Rosenfeld. I had copies of their exchanges with the foundation. What was I supposed to do? Correct him? *No, you're mistaken, Mr. Bellow. In fact, your lifelong rival beat you to it.*

I maintained my usual psychiatric silence.

We were each on our second glass of wine by now, and its uninhibiting vapors incited me to introduce the name of Nadine Nimier, a girlfriend of Bellow's from his Paris days. I had interviewed her that spring, and she sent her *meuilleurs sentiments*. He lit up and began questioning me intently: how she looked (stunning), what she was up to (formerly the wife of a well-known French novelist, she had remarried), and what she had said about him (I couldn't recall). I didn't have the nerve to ask if it was true that he had proposed they run off to Africa together, though in retrospect I probably should have if I was going to put it in the book. What if Nimier had made it up?[*]

Since we were on the subject of women, I brought up another old flame—a woman Bellow had met on a Paris-bound ship in 1948. He looked shocked; he hadn't heard from her in over fifty years. He had taken up with her after his marriage was over, he said. Alas, a lie. He didn't get divorced until 1952, four years after his shipboard romance. Maybe he didn't remember? "That can't be," I murmured, disgusted with myself. *What am I, Saul Bellow's keeper, that I have to catch him out in his adulteries?*

Yet his willingness to discuss these delicate and highly private issues—Peltz was right; he did want to talk about the women—had emboldened me. I asked about his first wife, Anita. It had been a difficult marriage and a difficult divorce. This I knew, or sensed, from his account of Tommy Wilhelm's acrimonious divorce from Margaret in *Seize the Day*, which, like all of Bellow's books, could be counted on to provide the basic facts about his life.[†]

"What happened there?" I asked.

Bellow looked away. "I don't want to get into that," he said. "I have a son. . . ."[‡] He trailed off.

---

[*] To require two sources for every story would make it virtually impossible to write a biography, at least not one that relies on interviews for anecdotes. One could always write "according to," but it's such a pedestrian phrase and has a journalistic feel to it. Wasn't it sufficient to write that so-and-so "remembered" or "recalled," verbs that clearly conveyed that a story was only *that* person's version? Like so much else about the writing of biography, the more you examined the premises of quotation, the more dubious it seemed as an instrument of literal truth.

[†] Fiction, he liked to say, was a higher autobiography.

[‡] He had three, all by different wives.

I was getting really nervous now. This was private territory—even for me. *Leave the man alone.* I shifted the subject, insisting that I wasn't interested in gossip but in the manners and morals of the period, life among the intellectuals in postwar America. But of course I *was* interested in the gossip. For the first time, it occurred to me that Bellow wouldn't just sit there and tell me everything I needed to know. We were engaged in what Janet Malcolm would describe as a "transaction," as all interviews necessarily are. He would tell me what he wanted me to know, and I would have to figure out the rest on my own. All he could do was straighten me out about the facts, quite a few of which I'd gotten wrong—or, as I would discover, *he* had gotten wrong.

As we drove back to Bellow's house at the end of the evening, I sensed again his loneliness. He had Janis now; she had saved him from, as he once put it to me, "falling down in the street." He had friends, and the busy existence that renown brings. But there was a penumbra of isolation around him that nothing could dispel. We're born alone, we survive the pain of life alone; we die alone: no one knew this better than the author of *More Die of Heartbreak,* a novel about a geniusy botanist named Benn Crader who feels estranged from the human race. One of Crader's favorite books is Admiral Byrd's *Alone.*

On an impulse (was I breaking our pretense of objectivity by inviting him to a social event?), I suggested we get together with my friends Robert and Patricia Towers, who had a place in Cambridge, New York, not far from our Vermont farmhouse. Bob was an English professor at Queens College and a critic whose work often appeared in *The New York Review of Books;* Pat was a veteran magazine editor I had known since my days at the *Times.* They were lively people, and I thought Bellow would enjoy their company. He liked the idea.

When we pulled up to the house, Bellow seemed in no hurry to go. We sat in his car, and he said in a heartfelt way that he'd had a very good time. He asked what to call me: Jim or James? The answer depended on how I felt about myself at any given moment. If I could live with who I was (the best-case scenario) and felt comfortable in my own skin, I was Jim—informal, unpretentious, a regular guy. If I was feeling shaky, I reverted to James—literary, pompous, stiff, assuming a British, butler-like identity. Things had gone well that night: I was Jim.

"There's always business to conduct," I said, handing him a letter I'd drawn up giving me permission to consult the files of Marshall Holleb, one of Bellow's lawyers in Chicago. He handed the letter back unsigned: "It's just legal stuff."

Driving back home over the mountains, I was weirdly elated. He'd said no—hardly a triumph. Yet here I was shouting to myself "It's fun! It's fun!" I didn't feel rejected: It *was* "just legal stuff." Besides, I was already conversant with the details of his divorces, the alimony fights, the near-jailing for perjury when he'd lied about his income. I didn't need Bellow's permission: the creative part, the original part, was my interpretation. *That's what biography is,* I consoled myself. It was a *game,* an exalted game. Though sometimes a dangerous one. Neither party could control the outcome. I would write what I wanted, my own "issues" barely under control, my unconscious free to roam unfettered by my superego; my subject would "resist," hiding or forgetting inconvenient facts. I could write an uncomprehending book; Bellow, ill-served by his passivity, could let me write a book that revealed more than he wished it to reveal. So yes, it was a game; but in most games, there's a winner. Here both could lose.

T hat same summer my agent forwarded an invitation from Bill Buford, the editor of *Granta.* Did I have anything for a special issue they were doing on biography? I was excited. *Granta* was a greatly admired journal in literary circles, and Buford was a legend: an American long resident in England, he had founded the magazine when he was a student at Cambridge, resurrecting an obscure college literary journal and turning it into an institution. It was Anglo-American, chic, and trendsetting: its "Twenty Under Forty" issue, featuring the best work by young writers, had burnished the reputations of Martin Amis, Kazuo Ishiguro, and Ian McEwan.

But it was August, and I was up in Vermont. The Bellow manuscript was in a cupboard back home in New York. The issue was on a tight deadline. Annie had to pack up my chaotic work-in-progress and deliver it into the hands of a young woman from the magazine's New York office who stayed up half the night faxing it—all four hundred pages—to Buford in London.

He got back to me a day later. He liked the book and could easily find an excerpt. "But those pages of your journal . . . that's the real stuff."

My journal? What could he be talking about? Then it dawned on me. Somehow the notes that I had rapidly typed out after my meetings with Bellow had got mixed in with the manuscript. How embarrassing!

Within a few days, Buford had carved out a seamless ten-thousand-word narrative, beginning with Bellow's early childhood in Montreal and taking him through the publication of his first book, *Dangling Man,* in 1944. The *Times* had assigned me on short notice a profile of A. N. Wilson, and Buford asked me to meet him at the Groucho, a pseudo-seedy Soho club right out of an Anthony Powell novel. Its name was inspired by the famous dictum of Groucho Marx that he wouldn't want to join any club that would admit him, but every writer in London aspired to belong to the Groucho, and its bar was always crowded with famous London novelists and journalists.

Buford was a brilliant editor, the Cyril Connolly of my generation. He was also impressively dissolute, a dedicated smoker (Marlboros) and drinker who could put in a long bibulous night without showing any ill effects.* As we sat going over the proofs (another anachronism) of my piece, he put away four Scotches—not a great deal, given the English measurement of drinks in drams (half the amount of an American shot), but it was followed by two bottles of wine; the second he examined with the squint-eyed concentration of a jeweler assessing an antique watch, in an effort to determine whether draining it to the dregs† would impair our next day's editorial work. He decided that it wouldn't.

B ack in the city that fall, I had lunch with Adam. He looked prosperous in an expensive suit; he was obviously rising up the ranks in publishing.

I chided him about a remark he had made to the writer Daphne Merkin that I "wouldn't get [his father] right." He was mildly aghast and explained that he had meant only to suggest that I might be too

---

° On assignment for a men's magazine, I recruited Buford to be my guide to private London drinking clubs, and we spent a long evening in a series of smoke-choked dives where you had to knock on the door and be scrutinized through a peephole before you were allowed to enter. But that was then: in the health-conscious world of the new millennium, I once spotted him striding onto a tennis court in snowy whites.

† It was a rich and viscous red that had, I seem to recall, actual dregs at the bottom. Bill made no show of it, but he was a connoisseur who would go on to write a best-selling account of working in the kitchen of a famous chef.

close to my subject, might idealize him, only to be disappointed later. He stressed that the side of his father he was afraid might be neglected was "the spiritual side"—that no critics had really managed to grasp the significance of this issue in his later work or in his life.

Bellow had been writing a big, ambitious novel called *The Case for Love* but had put it aside. "It's too hard for him to write a big book now," Adam said. "The rigging can't weather the storm."

He made clear that he was in favor of the biography—"I'll learn things about my father that I never knew"—and had told members of the family that I should be the one to write the book. He also reported that Bellow and Janis had had a good time when we all went to see Bob and Pat Towers.

I hadn't taken notes, and all I can remember now of that afternoon is that Bellow got into an argument with a writer named Marcelle Clements over something to do with feminism and that he asked Janis to fetch his cap in a way that Annie found condescending. I wouldn't even mention this incident except that it says something, I'm not sure what, about Bellow's relationship with Janis. That she was subservient? That he was exploitative? Or was it just that he wanted his cap—we were sitting in the sun—and was a man in his late seventies who didn't feel like getting up? If I live that long, I'll want someone to fetch my cap, too.

I was sitting in the kitchen reading the *Times* on a Sunday afternoon in January when the phone rang. It was Bellow.

It took me a moment to collect myself. He had never called me at home before. I didn't even know he had my number.

"I've had a bad conscience about your letter," he said. Which letter was that? I wrote to him all the time. It no longer bothered me when he didn't answer. He got a huge amount of correspondence. "That's okay," I muttered. "No hurry." There was a long awkward pause. "About the letters . . ." Ah! The letters. He had once again closed the archive, and I had written protesting his decision and explaining my case. (Looking back, I sometimes wonder if I *had* a case. They were his letters, after all.) "My feeling is that it's fine, as long as you let me see what you're

---

° I was off duty—living, not working.

quoting. I don't want to look silly.'" Perfectly reasonable, I assured him. He'd been a good sport. I suggested we follow the policy we'd adopted for the *Granta* excerpt: send him the excerpts from his letters that I wanted to quote for his approval. I did wonder about the word *silly*—it struck me as somehow frivolous, lacking gravity; the greatest writer in the English language had many defects, but being silly wasn't one of them.

"I liked what you wrote in *Granta* very much," Bellow said. A thrill of joy shot through me. "I thought it was very well written. I have just one small correction, since we're talking about it: and that is, you should be careful about what other people say who may have their own peculiar view of matters."

I waited in silence.

"That quote from Vicki Lidov," he continued.

There were women; there were always women. During the winter of 1947, while Anita was off in Chicago with her brother, Bellow had shared a farmhouse in the country with Vicki and her husband, Arthur, a well-known painter.

"She doesn't know what she's talking about. She's a woman who couldn't have children of her own. She's had a bad life." The vindictiveness in Bellow's voice was palpable. He explained that he would go into the city by train and come back the same night, getting his car at the station. "I was trying to finish *The Victim* then. There were no women."[†]

Maybe there weren't and Vicki Lidov was full of it. It was her word against his.

I had lost an opportunity to find out. Two years earlier I had made arrangements to drive up to the small town in upstate New York where Arthur Lidov lived. (Vicki had been jettisoned somewhere along the line.) I was eager to meet him: he and Bellow had a lot of history together.

A date for my visit is set. I rent an Avis car. Lidov has sent me a

---

[*] Bellow's position reminded me of Beckett's hedge to his first biographer, Deirdre Bair, that he would "neither help nor hinder" her efforts. Except that Bellow would do both.

[†] And what if there were? "A compact with one woman puts beyond reach what others might give us to enjoy," Bellow wrote in *Dangling Man*: "the soft blondes and the dark, aphrodisiacal women of our imaginations are set aside."

hand-drawn map: *James Atlas: This for Monday Jan. 7, 2:30 at my place*. Three days before my visit, his daughter telephones me: her father is dead, the victim of a heart attack. "I'm sorry for your loss," I tell the daughter, who has lost her father. But I'm just as sorry for my loss. Lidov would have been a great source.

It happened all the time. After a protracted negotiation, I had been on the verge of getting Bellow's third wife, Susan, to talk to me. Reluctant at first—their marriage, pitilessly chronicled in *Humboldt's Gift*, had been characterized by extreme ill will on both sides—she had come around once I was able to prove that I was in earnest. She lived a few blocks away from me: it would be easy to meet. Then her son Dan called: she had died suddenly, also of a heart attack. She was sixty-two.

But for every person "subtracted" (a Bellow word) from my narrative, another was added, often under the most peculiar circumstances. One day my mother called and told me she had just come from Teddy the hairdresser's, where she had started up a conversation with the woman in the chair next to her, who turned out to be from Chicago. They were talking about their children, and when the woman learned that I was writing a biography of Bellow, she made a face and announced that she had known Frank Glassman and his wife, parents of the now-dead Susan. She informed my mother that the Glassmans had disapproved of Bellow, thought him a penniless, unreliable ne'er-do-well. That would make a good detail: what Susan Glassman's parents thought of Bellow. But how would the footnote read? "The woman next to my mother at a beauty salon in La Jolla"?

Others I got to in time but still too late. Catherine Carver, Bellow's longtime editor at Viking, agreed by mail to be interviewed, but when I arrived at the address she'd given me in London, it turned out to be a nursing home. She'd had a stroke and couldn't speak. I sat at her bedside for an hour and silently communed. It wouldn't be true to say that I came away having learned nothing. I learned that biography is about death.

A few weeks later I made another trip out to Chicago to see Bellow. Janis had reminded him that it was Valentine's Day, "but that won't be a problem for us," he had written me.

I found him alone. He looked well, though he'd gained a little weight; his natty purple striped shirt was open at the bottom button.

You could see why he had been—and apparently still was—so irresistible to women, with those saucer eyes and fine-boned face. (More than one called him "stunning.") He offered to make tea, and we sat down. There was always a certain constraint between us—Bellow had poor eye contact, and I tried to maintain mine. Obviously, he knew that I knew a lot about him, which made me feel guilty; but wasn't that my job?

We talked about Dwight, whose biographer, Michael Wreszin, had just been to see him. Bellow asked me if I knew Dwight, and I babbled on about how he had edited my Delmore book and how important he had been to me. But Bellow didn't want to hear about it, any more than he wanted to hear that I'd been snowed in at LaGuardia, or that I'd run into his daughter-in-law with his granddaughter in a candy store. As a novelist, he was interested in *his* account of the world, in all its strangeness and mystery. His job was to study life and interpret it for the rest of us. If Victor Wulpy, the intellectual in that fine story "What Kind of Day Did You Have?" wants to tell us about how he got stranded at LaGuardia in a snowstorm, why, go ahead: thousands are waiting to hear. If *I* wanted to tell someone about what it felt like to be stuck at LaGuardia, I could pick up the phone and call Annie.

Most of the time I didn't mind our unequal stature and talents: *Go, you be the genius.* But sometimes I felt: *What about my life? Doesn't it count, too?* There comes, inevitably, a moment of rebellion, when the inequality begins to chafe. Biographers are people, too, even if we're condemned to huddle in the shadow of our subjects' monumentality. All the same, self-abnegation has its limits. A thousand pages along, a decade in, the biographer cries out: *What am I? Chopped liver?*

Yes. That's what you signed on to be, and that's what you are.

Deal with it.[*]

At the end of the afternoon, as the room was growing dark, Bellow fetched his family album from an antique desk and showed me his mother's passport again. There were also photos of Bellow's ancient grandparents, the grandmother sad-faced, the grandfather dying. Their garments were torn. "See how poor they were," said Bellow. Not

---

[*] Ross Miller, an English professor at the University of Connecticut, was Philip Roth's first authorized biographer. In an article in *The New York Times* about biographers who take on living subjects, Miller described himself and Roth as intellectual "equals." Miller is no longer Roth's biographer.

all the photographs were old: here was one of Bellow and Winston Moore, the head of the Chicago Housing Authority, standing in front of a monolithic housing project. "Writing your life is like writing the rise and fall of civilization," I said.

It had been a mistake to refer to writing his life, which we both continued to pretend I wasn't doing. Our secret, however mysterious, had its uses. It seemed to make Bellow less inhibited, and he could encourage his friends to talk to me without explicitly giving them permission to talk to me. But I was impatient to see the letters, and therefore had no choice but to bring the fact that I was his biographer out into the open.

I made my case confidently and without hesitation: that this was going to be the definitive book and that while he must feel uneasy after the Ruth Miller debacle, and though I had no claim, since he never asked that the book be written, he had also "tacitly assented" to it over the years and allowed me to interview him. I felt "impeded" by his restricting the archive. He listened, then broke in that he was concerned about the Ludwig episode: "I look so stupid." (So it wasn't a matter of protecting other people at all; it was about how *he* would look.)

Jack Ludwig was a third-rate professor whose itinerary for several years had closely followed the novelist's—right into his marital bed. The irony of Bellow's reticence was that he had already put this notorious episode into a best-selling novel—which was why it would be of considerable interest to his biographer: it was part of the work *and* the life. Ludwig is—not "modeled after," *is*—Valentine Gersbach in *Herzog*, where Bellow described in painful and riotous detail his cuckoldry at the hands of Sasha (Madeleine in the novel) and her crude lover, even as the unsuspecting Herzog is getting him teaching jobs. So why would Bellow care what I wrote about Ludwig? He had already written it for all the world to read.

Finally he told me that after much deliberation, he had signed the request I had sent him to look at specific items (it turned out that he had sent it over to the library on Friday, the last possible day before my arrival) and agreed that if he were provided with an itemized list of correspondents, he would most likely sign all but a few; then, very conciliatory: "Is that all right? I try to make these sessions humanly palatable."

They were far more than that, I assured him.

In the spring of 1993, Bellow moved to Boston, as he'd been threatening to do for years; Boston University had offered him a tempting position, and he would be closer to Vermont.

One July day the following summer, as I was preparing for my annual visit to Bellow's dacha, he called and said that he had a doctor's appointment and could we meet next week? We set a date, but for some reason he seemed to be hanging on the line. At last he said—rather shyly, I thought—"Do you have a moment? There's a matter I wish to discuss.° It has to do with the reviews of Allan's book."

"Allan" was Allan Bloom, who had died the year before at the age of sixty-two under circumstances that would furnish one of Bellow's last crises. Bloom's book was the posthumous *Love and Friendship*, a collection of essays on the subject of sex and eros in Shakespeare, Rousseau, Stendhal, and other classic writers in his beloved Western canon. It was a deeply moving if controversial book, much of it dictated from his deathbed. But it hadn't been reviewed anywhere, Bellow complained: "Even Wieselpiss"—Leon Wieseltier, literary editor of *The New Republic*—"ignored it."

As it happened, it *was* being reviewed, in *The New York Times Book Review*, which I knew because I knew the reviewer: it was Katha Pollitt, one of my closest friends from college and a well-known feminist who wrote a fiery column for *The Nation* and had published several books espousing her progressive politics. I hesitated. No one likes (no one "wishes") to be the bearer of bad news, but it seemed cowardly not to say something. Since I was this deep in, I felt obliged to warn Bellow that a review was scheduled and that it wouldn't be positive. Katha had told me so herself. From her perspective, Bloom had been a reactionary determined to challenge the values of the feminist movement. And knowing Katha as well as I did, I was certain she was going to lay all this out in the most emphatic terms.[†]

Bellow was annoyed. He launched into a tirade about "affirmative

---

° I loved Bellow's old-fashioned, somewhat mannered figures of speech: "I wish" instead of "I want to," "shall" instead of "will." He sounded just like Shils.

† Which she did, noting—among other contradictions—that Rousseau, "the big romanticizer of bourgeois marriage and sentimental parenthood, lived with an illiterate chambermaid and consigned their five children to an orphanage."

suction"—he had a weakness for bad puns—and said the editor of the *Book Review* had invited him to write a piece about Bloom, but he was reluctant: he didn't say why. I urged him to reconsider. "This is one of the matters I wish to discuss," he said darkly.

Five minutes later the phone rang again. It was Bellow. He and Janis were coming to Bennington. They had errands—he needed yellow legal paper—and it was hot in Brattleboro. For some reason, he seemed to feel it would be cooler in Bennington. Also, he wanted to go to the Army-Navy store for pants "with lots of pockets" so he wouldn't have to wear a jacket whenever he went into town.

I was excited, but I wondered why he wanted to drive all the way to Bennington, forty-five minutes over the Green Mountains on a steep curvy road, just to buy a pad of paper and a pair of pants. Because he wanted to talk about Bloom? That must have been it. How did I know? I was his biographer.

We met in front of the Army-Navy store on Main Street. I had just bought a beat-up paperback copy of *Seize the Day* for $1.04 at Now & Then Used Books next door. Bellow was wearing a blue-and-white-striped railroad cap identical to mine. Just at that moment, Janis came out of the store. "I wish I had a camera," she said.

We went to the Brasserie, a modest French restaurant a few blocks away, and sat down at a marble-topped table on the terrace. We ordered iced tea, and the conversation turned to the collection of essays Bellow was planning to publish. I listed the titles of essays I considered essential—most of which, it turned out, he had failed to include. Janis was concerned that no one had overseen the project. I nearly volunteered but was afraid that to be involved with Bellow's work in an editorial capacity would compromise my "objectivity."

I still believed in the concept of biographical impartiality—as if I were a juror charged with weighing the evidence instead of a younger man entangled with an older man in a relationship of infinite complexity, one that could never be sorted out but only lived through as it metamorphosed over time, now warm, now cold, now angry, now loving, now master/disciple, now punitive father/rebellious son. The biographer was as real as his subject; he existed in the world and took up space. He learned to listen but reacted to what he was told—and wasn't told.

It was mid-afternoon, and the Brasserie was empty. The waitress, a young woman with curly black hair,° came over to see if we wanted anything else. I had an impulse to say to her: *Do you know who this is?* But what if I did and the name meant nothing to her?[†]

I sensed that Bellow was having a good time. He never looked exactly happy, but his large movie-star eyes were less mournful than usual. He told a joke or, more likely, reported a witticism he had made. The previous Rosh Hashannah he had been in a Chicago synagogue when the rabbi began praising an essay by the literary critic Leslie Fiedler—a source of irritation to Bellow because of Fiedler's insistence on classifying him as a Jewish writer. Fiedler had come late in life to an appreciation of his Jewish roots and was lamenting in the essay that no one in his secular family would know how to say Kaddish when he died. Bellow claimed that he had spoken up, with heads turning, "I'll say Kaddish for him if he's willing to die now."

Janis and I laughed and laughed. Bellow's archive of jokes was deep. He knew many, virtually all of them of the Jewish variety, and he told them well, throwing back his head and chortling with pleasure. Some were not very good, but so what? He hadn't won the Nobel Prize for jokes.

"You should write a book about writing this book," Bellow said. It had occurred to me that maybe I should write a book about writing this book *instead* of writing this book. Here was where the real work got done, the work of trying to understand who this man was—not in the library but in the lab of life. Seeing how Bellow drank from his glass, grasping it in his long elegant fingers and fastidiously patting his lips with a paper napkin, revealed as much about him as all the interviews in the world.

While I was walking them to their car, Janis told me that she had reviewed Roth's new novel, *Operation Shylock,* and I promised to look it up. But I forgot the name of the magazine she'd written it for, and even in the Age of Google I haven't been able to track it down, though I did find her review of Roth's *Sabbath's Theatre* in *Partisan Review.*

° Bellow would have known how to describe it; he was very good on hair. In *Herzog*, Valentine Gersbach has "flaming copper hair that literally gushed from his head"; Anna, in *The Adventures of Augie March,* has "spiraling reddish hair"; George Grebe, the census taker in the story "Looking for Mr. Green," has a "tough curl of blond hair."
† It would be like the counterman at Burhop's all over again. Or maybe it was a coincidence, and they were the only two people in America who hadn't heard of Saul Bellow.

It was a spirited defense of the novel, which had caused a commotion, and it gave me a sense of Janis as not just "the young wife" but as a sophisticated reader who could hold her own in the fast literary company in which she traveled.

Did Bellow *want* the woman who brought him his cap to be conversant with contemporary American literature? Or did he just want his cap?°

Toward the end of August 1993, I drove over the mountains to the Bellow homestead for the signing of permissions. It had been a hard fight. We had been skirmishing for several years now as, worn down by my dogged requests, he yielded up one territory after another—manuscripts, some letters, more letters, like a general who sees the futility of resistance but resists until the battle is lost and he must sign a treaty—in this instance literally. The agreement I'd finally gotten was a good one and guaranteed my freedom: I would show Bellow the quotes from his letters and papers that I wanted to use, and he would initial his permission: SB.

I had told Bellow I would arrive at two-thirty, but I was fifteen minutes late. Even after several visits, I still had trouble finding the house.

° I found the answer (*an* answer) in an essay by Janis I came across years later. Entitled "Rosamund and Ravelstein: The Discandying of a Creator's Confession," it sounded a note of disenchantment with the way Bellow had depicted her in *Ravelstein*, the novella about Allan Bloom written in his old age. Among the minor characters is the wife of Chick, Ravelstein's admiring intellectual sidekick, a "pretty, well-brought-up, mannerly young woman" who had been a student of Ravelstein's—as Janis had been a student of Bloom's.

In her essay, Janis describes begging Bellow to remove Rosamund from the book: "What could so slight a character add to a story already teeming with vibrant human types? A specific pain attached to this request. Don't do this to me. You misrepresent me. I'm not that woman: servile, prim, obedient. Is that the way you see me? Wounded vanity might be endured. But to be invisible to the person you love?" Bellow responded, as he always did when confronted about his real-life models, that Rosamund was a character; he was writing fiction.

Bellow's portrait of his young wife is in fact highly sympathetic. When Chick becomes violently ill from poisoned seafood in the Caribbean—an episode based on real events—it is Rosamund who saves his life, getting him to the hospital in Boston and camping out by his bedside for weeks. She holds him up when they swim in the sea. So why was Janis so troubled by this touching depiction? Was it that instead of registering her own turmoil, her conflicts about serving him, her human complication, Bellow had depicted her as a "wife"?

Bellow and Janis were loitering by the front door when I pulled up. He looked at his watch and said, "You're always so punctual."

"Forgive me. I got lost." As always, I took a quick inventory of my motives: Was my tardiness hostile? Was I acting out? No, I reassured myself: I had told him that I would be coming *around* two-thirty," "after lunch." Yet somehow this had become, in both of our minds, two-thirty. I was always looking for some reason to feel guilty, even when there was none.

"If the Pope can forgive, I can forgive," Bellow said. And why shouldn't he? I was his worshipful subject—except when I was an apostate. (There must have been some middle ground, but I never managed to find it.)

He was wearing a kind of soft canvas pith helmet, tied around his neck like a bonnet, the many-pocketed khakis he'd got in Bennington, a jacket, nice loafers, and black socks with black ribbons. He looked well, his face now quite wrinkled and lined, but still the handsome Bellow face.

Janis offered me a cold drink, and we took chairs out to sit on the lawn. We talked for a while in a desultory way, but I was eager to get on with the business at hand. I was about halfway through the book, I estimated, having accumulated four hundred pages of typescript and gotten my subject to *Herzog*. I made him sign each page. He said he felt like Jean Valjean pursued by Inspector Javert through the sewers of Paris.

After two hours, he had initialed each page, except for those from chapter two, which were somehow put last. He came to a bad poem from his high school days that I had found among his papers and said, "I'm not going to sign this."

I was stunned. "You're kidding," I said. What could it possibly mean to him at this point?

But he wasn't. He wasn't going to sign.

"It *is* pretty bad," I blurted out, instantly alarmed by my own response: I never talked back. "But it's better than Sydney J. Harris's poem," I said, ingratiating myself in the hope that it would erase my involuntary verdict on his own poem. Harris was an old friend of Bellow's from his Tuley days and, like everyone else in that crowd, a once-aspiring writer. He had ended up writing a column for the *Chicago Sun-Times* called "Strictly Personal" that I read every morning at the breakfast table when I was growing up and that my father found "platitudinous." "You're a 'contrast gainer,'" I said, employing the comic Bellovian term in the hope that it would please him. *See how well I know your work?*

Bellow recited Harris's poem, and Janis chimed in at the end: she knew the poem by heart, too.

By the time I left, I was way over my limit of Bellow exposure—the amount of time I could spend around him before I got Bellow burnout. So much concentration, combined with the suppression of self, was exhausting.

When I came to the main road, I pulled into the parking lot of a Dairy Queen, retrieved my notebook from the glove compartment, and wrote down as much as I could remember.

It wasn't a lot. Months or years after one of these encounters, I would pull my notebook scrawlings from my files only to discover that they were disappointingly spare—Zen koans without the wisdom. What to make, for instance, of this laconic jotting, from what must have been a more detailed account of Bellow's time in Paris in the early 1950s: "I was very depressed"? What if, instead of "B knew Weldon Kees and Nigel Dennis, book reviewers at Time," you were to record your subject's life as it really happened, so many days forgettably the same?

Dr. Johnson breakfasted on a bowl of oats, then descended to the privy and took a shit while reading an old Gentlemen's Magazine. *By ten he was at his desk in the attic atelier at 17 Gough Square, laboring over his Dictionary; at one he had a lunch of cold mutton, followed by a nap.*

At least it would have been true.

Late one night in the autumn of 1993, I flew into O'Hare and got my car from the Avis lot. I loved this part of the job: tossing my suitcase into the back, hanging up my jacket on the plastic hook, and driving off in a bright-colored Chevrolet Impala, fiddling with the dial until I found WFMT, "Chicago's classical music" station, 98.7 on the dial. I'd been listening to it since I was a child and could still remember the names of the announcers from thirty years ago, Ray Norstrand and Norman Pellegrini, their quiet civilized voices murmuring through the teakwood speakers in our living room as they announced that we would next be hearing Berlioz's *Symphonie fantastique,* conducted by George Solti with the Chicago Symphony Orchestra. Once again

I was in "Chicagoland," soothed by the civilized murmur of "cultural programming"—advertisements for ethnic restaurants that offered "continental dining," wine and cheese shops, hi-fi shops, Toad Hall Books & Records.

As I stepped on the gas and nosed onto the Edens Expressway, I remembered Herzog in his rental car, "the teal-blue Falcon storming," on his way to confront his wife's duplicitous lover, Valentine Gersbach: "From the last slope of Congress Street the distortions of dusk raised up the lake like a mild wall crossed by bands, amethyst, murky blue, irregular silver, and a slate color at the horizon, boats hanging rocking inside the breakwater, and helicopters and small aircraft teetered overhead." Gorgeous.

It wasn't the fastest way, but I liked speeding along the lakefront at night, past the immense Greek-columned Museum of Science and Industry, past Soldier Field, turning off at 55th Street into Hyde Park, its tree-lined streets empty at this hour, and parking in front of the dowdy University Club, happy to be in that haven of higher learning, surrounded by the ghetto pressing in from the south and west, its wide bleak trash-strewn streets lined with metal-gated liquor stores.

I was living both my life and Bellow's. His friends had become my friends. I always called Dave Peltz when I was in town. Dave knew Bellow better than anyone. Together they had traveled to Africa, played squash, made dumb investments. But they were rivals, too, with Dave the inevitable loser; he was a successful contractor on the South Side but had unrealized literary ambitions and harbored, despite his decent heart, a resentment of Bellow, who had put him in the story "A Silver Dish" as Woody Selbst, a ruddy-faced contractor, "fleshy and big, like a figure for the victory of Americanism," with a powerful appetite for life, a great reader of books who took night school courses at an adult education school in the Loop. It was a gentle, affectionate portrait that I thought really captured Dave, but Dave didn't like it. He found it unsettling to have no control over how he was depicted—a common complaint among Bellow's friends and former friends, who waited with nervous anticipation whenever a Bellow novel came out to see if they were in it.

Dave was emotionally invested in my book and wanted to make sure I got things right. One Sunday morning he took me to the Russian Bath on Division Street, depicted in *Humboldt's Gift* as a decrepit steam room where "Slavonic cavemen and wood demons with hanging laps of fat and legs of stone and lichen boil themselves and splash ice water on their heads by the bucket" while a wizened attendant scrubs them with oak leaves. It felt strange to be sitting nude on a wooden bench with Dave. It was one thing to follow in your subject's footsteps, quite another to follow your subject's friend into the sauna.

On this visit, funds running low, I was staying at Zita Cogan's apartment in a modern building overlooking the lake. Zita had been one of Bellow's girlfriends at Tuley, and I got the sense she was still in love with him. I myself had close emotional ties with her; her mother had been a friend of my grandmother's. The whole world, my grandmother used to say, is "one piece string."

She gave me a bowl of vanilla ice cream—I recognized the blue fiestaware from my childhood—and showed me her shelf of Bellow novels, all in their original dust jackets and thus highly valued by rare book dealers, especially when the frontispiece contains a fond inscription: "From second-Story Bellow," "From your own personal Humboldt Park author." Books inscribed by the author to a friend or family member were known in the trade as "association copies," which made them even more valuable. But Zita wouldn't have been interested in selling them: they were the most precious possessions she owned.

The next morning we talked about Bellow's letters to her. It turned out that he had come with Janis to look through his papers "and taken some away." She was happy to let me see what was left.

I was furious. How could she just have given them away? Now it would be ten times as hard to get them back. She gave me a box of clippings—quite a good haul, actually—and I sat on the floor going through them. She had saved everything, including handwritten scraps of five words—"S. Bellow paid a visit"—but the only letter, amazingly enough, was a brief note that made clear his position on the book. He was no more enthusiastic about having his biography written than he was about reserving a plot for himself at 26th and Harlem Avenue. He wasn't sponsoring "Atlas," he wrote. I was on my own.

A wave of anger coursed through me. "There will be tears before bedtime," the critic John Gross had predicted when he learned that I was writing a biography of Bellow. And so there would.

That evening I went to meet Professor Shils for dinner at a bleak Chinese restaurant on Cermak Road. On impulse, I asked him if he would read my manuscript, which had already ballooned to seven hundred pages. I needed a Dwight Macdonald, someone as tough as

Dwight had been on *Delmore,* yet also capable of giving me encouragement. Shils was dying of cancer—a fact unknown to me—but he agreed.

The next morning I went down to the lake and sat on the beach, sifting handfuls of sand. I had been doing the book for so long that I had my own memories of Chicago over the last few years. I was struck by how fast things change: what had once been the International House of Pancakes was now the Fine Arts Building of Loyola, with a broken window covered by plywood. Howard Street, where I had gone to get my hair cut and buy smoked fish on Sunday mornings, was now a black neighborhood; there were FOR RENT signs in front of the apartment houses where Jews had once lived.

I felt sad as I watched the children frolicking around me. I had gone through the papers in the Regenstein; I had been interviewing Bellow for five years and had my story. It was good-bye to an incredible period in my life—so I did have one after all—good-bye to the place I had inadvertently called, talking to Annie on the phone the night before, "home."

Edward Shils

XXI

We biographers have always done our work amid a loud chorus of negativity. Oscar Wilde famously observed that biography "lends to death a new terror." Joyce feared "biografiends." Nabokov, too, derided the biographer's efforts: "I hate tampering with the precious lives of great writers and I hate Tom-peeping over the fence of those lives—I hate the vulgarity of human interest."* Then there was George Eliot, who asked, "Is it not odious that as soon as a man is dead his desk is raked, and every insignificant memorandum which he never meant for the public is printed for the gossiping amusement of people too idle to read his book?"

Even members of the profession disparage it. Edmund White, the biographer of Jean Genet, called biography the revenge of the little people on the big people. And Michael Holroyd, after a lifetime of helping to elevate the form, has decided that biographers are "parasites . . . intent on reducing all that is imaginative, all that is creative in literature, to pedestrian autobiography." We compete with our subjects, he contends in "Two Cheers for Biography," writing big bulky books that overshadow their beautifully crafted masterpieces. We trade on their fame.

To refute these sniping critics, the defensive biographer keeps at the ready a handful of counter-quotations. Emerson: "There is properly no history, only biography." Yeats: "We may come to think that nothing exists but a stream of souls, that all knowledge is biography." Virginia Woolf: "By telling us the true facts, by sifting the little from the

---

* Yet Nabokov himself wrote a biography of Gogol, and Auden, while complaining that biographies of writers were "in bad taste," was annoyed that J. R. Ackerley, in his memoir *My Father and Myself,* was "never quite explicit about what he *really* preferred to do in bed."

big, and shaping the whole so that we perceive the outline, the biographer does more to stimulate the imagination than any poet or novelist save the very greatest." Sometimes we get three cheers instead of two. (John Updike, alas, awards us only one.)*

In A. S. Byatt's *Possession,* a scholar named Mortimer Cropper delivers a lecture entitled "The Art of a Biographer" in which he offers a persuasive vindication of his craft: "Biography was just as much a spiritual hunger of modern man as sex or political activity. Look at the sales, he had urged, look at the column space in the Sundays, people need to know how other people lived, it helps them to live, it's human."

I believe this. Biography provides useful information. It adds, in the critic R. P. Blackmur's phrase, "to the stock of available reality." But it leaves unanswered the question: What does the life have to do with the achievement? You can no more "explain" the sources of a person's talent—what combination of temperament, cultural circumstances, parents, genes, history—than you can explain why we're here in the first place. If talent is innate, the whole project can seem futile. Why do any of these random factors matter when you're dealing with someone whose endowments, whatever they were, made him worthy of a biography? Bellow said he was born with a gift for words and had no idea where it came from. If that was true—which I think it was—what was there to explain? It was all in the biology. You might as well ask how Bach wrote his cello suites, how Turner painted boats in a storm, or why the stars come out at night.

So what *is* the biographer's purpose? Primarily, I would say, to show what other factors—besides genius—contributed to the making of the writer's life, the genesis of his books, the social and literary influences that formed them. Richard Ellmann described the connection this way: "Affection for one leads to interest in the other, the two sentiments tend to join, and the results of affection and interest often illuminate both the fiery clay and the wrought jar." The fiery clay is the life, and the wrought jar is the work that gives it form.

Toward the end of 1993, I wrote a piece for the *Times Magazine* about the increasingly tawdry reputation of biography. The immediate provocation was Janet Malcolm's book *The Silent Woman,* an

---

* "One Cheer for Literary Biography," *New York Review of Books,* February 4, 1999.

account of Sylvia Plath and her biographers. Deftly and mercilessly, she laid out her case. Biography was a spurious art; the narrative it created was an invention of the biographer; there were no such things as facts.

"Worse, the pretense of biographical objectivity conceals a darker purpose," I wrote, summarizing Malcolm's argument: "The biographer's real intent is to exact revenge." I quoted this chilling line: "'The writer, like the murderer, needs a motive.'"

Malcolm is a skilled anatomist of our profession, a sort of anti- or meta-biographer whose books focus as much on her subjects' surrounding cast—scholars, relatives, friends, and enemies—as on her subjects themselves; she plays the role of biographer as deconstructionist, and I find her books enthralling. The comparison of biographers to murderers, though, seemed a bit melodramatic. Hostile or punitive, maybe; unwilling to give our subjects a break, not unheard of. But homicidal? It was hard to imagine my scholarly, mild-mannered colleagues bringing concealed weapons to the library.

Malcolm's contention that facts themselves are constructs, the scaffolding around an edifice that doesn't exist, seemed to me the weakest part of her argument. There *are* facts, I argued, and they can be illuminating. To demonstrate my point, I used what seemed like a small but telling discovery from my own research:

> That Saul Bellow, two weeks after his 21st birthday, officially changed his name from Solomon provides a clue to the name changes of his characters. Charles Citrine, the hero of *Humboldt's Gift,* was originally Tsitrine; Tommy Wilhelm in *Seize the Day* was Wilhelm Adler; Dr. Shawmut, the narrator of Bellow's story *Him With His Foot in His Mouth,* came from a family named Shamus, "or, even more degrading, Untershamus." Surely this persistent literary theme is clarified by the biographical fact. Why did Solomon become Saul? And why did his two older brothers choose to be called Bellows, adding an *s?* Was Bellow asserting his independence? Defying his father? The biographer can only speculate.

Three months later I opened my *New York Times* to find a long editorial by Bellow about his notorious Proust and the Papuans remark, in which he claimed that "the interviewer" who spoke to him over the phone (though I had been in his office) had misconstrued it: "Nowhere in print, under my name, is there a single reference to Papuans or Zulus. The scandal is entirely journalistic in origin, the result of a misunderstanding that occurred (they always do occur) during an interview. I can't remember who the interviewer was."

You can't remember the name of the journalist who went on to become your biographer? I had suffered what Annie would call a narcissistic injury. And I resented being called the "interviewer." I was the biographer.

This Bellow still could not bring himself to acknowledge. He habitually referred to me as "people," as if discussing some cohort of biographers and journalists instead of the one person who followed him around in Vermont and Chicago; pored over his papers in the Regenstein Library year after year; tracked down his friends (and enemies); and read his work with fierce attention. Would the singular imply that he had authorized me?

In his op-ed, Bellow argued that even if he *had* made that remark about the Papuans and the Zulus, he didn't mean it in a condescending way. After all, he had written his senior thesis at Northwestern—I must look it up!—on "France and the African Slave Trade." And he had read widely in African literature. As evidence he cited a Zulu novel entitled *Chaka*, by Thomas Mofolo, "a profoundly, unbearably tragic book about a tribal Achilles who had with his own hands cut down thousands of people, including his own pregnant wife."

Bellow then launched into a spirited and eloquent defense of "the autonomy of the imagination," which continually found itself under attack by the "thought police," enforcers of the politically correct. "We can't open our mouths without being denounced as racists, misogynists, supremacists, imperialists or fascists." The effort to pretend that all societies were alike was a form of despotism, an expression of rage. Morality had been hijacked by the Left—especially the academic Left. You couldn't insist on a hierarchy of cultural values, or you'd never get tenure. "My critics, many of whom could not locate Papua New Guinea on the map, want to convict me of contempt for multiculturalism and defamation of the third world. I am an elderly white male— a Jew, to boot. Ideal for their purposes."

I was pleased to see Bellow fighting back against the bullying strictures of political correctness. And maybe he really *didn't* remember that I'd interviewed him. It was quite reasonable to suppose that an encounter that had been so momentous to me—interviewing Saul Bellow for *The New York Times*—was, to Bellow, just another interruption in his day. But one thing puzzled me: Why was he writing about this contretemps now? My piece had come out seven years earlier. There had been no "peg," no flaring up of the issue. No one had called him to account about his "Papuans" (*Polynesians!*) remark of late. What had goaded him to this entertaining but unprovoked diatribe?

My favorite passage in the op-ed was the opening, where Bellow gazes out the window of his apartment at a wintry Chicago scene: "Snowbound, I watched the blizzard impounding parked cars at midnight. The veering of the snowflakes under the streetlamps made me think how nice it would be if they were totally covered by white drifts." This was what Bellow was best at: observing a moment in time and capturing it in an image. A word—*impounding*—made to represent a car trapped by snow instead of locked up by the police. The writer writing. And if he wanted, for his own reasons, to make things up, or remember them one way when they had happened another way—why, that was his prerogative, I guess. That's what novelists do.*

A week after Bellow's piece came out, there arrived in the mail a four-page, single-spaced letter from Edward Shils, accompanied by notes written on the manuscript in a green felt-tip pen. Now, where had I seen that color before? It was the same color that was scribbled over the typescript of *Mr. Sammler's Planet* on display in the New York Public Library. Shils! Now he was editing my book. If he could edit Bellow—his own portrait yet—he could edit me.

Like Dwight, Shils had a vested interest in helping me get it right. Both men had had complicated relationships with my subjects and an intimate knowledge of their worlds (which were in many cases the same). Also, they had exacting minds and were offended by errors and imprecision, which they hunted down with a vigilante zeal. In his memo, Shils explained to me every facet of Bellow's life: his friends and enemies, the streets he had walked and the books he had read; the

---

* It's not what biographers do. One day Bellow said to me: "If my characters were as well-rounded as yours are going to be, I might have accomplished something."

"Yes, but you make it up. I'm in the realm of fact."

"You make some of it up, too," he replied.

historical events he had witnessed; his attitude toward women; even what went on in his head. Biographers tend to forget that the world they're writing about was real to their subjects, not a construct of their research. Shils made Bellow real to me.

He was more encouraging than I had expected him to be. "I think that you have done a good job in presenting the origins of a complicated personality in a coherent and intelligible way," he wrote. The pages I had sent him were "vivid" and "compellingly readable."

By the time the "nots" began to pile up, I was armored and ready for criticism. "You do not pay enough attention . . ." "You do not attend sufficiently . . ." I had done a huge amount of research; what I hadn't delivered was a sense of what it was like to inhabit Bellow's world, to *be* Bellow. I had been taken in by the romantic image of the writer as "a sensitive, isolated person, spurned by society while keeping aloof from society. I think this is entirely central in Bellow's life." Shils urged me "to place him in the wider setting of European romanticism which had seeped into the United States."

A second memo followed two weeks later. He had now read the entire manuscript, but his secretary was having trouble understanding his dictation, and he was "rather ill at present" (I still didn't know how ill); he didn't have the energy to proofread his memo. As I leafed through it, I quailed: Shils had written his own mini-biography of Bellow, longer than some of Dr. Johnson's *Lives of the Poets*. By comparison Dwight's letters and annotations seemed mild.

Shils and Bellow had fallen out by then, for a variety of reasons: Shils resented Bellow's maneuvers to install a girlfriend in the Committee on Social Thought ("pushing a screwee," he called it), and Bellow resented what he took to be Shils's intellectual condescension. The two men barely spoke.

At best grudging in his approbation—of anyone—Shils was eager to dilate on his former friend's flawed character:

"Bellow had no sense of obligation to any other human being or to any Institution."

"If he has a heart, he wears it on his sleeve 24 hours a day."

"Saul Bellow was certainly not a person who had great sympathy with the great sufferings of humanity."

These brutal observations were typical of Shils, and I would hesitate to call them objective. But he didn't allow his detestation of Bellow to snuff out every last spark of generosity—he was too devoted to the scholarly discipline of fairness—and he bestowed praise, however grudgingly, where he thought it was deserved. He was impressed by Bellow's "extraordinary empathy with the dregs of society," and he admired the novelist's heroic dedication to his art.

Shils was adamant on one point: my book needed to be cut. He had read half, which was already four hundred pages in typescript; at this rate, it would be "far too thick for comfortable reading and far too long for the importance of its subject." The summaries of Bellow's novels were too detailed, and there was too much tracing of the characters to their real-life sources. In addition, the structure was disorganized: Shils recommended "a stricter application of a chronological principle in your exposition." Biographers take note.

There is no such thing as Biography School, but if there were, Shils could have been its dean. Among the lessons he taught me: you had to place your subject in a historical context (you couldn't just say someone was a Trotskyite, you had to explain what Trotskyism was); you had to make people sound authentic (Alexander Goldenweiser, whom I had described as "a distinguished anthropologist," was, according to Shils, "an inveterate philanderer and he was dismissed from his post at Columbia and his name was obliterated from the *Encyclopedia of the Social Sciences*"); you had to listen to what people said and be skeptical about pronouncements that sounded smart but upon closer scrutiny meant nothing ("How should a good man live?"); you had to write well and abjure clichés like "the dark realities of his own time." And you had to think independently: "Your book suffers somewhat from the fact that you accept the self-diagnosis of a small group of Jewish intellectuals in New York and an even smaller group in Chicago as the expression of an 'area' or of a 'generation.'" Above all, you had to get your facts straight, however trivial they seemed ("There is no streetcar on 51st Street"), because if you got a fact wrong, even if no one noticed, it would set off a vibration of wrongness that made everything around it, all the facts and quotes and speculations, feel somehow off.

I found Shils's memo exhausting to read. Would I ever be finished? Finally, on the last page, he threw me a bone. "My congratulations to you on having got so far."

Ten months later he was dead.

Brent Staples

XXII

On August 3, 1994, war broke out on the Vermont front.

I arrived ten minutes late, again getting lost.

Janis showed me around the house: the spacious new library, now filled with books on floor-to-ceiling shelves, the antique desk from Chicago, her big study and computer. She was friendly and offered me iced coffee, remembering that it was my drink of choice in the summer. Then Bellow came in, looking crabby.

He was unhappy about a recent mention of Adam in the *Times* that referred to his appointment as editorial director of the Free Press. Why did the paper always have to identify the books he published as "conservative"? Why did they have to give everyone an ideological label? Then he got on the subject of an article by Brent Staples, a writer on the *Times's* editorial board who had written a memoir, *Parallel Time*, about growing up poor and black in the slums of Philadelphia and winning a fellowship to the University of Chicago. An excerpt had appeared in the magazine over the summer.

Staples loved Bellow's work, but he was wounded by the derisive remarks about blacks in the novels, where they are variously referred to as "crazy buffaloes" and "porkchops," and where the black pickpocket exposes his "large tan-and-purple uncircumsized thing" to Sammler in the lobby of his building. "I wanted to be near him," Staples had written, "but not too near."

In an attempt to resolve this deep ambivalence, he had begun stalking Bellow, hoping to encounter his obsession/nemesis on the streets of Hyde Park. I'm not sure Staples knew what Bellow represented to him. A potential mentor? An enemy? Both? (These things often go together.) Nor did he seem to have a plan for what he would do if he ever did manage to confront Bellow. "I wanted to trophy his fear," he wrote, verbifying a noun, to frighten Bellow and make that experience the emblem of their relationship—the only one he felt was available to him.

Brent was a big guy—I knew him from the *Times*—and it was a point of honor for him to dress in scruffy clothes, as if to say *this is who I am*.

Bellow was appalled at the idea that Brent had been lurking in the shadows of Dorchester Avenue. It was "barbarous," he said—a word right out of *Mr. Sammler's Planet*. I defended Brent and described his devotion to Bellow's work: he could recite whole passages from the novels by heart. Bellow didn't want to hear about it. Why didn't Brent just come see him, instead of tailing him like a mugger?

I turned to Janis and asked, "What do you think?"

"No comment," she said.

Here was a tangled web. As it happened, I had edited Brent's piece in the *Times Magazine* . . . no, not as it happened. I had plucked the excerpt from the galley myself. It was beautifully written; it was about Bellow; it was news. A black journalist stalking a white Nobel Prize–winning novelist known for his controversial views on race through the streets of Chicago . . . what a story! But there must have been other factors involved in creating the awkward situation in which I now found myself. Could I have been making Brent's aggression a stand-in for my own? Then there was the most obvious motive of all: it would be good for *my* book.

I confessed to Bellow my role in the publication of Brent's piece. There may have been a tangled web, but at least there was no deceit, just the usual murk of mixed motives—unconscious acting out, ambivalence, good intentions, bad faith, enthusiasm, opportunism, and a thousand other impulses, all of them imperfectly understood.

I followed him into his study and began to tell him about the brilliant essays on John Dos Passos, Sherwood Anderson, and James T. Farrell that had turned up among his papers in the WPA archive at the Illinois State Historical Library—a real find. He wasn't interested. He rebuked me sharply for putting my iced coffee on a book, then went over to his desk and got out his mother's old passport. "Have you seen this?"

I thought he wanted to tell me the story about his family's arrival in the New World again, but no: he wanted to make a point. "Why did you say my name is Bellows?"

Suddenly I remembered—it was the article I had written the previous winter in defense of biography, the one in which I noted that

Bellow had changed his name from Solomon to Saul. Now what had I done? A favorite saying of Bellow's flew into my head: A fool throws a stone in a pond, and ten sages knock themselves out trying to find it.

"I made a mistake," I said. "Maybe I wanted my independence. I can't come running to you every time." I was scared, but I defended myself as best I could. "Besides, I wasn't entirely wrong. There was *some* issue about your name." He had talked about it before, I reminded him—to Terry Gross on National Public Radio.°

Bellow didn't reply, instead launching into a tirade on the critic Hilton Kramer, who had attacked him in *Commentary*.

He was surprised there hadn't been more letters in the magazine protesting Kramer's piece. He felt persecuted by the editor of *The New York Times Book Review*. He had offered a piece to her, but she wanted him to cut three pages—including one in which he referred to "a fat woman." He disparaged Peter Prescott's review of his collection of essays, *It All Adds Up*: "They were out to get me." *They?* Was this another instance of Bellow's tendency to pluralize his enemies, robbing them of their identities as individuals? I had never seen him so angry before.

Not that anger in Bellowworld was anything new. Sometimes I thought anger was his nature, the emotion that dominated his life. There were many others: irony, spiritual feeling, a sense of fun, deep insight, generosity—especially toward his relatives and, fitfully, old friends. But then he would refer to a woman writer who annoyed him as a "cunt" or make a joke about "Afro-American Jim." I was always amazed that Bellow would say these things in front of me: Didn't he realize they were on the record? Or was that the whole idea? He would say whatever he liked, and I would publish the words I chose to publish, and somehow the fact that they were being channeled through his biographer would soften their effect. This arrangement suited me.

The day wasn't over yet. We had a long wrangle about the papers. Bellow wouldn't give me permission for the latest batch of excerpts I'd brought him for initialing unless I explained how the passages were being used. Finally he relented a little: "I'll give you all the stuff that makes me look good," he said with a laugh.

° In fact, I'd made no mistake, except of judgment. I'd never claimed that Bellow had called himself Bellows. It was his brothers who had changed their names, as I noted in my *Times* piece.

But he was still "sore." He glanced at his watch, something he'd never done before. He wanted me to leave. They were going out to supper.

Janis was in the garden. "We had a fight," I told her.

"Bring your swimsuit next time," she said cheerfully. "It will be more fun."

It blew over, as our quarrels always did. What choice did we have? There was no going back now.

Three weeks later, having sent Bellow thirteen pages of "context" notes, supplying the sentence before and after each quote, I called to find out whether they were adequate. Janis answered and told me he was sleeping.

I still didn't know how to address him. I was James or Jim, like a handyman; he was always Mr. Bellow. This time I settled on "the great man." We agreed that I would call back at five, which I did, letting the phone ring awhile. (They didn't have an answering machine.) No one picked up.

I went outside, and a few minutes later Annie called me. Bellow was on the phone.

He had been in the garden, he explained when I picked up. "I wasn't going to break my ass answering the phone." But his tone wasn't confrontational. The letters seemed harmless, he said. We set a date for "the signing"—as I had come to refer to our initialing ritual.

When I drove up a few days later, right on time, he said: "You're like the Illinois Central."

We sat down under the tree in the yard, our own Vermont Yalta, and he said, giving me a forthright look, that he had never meant to interfere in my project; I had misunderstood him. He just wanted to know what I was quoting. He was concerned about what "certain people" were saying about him. How would I know to be fair?

It was my job, I answered. I knew how to judge character.

"But you're not the catcher in the rye," Bellow retorted.

"It's true," I replied. "I can't save you every time." We both laughed.

We went into the house and sat down at the kitchen table. Bellow was businesslike and went through the papers page by page, initialing each as if it were a legal document (which, in a sense, it was). It took us two hours to get through the papers. "What can I do about all this crap?" he said with a sigh as we neared the end. Then: "This is tiring."

When we were done, he got up from the table. He didn't want me to stay.

As I drove off, he stood on the porch and waved. I waved back. He seemed so alone.

When I got home, I hunted down a copy of *The Catcher in the Rye* and leafed quickly through it until I found the scene I was looking for. Sitting on the bed, Holden describes to his sister, Phoebe, the one job he'd like to have:

> Anyway, I keep picturing all these little kids playing some game in this big field of rye and all. Thousands of little kids, and nobody's around—nobody big, I mean—except me. And I'm standing on the edge of some crazy cliff. What I have to do, I have to catch everybody if they start to go over the cliff—I mean if they're running and they don't look where they're going I have to come out from somewhere and catch them. That's all I'd do all day. I'd just be the catcher in the rye and all.

I sat on the couch and wept. My job was even harder than Holden's. It wasn't some little kids I was supposed to protect, but the greatest novelist in America. And I . . . well, I was Holden. But I was also the cliff.

J. A. FROUDE.

Carlyle's Speaking Likeness (grimly)—
"AFTER MY DEATH I WISH NO OTHER HERALD,
NO OTHER SPEAKER OF MY LIVING ACTIONS,
TO KEEP MINE HONOUR FROM CORRUPTION,
BUT SUCH AN HONEST CHRONICLER AS—FROUDE."

James Anthony Froude

XXIII

Among the pronouncements on biography I had filed away was this one from Johnson's column in *The Rambler*: "If a life be delayed til interest and envy are at an end, we may hope for impartiality, but must expect little intelligence; for the incidents which give excellence to biography are of a volatile and evanescent kind, such as soon escape the memory, and are rarely transmitted by tradition."

But there are hazards, too. When you write about someone who is still living—or someone you knew—you risk becoming embroiled in the feuds and skirmishes of the day, the gossip, the scandals, the struggle over who gets to own the narrative. "Rarely does a month pass without some new biographical 'controversy' making the headlines," noted Ian Hamilton in *Keepers of the Flame*: "Two widows have been at each other's throats; a family is divided; an authorised biographer has been expelled."* Grief rarely brings out in people the spirit of conciliation.

This was especially true of Victorian biographers, who often knew their subjects. Mrs. Gaskell's biography of Charlotte Brontë, published two years after the novelist's death, caused a tremendous uproar in its day. The book had been authorized, more or less—the biographer had been allowed to read the novelist's letters—but no one in the inner circle was happy about the revelations it contained, according to Juliet Barker, one of Brontë's more recent biographers. The novelist's husband, Arthur Nicholls, was disturbed by the suggestion that she had been less than enthusiastic about his marriage proposal; her father denied that he had forced his daughters "to live chiefly on vegetable food," ruining their health; and the little remembered writer Harriet Martineau, whose negative review of Brontë's novel *Villette* had ended

---

* George Birkbeck Hill, an early biographer of Boswell, reported that he had "once tried to penetrate into Auchinleck" but had been "most rudely repulsed."

their friendship, wrote angry letters to the newspapers spinning Mrs. Gaskell's account of their contretemps. The only one who came across as objective was William Dearden, a local schoolmaster. Trying to bring the controversy to a close, he wrote, "The passing affairs of this life— which too much occupy the attention of passing mortal man, are but dust and ashes, when compar'd with the concerns of eternity."

How far all this commotion was from Gaskell's actual biography, a masterpiece of sympathetic insight and scrupulous research. Herself a well-known novelist, she had been approached by Brontë's father to write the book based on a perceived emotional sympathy with his daughter. It was a sound instinct. The two writers had spent only a few days in each other's company; Charlotte came to Gaskell's house in Manchester on three occasions, and Gaskell went once to Haworth. Why, then, did she refer to her subject as "my dear friend Charlotte Bronte"? If they hadn't logged as many hours in each other's company as Boswell and Johnson, they had nevertheless developed a strong bond, based on shared spiritual and literary affinities.

Mrs. Gaskell made no claim to biographical omniscience. "I do not pretend to be able to harmonize points of character, and account for them, and bring them all into one consistent and intelligible whole," she wrote with a candor rare in our profession. And whenever she arrived at a place in the narrative that was resistant to authorial certainty, she let the reader know: "I now come to a part of my subject which I find great difficulty in treating, because the evidence relating to it on each side is so conflicting that it seems almost impossible to arrive at the truth." Many biographers would have plowed ahead anyway, choosing the evidence that supported their position while *pretending* it was the truth.

Still, her personal acquaintance with her subject served Mrs. Gaskell well. Her use of *I*, infrequent and judicious, reminds you of her presence in the narrative while maintaining the biographer's customary self-effacement. It's with a shock that one reads her first impression of Brontë's "reddish face; large mouth & many teeth missing" (a startling detail to the modern reader, who tends to imagine missing teeth only in some homeless crone). Then there are the eyes, often remarked upon for their singular intensity: "The usual expression was of quiet, listening intelligence; but now and then . . . a light would shine out, as if some spiritual lamp had been kindled, which glowed behind those expressive orbs." Or this: "Her hands were the smallest I ever saw; when one of the former was placed in mine, it was like the soft touch of a bird in the middle of my palm."

Ignoring its literary qualities, the principal and minor figures chose to focus on themselves and instantly fell upon one another. Gaskell's *Life* arrived "on a tide of pathos, publicity, and near-scandal," wrote Winifred Gérin, author of what was generally considered the definitive biography of Brontë until it was superseded° by Juliet Barker's group portrait of the family. But the conflicting accounts, the concealments, the dramatis personae airbrushed out of the picture, and the outright lies continued to fester into the next generation, where the contested facts, instead of being reconciled, become even more hotly contested. Thus we learn, many years after the publication of her book, that Gaskell herself suppressed references to several manuscripts that might have offered us a less positive view of her subject, most notably *The Professor,* a thinly veiled portrait of the still-mysterious M. Heger, a Belgian schoolteacher with whom Brontë had been in love and who had in his possession letters to prove it. "What he *knew,* and the material he possessed," writes the usually restrained Gérin in excitable (and starkly idiomatic) terms, "was gunpowder in unscrupulous hands, and could blow Charlotte Brontë's reputation sky high." Perhaps so, but over time the curiosity surrounding Brontë's relationship with M. Heger has served only to intensify interest in her life. Mrs. Gaskell, the first responder, was trying to put out flames that later biographers would fan.

James Anthony Froude also ran into heavy weather in his biography of Carlyle, one of the monuments of Victorian biography in a literary graveyard crowded with them.

Author of a twelve-volume history of England and a novel, *The Nemesis of Faith,* that his future subject uncharitably characterized as a "vomiting up [of] interior crudities, dubitations and spiritual, agonising bellyaches," Froude would appear at first glance a peculiar choice as Carlyle's biographer. But a decade later Carlyle seemed to have forgotten, or at least forgiven Froude's poor performance:

° This inevitably happens and is one of the heartbreaks of the profession.

Late one afternoon, in the middle of winter, Carlyle called on me, and said he wished to see more of me—willed me in fact to be his companion, so far as I could, in his daily rides and walks . . . and from that date, for twenty years, up to his own death, except when either or both of us were out of town, I never ceased to see him twice or three times a week, and to have two or three hours conversation with him.

Carlyle was ambivalent about a biography. At the beginning of their friendship, he told Froude he didn't want one, but this reluctance soon turned to resignation: "Whether he wished it or not, a life, or perhaps various lives, of himself, would appear when he was gone." To this end, Carlyle handed over letters, journals, manuscripts—"the accumulations of a life"—with the directive, according to Froude, "to burn freely as I might think right." So the biographer is supposed to burn his subject's papers? That's a new one.

Still, he might have been tempted to consign them to the flames. Writing Carlyle's biography would turn out to be a big job. For a man who did little but sit in his study writing, Carlyle had led a complicated life. His marriage to Jane Welsh Carlyle was so famously storm-tossed that it nearly killed them both. Carlyle took up all the oxygen in the parlor of their townhouse on the Thames; the displays of harassment, arias° of self-absorption, efforts at talent-suppression, and neurotic bullying to which the lionized writer subjected his equally talented but stifled wife were legendary. It wouldn't be a stretch to attribute Jane's premature death, of a stroke while being driven around Hyde Park in her carriage, in part to Carlyle's fulminations.

Their capacity for damaging each other was limitless: "The morning after his wedding-day [Carlyle] tore to pieces the flower-garden at Comely Bank in a fit of ungovernable fury." They slept in separate bedrooms; they fought and screamed at each other until the neighbors complained. "For the first time," writes Froude, describing the effect that reading Jane's private papers had on him, "I realised what a tragedy the life in Cheyne Row [their house in Chelsea] had been—a story as stern and real as the story of Oedipus."

The "blue marks" on her arms that Jane Carlyle described in her journal bore testimony to Carlyle's capacity for literal, not just psy-

---

° I see that I've picked up this Bellow word.

chological violence. Then there was the delicate issue of Carlyle's impotence—what his beleaguered wife tactfully described as an "inability to love"—a deficit confirmed by Jane's friend Geraldine Jewsbury[*] but known to no one else. Learning that Carlyle couldn't get it up, instead of producing one of those *aha!* moments biographers live for, made Froude uneasy. "Froude was now seriously troubled," writes Ian Hamilton in his account of the Froude/Carlyle biographical debacle: "He knew more than he wanted to know." I doubt it—biographers can never know too much—but I see what he means. How do you handle incendiary facts that threaten to undermine your subject's integrity of character? Treat them in a gingerly manner; be truthful, but—if you can—be generous. And if you can't, well . . . you're just the messenger.

Carlyle himself was deeply divided about how much of his private life he wanted to be made known. The note attached to the manuscript of his *Reminiscences* is almost comic in its ambivalence: "I still mainly mean to *burn* this book before my own departure; but feel that I always have a kind of grudge to do it, and an indolent excuse, 'Not *yet;* wait, any day that can be done.'" However, in the event that he *didn't* burn it, be it known that the manuscript was for "*friends* only." And if he ever *did* consent to its publication—which would never happen—it would have to be heavily revised.

After much agonized vacillation, Carlyle chose the third option, and the *Reminiscences,* edited by Froude, appeared just a month after his death. He had revealed a great deal about himself, and his candor did his biographer no good. "There was outcry on all sides," reports Hamilton:

> How could Froude have allowed Carlyle's remorse, his dark domestic secrets, to be advertized in such appalling detail; why had he not censored certain off-the-cuff acerbities (in particular those aimed at the living and the not-long-dead); why had he been in such a hurry to blacken Carlyle's name? Froude genuinely believed that he had cut out "everything that could *injure* anybody," and he knew (as the readership did not) that he had suppressed secrets much darker than the ones he had revealed.

---

[*] I've always been curious about this name: who put the Jews in Jewsbury? But it turns out to be a derivative of Duesbury, from a village in Yorkshire, recorded as Deusberia in the Domesday Book.

He was just doing his job, the job he'd been commissioned to do.

The critical reception of the *Reminiscences* portended ill for the biography, which took Froude a decade to write and was published when he was sixty-four. "Even when it was praised," writes Hamilton, "he did not feel that the complicated, tragic point of it had been quite grasped." In being honest, in laying bare Carlyle's faults—his monstrous egotism, his fits of rage, his disregard for the feelings of others, his sadistic treatment of his wife, his dyspepsia, his preoccupation with his ceaselessly churning bowels—Froude was depicting the man as he really was. And remember, Carlyle had *urged* his biographer to be candid: for that alone, the biographer deserved a pass. Froude wrote his sister-in-law Mrs. Charles Kingsley, herself a biographer: "Let [others] look into their own miserable souls, and ask themselves how *they* could bear to have their own private histories ransacked and laid bare." Candor demanded courage.

Froude knew his book would be controversial, but he could scarcely have anticipated the loud outcry that followed fast upon its publication. Attacked in the press, denounced by Gladstone in the House of Commons, Froude believed his reputation was irretrievably damaged. He had suffered "some deep inaccessible hurt," writes Julia Markus in her fine biography of Froude; friends noted his "vulnerability" and sensed that he was "disappointed in himself." He wasn't only a victim. He bore some responsibility for the debacle. He had failed to make his case. "Up close he would see Carlyle's human feet, clay as are ours," intones the always eloquent Markus: "But there was a part of Carlyle that was immortal, a part that was the truth teller, who if he hadn't led mankind out of the desert of contemporary spiritual obliqueness, in the future, after democracy had its day, still would." It was this heroic Carlyle that critics had missed in Froude's biography, preoccupied as they were with the salacious details of his sex (or was it nonsex?) life—the great biographer, the world-historical figure whose books would survive his time. This was the book Froude had intended to write.

In *My Relations with Carlyle*,* an exculpatory manifesto published after Froude's death, the biographer threw down a bitter challenge:

---

* This manuscript was found among his papers by his doting children and published in response to a volume called *New Letters and Memorials of Jane Welsh Carlyle*, edited by Carlyle's nephew Alexander.

"If anyone will suggest what unworthy motive I can have had, he may perhaps assist me in discovering it. I cannot discover it myself." Not for lack of trying. Victorian England was pre-analytic—people didn't question their ostensible motives—but Froude was unusually self-aware for that era, and his anguish rises off the page like a damp mist off a pond: "Mrs. Carlyle's pale, drawn, suffering face haunted me in my dreams." Had he revealed too much? Too little? Should he have mentioned the blue marks? Carlyle himself had referred to them in an unpublished memoir, with the injunction that it was "never to be destroyed." That's how biography was supposed to be practiced, even in that more guarded day: nothing should go unsaid. This was not just Froude's view; it was Carlyle's: "The lives of great men are scrutinised to the bottom. Mankind will not rest till they have learnt all that can be discovered about such men."

The deeper problem had to do with how Froude felt toward his subject. "My admiration of him had never wavered," he wrote, "but the contempt with which he treated everybody and everything, the anecdotes which I had heard from his wife, and his manifest forgetfulness of every other person's interest or comfort where his own wishes were concerned, had made it difficult for me to *like* him in the common sense of the word." When that requirement went unmet, trouble followed. The biographer's feelings seeped through the facade of objectivity. The truth emerged, whether welcome or not. It always did.

Froude's posthumous self-defense was promptly answered by Alexander Carlyle, who laid out his case in a book of his own entitled *The Nemesis of Froude.** Rumors about the biography that had begun as "mere gaseous gossip," he noted with fierce contempt, "have become gradually congealed and glued to [Carlyle's] name with many offensive accretions." That his uncle's hated biographer, having died in the interim, could now be referred to as "the late Mr. Froude," did nothing to moderate his wrath.

With lawyerly officiousness, Alexander made his case. The marriage, far from being a death-match between two high-strung screamers, had been happy. To Ralph Waldo Emerson, visiting from America, the great writer and his wife gave the appearance of a happy couple, sitting cozily by the fireside. "Carlyle and his wife live on beautiful terms,"

---

* The book had a co-author, Sir James Crichton-Browne, a physician who had addressed the matter of Carlyle's impotence in a British medical journal.

Emerson wrote in his journal. Sure, they squabbled now and again: "They had their little differences and misunderstandings and sometimes sharp encounters. What married pair has not?" But for the most part, it was a companionable union.

As for the matter of the "blue marks," how reliable is Geraldine Jewsbury's allegation that Carlyle suffered from "a physical defect under which, it is alleged, he laboured, and which made his marriage no marriage"? Jane's letters show her not to have been "amatively disappointed," and besides, Jewsbury herself, the authors suggest, was secretly in love with Jane! A letter is quoted: "I cannot express my feelings even to you—vague undefined yearnings to be yours in some way."

Since the existence of the blue marks can't be denied, some other explanation must be offered. Alexander Carlyle speculates that they may have been caused by

> the operations of her *bête noir,* the bug, if an insect may be so designated, which, in spite of her vigilance, several times invaded 5, Cheyne Row, and her hunts after which she has described with the exciting realism of one of her favourite novelists, Fenimore Cooper, and the wrist is a favourite point of attack of the *Cimex Lectularius.*

Of course! Why hadn't Froude thought of that?

Froude and Alexander Carlyle disagreed about everything. The biographer assailed Craigenputtock, the Carlyle family homestead in Scotland, as "the dreariest spot in all the British dominions." But Alexander claimed that Jane loved the place. Her letters from Craigenputtock were "as bright as the unpolluted sunshine on the mountain, breezy as the atmosphere that undulated around her; lucent and hopefully babbling like the streams that hurried to the valley below."*

As *The Nemesis of Froude* draws to a close after 130 pages, Alexander Carlyle ratchets up the vitriol. *The Life of Carlyle* is a "grisly biography," he splutters; Froude has offered up a portrait that is "blotched

---

* I checked out the house online, and it does look pretty nice—even discounting its mildly obscene-sounding name—with lots of rolling hills and open views. But it's also in the middle of nowhere—the kind of place where you'd want to spend the last two weeks of August and no more.

and discoloured," "literary garbage." And why did the biographer write it? He had "pecuniary" motives.[*]

What a melancholy tale, I thought as I laid this last installment atop my tottering pile of Froudeiana. You were damned if you did and damned if you didn't. If you told the whole story, it would inflame the literary world. If you didn't, you would be accused of suppressing the facts.

I hoped Froude had derived some consolation from a pamphlet in his defense written by his co-executor Sir James Stephen:

> In order to present a true picture of him as he really was, you, well knowing what you were about, stepped into a pillory in which you were charged with treachery, violation of confidence, and every imaginable base motive, when you were in fact guilty of no other fault than that of practising Mr Carlyle's great doctrine that men ought to tell the truth.

Relations between subject and biographer aren't always so acrimonious. I was comforted by the example of Dickens and John Forster, his first biographer, who merits a biography himself.[†] Born in 1812, just two months after Dickens, Forster maintained a high profile in the London literary world; a contemporary described him as "a flamboyant character with a taste for oysters and grog." His seven-hundred-page biography of the playwright Oliver Goldsmith had made him famous. Mrs. Gaskell found him "little, and *very* fat and affected, yet *so* clever and shrewd and good-hearted and right-minded." She undercut her already double-edged praise with a sly put-down: "His friendship was deeply valued, perhaps even slightly more than his presence."

Forster's three-volume work,[‡] published two years after Dickens's

---

[*] This is one charge literary biographers working today needn't worry about. Ours is not a lucrative trade. Don't urge your children to go into it.

[†] But of course it turns out there is one: *John Forster: A Literary Life*, by James A. Davies.

[‡] I own the first two volumes, plucked from the secondhand book bin in front of Blackwell's for 25p (the price written in pencil on the frontispiece); they have burgundy-colored boards and a facsimile of Dickens's signature embossed on the cover in gold leaf. What's most notable, though, is the type size: it's the tiniest I've ever seen. How

death, was an amiable portrait that depicted the great novelist as a genius whose fevered, explosive imagination and "generous nature" made him an attractive figure. I won't call Forster's *Dickens* a hagiography, but their relationship was marred by no rift, no tension lurking just beneath the surface. They hung out together in Bath and Edinburgh and the clubs of London, the dutiful biographer taking dictation in direct quotes of suspicious length that not even the master scribe Boswell could rival. Forster read Dickens's work in manuscript and again in page proofs; accompanied him on holiday; and advised him on business deals. He was Dickens's closest friend, "a member of the family," according to Forster. It was Forster who informed Dickens of the death of his child, Dora. And it was Dickens who consoled Forster on the untimely death of his brother: "You have a Brother left. One bound to you by ties as strong as Nature ever forged. By ties never to be broken, weakened, changed in any way." (Their chumminess didn't prevent Dickens from satirizing Forster as the pompous Mr. Podsnap in *Our Mutual Friend*.) "They were always at ease with one other, with no need to pose or pretend," Claire Tomalin observed in her exemplary biography.

This intimacy, though it compromised the book's usefulness as an "objective" biographical work, was edifying. Forster's biography captures Dickens's "sparkling, clear, and sunny utterances" intercalated with "bits of *auto*-biography unrivalled in clearness and credibility." The story—told in every biography—of the novelist going by a grand home on Gad Hill as an impoverished child and dreaming that he would one day occupy it, acquires a deeper resonance when it's recounted by the author in the first person: "Very often had we travelled past it together, many years before it became his home," the biographer writes in the opening pages, "and never without some allusion to what he told me when I first saw it in his company."

---

can anyone have been expected to read this minuscule font? The thin paper is dotted with melanoma-like blots. The epigraphs from Boswell ("I cannot conceive a more perfect mode of writing any man's life") and Carlyle are in such small type that I had to hold the page an inch away from my face to read them. Carlyle's, which is quite long and is identified as a *"Letter to the Author,* 16 February 1874," says, in part, "I incline to consider this Biography as taking rank, in essential respects, parallel to Boswell himself." A blurb! I'd never seen one from the nineteenth century before. This must be what Darwin felt when he came across the beak of a dead finch: *Here is where it all began.* I hadn't known that blurbs dated back so far in the evolution of literature.

Reading Forster, you can trace the origins of these stories directly to their source, without the spurious omniscience of later biographers. Dickens's traumatic labor as a boy in a blacking factory, an episode that would eventually become mythologized as the formative episode of his life—or was mythified as such—would never have come to light, Forster asserts, had it not been for the accidental revelations vouchsafed by their mutual friend Mr. Dilke of a visit Dickens's father had once made to "his uncle Barrow," who told him . . . ten readings of this passage in its minute type can't unravel the sequence of events, or whose father was whose uncle. But at least we learn—sort of—how *David Copperfield* came to be written.

How much did Forster leave out? From the prying perspective of our time, a great deal. Only by scouring the appendix do we learn of Dickens's affair with the actress Ellen Ternan, whom he met when she was eighteen and he was forty-five, which is widely regarded as responsible for the dissolution of Dickens's marriage. Leave it to others to write the warts-and-all* accounts. For now—I would say if I were reviewing Forster's triple-decker in *The Edinburgh Review* in 1872— we have an admiring portrait that conveys the vitality of Dickens's genius and brings us closer to the man. So what if it's not objective? All it has to be is true.[†]

Another way the biographer/subject relationship can go wrong: you start out a friend of your subject and end up hating him, as Lawrance Thompson did in his notorious biography of Robert Frost. Every biographer is familiar with this train wreck; Jay Parini, Frost's most sympathetic biographer, called it "a three-volume assault on Frost's character in the shape of a literary biography." Thompson died before he could complete the third volume, to the relief of all concerned, and it was finished by his student R. H. Winnick, but the damage was done.

---

* Why do I so dislike this cliché of the biography trade? How many biographical subjects, besides the wart-flecked Cromwell—the phrase derives from his directive to a portraitist—have actually had this disfiguring trait?

† "Narrative truth can be defined as the criterion we use to decide when a certain experience has been captured to our satisfaction; it depends on continuity and closure and the extent to which the fit of the pieces takes on an aesthetic finality." *Narrative Truth and Historical Truth: Meaning and Interpretation in Psychoanalysis*, by Donald P. Spence, a book every biographer should read.

His biography stands as a monument to the danger of writing about someone you know.

It began as a promising match. Thompson wasn't just Frost's biographer; he was the authorized biographer, appointed by Frost after he read an admiring book Thompson had written on his poetry. The admiration was apparently provisional, since it didn't prevent Thompson from giving a hostile review to a play of Frost's in the *Times Book Review* or, stranger still, having an affair with Frost's mistress, Kay Morrison, the wife of Theodore Morrison, a poet and professor of English at Harvard. Now that's access. Is it enough to call this a conflict of interest, or is it transgressive?

"Thompson's intimacy with Kay allowed him to participate in and even change the course of the life he was writing," wrote Jeffrey Meyers, one of Frost's many biographers. He urged Morrison to reject Frost's proposals of marriage and be "tough" with him, even though Thompson knew—it was his job to know—every detail of their affair.* I can't help wondering what their pillow talk was like.

Thompson's animosity toward Frost was hard to miss. As Jay Parini points out, the index includes the derisive categories "Anti-intellectual," "Brute," "Charlatan," "Hate," "Insanity," and "Monster," among other opprobrious terms. Thompson loses no opportunity to snipe. Frost's creative process, he writes, "caused him to mingle self-deception with little falsehoods; it even caused him gradually to convince himself that some of these fictions were genuine truths." The young Frost was characterized by "jealousy, sulking, temper tantrums, vindictive retaliations and self-pity in the guise of threatened suicide." He cheated at card games and tennis.

It's true that Frost was a flamboyantly terrible man, not your average bad-boy poet but someone who once started a small bonfire at a rival poet's reading to call attention to himself, and is said to have threatened his wife with a gun, insisting their daughter choose between them. Even so, Thompson's hatred of his subject seems at times pathological. How account for it? Maybe he had authority issues. Maybe he was disappointed about his own failed career as a poet. Maybe he just didn't *like* Frost—many didn't. But what's so fascinating about this

---

* What if Morrison had ignored Thompson's advice and married her lover's rival/subject? We would be in uncharted biographical territory indeed—the biographer not only writing a narrative but creating it. From there it's only a step to writing the biography *before* the life is lived. Isn't this the kind of autonomy biographers instinctively seek?

"case" is how unanalyzed Thompson was. He was willing to destroy his own book, the work of decades, in order to destroy his subject.

But is that the whole story? I was electrified when I came across an essay about Thompson's heroic efforts to "get" Frost (in the analytic, not the threatening sense) that laid out the steep challenges facing even a self-aware and psychoanalytically sophisticated biographer. Its author was an English professor named Donald Sheehy who had gained access to two thousand pages of Thompson's notes in the University of Virginia Library. It showed how hard he had worked to understand his obdurate, prickly subject, who defied whatever sympathy a biographer could manage to extend. Frost had gone through four biographers by the time he settled on Thompson; one actually produced a draft, only to have it rejected by Frost on the grounds that the biographer's "long-standing affection" for his subject had spoiled his objectivity; another one died. Frost didn't want a biographer who focused on the "dross and dirt" of him, but he didn't want a biographer who adulated him either (or so he claimed).

As a guide to better insight, Thompson turned to Karen Horney's *Neurosis and Human Growth: The Struggle Toward Self-Realization*: "If it had mentioned Frost on every page it couldn't have come closer to giving a psychological framework to what I've been trying to say in the first volume of the biography." According to Horney, self-knowledge is the key to the development of an integrated personality. But a hostile environment like the one in which Frost grew up—his father beat him, his mother was overindulgent—could have a disastrous influence on character; the drive to excel could become "vindictive." In such a scenario, "the motivating force stems from impulses to take revenge for humiliations suffered in childhood." Achievement expresses itself as a form of aggression. It was this dynamic, Thompson argued, that made Frost capable of such vicious behavior. He had to win in order to validate himself.

In the end, Thompson's close personal relationship with Frost, rather than providing greater opportunities for insight, proved a hindrance. He spent whole summers on Frost's farm, accompanied him to Israel and Russia, and kept a detailed journal of their conversations.°

° But was the journal accurate? "I've noticed that when I tell a story of something Frost told me years ago," Thompson confessed in his journal, "I feel quite sure that I can quote him verbatim on a little phrase, because the phrase has such pertinence. But later, when I happen to be in my 'Notes on Robert Frost,' I frequently come across

But the biographer's intimacy with his subject conspired against him in ways he couldn't have foreseen. "The very objectivity that Frost had sought in choosing Thompson had brought them into a relationship far closer than either had expected," Sheehy noted. "Such a relationship precluded the impersonal biography of ideas that Frost had originally hoped Thompson would write."

Only how adversarial was it? Thompson warned that Frost's correspondence would reveal the private man's "periods of gloom, jealousies, obsessive resentments, sulking, displays of temper, nervous rages, and vindictive retaliations," but his interpretation of this volatile mix went a long way toward exonerating or at least explaining Frost:

> Permit any excruciatingly sensitive young man to develop all the ambitions and drives of an incipient artist. Let early failures make him self-protectively proud and scornful of scorners. Add extra measures of physical illness, often inseparable from emotional and mental anxieties. Enable him to succeed at nothing he thinks important through years of more intensely ambitious effort than he would ever be willing to acknowledge afterward. Give him enemies enough; and even give his enemies reasons to mock him for his pride, arrogance, and failure, until he is nearly forty years old. Then suddenly grant him unexpected attention and fame—abroad. Let him come home to the vicissitudes of criticism and praise, but let him keep trying, striving, driving until he has earned a steadily increasing recognition and adulation. Under these circumstances anyone might become unbearably vain. Robert Frost did not; but his later letters indicate an unquenchable thirst for honor and glory, as though the ultimate balm of innumerable tributes could never quite heal the wounds he suffered in those agonizingly long years of failure.

What comes through, writes Sheehy, is "a sincere, if troubled admiration for the man." If Thompson sometimes lost it, he tried mightily to be fair:

---

my first recording of the event—the recording made immediately after the conversation. And I find that there I quote him verbatim in a way which is quite different from my later quoting! Oh dear!" *Oh dear* is right. I call this the Polynesians/Papuans Conundrum.

It's easy enough to get mad at that old bastard, but when you get down deep enough to understand that he was victimized by a whole set of drives that he couldn't control, then the value of explaining the complication is the value of treating them sympathetically and of giving him credit for having intermittently triumphed over his troubles as well as he did. . . . The point is that here was a man who actually achieved a well-deserved and lasting fame as an artist-poet; a man who in spite of his flawed human qualities, was at times extremely lovable; a man, who in spite of his meanness to so many people, really went out of his way to help certain people—and did help them. I must keep reminding myself of this.

I was moved by this self-hortatory, somewhat tortured expression of impatience. Read in its belated context, after the damage has been done, it shows the biographer fighting to overcome his own distaste for his subject—and failing. Yet Thompson came to his task better equipped than most biographers. His job was to understand not only his subject but himself. Critics complained that he was biased. No one knew that better than he did.

I found the story of Andrew Field, Vladimir Nabokov's first biographer, even more unnerving than Thompson's debacle. Field had written a smart but fawning critical study, *Nabokov: His Life in Art*, and the exacting novelist had pronounced it "superb." Not long afterward he made Field, then only twenty-nine, his "first" biographer.

It was a peculiar decision, given Nabokov's reclusive nature. "He had a hypertrophied sense of privacy," observed Brian Boyd, Field's successor. He was a control freak* who at one point decreed a fifty-year ban on the papers he deposited in the Library of Congress; stipulated that interviewers had to write out their questions in advance; and insisted on the right to read Field's book in manuscript as a condition of quoting from the work.

---

* I have circled around this phrase, deleting and restoring it several times. It feels somehow *too* idiomatic, and therefore inappropriate, even faintly insulting to a master of usage like Nabokov. But isn't the goal in writing to approximate ordinary speech? And Nabokov *was* a control freak. Stet.

Their collaboration—for that's what it was—got off to what both thought was a promising start. Field set up shop in Nabokov's suite at the Palace Hotel in Montreux, transcribing his subject's recollections of Russia—preliminary notes for the classic *Speak, Memory*—while Nabokov, turning the tables, played the biographer. Joining Field after a nap, the novelist conjured up a description of himself as he imagined the biographer would see him: "I remember him shuffling in looking old and wretched, and a moment later he was bubbling with good spirits." In the biography, boldface indicates that Nabokov is speaking. Or maybe Field is quoting him or imagining what Nabokov would say. The point is that the biographer has broken down the wall between reader and subject that exists in a formal interview, where only one party is permitted to ask questions and one to answer them, and made of it a conversation. Biography as dialogue.

Things started to go wrong when Nabokov learned that Field was—quite reasonably—interviewing people who had known his subject. Didn't he have all he needed with the papers and interviews with the author himself? Nabokov wrote Field in the third person (perhaps hoping to dissociate himself from the book he himself had enabled): "V.N.'s biographer can learn very little by getting in touch with V.N.'s sporadic relatives, schoolmates, literary acquaintances, or academic colleagues, and the worst he can do is to collect the vulgar gossip that always buzzes around a ripe old author ready to be biographized."

It got worse when Field began to share with Nabokov his work-in-progress. "On January 28th"—the enumeration of the date sounds ominous, as if we're reading a police report—"Nabokov began reading Field's typescript. He thought he had braced himself for the worst, but what he found outdid his gloomiest apprehensions." Over the next three weeks, Nabokov "clocked up a hundred hours of work on the ms," according to Boyd. By page 285, he could write his wife, Vera: "The number of absurd errors, impossible statements, vulgarities and inventions is appalling." His corrective memo came to 180 typed pages. They spent the next four years communicating through lawyers.

Field's biggest mistake was deciding to go it alone. "Upon rechecking this collection of quotes and notes," wrote Nabokov, "I find myself wondering what strange 'block' prevented you from simply consulting me in hundreds of instances when my wife and I could have come to your assistance." He was particularly irate about scenes that he felt Field had invented or embellished to fill in the picture: "The little feet of the limping anecdote have to be orthopedically shod. And since by no amount of imagination can one conjure up the details one does not know in a setting with which one is not familiar, the description of the event becomes at best a clumsy cliché and at worst an offensive farce."

Nabokov's determination to protect himself inflamed Field—to know why, one would have to write *his* biography. As with a love affair that goes off the rails, enchantment led to disillusion. "There is an absence of that glow of affection I felt for *Speak, Memory*," Nabokov complains to his biographer, predicting the end of their harmonious relationship: "It will not be violins, but trombones." It's poignant that a writer as famous as Nabokov cared what his biographer thought: no one is exempt from the need for approval, not even geniuses.

The problem was that Field couldn't tolerate the self-suppression that biography requires, the willingness to subjugate one's ego to the task at hand. Instead, he put himself in an adversarial position: he charged Nabokov with "avoiding facts" in *Speak, Memory*, that lyrical classic of remembrance, and claimed that it was unreliable. Determined to prove his independence, to show that he was "his own man," he made it clear that he no longer needed Nabokov's help. After all, what did he know about his own life? All biographers feel this way at least some of the time, but Field admitted it, declaring in the first chapter that he was his subject's "competitor." A competitor of *Nabokov*, one of the greatest stylists in the language? Give me a break.

Field's reading of the work is heavy-handed, his narrative meandering, his research—what Dwight called "kitchen-work"—lazy: "Someday no doubt registries and municipal records from the 19th century will be able to be examined in key Siberian shopping places." Aren't *you* supposed to be doing that? Yet there's a kind of intimacy about this odd biography that makes it feel entertaining and true (even when it's false). In one scene, where Nabokov has to lend Field a jacket for the dining room, he says, or Field has him say, or maybe just think: "Now I can see for the first time how I look in that coat. I never realized that there was so much yellow in it." Wearing his clothes: how much more inside your subject can you be?°

Boyd, whose two-volume "definitive"† biography followed Field's by

---

° Which doesn't mean you've learned anything. What did I learn from wearing Bellow's hat?

† *Definitive* until when? Until it's supplanted by something better—or just later.

just two years, is the good cop to Field's bad cop.° A conscientious biographer, he clops through the chronology for twelve hundred pages—"A week later . . ." "A month later . . ." Boyd is a master of his trade, firmly in command of the mass of material generated by an incessantly productive novelist, critic, poet, playwright, lecturer, and correspondent over more than half a century. He has read and absorbed every word Nabokov ever wrote and every word written about him in English and Russian; he interprets the work with authority, the person with sympathy and wit. There is no fact he doesn't know: should the reader wish to learn Nabokov's income from Czech translation rights in 1934, when he was living in Berlin, the number is right there: 103 Reichsmarks.

Boyd, unlike Field, keeps himself mostly out of the narrative. On the rare occasions when *I* appears, it is unobtrusive, and even gives the book a kind of casual authority ("Many readers—and for a long time I was one . . ."). It is only from his engaging collection of essays, *Stalking Nabokov*, published twenty years after the biography was complete, that we get the full story. The note of aggression in the title is ironic, or perhaps unconscious; the essays radiate warmth. Boyd's intense scrutiny of the work is in itself a tribute, and he describes with enthusiasm the long hours ("from morning until after midnight") spent scrutinizing the vast archive of manuscripts and letters. His genial attitude toward his subject is reflected in the biography, which manages to be at once indulgent and critical.

Frustrated by the "garbling" and "decomposing gossip" in Field's book, Boyd lauds with heavy sarcasm his predecessor's "gift for mistranscription, misreporting, mistranslation, and misconstruction." In his own telling, Boyd is the real biographer, so dedicated that in his early days as a Nabokov scholar, he would board a Greyhound bus after the Cornell Library closed, ride all night on a cheap student's pass to avoid spending money on a hotel, and return to Ithaca in the morning, "not very fresh or very clean," to resume his research. The novelist is never far from his thoughts. Shaving, he thinks of a passage in *Pale Fire* where the poet John Shade describes the inspiration he gets from the same quotidian act: "That's how close my Nabokov can be."

It's not until the end that Boyd really loses it. In three lengthy foot-

---

° Field teaches in Australia, Boyd in New Zealand. What is it about that antipodean realm that produces biographers of Nabokov?

notes, he lays out the evidence against his rival as if he's conducting a criminal trial:

> Exhibit A: The effect of inflation in Berlin during the 1930s on Nabo-kov's decision to stay in Berlin; "averse to chronology," Field got the dates wrong.
>
> Exhibit B: "As his bibliographer and biographer, Field should have known that *before* Fondaminsky [Ilya, editor of a literary journal] called on him in Berlin, Nabokov had published the whole of *The Defense* in *Sovremennye zapiski*."
>
> Exhibit C: In chronicling readings by Nabokov in Paris during 1936 and 1937, Field had again gotten the dates wrong and, even more grievously, conflated two occasions for Nabokov's famous meeting with James Joyce, producing "a muddled mirage."

Field couldn't even get the facts about himself right: he was mis-taken about the date of his first meeting with Nabokov, according to Boyd, as well as the street his own hotel was on—not the Grand-Rue des alpes, but the Avenue des alpes.° Well, it's easy to make fun of pedantry. What interests me here isn't so much the wrong dates as the *tone* of Boyd's corrections. In laying out the facts, he resorts to martial language: Field had "retaliated," "fired his first salvo," "seemed to be preparing an attack." As far as Boyd is concerned, Field's biography was an act of war.

On a visit to Montreux, Boyd leaves a message at the front desk of the Palace Hotel, but he never does meet Nabokov—in the end, I sus-pect, a missed opportunity that turned out to be a piece of luck.

° Actually, it's the Avenue des Alpes. Boyd wasn't infallible either. And why, for that matter, trust Nabokov himself? In *Vera*, her scintillating biography of Nabokov's wife, Stacy Schiff writes: "Friends had long complained that he winked at his interlocutor on the rare occasion when he spoke the truth."

New Yorker illustration of the author and Saul Bellow

XXIV

I n the middle of my labors, Bill Buford was appointed fiction editor
of *The New Yorker,* and I soon got a note from him asking about
my "Bellow journals"—the notes Annie had sent to *Granta* by acci-
dent. Was there something there that might work for the magazine?

How could I resist? Or rather, how could *I* resist? A more prudent
biographer might have considered the possible consequences and
demurred. But despite considerable evidence to the contrary, I had
become accustomed to thinking of Bellow not only as a father figure
but as a father, whose unconditional love—or at least forgiveness—I
could count on no matter what I did.

So it was that in the summer "reading issue" of June 26 and July 3,
1995, a selection of entries from my journals appeared, accompanied
by a drawing of a skeptical-looking Bellow, his "biographer" peering around the edge of the frame. It was titled "The Shadow in the
Garden"—Bellow's description of the biographer. Of course, that, too,
turned out to be slightly off; I later discovered, in reading through my
journals, that the biographer was "the shadow of the tombstone in the
garden"—not as poetic but perhaps even more unsettling. The tombstone was the biography.

And the biographer was the gravedigger. I had life-giving impulses,
too—a love of Bellow's work, a love of my craft, a wish to commemo-
rate a great American writer by telling his story—but I seemed to be
in an awful hurry to bury the person I was raising up. Had it been
prudent to describe as a "difficult, prickly character" in the pages of
The New Yorker someone who was no character at all, but a flesh-and-
blood man who would read those words in his wicker rocking chair on
the front porch and think: *Oi.* On the Monday it came out, I opened
the magazine in a state of excitement and dread. It was a great issue,

with contributions from Philip Roth, Martin Amis, and Paul Theroux, among other literary heroes of mine. There is a Yiddish expression: *Gottenyu.* Dear God.

That August, after a period of agonized waiting, I called up Bellow in the hope of arranging our yearly visit in the country. It had been two months since my tactical blunder, and I was hoping, absurdly, that he had once again forgiven me. Besides, calling was the only honorable course: not to call would have been a tacit acknowledgment of wrongdoing.

Bellow answered the phone himself. His voice sounded strong.

"Hello, Mr. Bellow," I said, my own voice—not without reason—timid. "This is Jim [not James today] Atlas."

"Hello, Mr. Bellow," he replied—a slip so complex, so *nuts*, that I could scarcely believe my ears. It's one thing for the biographer to identify with his subject to the point where he feels as if he *is* his subject. But for the subject to confuse himself with his biographer . . . Now we not only wore the same railroad cap; we were the same person.

"Well, I'm in Vermont," I said, "and I thought I would give you a call, see how you're doing, and whether I might come and see you." Usually I wasn't so nervous, but this time I could barely stammer out the words. Why didn't I just say: *So what did you think of my journals?*

"I've had health problems," he said shortly. *Uh-oh.*

"Yes, I know," I broke in, eager to demonstrate my familiarity with every aspect of his life, "but people who've seen you at Marlboro"—the summer classical music program at Marlboro College, just a few miles from his house—"say you look well."

"I may look well, but it's like a jukebox: all aglow on the outside, but full of complicated machinery on the inside. Also, I'm trying to finish a book, and I've had heavy teaching responsibilities at BU. So I really don't see where I would have the time." *What did you expect, idiot?*

"As you wish," I said in a chastened voice.

"It's not as I wish, it's the way I am," he answered sharply. *And as my biographer, you should know that.* After an unnervingly long pause, he continued: "I'll tell you a story: A wise man is asked, 'What is the difference between ignorance and indifference?' He answers: 'I don't know and I don't care.'"

I laugh. "I'll write that down and think about it."

"You do that."

"I wish you well," I said, hoping to convey an apology without apologizing. *Accept the consequences of your acts.*

I hung up, shaken. This time I had really done it.

I never missed a Bellow reading at the 92nd Street Y, and my heart gladdened when I read in *The New York Times* that he would be appearing in October.

I had heard that the house was sold out, and I congratulated myself on having ordered my ticket early, as was my custom. When I arrived, I spotted a friend in the lobby. He asked me if I was with anyone. "No," I said. "I'm just a lone fan." He, too, was alone. Going to hear Bellow wasn't a social event: it was an act of witness.

Rust Hills, the crusty fiction editor of *Esquire*, introduced Bellow. "It's a wonder there are any awards left," he joked. "Why doesn't he give some back?" Then he turned earnest: "I don't just mean that at eighty he's still here. That's swell. But I mean longevity. Every decade, because of him, the canon of American literature grows."

When Bellow emerged from behind the curtain, the applause was thunderous and sustained. He looked well. His face showed few new lines; his hair was white but still there. He wore a conservative gray suit. I was struck, once again, by how handsome he was. I could see why women—Evelyn Stone notwithstanding—fell for him.

"This is an extremely large audience," he said, peering out at the sea of fans. It was an older crowd, verging on the geriatric, but there were lots of younger people, too, in their thirties and forties. Bellow was read now by a new generation; he still had the goods.

"My first thought is, 'What if I were to close the doors of the hall and perform a Vivaldi concerto on the recorder? What a delicious torture!'"

He read from *The Bellarosa Connection*, a book I'd never been crazy about. The narrator, an elderly Jew who lives alone in a vast, lavishly furnished house in Philadelphia (why Philadelphia?), spends his days absorbed in the past and finds himself ruminating on a distant relative, Harry Fonstein, who was saved from the Holocaust by the Broadway impresario Billy Rose. The story had always struck me as contrived, but now, as Bellow read from his novella, a "late" book written when he was in his mid-seventies, I finally heard its pathos. It was a book about memory, "which is life itself," the unnamed narrator muses. He had put the people he most loved "in storage," "a mental warehouse" closed off from his true feelings. He had gotten it wrong. In a terrible dream, Fonstein comes to the realization that "the best he could do was not enough." "I was being shown—and I was aware of this in sleep—that I had made a mistake, a lifelong mistake: something wrong, false, now fully manifest."

After an hour of reading, his voice still strong though tinged with the hoarse octave of old age, Bellow said, "My strength is going here," and broke off. The applause was even louder this time.

The moment had come for the ritual of answering questions drawn from file cards that the ushers had handed out before the reading. Bellow leafed through the cards and paused at one he seemed to like: "What do you think of Mr. Atlas's biography?"°

Bellow gazed out at the audience and said, after a pause: "It's like being measured for your coffin. All kinds of shameful matters . . ." He trailed off.

Other questions followed, some self-written, I presumed, others from members of the audience. Did people still interest him at eighty? "Part of your business as a writer is to discover the fascination of people. You think they're perfectly ordinary, but they never are." On Delmore: was he the most brilliant person Bellow had ever known? "He wasn't the most brilliant. He was one of the most charming." On his own early works: "I feel an urge to cut them."

He told a funny story about Isaac Bashevis Singer. A friend of Bellow's had once picked up Singer at the airport for a reading, and Singer had asked him to pose a question that night about "the parallels between Singer's work and Chagall's."

Dutifully, Bellow's friend had stood up after the reading and asked: "Are there any parallels between your work and Chagall's?"

Singer: "What a stupid question."

A great roar of laughter erupted from the audience.

The next summer I waited until almost the end of August to call. I was scared. But I didn't want to leave our quarrel unresolved. Also, it seemed rude *not* to call. I looked forward to visiting Bellow

---

° Confirmation that Bellow wrote his own questions: no one else called me Mr. Atlas.

each summer ("to see your bubba," he said). As far as I could tell, he enjoyed it, too. At least sometimes.

It was Janis who answered: "This is Mrs. Bellow." She was friendly when I announced myself. "Hello, Jim Atlas," she said pertly, and asked me how my summer had been. I asked if I could "have a word with Mr. Bellow." I wouldn't have dreamed of calling him "Saul," even at this late date. Or ever.

"James Atlas," Bellow said, intoning my name—as if in calling me James, he was upgrading me, giving me respect. I felt a surge of gratitude.

I asked if I could come and see him, and though he sounded congenial, he put me off. "Janis's parents are coming, and I have three children and four grandchildren."

I was silent. He had often put me off, only to relent. Sure enough: "But maybe next week. I'm not good at remembering these things. Why don't you call me on Sunday?"

"Great," I murmured. "Fine."

Suddenly awkward, we muttered shy good-byes to each other—"like two boys making up after an argument in the locker room," Annie said when I recounted our conversation.

Significantly, I have no recollection of whether a subsequent meeting took place that summer, and no record of one. I was beginning to slip away from Bellow's influence, shrugging out of its once-tight bonds. I was deep into *my* Bellow now, asserting my freedom—the freedom that art grants the biographer to "kick around the facts," as Dwight had put it. Not to fabricate them, but to choose and order them in such a way that they create a likeness—a likeness that was mine. Foolishly and generously, out of kindness and vanity, innocence and egotism, Bellow had allowed me a glimpse of his many-selved character. For the better part of a decade, I had observed and made notes. The data had been collected. That work was done. Ahead lay the harder work: making sense of it.

Rosenfeld, Freifeld, and Glotzer

XXV

I was sitting at my desk one morning, working on my book, when the phone rang. It was Alfred Kazin—"Alfred," he said. My heart quickened. (Though now nearing fifty, I still couldn't call Kazin by his first name.) When I was a child growing up in Chicago, my parents had taken me downtown to see the Bolshoi Ballet: there was an act where two caped wrestlers grappled with each other until the cape was thrown off to reveal that we had been watching a master contortionist and there was only one. That was my relationship with the New York (Jewish) intellectuals.

Kazin and I had quarreled, often bitterly, but a strong bond held us together: my literary and emotional involvement in his work, and the pleasure he derived from it. He approached literature not as a job or career but as a vocation. His books on American literature—the only subject that interested him—are less critical assessments of the canon than celebrations of it, hymns to the greatness of Melville and Hawthorne and Dreiser, the "big" writers who had taken as their theme the nation's boundless immensity, its physical and spiritual largeness, its implacable grandeur, and above all, its capacity for intensifying our experience of life in all its infinite possibility. *Big* was one of Kazin's favorite words: he was always at work on a "big" book, never just a book. The scale of his ambition was large. The titles themselves—*The American Procession, Bright Book of Life, A Lifetime Burning in Every Moment*—give a sense of his tireless and urgent quest to make literature matter.

This dedication had come through powerfully in a letter he wrote me years earlier, when I was working as an editor at the *Times Book Review*. I had written asking him to review a book, and he had replied from Indiana, where he was teaching at Notre Dame:

The winter is so peculiarly harsh here (yesterday coming back from a lecture at Washington U in St. Louis it was "minus 12" and minus is just le mot juste) that I am torn between gratitude for having a chance to work from dawn to midnight on my big book, certain characters like H. Adams and E. Dickinson etc. etc. between the two great wars—1865-1915—and a feeling of total emptiness, unreality. New York may be awful in many ways but at least people talk there. . . .

Since my favorite character in history is A. Lincoln, who detested vindictiveness, I have to admit that I forgot long ago about your article° and have long wanted to clear up certain things. But having also a highly Jewish sense of the absurd, I cannot help laughing at the contrast of my "apparatchik" self in South Bend, Ind., the land-bound icebound frozen and already numb and numbskull capital of nothing, with New York and especially New York Times Book Review, where the railroad men direct and redirect the switches that make it possible for certain prominent books to come roaring down the rails. Man, that is power! Or is it? But I never wanted to be on any magazine or review.

Now, on the phone, Kazin sounded as shy as I felt. *The New York Review of Books* had asked him to review Bellow's new novel, *The Actual,* which he "didn't like," but it occurred to him that it would be "a natural tie-in" with my biography. When was it coming out? "I'm dying to read it." I was chilled by his choice of words. I'd heard that he had cancer—now he alluded to it himself. "I'm sure you've done a wonderful job, but I'm not going to be around that much longer." Could I at least send him a few chapters?

"I'm writing as fast I can," I assured him, "but there's just so much stuff."

"I'd appreciate it," he said humbly. "Sorry to bother you. It was nice to talk to you." A shudder of grief coursed through me as I hung up the phone. How time wastes everything in its path! I wanted Kazin to read the book, but I was afraid—I wasn't sure I was ready to have my

---

° In my callow literary youth, I had insanely referred to him in *The New York Times* as a "culture *apparatchik*"—as if I even knew what the word meant.

work-in-progress commented upon by one of the most important literary critics in America. Then again, he might have liked it.

I would never know. A year later he was dead.

Others were eager to see the book for the same reason: time was running out. Bellow's old Chicago friend Al Glotzer had written me: "I shall soon be 88 but I'm hanging on till you finish your biog. on Saul simply because I want to read it and who knows, the Cubs [Chicago's famously hapless baseball team] might take it all, or just a division title."* But he was dying of lung cancer. "I know you are basically finished with the book, I know there are corrections, additions, deletions, sculpturing the syntax and so on, but is there not some light at the end of the tunnel saying the book will appear on such and such a date? You understand now why I ask."

I did, Al. But he, too, died before the book was done.

B ellow's portrait was beginning to darken, like a negative exposed to light. Even his friends had unkind things to say. Their testimony was often harsh, and they didn't seem to care if it was on the record. His Tuley classmate Sam Freifeld told a reporter for *Newsweek* that Bellow was "a great writer but a lousy friend."[†] And I had a disagreeable interview with Mel Tumin, a professor of sociology at Princeton who had been a member of the Tuley crowd. Tumin was hostile; he dwelled on his recent gallbladder operation, disparaged biography ("There's no such thing as truth"), and assured me that Bellow's girlfriends at the University of Chicago "weren't pretty." He was no fan of Bellow's work:

---

* He would have had to live until the age of 108.
† Of course you could write a whole book about their relationship (you could write a whole book about anything) and not get to the bottom of it. Freifeld's worst offense, apparently, was to warn Bellow against underestimating his income in one of his divorces—advice Bellow disregarded, almost ending up in jail. For Freifeld's trouble, Bellow depicted him in *Humboldt's Gift* as a chiseling lawyer with "a broad can, Roman nose, and mutton-chop whiskers." The point being: Is any quote fair? Isn't the truth of every utterance compromised by the circumstances in which it was uttered? The history behind it? The unconscious animus that shades its expression? Saul Bellow may have been a lousy friend to Sam Freifeld, but at what stage in their lives and why? They had been friends at Tuley High School, members of the Russian Literary Society that met at a hot dog stand on Division. Saul Bellow was a lousy friend when Freifeld was being interviewed by a reporter from *Newsweek*. Had he been a better friend in their hot dog–stand days?

"I fell asleep reading his books." And he was no fan of Bellow the man either: "I don't like him."

Tumin was only one witness out of the two hundred or so I interviewed. Clearly his ill-tempered testimony was unreliable, but at least he had made his position clear. What about the others? What if they hadn't stated their feelings so bluntly? How would I know how to "read" them? I sorted my interlocutors into categories: "likes," "dislikes," "admires but dislikes," "loves," "hates," "loves *and* hates," and so on. It was a highly imprecise system, but it helped to organize the storm of random feelings that pelted me from every side as I went about my research.

That I was writing a biography of a living person was beginning to give me doubts. It wouldn't be the final word, for one thing, and it might cause embarrassment to people in the book—including the subject, who would live to see himself depicted as a philandering misogynist, and the author, who would be scolded for providing the evidence. There were times when I wondered if knowing Bellow in the flesh offered any advantage. "If a man has not supped with his subject, he cannot know him well enough to write his biography," proclaimed Dr. Johnson. Was he right? I had never met Delmore, but I was floundering with Bellow, whom I had supped with on more than one occasion. Somehow knowing him was proving a hindrance to understanding him. I had conducted many hours of interviews, but instead of bringing my subject closer, they had distanced him from me. It was as if his own huge personality was getting in the way, obscuring my sightlines. He loomed over me like one of those carved wooden bears you see at the entrance to national parks, casting his giant shadow. The bear who doesn't go with me . . .

Then there was the matter of our relationship. Bellow protected himself by subterfuges—fidgeting, laughing insincerely, displaying unfelt modesty, grimacing when he had meant to smile, losing his temper, raising his voice, pretending not to hear. Being human: in other words, impossible to understand. It would have been fine if I had been writing a memoir, but I was writing an "objective" biography, and Bellow wouldn't sit still. Biography, he once said, was "a spectre viewed by a spectre." And here we were, two ghosts invisible to each other: one determined to see, the other equally determined not to be seen. The blind misleading the blind.

"I will make the record in my own way," says Augie March. So would

I. And if it turned out to be a little tough at times, well, what could I do about that? Bellow had said his job was to study the clover flowers; mine was to study him. And as Augie noted, "in the end there isn't any way to disguise the nature of the knocks by acoustical work on the door or gloving the knuckles."

Saul Bellow

XXVI

It was August 1998, time for my annual summer visit to Bellow. For some reason—he wanted to make it short? to get out of the house?—he had asked me to meet him in Wilmington, the little town a few miles from his house. Wilmington isn't a picturesque Vermont village, though it has its charms: a bookstore, tchotchke shops, and a white-pillared hotel with wicker rocking chairs on the porch. We had agreed to meet at a bar called Poncho's Wreck, and I arrived there promptly at two, only to discover that it didn't open until four.

I was apprehensive about the meeting. *The New Yorker* was planning to run an excerpt from my book, and it was all about Jack Ludwig's affair with Sondra. Why would Bellow want to be reminded of that ignominious episode in his life? The very one that had—or so he claimed—made him resist a biography in the first place?

When he pulled up in his dark green Range Rover, I pointed out that Poncho's Wreck was closed, adding, "It looks a little rough, even for Chicago boys." (I briefly wondered if it was presumptuous to link myself with Bellow in this way, but he didn't seem to mind.) We agreed upon a restaurant whose name I can't recall despite trolling through Yelp and TripAdvisor; anyway, it would have had a different name in that pre-gentrification era. (It wasn't the Cask & Kiln or Harriman's Farm to Table: that much I know.)

The restaurant was empty. The chairs were vinyl upholstered, and the red carpet was threadbare—just the kind of place Bellow liked. We sat down at a table by the window, and he tossed a manila envelope containing my latest "submissions" onto the table. "I don't have any problem with this," he said.

The only letter he declined to initial was one written in his twenties to his Tuley classmate Oscar Tarcov about a quarrel with his father at the family shop. Beneath it, Bellow had written: "No because it's so boring."

"Boring!" I protested. How could he say that? For one thing, this happened *sixty years ago*. And it was a moving letter: it showed the passion and intensity of their relationship, the young man's proud assertion of independence, the fierce conflict between his insistence on becoming a writer and his father's demand that he go into the family business. In fact, it said a lot about both of them; it was a precious snapshot of a father and son at odds but not grimly beyond reconciliation. When, sixteen years later, Bellow published *The Adventures of Augie March* to great acclaim, his father Abram wrote him a *kvelling* letter in the best Jewish tradition of paternal pride. So what if they'd had an argument? Shouting at each other was what fathers and sons did (especially businessmen fathers and literary sons).

I was mildly annoyed; by this time I was spoiled by Bellow's genial concurrence with my quotations from his letters. But I was also touched: he'd given me permission—incredibly, I sometimes thought—to quote letters from his girlfriends, his enemies, his enemies who thought of themselves as friends, his friends to whom he confided about his children, his financial chicanery, his literary feuds, even his infidelities— but not this innocuous document. I tried to argue him out of it, but nothing doing. I guess he still had "dad" issues, even at eighty-two.*

In April 2000, six months before the publication of my book, Brent Staples, my colleague at *The New York Times* who had written about his non-encounters with Bellow in Hyde Park, published a piece on the editorial page about my collaboration with Edward Shils, describing the thirty-one-page single-spaced memo Shils had written me shortly before his death. "I sat at a keyboard with this memo, communing with a dead man," I had told Brent, as always failing to be on my guard.

Like Dwight, Shils had become emotionally involved with my book out of powerful feelings for an estranged friend, intellectual curiosity, devotion to the Great Ideas, and a wish to keep thinking and working in his health-dampened last days. All this was in Brent's piece, but its last line struck an unexpectedly sinister chord: "We have known for

---

* He must have relaxed in the end, because I quote from the letter at length in my biography.

half a century what Mr. Bellow thinks of Mr. Shils.° Come the biography, perhaps we can glimpse, at least after a fashion, what Mr. Shils thinks of him."

What fresh tzimmes was this? As far as I was concerned, Brent's piece was about Shils and Bellow: What had Shils thought of Bellow? What had Bellow thought of Shils? It was a fascinating question, and my book addressed it from both sides. Brent made it sound as if Shils were rising up out of his grave to avenge himself on his former friend, poised to plunge his green felt-tip pen, like a dagger, into Bellow's heart.

Bellow was apoplectic over Brent's piece, as I learned when his agent called me the morning it appeared. It was the last straw; he'd had enough of this biographer; he would rescind permission to quote from his papers.

I immediately sat down and wrote him an apologetic letter, explaining that I had asked Shils to walk me through the historical issues and people I had written about in the book—to do what Dwight had done for *Delmore*: "I sized up Shils as a guy who would say exactly what he thought about my work-in-progress, and that's exactly what he did." I added that I had put in that Bellow had tried to see Shils on his deathbed and been turned away—an act that showed him in a highly favorable light.

Amazingly, he got over it. Bellow's grudges, which could last a lifetime, were for some reason—fear? indifference?—of short duration with me. I sometimes wondered if he forgave me so easily out of reluctance to pick a fight with his biographer.

I am putting the finishing touches on my biography (having a little trouble writing the last chapter, as you can imagine)," I wrote Bel-

---

° Bellow's literary portraits of Shils had soured considerably since *Mr. Sammler's Planet*, in which he was depicted as a worldly and world-weary refugee from the ruins of postwar Europe, a deep-thinking polymath at home with the whole of Western culture. In *Humboldt's Gift*, in the person of Professor Richard Durnwald, he was still imposing, "one of the most learned people on earth," and a decent character, "cranky" but "kind." By *Ravelstein*, Bellow's last book, Shils would metamorphose into Rakhmiel Kogon, an eminent sociologist and closeted gay (there was no evidence whatever for this in Shils's own life), "a dangerous person, ruddy, with a red-eyed scowl and a face in which the anger muscles were highly developed."

low early in the summer of 2000. "Every time I come up with a good ending, some new and remarkable event transpires in your life." First there was the baby, Naomi Rose, born just before Christmas 1999— new life, but a heavy responsibility for a man of Bellow's years. This momentous event would receive only a passing mention in my book: should I lean over the infant's crib with my notebook in hand, recording each mewl and puke?

I worried that he had taken on too much, but he still had lots of energy, and his capacity for provoking uproars was as robust as ever. In the spring of 2000, he published *Ravelstein*, a slender novella about Allan Bloom. Basing a character in his work on a real-life figure was nothing new for Bellow; it was the revelation that the charismatic professor Ravelstein "liked pretty boys" and appeared to be dying of AIDS that got him into serious trouble. As Bloom's acolytes saw it, Bellow had "outed" his dear friend.

Bellow insisted that Bloom had urged him to write an honest book, but he also admitted to "a feeling" that Bloom might have minded his candor.° In any event, the fallout was heavy—though I was glad to see there were still critics around capable of recognizing *Ravelstein* for the great book it was, especially when you considered that its author was eighty-five years old.† For me, it was a vindication of biography as a literary form that could attract the greatest writers of fiction—even those who questioned its legitimacy. The book was in essence a brief life on the model of Johnson's *Lives*—Bellow mentioned it as a source and constructed his portrait of Bloom out of what Boswell called "the minute details of daily life," the specific features that bring a person before us in all of his contradictions and complexity. "If these are left out of my account of his life we'll see only his eccentricities or foibles,

---

° I was stunned to learn from Zachary Leader's biography that Bellow had claimed my own eagerness to out Bloom as a defense for doing so himself. In a letter to Clifford Orwin, a disciple of Bloom's, he explained that his biographer ("James Atlas") "would have liked nothing better than to break the story of Allan's illness to a public of scandal-consumers." ALLAN BLOOM DEAD OF AIDS—*read all about it.*

† I can't think of a major novelist who accomplished anything important at that age, or even close to it, except Thomas Mann, whose expanded version of *The Confessions of Felix Krull* was published after his death; and even in that case an earlier version had appeared a quarter of a century earlier in a collection of short stories. As for becoming a father at eighty-five, I had to search the Internet to find someone who had beaten Bellow's record: a ninety-six-year-old Indian farmer named Ramajit Raghav. ("I do it three or four times a night.")

his lavish, screwy purchases, his furnishings, his vanities, his gags, his laugh-paroxysms, the *marche militaire* he did as he crossed the quadrangle in his huge fur-lined coat of luxurious leather." Here were the minute details—in spades.*

One afternoon that same summer, we sat around the kitchen table in Vermont, papers spread out before us, like two real estate brokers closing a deal. I just needed permission for two last items: a letter to a girlfriend, written in 1947, in which Bellow tried to extricate himself from their affair; and a lengthy quotation from a random note (he seldom kept a journal) that I'd found among his papers. I prized it for its candor; in just over a hundred words, Bellow provided a portrait of his character—a difficulty establishing emotional connections "because of attachment to something in childhood"; an inability to accept the responsibilities of parenthood ("a brother rather than a father to the children"); and most revealing of all, a revelation of how much his struggle to become a writer had cost him: "And the great fatigue of a struggle of 50 years. Feel it in my arms, in the very fists." There was also a note of self-forgiveness in this frank appraisal of his failings: "Miraculous to have accomplished so much in the world while in such bondage."

It *was* miraculous; Bellow had worked so hard against himself that the magnitude of his achievements as a writer was all the more impressive. He had often sabotaged his genius—the multiple marriages and general chaos of his life exacted a high toll—but he had just as often persisted. He let me quote the whole thing. On the matter of the off-putting love letter, he demurred, at least for the moment, on the grounds that "the context [had] vanished." (In the end, he allowed it.)

Bellow said a benediction in Hebrew—I didn't understand it but was embarrassed to let on. Then he asked me what I'd learned over the last ten years.

I quoted Herzog's axiom—identifying the source in case he didn't remember—"Each man has his batch of poems." It worried me a little to recite this phrase, which could have been construed as suggesting that Bellow repeated himself. (Also, I'd searched through the book the

---

* The detail that sticks most vividly in my mind from Bloom's last years is described by Bellow in his eulogy. As he lay dying, a saleswoman from Loeber Motors called him at the hospital to discuss the details of the Mercedes he had ordered. Did Bloom want a CD player? Gray upholstery or black?

night before and hadn't been able to find it.) I'd learned something else, too: "That you can never really know another person, no matter how hard you try."*

"That will do," Bellow said. Meaning: *That's enough to justify your labors.* Or, if said in a stern voice, which it might have been but I don't think was: *That's enough out of you, young* [not so young] *man*.

I t would be our last encounter.†
     We had agreed to meet at the Vermont House in Wilmington. I was standing out front when Bellow drove up.

"Punctual as usual," he said with a smile.

We sat in the back room. Bellow ordered Sprite, and I ordered a Coke. I handed him a present I'd bought at Austin's Antiquarian Books down the street: a fine old edition of Blake's *Songs of Innocence and Experience.* Blake was one of Bellow's favorite poets: for many years he carried around a copy of *The Portable Blake*, and he had once confided to his friend Richard Stern that he'd had in mind the lion imagery of "Little Girl Lost" when he was writing *Henderson the Rain King.* He looked pleased.

He still wasn't going to let me quote from his high school poem, but he gave permission for all the letters, signing the bottom of each page with his initials: SB. He didn't want to grant permission for me to use the family photos: "I've given it a good deal of thought. It would mean I was authorizing the book, and I don't know what's in there."

He hadn't read the excerpt in *The New Yorker.* "I make it a point not to read about myself," he said. "I find myself boring. That's why I write fiction." He was proud of the newsletter that he and Keith Botsford, who had been his co-editor on *The Noble Savage*, put out on an irregular schedule; it had only four hundred subscribers, but Bellow preferred it that way: at least they were loyal.

He talked for a while about the death of American culture: no one read books, no one cared about classical music. We were inundated with pointless information—"crisis chatter." I'd heard it all before, but

---

* "Never say you know the last word about any human heart," warned Henry James.
† Dwight Garner, in his review of Leader's biography in the *Times*, wrote that Bellow "lost faith in Mr. Atlas and stopped co-operating with him before the book was published." Whether he'd lost faith in me or not, he co-operated right up to the end.

it didn't matter. I sat and listened, like the little dog with his ear to the phonograph speaker.

Our hour was up. Like a psychiatrist, I kept track of the time; I was always nervous about keeping Bellow too long, even when he seemed to be enjoying himself. Afraid of counter-transference?

The bill came to $3.30. Bellow reached for the check, but I got there first. "Now we're going to have a fight about who pays," I said. He gave a brief laugh.

Before we parted, he told me, for what must have been the third or fourth time over the decade-long course of our conversations, the joke about the soprano in the opera house, where the raucous audience cries *ancora!* until the exhausted singer can sing no longer. Finally someone cries out, "You're going to sing it until you get it right!"

This time, though, Bellow added, "One of the great tragedies of human life is that you have to get off the stage before you've gotten it right, and leave those cracked notes lingering forever."

Lou Reed

XXVII

W hen is this book of yours coming out?" Bellow wrote me a few weeks before publication day. "I feel as if I should go off to Yemen." When Ruth Miller's biography was on the verge of publication, he had expressed a wish to disappear into "a remote part of Madagascar." In the end, he would stay put.

As for me, I had already returned from my exotic travels: it had taken me eleven years to write my biography of Bellow, and now I was at the mercy of critics who would spend a few days—if I was lucky—reading it and writing their reviews under the pressure of a deadline. Even more irritating, they would pass off my research as their knowledge; I used to do it all the time in my youthful days as a critic.

Things started off with a bang. John Leonard, in the crucial *New York Times Book Review*, gave the book a rave—or what I thought was a rave. Heralded by a black and white photograph of the Bellow family in Montreal on the cover, it occupied two whole pages within and showed, as always with Leonard, a tremendous depth of learning casually displayed. It was also very funny: "If you know Bellow and aren't dead, Atlas will have talked to you. If you had an opinion but bought the farm, he's read your diaries, your F.B.I. dossier and maybe your genome." Friends wrote to congratulate me on "a dream review," "a spectacular review," one that amply rewarded my long labor. It was one of the happiest days of my life.

The critical honeymoon didn't last. A phrase from Leonard's review—"wary disapproval"—should have put me on alert; he was describing my general attitude toward my subject. Then there was this arresting sentence toward the end, after an ecstatic riff on his love of Bellow's prose: "Atlas must have felt the same way before he began this long journey into knowing too much." Yes, I thought: *If only I could have preserved that innocence of early discovery.*

Then it all blew up. Flames of rage engulfed my book. Reading the splenetic reviews,° I thought of something Carlyle had written:

> The English biographer has long felt that if in writing a man's biography anything appears that could possibly offend any man, he had written wrong. The plain consequence was that, properly speaking, no biography whatever could be produced. No man lives without jostling and being jostled; in all ways, he has to elbow his way through the world, giving and receiving offence.

My subject had done both, but so had I, and I would have to pay.

However hurtful the critical lashings, the misery they caused me was insignificant compared to my own self-review. Had I disparaged Bellow's intellectual pretensions? Was I as hostile to my subject as my critics claimed? Had I gone on too much about the women? Whenever I walked past the shelf in my living room where my book stood wedged between Deirdre Bair's *Beckett* and Fred Kaplan's *Carlyle,* I winced at its thick spine, its presence as malign as the heart of the old man, murdered by the narrator in Poe's "The Tell-Tale Heart," that beats loudly beneath the floorboards: "Dissemble no more! I admit the deed!"

One day I sat down with a stack of yellow Post-its and went through my book page by page, marking the places where I felt I had gotten it wrong—not in fact but in tone, a thing much harder to get right. I referred to these as the Twelve Errors. (The number has a canonical sound, but that's how many I discovered.) Some were ungenerous assertions: "Bellow wasn't a nurturing person—to students, children, wives, or parents. *He* wanted the nurturing." Others were snotty: "Writers who posed a threat to Bellow's hegemony got the cold shoulder." A few were judgmental, the worst sin of all: "In Bellow's self-serving and sanctimonious account . . ." How I longed to edit these sentences. Like the pockmarks from a medieval ague, they would disfigure me forever, unsalved by the ointment of self-knowledge.

Over the years, I would take the book down from the shelf and study these Post-its, curled and faded by time, revisiting the outbursts of spite that had occasioned them; every few years, in a fit of charity to myself, I would peel one off, convinced that my sharp criticism had been right after all. That Bellow "wasn't a nurturing person" was a fact,

---

° There were also many positive ones, but who remembers those?

however unpleasant to a sympathetic reader or critic or family member of Bellow it might be. I had also written: "As he grew older, the bones of a deeply conservative, xenophobic vision of life emerged more clearly." Eventually the Post-it identifying this sentence was removed, along with several others ("Leave before you're left," "The genius and the self-regard are of a piece"), on the grounds that they were true. By the end, only six Post-its remained, marking statements too neurotic and small-minded to be forgiven, even by their author. ("For admirers, the busy novelist had plenty of time.") Subsequent efforts to further reduce their number have proved of no avail.

I pick up the phone, and the voice on the other end of the line says: "Is this James Atlas? It's Elizabeth Pollet."

It is 2008, and thirty-one years have passed since the publication of *Delmore*. Why is his widow—one of his widows; the first wife, Gertrude Buckman, must almost certainly be dead*—calling me? Her voice is faint, enfeebled . . . the voice of an old woman.† She must be . . . I do a rapid calculation, biographer's math: nine years younger than Delmore, 1913 + 9, b. 1922 would make her . . . eighty-six. She had been just over fifty when I interviewed her at Westbeth, the artists' residence in the West Village. She was beautiful then, blond and blue-eyed—"like an airline stewardess," a friend recalled.

I greet her in a friendly way, but I have no idea why she's calling. "I just read the biography," she says.

Why did she wait so long? "I couldn't bring myself to read it until now." She liked it, she tells me. I really captured Delmore. She learned a lot.

"He was my first love. I devoted fourteen years of my life to him. I had twenty years of the best relationship I ever had until my partner died a year ago." Wait: What does the "twenty years" refer to? Is she telling me about someone else? Her most recent—probably her last—relationship? And what does she mean by "partner"? Her late husband? Or did they never marry? Or could it be that she was gay?

---

* If not when I was writing this passage, then surely by now, unless I were to come across her photograph in one of those morning TV shows that celebrate the birthdays of centenarians.
† Am I being "ageist" here? Listening to myself on our answering machine, I'm disheartened by my own "old-man" voice.

Elizabeth has a grievance. (Who doesn't?) "I felt you didn't make an effort to talk to me. You only came once."

"Maybe I was shy," I venture. I often was in those days with my subjects' wives and girlfriends. What right did I have to ask all these questions?

"You're wrong to say I was living in a state of siege. . . . I didn't take the car. . . . I was more worried about the cat than about Delmore. . . ."

I've stopped listening. "I'm fifty-nine," I say. "I'm not going to correct the record."

A year later I hear from a friend of hers that she's dead.

I am not done with Delmore.

A letter arrives in the mail.

The writer identifies herself as Trina Doerfler, and she . . . but let her explain:

> My biological father was Delmore Schwartz and I was conceived in 1956 while Delmore was married to Elizabeth Pollet. My mother, Eleanor Goff, married my stepfather Walter Doerfler when she was seven months pregnant with me and he raised me as his own. Out of respect for him and a desire to remain out of the spotlight, I have not come forward until now.

A physician in Seattle, Trina had—as everyone does—a story. She was "coming out of the closet" in midlife because her fifteen-year-old daughter, gifted like her grandfather, had aspirations to be a writer. "I am looking for her to connect to her lineage, at least the part of this one that has lent her the gifts she demonstrates in writing."

I knew some of the story. We had met. After a lecture, a young woman had approached, and the unmistakable apparition of Delmore's face, with its sensuous eyes and lips, its faintly Slavic features, a face I had never seen but instantly recognized, loomed up out of the crowd. She had introduced herself as Delmore's daughter.

I wrote her back, recalling our encounter, only to discover that Trina had no memory of it. She did have other memories:

> I can tell you that your book came out while I was studying dance at Brooklyn College in Flatbush, and had the extraordinary expe-

rience of seeing for the first time pictures of my grandparents, Rose and Harry, in your book, while sitting on the steps of Brooklyn College, a stone's throw away from where it was all lived. It was an extraordinary moment and that book was the family album for me for that side of the family.

"There is but one notation in Delmore's journals in the spring of 1956 that mentions me," she continued. "'Baby this summer,' and there is a mysterious dedication in a poem of that last book to little Katherine Schwartz, dated 1961. My given name was Katherine. I believe that poem also has a line in it, 'Where is my father and Eleanor?'"

Trina was still on a quest: "I met Delmore's brother Kenneth in Los Altos, California, in 1986 or so, but we lost touch and I understand he died in 1993. I am looking for Albert Schwartz, who I believe to be a cousin, and who may be living in Seattle, lecturing on theosophy." Albert Schwartz? Who? And theosophy? I could have introduced him to Bellow. If you find Albert, let me know. Actually, don't.

Trina's daughter sounded like a remarkable person. "She wrote a novella for her eighth grade project last year based on Entanglement, a principle of quantum physics and surely human psychology as well."

They would be coming to New York that summer, Trina informed me. Would it be possible for us to meet?

I was excited by the prospect, but I never heard from her again.

Another day a letter arrives in the mail from a person named Jerome Weinberger: he's writing in regard to Delmore's grave plot. I had contributed a hundred dollars toward its maintenance, and Mr. Weinberger is bringing the account up to date:

Mr. James Atlas $100.00
Mr. Saul Bellow $300.00
Mr. Lou Reed $300.00
Mr. Jerome Weinberger $495.00
Perpetual Care Trust Fund—Cedar Park Cemetery
Westwood, New Jersey
Block 36, Line G, Grave 18
Emes Wozedek
C 34483 T12

Estimate for Perpetual Care
Endowment: $1,200
Plant Taxes: $300.00
Seasonal Care: $385.00

I was in good company: not only Bellow, who had fixed Delmore forever in the pantheon of great characters in literature, but Lou Reed, founder of the Velvet Underground, the gritty Lower East Side band that was such a defining presence in the 1960s. Reed had been a student of Delmore's at Syracuse.* How cool was that? The endowment must be long gone now, as are two of its benefactors—if not three. I never did find out anything more about Mr. Weinberger except what I learned from his letterhead: that he lived at 15 East Ninth Street, apartment 18M, and had two phone numbers, work and home/fax. But I'm grateful for his ministrations to Delmore. I wonder if Mr. Weinberger, if he *is* alive, continues to pay the "seasonal care" fee, or if the grave has gone to seed, tufts of tall grass growing over the stone. And what about Emes Wozedek—is *he* still alive? And if so, is he still the grave tender at Cedar Park Cemetery? Or does Mr. Wozedek have a grave tender of his own?

B*ellow,* too, elicited correspondence and the occasional phone call long after my book had disappeared from the shelves.

I heard from a contemporary of his, Olga Adler Titelbaum, who, like Bellow, had once been a writer for *Encyclopaedia Britannica.* Over several closely argued paragraphs, she rehearsed her grievances against this apparently heartless bureaucratic project (which eventually "terminated" her): "I resent (as Bellows [*sic*] would have done) the fact that text written by me stands in many EB articles without an iota of credit to me." Furthermore, she informed me with the kind of tedious precision that often attends recounting of wrongs, however long ago committed: "I reviewed and edited all language, culture, and ethnolinguistic articles to resolve any discrepancies between maps and texts." "I rewrote . . ." "I compiled a list of queries . . ." And yet! "My

---

* Why did I never interview Lou Reed? What a missed opportunity: a rock star in the 1960s, the height of my own rock'n'roll–obsessed youth. Too late now—the refrain of old age.

name appears in the EB list of credits only in the 1974 volume, and even then, my maiden name (which is part of my identity) is not given. It's not right." I agree, Mrs. Titelbaum. Life isn't fair. But what can I do about it? I'm Saul Bellow's biographer, not a member of the editorial board of *Encyclopaedia Britannica* half a century ago. Go complain to them. (But of course, you can't, which is why you're writing to me.)

From time to time, I would be ambushed by a critic who, like a soldier stumbling out of the jungle, didn't know the war was over. One was Steven Zipperstein, the biographer of Isaac Rosenfeld, who charged me in the *Jewish Review of Books* with reducing Bellow to "a crabbed man, as vain as a movie star and as promiscuous as an alley cat." I was incensed. Look, Steve, I lectured him in my head, we all do this kind of thing, we're all capable of treachery; but say I *did* depict Bellow that way (and I don't think I did): you still couldn't have written your book without me. I'm the one who salvaged Rosenfeld's papers! Don't be a jerk.

But then, life being the unaccountably strange experience it is, I rise from my desk, where I've been tinkering with this passage (would "Grow up" be less harsh than "Don't be a jerk"?) to go hear a reading by Philip Roth at the 92nd Street Y, only to find myself seated next to . . . Zipperstein! I refuse to shake hands and say to a woman seated beside him, who I presume is his wife (no alley cat he), "Steve did a bad thing: he took a swipe at me after I saved Rosenfeld's papers." Zipperstein seems flustered and says, "Let's not talk about that now. We have other things to talk about." And we did: Roth, Bellow, brief biographies (he was the editor of a series called Jewish Lives). Let it go: I was too old for these feuds. He gave me his card, and we parted friends, or at least not enemies.

There were also periodic phone calls from a woman who'd had an affair with Bellow in the 1940s and wanted "to catch up"—we had Bellow in common. One time she launched into a confession about an affair she'd had while married to her husband, who had died the year before. She had never told anyone about it. *But I'm only interested in your affair with my subject,* I felt like saying—*not your affairs in general. What is your adultery to me?* All the same, I listened. For a biographer, there is no such thing as retirement.

One of the most poignant letters was from a woman who had known Isaac Rosenfeld's son George; she had been in his seventh-grade class at a school in the Village:

When I think of him now, I see him as he was at 13: smart, curious, perceptive, humane. I see him living on Barrow Street with his mother and sister, surrounded always by books, music, and animals, especially reptiles. All vibrant . . . Since I will never learn the answers from him, I must ask: what branch of medicine did he study? Did he get married/have kids? Did he remain close with his mother and sister? Did music continue to be a joyful thread in his life?

By the answers I hope to be reassured that he did not die of a broken heart.

I couldn't say. But in the literal sense, he did. George died of a heart attack in 1994, at the age of forty-eight—a decade older than his father had been when he dropped dead in his cheerless (or not) apartment on East Huron Street.

XXVIII

A dam Bellow and I had kept up. One day about a decade after my book was published, I got an e-mail from him suggesting lunch.

It was a sunny summer day, and I didn't recognize him at first when he came through the door. He was heavier than I remembered—not the young man he'd been when we first met—but handsome like his dad. Those eyes! I could only imagine how old I must have looked to him—a round-faced, white-haired man of sixty-two.

We sat down, and I made a little joke, calling him "lad." His face crinkled, and I recognized with shock the same expression I had studied for so many years, passed on to the next generation through the miracle of genetics. Sometimes it was a nose, a chin, a mouth. Adam had gotten the whole face.

Since Bellow's death in 2005, Adam had grown more estranged than ever from his father's world. Philip Roth had walked right by him on the street: "I was stunned. What had I done?" He recalled in a wistful voice the time when he had spotted Roth and the Israeli writer Aharon Appelfeld in the window of the Éclair Bakery on West 72nd Street, and Roth had beckoned him to join them. "I remember thinking, 'This is good.' Now I've been cut out of the story. It's as if I don't exist."

He told me about his father's funeral. It was at the cemetery in Marlboro, Vermont, not far from Bellow's summer home. His three sons were there, and Janis with Rosy, and Bellow's old friends; not many were left by this time. "The literary crowd"—Martin Amis and Leon Wieseltier and the critic James Wood—"sat off by themselves. They had closed ranks." When Adam tried to approach Philip Roth, Roth waved him away: "He was off by himself in his pain."

Adam referred me to Roth's account of the nameless protagonist's

Bellow and his boys

funeral in *Everyman*. "You weren't there," he said, clarifying my absence in his mind. A strange thought: how could I have been there, given the way things had turned out? That wasn't how Adam saw it: as far as he was concerned, I was the Biographer, not the Enemy.

It had been hard for the boys, Adam told me. "Greg threw a handful of dirt on the grave and said, 'Rest easy, Pops.' I couldn't lift the shovel. I was numb and overcome with an emotion I couldn't even explain to myself until I figured out it was rage."[*]

A few weeks after the funeral, Adam and his younger brother, Dan, had driven up to the Vermont house in a U-Haul to collect Bellow's old rolltop desk, which he'd bequeathed to Dan.[†] Bellow's lawyer, Walter Pozen,[‡] had greeted them, explaining that Janis was upstairs; Adam had to ask to see her. She came down and sat in the kitchen and explained that she was "taking time off" and didn't want to correspond or talk with the boys for a while. Then she excused herself and went back upstairs.

Adam's original bequest was five hundred books, but the will had been changed—as he had discovered when a revised version came in the mail. When he wandered into his father's library to take a final look around, Pozen rushed in after him as if he were worried that Adam was about to steal a book. "Yes, it's too bad," Pozen said. But he was still reluctant to leave Adam alone. As he was leaving, Adam asked Pozen if Janis would be willing to send him a recorder of Bellow's—"one of the older ones, worn smooth and oiled by his fingers and lips over many years of playing." Six months later a "newish" model came in the mail, "along with a pair of Saul's glasses—broken!"[§]

---

[*] When I got home, I looked up the passage from *Everyman*. It was virtually the same as Adam's description, except for Roth's attribution to the son of a lack of feeling for his father: "'Sleep easy, Pop,' Randy said, but any note of tenderness, grief, love, or loss was terrifyingly absent from his voice." I doubt that was how Greg felt. On the other hand, I reminded myself, Roth had written a novel, not a memoir. Randy didn't have to feel the way Greg felt.

[†] Advertisement in *The New York Review of Books*, February 16th, 2016: "FOR SALE: Saul Bellow's Desk $10,000 mahogany roll top, leather writing surface, pigeonholes. Part of the furniture of his house, appears in book jacket photo."

[‡] Known in the family as "Walter Poison."

[§] "Apparently these objects were too numinous to part with," Adam wrote me: "Which is of course exactly why I wanted one."

He wasn't even allowed access to letters from his father, which he had turned over to the Regenstein. "Not that he wrote that many," Adam said ruefully. "They were mostly postcards: 'This is a castle.'" He noted bitterly that his father had played the boys off against each other. "He would tell each of us that we were his favorite son. He never liked having us all together. He feared us, like old Karamazov."

Adam told me an amazing story. He had been invited to speak before a conference of psychoanalysts in Boston about what it was like to be the son of a famous man. Joining him on the panel was the daughter of the psychologist Erik Erikson and the daughter of Supreme Court justice Harry Blackmun, "who went on and on about how little time her father had for her, but it didn't matter because 'Roe v. Wade was for all women.'" When it was Adam's turn, he told the eager crowd that he hadn't prepared anything. "So I'll just wing it."

Then, to his own astonishment, he declared: "I have two things to say: I'm glad he's dead and fuck you. You all have father issues or you wouldn't be here." There was a stunned silence, followed, after a long pause, by a roar of laughter. The joke was on them, but it was funny anyway.

We laughed until tears came to our eyes. "Back went the head, down came the lids, up went his chin, and there it was," as Amis once described Bellow's laugh. Adam had it, too.

I had listened to his account with mesmeric attention. It was a part of the story I knew nothing about—Bellow's life after the publication of my biography, Adam's life after Bellow's death. The story I'd missed. The sequel. The end and the post-end.

Now, still agonized after a decade, I poured out my doubts about my book. I'd been unfair to his father; I'd gotten it wrong. I told Adam about the twelve Post-its I'd attached to pages in the Modern Library edition to indicate where I'd been snippy or unkind. I could have fixed the whole thing in three hours.

"I never felt like I knew him," I said to Adam. "I never felt that I *got* him."

"You got him," Adam said firmly. "You have to own your book. It's part of you." I fought off an impulse to ask Adam what his father had thought of my book. I didn't want to know—and anyway, I probably *did* know. Sammler: "Both knowing and not knowing—one of the more frequent human arrangements."

Out on the street, we shook hands, awkward but connected in some deep way. I recalled my encounter with Adam and Dan after Bellow's last reading at the Y. I'd seen them standing in the aisle and was weighing the possibility of trying to slip past when Adam called out: "It's the last brother!"*

My eyes filled with tears. Only this time they weren't from laughing. "It's the eternal same story," Dr. Tamkin says to Tommy Wilhelm, trying to comfort him after Wilhelm recounts an argument he's just had with his father: "The elemental conflict of parent and child. It won't end, ever. Even with a fine old gentleman like your dad."

And he wasn't even my dad.

Two years later I get an invitation to attend a memorial service for Adam's mother, Sasha, who has died at the age of eighty-one. I met her only once, when I interviewed her for my book; it's out of feelings for Adam that I decide to go.

The service is held in a nondescript modern church with redbrick walls and shiny pews and a linoleum floor. It's a good turnout, maybe just over a hundred. Adam spots me when I come in and seems glad to see me. I walk over and shake hands. He looks handsome, with that fine-boned Bellow face, relaxed and confident. Greg is also there, dressed in an olive-green corduroy suit; his walrus mustache makes him look like Mark Twain.

Adam reads a fine eulogy, recalling his mother's hardships raising him on Long Island. Divorced at twenty-nine, she had no money and couldn't pay the phone bill; she supported them by going into the city to write abstracts for an engineering journal. She designed jewelry that she sold at the crafts fair on Columbus Avenue. She didn't want her son to be deprived of culture. She dragged him all over Europe to see every church, every painting, every monument; stuffed books down his throat; made him learn Hebrew and French. Adam reads from a story Sasha wrote on his old high school typewriter about a woman, eclipsed by her movie star husband, who has an urge to lie down on the street. It's very well written. She doesn't lie down.

Afterward we go down to the basement for a Zabar's spread of cold

---

* A reference to Joe McGinnis's biography of Ted Kennedy, *The Last Brother.*

cuts and a big birthday cake. This would have been Sasha's eighty-second birthday.

I see Maggie Simmons, and we embrace. Maggie maintained a close relationship with Bellow for half a century and was, according to many, the love of his life. With her short cropped hair and big teeth, she's still beautiful, a stunner with blue eyes and golden hair and "the sort of face you might have seen on a Conestoga wagon a century ago."

I learn at the funeral that Adam is working on two books, including one about the evolution of his politics. Greg tells me he has written a memoir of his father. "Bloomsbury is going to publish it. I just said what I had to say, without notes—I wanted him to be seen as a human being."

"I thought I did that," I say.

"No, but not as a biographer. It's called *Saul Bellow's Heart.* You'll enjoy it, though I take you to task once or twice. I thought you got carried away by your admiration for Saul." Greg is irate about the edition of Bellow's letters that has just come out: they can still hurt people, including him. "Why does he get to have the only version?" He tells me that the villainous cuckolder Jack Ludwig is, incredibly, still alive. Zach Leader, the new biographer, interviewed him. "He's a digger," says Greg.

The idea of this biographer interviewing Ludwig claws at my heart.[*] Why hadn't I made an effort to track him down? Had it been some unconscious reluctance to meet a figure so crucial to the story? The person Bellow conjured up in *Herzog* was more real than the person I would have interviewed. How could any corporeal being compare in vividness, in the sheer power of being, with the imaginary one?

Whenever I thought about all the people I hadn't interviewed, I was gripped by a maddening sensation of incompleteness. Ludwig, the family in Cincinnati, people in Israel, the secretary he saw every day, for God's sake! I'd had research fatigue. The new collection of Bellow's letters introduced names that were unfamiliar to me. Who was Sam Hammersmark (the owner of a bookshop on the Northwest

---

[*] A year later I learn that Leader *hadn't* interviewed Ludwig. They had only exchanged e-mails, in the course of which Ludwig complained that I had "Swiftboated" him—as if a literary biographer with liberal politics left over from the 1960s could be mistaken for the angry veterans who sank John Kerry's presidential bid. It gave me an aura of military swagger that improved upon my self-image as a timid scholar groping, mole-like, among his books.

Side), or Ilya Konstantinovski, a Russian émigré novelist Bellow got to know in Paris? What about Bellow's uncle William, a brushmaker? (A *brushmaker?* What kind of profession was that?) And who knew what manuscripts were still out there? I had come across a reference somewhere to a novel called *Ruben Whitfield* that had vanished. And what about the "lost cache of *billets-doux*" written to Bellow's high school girlfriend Eleanor Fox?

You could never get it all down. The story would always remain unfinished. It was a hazard of the trade.

One day I came across a passage on the last page of Kohut's *The Analysis of the Self*: "Patient and analyst may, upon the termination of the treatment, share in the acknowledgment of the fact that the analysis itself has of necessity remained incomplete." His words struck me with tremendous force. Biography, like analysis, remains incomplete; the subject, like the patient, remains unknown. I was reminded of a passage in *Herzog*: "The dream of man's heart, however much we may distrust and resent it, is that life may complete itself in significant pattern." Isn't that the biographer's dream? To find the pattern in a life, even if it isn't there?

W hose life was it, anyway? It's not only money that the survivors of the deceased fight over, not only the silver and the Steinway piano. The emotional legacy—who was loved the most—is just as hotly contested. What could be more valuable than knowing you had a special bond, that you were the one? The dead can no longer love us, but we can imagine that they do—and for a biographer, everyone who loved your subject has a different story to tell.

Bellow had three sons: Greg, Adam, and Dan.

He also had three disciples: James Wood, Leon Wieseltier, and Martin Amis. These three were—I won't say pseudo-sons, because their affection for Bellow was so deep as to be almost filial—but surrogate- or substitute- or perhaps alter-sons, whose love was uncomplicated by anger and the unruly demands of hereditary sons. Easier to choose your sons than to deal with the ones you have.

Eight years after Bellow's death, in 2013, Greg published the memoir of his father that he had told me about at Sasha's funeral. *Saul Bellow's Heart* is a raw book in which the oldest son accuses his father of neglect, emotional manipulation, and other kinds of parental malfeasance even as he tries (with some success) to forgive him. His purpose, writes Bellow *fils*, is "to reassess my patrimony as a writer's son, and to have my say."

Born in 1944, Greg was the progeny of what was sometimes called in intellectual circles in those days "the first wife"—the one who lived through the early stages of a writer's career and set up a bourgeois household that eventually became suffocating and ended in divorce. This was the kind of home Greg grew up in—though his mother, Anita, was herself a person with a formidable intellect and drive.

His parents divorced in 1952, producing the usual heartache of a broken home. "I was lonely, sad, and now a latchkey kid living with a depressed mother," he wrote. Saul was an absent father. When he picked up Greg for a visit to the Museum of Modern Art, "he was often late and sometimes did not show up at all."

Yet there was another side to the story. Greg claims in the book that his father was his "best friend," and I believe him: "Saul understood my black moods because he had so many of them, and because he felt responsible for my sadness." Sometimes, when he wasn't being a friend, he acted like a parent. When Anita died, Bellow tried to comfort his sobbing son: "Come to Chicago. Your loving father will be waiting." They fought the way only fathers and sons can fight: stubbornly, needily, and with a sense, not always acknowledged or even understood, that their consanguinity was the source of their bond.

When we write about the dead, we imagine that we're mourning them, and often we are, but just as often we're doing other things, too: asserting our place in the narrative; dictating the way we would like the subject to be depicted; dictating the way *we* would like to be depicted. As usual, it's all about us. Greg's complaints about his father's prolonged absences sounded a bit whiny at times, but the memoir was poignant; you feel that his aching need for a father will never go away.

Adam, too, had his struggles with his father's legacy. "Missing: My Father," published on the editorial page of *The New York Times* two months after his father died, gave a sense of how *he* saw their connection. Like his siblings, Adam had "a fond but highly attenuated bond with a frequently distracted, often absent, and much older father," "a father who was never there"—even when he was. They rarely spent holidays or family vacations together. "He just sat up there like Wotan on his mountain, in Vermont, or in his aerie overlooking Lake Michigan, and I made pilgrimages by bus or car or plane." Still, they had a bond. Bellow, "though absent," was "deeply, unpredictably, stubbornly present" through the agency of his son. To nip and tuck Wordsworth's celebrated line, the man is father to himself.

Not long after the appearance of Greg's memoir, James Wood, a member of the "other," nonconsanguineous brotherhood, published a curiously harsh review of it in *The New Yorker*. Wood read the book as "angry," "a child's complaint" that "displays an unconscious hostility toward his father's writing." It was "a migraine of unreliability," "a fake narrative of psychic closure." "He seems to struggle with resentment at the very idea of Saul Bellow's having an independent literary existence; which is to say that he finds it hard to credit that his father was a writer at all."

At least Wood was up-front about his partisanship: he mentioned that he had co-taught a course with Bellow at Boston University. And if you looked back to a tribute in *The New Republic* Wood had written eight years earlier, just after Bellow's death, it emerged that they had been close friends: their daughters had played together; Wood and Bellow had played piano (Wood) and recorder (Bellow) duets. And they grew still closer toward the end: "In the final year of Bellow's life, as he became very frail, I would read some of his own prose to him." I was envious. How lucky for Wood that he could appreciate Bellow without having to judge him.

Leon Wieseltier, writing in the same issue, recalled a summer afternoon in 1977: "We were sunk in Adirondack chairs on the grass behind the shed of a house that he was renting in Vermont, and sunk also in a sympathetic discussion of Owen Barfield's theories of consciousness." Barfield, a knotty British philosopher whose work Bellow admired, caused even the intellectually agile Wieseltier to balk; it was a relief to be brought back to the world of literature. "Soon it was twilight. For a beautiful hour we sat before the fire and Saul read from the 'Zetland' manuscript"—the novel about Isaac Rosenfeld—"which was again in his typewriter." Thus does another son step forward to claim the right to call Bellow "Saul."

I'm just being spiteful: Wieseltier had earned his familiarity. Bellow's long letters to this most enthusiastic of disciples validate his claim: "It made me happy to see you." "We have a good deal to tell each other." And they did: they corresponded about "that superior Krautess" Hannah Arendt, Israeli politics, the Holocaust, and other weighty topics. I recognized the Bellow described in Wieseltier's tribute, a charmer "with melancholy eyes, except when they sparkled," and "a recreational savager of pieties."

The most famous "son" was Martin Amis, who met Bellow in 1983, when *The Observer* sent him to Chicago to interview his literary hero on the publication of *The Dean's December*. Their affinity was instant and would last, with growing intimacy, until Bellow's death in 2005. On Amis's part, the disposition toward friendship was already there. "Bellow has made his experience reverberate more than any living writer," he would write in *The Observer*.

But it wasn't just about the books. Amis also had father issues, as he freely acknowledged—not that you would have had to look far to find them on your own. Both Martin and his father, Kingsley, who enjoyed a reputation as England's major novelist until his son entered the scene, made public acknowledgment of Amis senior's dismissive attitude toward the novels of Amis junior. Kingsley was "suspicious" of his work, Martin confirmed with admirable docility in his *Paris Review* interview, while claiming that his father had once flung *Money*—one of Amis's best books—across the room.

We all need fathers, and it was natural for Amis to fix upon Bellow as a substitute for the defective one he had. Here was a great novelist who would return his affection and appreciate his books without ambivalence. And just as Amis loved Bellow like a father, Bellow loved Amis like a son. The day Amis's father died, he called Bellow and said, "You'll have to be my father now." Bellow replied: "Well, I love you very much." Theirs was no ordinary friendship.

Amis visited Bellow in Vermont and Boston; accompanied him to a conference on Bellow's work in Jerusalem, where they had their first "nonprofessional" encounter, tea on a rooftop overlooking the city; and talked regularly on the phone. (A footnote in Amis's Bellow-heavy memoir, *Experience*, reports: "Today—10/6/99—is the author's eighty-fourth birthday. He is due a call.")

That there were other, "real" sons in the picture wasn't lost on Amis, and he wasn't insensitive to the jockeying for position: "I mustn't encroach on the territory occupied by Gregory, Adam, and Daniel." But he did, despite his best intentions; they all did.

I, too, had wanted to be a son—only to discover the spot was taken by several others.° Anyway, I was the biographer—assigned to be objective. Like the designated driver, I needed to have a clear head.

At his father's funeral, listening to the literary troika deliver its tributes, Greg thinks to himself: "What is it with all these filial narratives? Did they all have such lousy fathers that they needed to co-opt mine?" As the three brothers drove away, he recalls in *Saul Bellow's Heart,* he asked Dan how many sons he thought were in attendance. Dan's answer, literally correct, was three. "I disagreed, feeling that almost everyone there considered him—or herself to be one of Saul's children."

I was moved by Greg's indignant cry, which expressed the thwarted longings, the desperate competition for attention, the anguish of unmet needs that torment the forsaken son: "After all, he was *my* father!" That's what you think.

One day Greg calls up out of the blue and invites me to lunch. He's friendly but states his agenda: he wants to talk about his father. We meet at an outdoor café in Chelsea. Greg's resemblance to his father is eerie: he has Bellow's eyes, his voice, even his taciturnity.

He tells me about his children. He's visiting his granddaughter; his daughter is a professor of art history. He's a psychiatric social worker living in a suburb of San Francisco, just retired after forty years. He's become obsessed with biography and has just read James Breslin's book on Rothko—I tell him that Breslin had invited me out to Berkeley for a conference a few months before he died of a heart attack at the age of sixty. It turns out that his widow is in Greg's book group.

At this point, my biography has been out for over a decade, but I *still* don't know how to refer to Bellow. "I'll call him Saul," I say boldly, "something I could never do in his lifetime." Sometimes Greg calls him Bellow. Sometimes I call him "your father" or "your dad." It's not a good sign that even now I can't resolve this nomenclatural issue.

Greg thanks me for having given an accurate and sympathetic depiction of his mother. I apparently described Anita as "the 'real' wife"—I

° Let's say I was an *honorary* son. "Jim wrote the book as if he were a son," Adam told a friend, who reported it to me. A son who could neither idealize the father nor win his approval. A bad son.

have no memory of this, but I can see that it was important to him. His feelings toward his father are clearly more conflicted. "My father wanted me to do what he said, the way his father was with him. I had a bad time in Stockholm, when Bellow won the Nobel. I didn't want to be part of that world. My feeling was, 'Fuck that. I'm not going to put up with this shit.'" Wow. The anger is still there.

Greg has two questions: What was it like for me to write my book? And what happened afterward? I try to be succinct, though I could go on for as long as Mr. Memory in *The 39 Steps*. I describe my regrets about the Twelve Errors (since narrowed down, you'll recall, to six); my wish that I'd written more about the books and less about the women; and the fear that I was too much of a scold and should have given Bellow a pass on his promiscuity. "I never bought into the idea that genius exempts you from playing by the rules."

"He made up his own rules," Greg says. Then, mildly alarmed by my anguished outpouring: "I didn't mean to stir this all up."

"You didn't stir anything up," I assure him. "I've thought about it for years."

Greg mentions an angry letter he wrote to "Saul" when he was an adolescent. "I didn't see that," I say. "Yes, you did," he reproaches me. "You quoted from it." I feel foolish. I can't even remember what's in my own book.

I ask about Janis and the estate. She, too, has claims on Bellow's posthumous affections. She is "ungenerous," Greg says, confirming that the boys have been denied access to the archive at the University of Chicago. He has written Bellow's agent, who didn't reply. "They're stonewalling me."

Greg *has* stirred things up. After he leaves, I go back to my office and sit at my desk for a long time. In the end, my "overt" biography, for all the Chicago connections I shared with my subject—the schools and old neighborhoods and family friends—camouflaged a profound disparity between us.° While I was ambling through the Dinosaur Hall at the Museum of Natural History with my children, Bellow was off

---

° Would a biographer who was gay or a woman or who had a divorce or two under the belt have told Bellow's story differently? Probably, if they wished to write his story at all. Maybe the author's note should be more transparent—not *James Boswell is a barrister and a regular contributor to* European Review; but *James Boswell is a sot, a frequenter of prostitutes, a terrible husband and father, and a man with a strong inclination to worship famous men.* This way the reader could be on the lookout for bias.

somewhere* writing the beautiful stories in *Something to Remember Me By*. His work was the center of his life, which makes sense: he was a genius, and geniuses don't have unlimited time. "How, really, could the drama of paternity have competed with the drama of creativity?" asked Wood. For Bellow, "The writing *was* the living." But couldn't he have put his work at the center of his life and still left some room around the edges for others? I could never understand Bellow's almost boastful confession that he had "turned into a beast" when he was writing *The Dean's December*. It's not even that good.

As the years passed and the number of Post-its in the pages of my *Bellow* dwindled, I began to realize that it wasn't the Twelve Errors that had made me dissatisfied with my book. And it wasn't anything that could have been fixed in three hours, as I had said to Adam Bellow. Maybe it could have been fixed if I'd written the book now, toward the end of my life, and known more about its capacity to wound. Maybe it could never have been fixed. The key to writing biography is the capacity to be empathic; Holmes's image of the biographer extending "a handshake" toward his subject stayed with me. At some point, without realizing it, I had withdrawn my hand.†

Why? Maybe I had failed to grasp the extent of Bellow's suffering—or he had failed to make it seem authentic. Despite the psychic misery he inflicted on himself with his multiple marriages and public provocations, Bellow enjoyed his life when he wasn't tearing it up. He told jokes, he wrote great books, he slept with a lot of women, he traveled and had friends; he received a tremendous amount of attention. (He said to the photographer of *Newsweek*'s cover story on him, "I can't get any famouser.") He made light of his anguish: "I am to suffering what Gary is to smoke."

And he did suffer. One has only to read the opening scene of *Herzog*, where "*that suffering joker*" lies on a sofa in his New York apartment and tries to take in the fact that his imperious wife, Madeleine, is divorcing him: "He dreaded the depths of feeling he would eventually have to face, when he could no longer call upon his eccentricities for relief." She makes her announcement while Herzog is putting up a storm window. I could only imagine how painful that moment must

---

* Not even the most assiduous biographer can keep track of his subject's whereabouts at every moment.

† Or was Bellow's grip on it so tight that I had to let go?

have been, whether it happened to Herzog or to Bellow, or to both. But hadn't that been my job? To imagine another's pain?

Anyway, it's not as if he got away with it. There was a lot of wear and tear. He was battered by alimony fights and operatic love affairs. As a father, he was a disaster. Even Janis, whose love for Bellow was unconditional, acknowledged in an interview after his death that "he failed his children; he left them, and it was a wound he carried around."

Of course, Bellow was famous as a writer, not as a father, and no biography should devalue a writer's achievement just because the writer's family has been thrown under the bus. His Nobel wouldn't have been rescinded if he fell behind on his child support payments. But did the greatness of the work mandate the censoring of the life? Could the biographer ignore the sexual adventures and misadventures that fueled Bellow's fiction and wreaked havoc on his domestic arrangements? They were crucial to the story.

I had never been able to convince myself that it was justifiable for Bellow to diminish his friends and family members by making them "material." When Dave Peltz reprimanded him for putting a story Peltz had told him in *Humboldt's Gift*, Bellow lectured him about the sanctity of the artist: "I should think it would touch you that I was moved to put a hand on your shoulder and wanted to remember you as I took off for the moon."

I remain unpersuaded by the casuistical argument put forward by James Wood: "The number of people hurt by Bellow is probably no more than could be counted on two hands, yet he has delighted and consoled and altered the lives of thousands of readers." Was I missing something in this creepy moral calculus? Was Wood suggesting that it was okay to hurt your own wives and friends and children in the service of literature? "Does the reader care that Dave Peltz was a little wounded?" I did. Dave was my friend.

As I sat there thinking about the sons, I realized that my disapproval and Wood's excuses were equally misplaced. It wasn't his job to defend Bellow any more than it was mine to judge him. The work and the lives that inspired it were intimately connected, but they could not be placed on the same balance sheet. Wood explained away his math as "an awkward but undeniable utilitarianism." Dwight would have called it a weasel.

XXIX

A decade or so after the publication of *Bellow*, there "came into my hands" a manuscript from which I would learn more about my subject than I had in all my years of tracking him down, puzzling over his work, both published and unpublished, reading his correspondence, studying his manuscripts and his books, and all the other labors that I undertook in my efforts to understand this man. It was a kind of epistolary memoir—letters back and forth, interspersed with commentary—by a woman from the Chicago area, a decade younger than Bellow, who had written him in 1956 to ask if she could show him a novel she had in the works.

The writer was a housewife in a midwestern university town, taking courses, doing the laundry, and trying to raise two young children while writing her novel. Her name was Bobby Markels. She had moved out to California in the 1960s and ended up in Mendocino, where she wrote a column for the local paper called "Babbling with Bubbeleh." She had been on my radar, but I had never managed to track her down.

Bellow was patient with Markels; he read the novel carefully, offered advice, and persuaded her that it was a thing worth doing. None of this prevented her from having a nervous breakdown. Her memoir of their relationship, one that would last for almost half a century, offered a more vivid portrait of Bellow than any I had ever read. (In later years, it was platonic, but they stayed in touch until the end.)

When they finally met, in New York, after corresponding for a year, Markels was excited: Bellow reminded her variously of someone who hung around pool halls, Humphrey Bogart, and "a Jewish shoe salesman." They talked awhile, then Bellow announced that "he had a friend in the loony bin (Delmore Schwartz) he had to go and see and he added, 'Why more people aren't there I'll never know.'"

Bobby Markels

Over the next year, they continued to write, Bellow from Yaddo and the White Elephant, his Victorian estate in Tivoli, New York; Markels from Chicago and Columbus, Ohio. He cautioned her against writing too much about herself: "This is the danger of the autobiographical element; it causes the nostrils to swell with infatuation."

Markels's description of Bellow lacked literary art but brought him to life: "Saul was not a large man physically but he was a huge presence—bright and overflowing with humor, gaiety, laughter, verbosity, intelligence and his energy, his aura, his psyche, whatever you want to call it, was tremendous." She recalled a dinner in Tivoli: "Saul dominated the whole evening; he was the captain of a ship stalled in harbor with the crew sitting around the table listening to his commands, his jokes, ribald laughter. . . . He loved having people around, he loved 'performing' for and with them but unlike a lot of egomaniacs he knew how to listen." He could be attentive, too:

I have heard many times that Saul was unkind to other writers. I have heard that he was not too great as a father, or a husband and I'm sure what I heard was correct. He was a Don Juan; a vain man who made serious mistakes and was often foolish. That he was brilliant, yes; a wonderful writer yes; disciplined, hardworking, yes—funny, yes—all that and more has been written about him and is certainly true. But when I look back I see that no matter how foolish my actions, how bizarre my letters, he never deserted or abandoned me—he was *there*—patient, generous, and kind. . . . Here was a man who never ceased growing, searching, loving and no matter how high he soared, kept in touch with old friends, old loves, old times and matters of the soul.

There was a vulnerability in Markels's portrait of Bellow that I hadn't encountered before, a longing for others' approval: "Though he often asked for sympathy, understanding, even pity, what he wanted more was approbation . . . that people should think he was right, had the right tie, suit, woman, shoes, briefcase, bottle of wine, to make him look good." His jauntiness concealed a darker side: "There was something about him that was sad. The natural state of his deep dark eyes—when he wasn't laughing—seemed to be not just looking in neutral but imploring. His face was deeply weathered; he had the look of an older man and when he was in repose there was something infinitely sad in him, wrecked and disappointed." *Wrecked.* Being Saul Bellow wasn't easy.

One of the most fascinating things about this newly discovered manuscript was its depiction of Bellow's sex life. It's not that Markels was explicit (although she was); it's that for the first time I *got* what made Bellow's experience in this department so difficult, so charged with failure and anxiety. He himself had once intimated to me that his therapeutic sessions with Dr. Ellis focused on the problem of *ejaculatio praecox* (Herzog's problem, too). Markels provided plenty of corroborative evidence. But her account of a memorable night they spent together awarded him high marks:

> It was wonderful. He was so *present,* he was so *there.* He was not a great lover; it was not great sex, whatever that means, but it didn't matter, it was of no consequence; for the first time we really kissed the way people do who are going to make love, who love and passionately want each other, all the time saying, "I love you. I love you so much," until finally we lay with our arms around one another and he kept saying, I love you and I kept saying I love you and then we fell asleep.

The next morning, as he was getting ready to go back to Sasha, Bellow started to cry. I found this disturbing. I'd never heard of Bellow crying before.

Markels had told me everything I needed to know—and more—about this aspect of Bellow's life and why it caused him so much anguish. Her manuscript validated my own sometimes maladroit speculations. And yet reading about their carnal activities made me uneasy. What if I had gotten my hands on it (or rather, it had come into my hands) while I was writing my book? The biographer is determined to know everything, but everything sometimes feels like too much. Boswell claimed of his *Life* that it would depict his subject "more completely than any man who has ever yet lived." But he also believed, as he wrote in his dedication to Sir Joshua Reynolds, that "the whole truth is not always to be exposed."

The more I read about Bellow's grappling bouts with Markels, the more I began to see how desperate he was. In one frightening story, when Sasha announced that the marriage was over, he told her he had tried to kill himself. Saul Bellow a suicide? I couldn't think of anyone who loved life more.

Markels never stayed angry with Bellow for long. "He was Saul and that was the way he was." They were often quietly happy together, their lives in Tivoli out of a Seurat: "He painted [screens,] and I sat with the sun on my face filled with joy and admiration and love."

Bellow's own letters sound a rueful note. It "depresses" him to be apart from Markels; she is "dearer" to him than his own siblings; she should come to Tivoli: "Bring the kids, we'll raise lettuce and tomatoes." But was it Markels he needed, or just a love object? There was no "chemical rush," she noted. "Little did I know at that time that Saul didn't have to have a 'chemical attraction' at first play, or deep affection later. You had merely to be a woman and alive."

She had her needs, too, mostly literary, and often got her way: "*I wanted to be a writer*. That was my goal." Bellow gave in to her pestering requests: he referred her to his agent, submitted her book to his editor, and tried to get her published in *The Noble Savage*, while noting tartly that she had never asked him one thing about himself. He had his own problems. Two of his brothers—"the only ones I had"—had died within a month of each other. He'd gotten divorced again. "I seem to have a bad character—a character that demands a test, and then after a struggle fails." At the same time, he saw himself as a victim: "I didn't invent my faults. Many were inherited." He had a "disorder," he explained. "Do you think I want to *be* like this?"

Their last meeting, when both are deep in old age, is at the San Francisco airport. "We don't have much time and I want to tell you something," Bellow says. "All that sexual business. You had nothing to do with that. It was my fault. Not yours. It was my dysfunction. Not yours. There was nothing wrong with you. It was all me."

Her account of their last phone call made me laugh out loud:

He says something I wouldn't expect him to say—ever. I am almost 79 and he, what? 91? 92? [89, probably: he died just short of 90] and he uses a phrase so current, so hip, it charges through my mind like lightning and I am filled with the same spirit and energy and optimism that he poured into me years ago. He says, "You go, girl."

When I get to the last page of this incredible manuscript, I have an impulse to look up its author online. To my great shock, the first entry that comes up when I type in her name is: Roberta "Bobby" Markels Obituary. She had died, according to the *Fort Bragg Advocate-News,* "in the wee hours of Friday, Feb. 28, 2014," just two months earlier.

It's a well-written obit, full of interesting facts: she had grown up in a wealthy Chicago family, been a "wild" girl," was packed off to live with friends of her parents, been married and divorced, had an affair with Bellow, moved to Mendocino and bought a house for a thousand dollars that she made welcome to "an ever-shifting assortment of boarders, guests, pals, suitors, vagabonds and waifs." She was a Buddhist. She wrote a children's book called *I'm a Human Bean* and was at work on a novel called *The Seduction of Nony Stein* when she died. She suffered from a chronic autoimmune disorder called scleraderma. "She was annoyed at the prospect of approaching death,° but not at all afraid, and was serene and fully conscious in her last hours."

There's also an interview on a local TV show, *Senior Perspectives* (is there *anything* you can't find on the Internet?), in which Markels makes it clear that time is running out. "You have to clean up your bathroom shelves, clean out your closets," she tells her interviewer, an affable, white-bearded guy maybe a few years younger who's dressed in a blue warm-up jacket; he reminds me of my high school tennis coach. "I've got to get rid of everything," she says, including a book she's been working on for "forty or fifty years"—probably some version of the one I've just read.

How old is Markels at this point? I do the biographer's math—1926 to 2014. That would make her eighty-eight. She looks terrific: a well-coiffed head of brown/platinum hair, a long face, a strong jaw. She's wearing an elegant sea-green chemise. She's so charming, so *alive,* that I miss her without having known her. Though, having read her book, I feel as if I did.

On the show, Markels mentions Bellow only once, to note that he endorsed her book. This is about her.

° I liked the idea of being "annoyed" at the prospect of death, as if it were some minor nuisance to be waved away.

XXX

Not long after my biography of Delmore came out, I had received a letter from his dear friend William Barrett. "I wish you godspeed on your journey," Barrett wrote, "and may you safely avoid the shoals and reefs that wrecked your protagonist."

Looking back, I mostly have, though I ran aground a few times and nearly went under once. It turned out that in writing about Delmore forty years earlier, I had drawn on knowledge I didn't know I had. My own susceptibility to the biological and mental illnesses that destroyed him enabled me to understand Delmore better than I understood Bellow, whose afflictions, excruciating as they had been to him, seemed to me of a different and less extreme kind.

My collision with the shoals and reefs Barrett had warned me against occurred when I was in my mid-sixties and struggling not to drown in a cascade of career reversals. Depression seized me in its grip and wouldn't let go; it confirmed for me Leon Edel's observation that "an individual who hasn't been in the depths of depression has no conception of what depression means."

I was diagnosed with Delmore's main impairment, bipolarity, after a parade of psychiatrists had missed the symptoms, or in fairness, had understood them as temperamental or characterological, the fashion throughout almost the entire period during which I was under treatment—one that spanned, alas, given the expense and its lack of meliorative effect, close to five decades.[*] It wasn't until near the end of

---

[*] Excerpts from my journals of those years: "very sad; obsessive devastating feelings of isolation, of not-belonging, even of annihilation of self . . . happiness . . . mood dip . . . total melt-down . . . terrible tennis . . . great tennis . . . losing in tie-breaker with inept forehand . . . excellent day, writing, looking out the window at beautiful, fragile New York in the twilight . . . no friends . . . lots of friends . . . fun . . . fun! . . . strong day . . . paranoia . . . joy at the first bite of pesto risotto . . . sick of mind . . . happy on the porch

Delmore in Washington Square Park, 1961

the twentieth century that antidepressants came to the rescue. In my case, they helped, restoring me to what Freud called "normal unhappiness" and often happiness itself. Anyone who has experienced clinical depression will know what a gift this is.

There were times when I wondered if my obsession with biography had been unhealthy. Had I become Bellow's Humboldt, "gray stout sick dusty," eating a pretzel in the street? No, though I had the beginnings of a belly and sometimes wolfed down a hot dog from a cart, ashamed of my mustard-stained fingers as I shuffled up West 77th Street. *Gray?* It was closer to chalk white. *Sick?* Yes, if you caught me on a bad day, my face drawn and pinched with worry. *Dusty?* Maybe Humboldt had walked by a construction site. Even so, Bellow's description of Delmore was unnervingly familiar, and not just in the literary sense. I identified with this character, both the one Bellow had brought to life and the one who had lived, in a primal way. It wasn't a matter of *Delmore c'est moi.* I didn't have his talent, and I hadn't lived his life.* All the same, I *knew* him. The heavy bear who had gone with Delmore now went with me.

One day in the summer of 2006, I opened my Sunday *New York Times* to find a long article about the discovery of a diary from the 1930s recording "the life and times of a smart and headstrong New York teenager, a girl who loved Balzac, Central Park and male and female lovers with equal abandon." Her name was Florence Wolfson, and I had mentioned her in my book. Now the diary, recovered from a dumpster on the Upper West Side, had been edited by a reporter for *The New York Times* and published under the name of *The Red Leather Diary.*

At last I could find out who Florence Wolfson was, and why Delmore had ended up at her "salon," as the author referred to the group of young intellectuals who gathered at her parents' apartment on Riverside Drive. When the book appeared, I leafed through the photographs at Barnes & Noble and put it aside. It was disconcerting to read

---

as I looked out at the birds in the wet grass . . . I grabbed my own neck in anguish . . . suicidal ideation . . . the clarity of the city in the snow . . . came home tremulous, wired . . ." I was riding Delmore's "roller-coaster."

* I had a high-functioning family, a spacious sun-filled apartment on the Upper West Side, and a mantel crowded with photographs of the family on ski trips. Delmore never went to Stowe.

about Delmore's last meeting with his father, which Wolfson claimed had taken place with his brother in the rain in Times Square—how he "brushed against their father's sandpaper cheek in a good-bye kiss through the window of the cab, which took off into the night." Where did she get this rich material? But it was too late. Whatever I didn't know I didn't want to hear about now.

In 2004 New Directions issued a new edition of Delmore's stories with an introduction by Cynthia Ozick. Her knowledge of the poems and stories was thorough; she quoted at length, reminding us of what was great in Delmore, and she captured the pathos of "a catastrophic life—turbulent, demanding, importuning, drinking, pill-swallowing, competitive, suspicious, litigious." Ozick saved the bad news for last: "Delmore Schwartz, some* dare to say, is in eclipse. With the acceleration of the generations, his fame is long dimmed; the *Wunderkind* he once was is unremembered." Whoa. So the half-life of Delmore's reputation is less than thirty years? That's it? Without my knowing it, he had come and gone, a victim of our brief attention span and hunger for the new.

My own fixation on Delmore was weakening its hold. There were times when I missed him, though I no longer grieved for him—a crucial distinction, for it meant that he lived on in my memory if not in my heart. Even so, he continued to exert his ursine power.† Whenever I took my biography down from the shelf (which wasn't often), I felt a clutching sorrow. The copy I had was in Dorian Gray condition, the pages still white, the spine firm, the jacket unfaded and shiny. But Delmore was gone.‡

Or was he? One day I was walking across Washington Square in the weak sunshine of a late spring afternoon. As I strolled past the chess players at their concrete tables, the guitarists perched on the lip of the fountain, the couples hand in hand, my eye fell on the curved bench

---

* Who?

† His name shows up in the routine transactions of my daily life. My passwords include various iterations of Delmore; the name on my business credit card is Delmore Inc. (Bellow, too, has been put to this utilitarian use: bellow64, bellow65, Bellow66 . . . you can see where this is going.)

‡ Within is a publicity photograph of his twenty-eight-year-old biographer, a portrait of orthodontal disaster, sartorial innocence—cord suit, Trotsky glasses—and well-coiffed raven hair taken on his wedding day. Like Milton's Adam, he's at the beginning of his life: the world is all before him, where to choose. So he chooses to be a biographer . . .

where Delmore once sat in a rumpled suit, a cigarette gripped between thumb and finger, staring out with paranoid eyes at the terrible future, and for one electrifying instant, he was there: a corporeal presence, resurrected, *real*, the one I had been seeking for nearly four decades. A line of Delmore's flew into my head: "Calmly we walk through this April's day."

It was the title of a poem, I discovered when I got home and looked it up. Here are some lines:

What will become of you and me
(This is the school in which we learn . . .)
Besides the photo and the memory?
(. . . that time is the fire in which we burn.)

In a late journal, Delmore posed the question: "Why are people alive on earth?" The answer: "Because they are living and have not yet died."

And Dwight? He wasn't just dead, but more dead, receding further and further into the past. For a few years I had kept up with him—my savior with the red-felt-tip pen—but it wasn't the same. Our bond, the source of our friendship, had been Delmore, and once Dwight had discharged his obligations as Delmore's literary executor, we had less to talk about. Gradually we drifted apart, and by the time he died, I hadn't seen him in years.

Another Sunday morning I opened the *Book Review* to find an essay by James Wolcott that startled me: it was titled "Dwight Macdonald at 100." And there was a photo of Dwight with his omnipresent cigarette and billy goat beard—a dead centenarian. I still missed him, but I was glad he hadn't lived that long. I wouldn't have wanted to think of him in some nursing home where, forbidden alcohol and cigarettes, he spent his days thumbing through old *New Yorkers* with trembling hands. Wolcott's thesis—no doubt correct—was that Dwight had been scrubbed from the record, a victim of history's ruthless drive to obliterate from memory even the most vivid of our species: "Today, he and many of his concerns could hardly seem more dead." He'd had plenty of other problems, too, Wolcott reported: "For years before his death in 1982 from congestive heart failure, Macdonald had been battened down by booze, pressing doubt and writer's block; frustrated, fatigued and plagued by the feeling that he had failed to climb the masthead of his talent by writing a major, original work."* To a young woman who came up to him at a cocktail party and asked him what he "did," Macdonald replied with the stammer I remembered so well: "Well, I, I, I was a writer."

Edmund Wilson, too, had become a diminished figure in his last years. As early as the mid-1950s, he identified himself with "a half-obsolete group of survivors from the Victorian age." His later work is curmudgeonly to the point of self-parody; the journals of his sixties and seventies recount a desolate cycle of drink and depression, exacerbated by dwindling sexual powers. Wilson's lifelong quest for sexual adventure had a poignant source: he confided to Mary McCarthy that at the root of his trouble with women was his fear "of not being loved, which I have carried all my life from childhood." His biographer Jeffrey Meyers conjures up a dolorous image of Wilson in old age—"the dark defile," as he memorably called it—sitting on the toilet and reading old reviews of his books to boost his morale.†

Whenever I walk past Wilson's books on my shelf, the plump volumes lined up in a row, I think of how hard he found it to let go, despite a long life of suffering. In one of his last journal entries, he wrote: "I am glad to have had some share of the life of this planet." I feel that way, too, on a starry night in summer, when the fireflies blink on and off in the field, or watching dark water swirl beneath a covered bridge on the Walloomsac River. But not so often now.

Should I have written Wilson's biography? It would have been a propitious moment; he was recently dead but still important. His books were read by anyone who cared about literature. Today he's out of fashion. Writing his biography at this point would feel as archaic as composing a book on a Smith-Corona typewriter.

His time may come again. Each generation needs its own biography,

---

* This demand that one write a "big" book has caused untold misery in the lives of writers who wrote a few small books or none yet still had honorable careers.
† My own bathroom reading these days isn't old reviews of my books—I doubt they would boost my morale—but a weather-beaten copy of *Boswell in Holland*, its cover as warped as if it had been left out in the rain. After a decade of leafing through its mildewed pages, I'm never bored. "My Lord Marischal was most entertaining company, and the Turkish lady talked extremely well when indolence did not keep her in silence." We won't be hearing from her again. Yet Boswell incited her to speech.

argued Virginia Woolf. The "facts" need to be reinterpreted: "These facts are not like the facts of science—once discovered, always the same. They are subject to changes of opinion; opinions change as the times change." In the preface to his *Shelley,* Richard Holmes preemptively parried any objections that he might be going over familiar ground. Shelley's life had been well trod by scholars and by the poet's contemporaries, most notably his friend Edward John Trelawny (whose *Recollections of the Last Days of Shelley and Byron* Holmes dismissed, not unfairly, as "semi-fictionalized"). But these books belonged to another time, as did the musty volumes shrouded in what Holmes called "the penumbra of Victorian proprieties." Holmes carried the story forward by making Shelley real for *us.* His Shelley, he insisted, "stands there for anyone who has eyes to see, ears to hear, or heart to feel, sometimes so close that Shelley's life seems more a haunting than a history." It exists in the present, not in the past.

History is ever regenerative. New subjects arise as the old ones disappear—including people we never heard of. Virginia Woolf asked: "Is not anyone who has lived a life, and left a record of that life, worthy of biography—the failures as well as the successes, the humble as well as the illustrious?" What about all the people I've known who didn't leave records of their own lives? Don't they deserve biographies, too? Sing now of Scottie A., my best friend when I was growing up in Highland Park, Illinois, who built snow forts with me in the days when there was snow, and who died of cancer at the age of fifty-eight, which maybe wasn't such a terrible thing as he was about to be put on trial for securities fraud; of Mr. Gillespie, my seventh-grade Latin teacher at Nichols Junior High, who gazed at me with a doleful eye when I stumbled over my conjugations; of Susan M———, a blond, blue-eyed stunner who lived across the street from me and who I thought of when, years later, I encountered the much-revised sentence in *Ulysses* where Bloom gazes at some mannequins in the window of a department store ("Mutely he craved to adore"); and a hundred—a thousand—others. Who will write their biographies, or—the most common fate—will they remain unwritten about for all eternity? Biography, in the end, is a stay against death. Most of us don't get one.

One day I packed seventy-three biographies into a shopping cart and wheeled it down the street to HousingWorks, the thrift shop that donates its profits to AIDS research. I had been a judge for a biography award; books had landed with a sharp report on my doorstep several times a day for months, so many that even the closets were soon overwhelmed. It was a cold afternoon in January, the sky darkening at four o'clock, and as I trundled my cargo along the icy sidewalk like a homeless person pushing a shopping cart loaded with empty cans, I thought back to the days when I used to call up Fred Bass, the genial buyer at the Strand Bookstore, to alert him that I had a new cache of review copies. He was always glad to hear from me and would arrange a time for Dennis, his ponytailed driver, to come pick them up. The last time I'd called Fred, he had told me they were accepting only large collections. "It's not worth the time or the gas to go up there anymore." *Gas*: it seemed like such a trivial expense.

Spare me the elegies, right? The world is ever in flux, each generation forced to undergo its own obsolescence. I try to keep up and have learned to stab at the letters on my iPhone keyboard like a chicken pecking corn. (Let others employ their simian thumbs.) I read on a Kindle, adapting to "locations" instead of numbered pages, use search buttons instead of having the maddening but pleasurable experience of leafing through a book in search of a particular passage for half an hour, then stumbling upon it and being rewarded with a pop of dopamine.

But what about the "book"? Will it go the way of the gramophone, destined for a glass display case in the Smithsonian? And what does this looming disappearance into the dustbin of technology portend for biography? Its tools will be audio, video, and who knows what else. The questions biographers of my generation ask before embarking on a project—Are there letters? Where's the archive?—won't be the questions the next generation asks. The only archive will be the cloud.* And just as the means of depicting another person are transformed by technology, so will be our ways of interpreting the data we collect. What we see and hear will shape our portrait more than what we read.

Biography will survive, but not biography as we've known it. E-mail spells the end of written correspondence; the letter is dead.† Future biographers will scroll through "texts." (I never thought I'd see the

---

* Isn't there something now called Snapchat where the message just fades away? *Dear T. S. Eliot: It was with the greatest . . .*

† Never again the letter in the mail, the pulse-quickening experience of spotting a hand-addressed envelope among the bills and flyers.

day when that sacrosanct noun would become a verb.) The interview where you sit across from your subject with your notebook on your knee will be supplanted by the interview conducted on Skype. Human character will be assessed by new criteria: How does the subject perform on camera? Is he graceful? Articulate? What about the timbre of his voice? His sartorial style? And who will "write" these books? The new generation of biographers will include filmmakers, multimedia artists, and oral/visual historians—a profession that doesn't even exist yet—who produce biographies assembled from podcasts and documentary clips. Biographers will continue to determine who gets to live awhile in the evanescent ether of posterity and who dies in obscurity, unbiographed and unknown. It's just their tools that will be different. And I won't have to learn how to use them.

Phew.

I sit in my study and contemplate the stacks of biographies strewn about the room. The shelves long since full, I've taken to piling them up on the floor. I've read most (a lot?) of these books, some several times, but I like to hold them in my hand and turn the pages. Here is Harold Nicolson's *The Development of English Biography*, published by the Hogarth Press, the imprint founded by Leonard and Virginia Woolf. Bound in dark blue cloth, it's compact, its dimensions barely larger than a postcard; copious notes fill the blank front pages: "70 first use of the word 'biography'"; "**79 biography as 'creative literature'"; "87 Boswell 'invented' actuality." And here's a beat-up old book published by Doubleday, Doran & Co. in a series called the Master Classics; it's an anthology of passages from Boswell, Macaulay's *Byron*, Carlyle's *Dante*, and others, also heavily annotated. Macaulay's *Life of Johnson* (1928) is equipped with "Study Helps and Questions" for students: "If Boswell 'could not reason, had no wit, no humor, no eloquence,' why is it that his writings 'are likely to be read as long as English exists, either as a living or a dead language'?" For once I was sorry I wasn't taking an exam: I could have nailed this one.

Not all my books are antiquarian: I'm excited to come across a galley of volume two of Holmes's *Coleridge*. Clearly unread (its spine is uncreased, and my last note, "weird unsparing exactitude," is on page 14), it now induces in me a kind of hypnotic attention right from the first page, in which the poet watches "the lights of England recede along the Cornish coast through the brass porthole above his narrow berth" as he sets sail for Malta.°

In his afterword, Holmes muses on the contradictions that shadow his monumental undertaking. "Coleridge's life continues in one's head, and mixes with the sounds of one's own existence, and starts up again somewhere else in other hands with a different interpretation," he writes. "This is the peculiar music of biography, haunting and uniquely *life-like* for a moment, but always incomplete and unsatisfactory and sending out many echoes into the future." *Incomplete and unsatisfactory*: yet Holmes devotes his life to the effort.

When Delmore was seventeen, he wrote a strange epistemological treatise called "Having Snow"; its theme was "the attempt to know." His intent was to explore "the existence of objects which do not preserve their identity, for even as we form an idea of what they are they are becoming something else." Isn't this what the biographer does? Delmore assigned his friends "grades of permanence"; some lingered in his mind longer than others. In the same way, our subjects elude the porous net of facts we cast over them; they shape-shift over time, and so do we. I had devoted my life to an art whose assumptions couldn't be tested. Still, its rewards could be great—the challenge of reconstructing someone else's world; the opportunity to educate yourself; the serendipitous encounters and unlikely finds. I found this invigorating. You could never hope to get it right: even Holmes said so. But if, over many years, you worked very hard and extended your hand, you could write a book that earned a high degree of permanence.

One day as I'm walking up West 79th Street, I pass the apartment building I first lived in when I came to New York in the fall of 1977—forty years ago, I calculate as I stop by the front door and peer into the lobby. What was the doorman's name? Albert. What has happened to Albert? Where is he now? He had a weathered-looking face, as I recall, and thinning cottony hair; his skin was lacquered like an old

---

° It reminds me of the passage in *Lord Jim* where the young sailor on the deck of a ship bound for the East watches "the big ships departing, the broad-beamed ferries constantly on the move, the little boats floating far below his feet, with the hazy splendor of the sea in the distance, and the hope of a stirring life in the world of adventure."

wooden floor. Let's say he was sixty: that would make him ninety-eight. Take off a decade, and he's still pretty old. But what if by chance he's still alive? Where would I find him? Not by publishing one of those letters from biographers that appear in *The New York Review of Books*: *I am at work on a book that features someone named Albert who was a doorman at 147 West 79th Street in the 1970s* . . . I wonder if he'd be a good subject.

My encounter with the ghost of Albert reminded me that my own archive wasn't in order—a shameful situation for a biographer. The painful but fascinating adventure of life would soon draw to a close, whether in two years or twenty. (Bellow's description of death: "The pictures stop.") On an impulse, I decided to go through my papers in the hope of getting rid of them, or most of them, to spare my children the trouble. I've stored the few letters from famous writers I corresponded with over the years in a separate accordion folder. *Bishop, Mailer, Malamud, Oates* (a blizzard of blue postcards), *Updike,*° *John Irving, Walker Percy*: the wily book dealer Glenn Horowitz should be able to get a few thou for these.

So much *stuff*: I sit cross-legged on the floor and leaf through the pile. Yellowing stacks of *The Nation* with my early reviews; letters from high school girlfriends; report cards; short stories, written when I was in college. I read the first sentences: "Herman Traps awoke to find a stranger sitting by his bedside." "When she asked me to go with her it was late in the evening." I lay them on the "discard" pile. But here's an intriguing document: a manuscript typed on legal paper, defaced by brown splotches like faded sunspots, the pages yellowed to the color of parchment, held together by a rusty paper clip. At the top is an address where I lived in the mid-seventies: 111 Magazine Street, Cambridge, MA 02139. The title is typed in caps at the top of the first page: THE LETTERS OF LEON STEIN. There is a long introduction by David Blum, a friend of Stein's. The letters, all quite long, are addressed to

---

° Biography New World: In 1973, I copied out Delmore's letters to his publisher, James Laughlin, by hand at the dining room table of Laughlin's white-clapboard home in Norfolk, Connecticut, while sheep trotted past the window. Four decades later Updike's biographer, Adam Begley, shows up at the door and photographs my correspondence with Updike on his iPhone. Again, forgive my archaic laments, but I remain convinced that something about writing down words in your own hand—or even typing them—imprints them on the mind and brings some new depth of understanding. This is probably nonsense.

Leon's father Herman,* to Thomas Mann, to his girlfriend, Miriam, and to himself.†

It's the draft of a novel I wrote in my twenties, seventy-five pages long, and I can't put it down—it's brooding and strange, about a twenty-four-year-old intellectual with a depressive existential head who reads Spinoza and maintains a weak allegiance to the University of Chicago—one of those disaffiliated Jews defined by "Marxism, *Angst,* implacable rebellion, and a high I.Q." Leon was familiar with the Banach-Tarski theorem and had memorized the entire works of Balzac, transcribing them on index cards in a minuscule hand. His erudition was formidable; in a footnote, Blum claims that he was conversant in Russian, Yiddish, French, German, Italian, and Polish and possessed a reading knowledge of Hebrew, Hungarian, Serbo-Croatian, Chinese, and "several Paleosiberian dialects."

To my surprise, I find that Leon Stein is vividly drawn: "He had sharp, angular features, the sort that create shadows and recesses in the face, begrimed spectacles that appeared to balance like pince-nez on his nose, and that exacerbated an impression, like smudged windows in midwinter, of unrelieved pallor." He belongs to no institution and has no job. After the death of his father, he leaves home and rents a room above Walgreens, where he opens a shop called Eisenstein Enterprises.‡ Its motto is "We Solve All Problems," and it's staffed by "a group of capable Ph.D.'s" who turn out to be Leon alone. (His first and only customer is a woman seeking the definition of *oneiric,* which he supplies for a dollar.)

Life is an ordeal for Leon. "What I love isn't available in this world," he writes Miriam: "the simple experience of living." On the last page, he plunges into Lake Michigan with a fifty-five-volume set of Balzac's collected works tied around his waist (or "torso," as I have it). I'm giving the plot away, but so what? No one's going to read it now.

I decide to save it anyway.

Little else survives: I throw out old journals ("reading Boswell with keen enjoyment"); manuscripts labeled "foul matter" (the weird publishing phrase for drafts); notebooks with interview fragments: "I

---

* So what's with the *Herman*? That was the name of my grandfather, as noted earlier; also, with a second *n,* of Kafka's father.

† I must have read *Herzog* by then.

‡ I was a perfervid fan of the Russian director.

complained that his dog relieved himself in the herb garden; he was outraged when I took a swipe at the dog with a broom." (This must have been Bellow on Ralph Ellison when they were sharing the house in Tivoli.) Everything—or almost everything—must go.

It's no great loss. I'm safely in Carlyle's land of "No-biography," though once in a while I find my name lodged in the index of some literary chronicle between *Atlantic, The* and *Auden, W. H.* One of the consolations of achieving less than one had hoped is being spared this prospect. There's little here of interest to anyone else.

But wait. What's in this small manila envelope? I've written on it: "Isaac Rosenfeld family—friend of Bellow. Okay to throw out." I guess: his wife is dead, his son is dead, his daughter Eleni is a Buddhist nun who lives in a monastery in Bordeaux. I open the envelope and study the photographs: old snapshots with scalloped edges and a sepia tint. Isaac in swimming trunks; Isaac in a Hyde Park playground, cigarette in hand; his wife, Vasiliki, in a long fur coat, leaning against a tree. The prohibition against destroying photographs is atavistic. It feels like desecrating a tombstone. I put them back in the envelope and toss them on the "keep" pile.

Three hours later I've filled a large green garbage bag with the detritus of a writer's life: book reviews, manuscripts, journals, profiles of famous American novelists, and articles for travel magazines. I carry it out into the hall, set it down by the service elevator for the porter to pick up (no bonfires in Manhattan), push the button, and head back to my apartment with hurried steps before I can change my mind.

Acknowledgments

Books are supposed to be composed in solitude—the writer in his lonely lair, struggling to get words down on paper as the window darkens and night comes on. I've had my share of such days, when my only companions were long dead: Boswell and Baron Corvo and Lytton Strachey and all those other strange figures out of literary history whose voices have long haunted my imagination. But I also had days when the legendary editor Alice Truax made a house call to excavate from the depths of my unconscious the buried material of this book. Alice, I have kept a bottle of your Kombucha Wonder Drink in the fridge to remind me of your enlivening presence. And after Alice came the beloved Deb Garrison, to whom I first confided my fugitive early reflections about a book to be called *The Shadow in the Garden*. Deb got it before there was anything to get. Twenty years later, when I finally had a manuscript to show, it was Deb I thought of first. She and her colleagues at Pantheon—Dan Frank, Sonny Mehta, and Todd Portnowitz—have produced a book that is beautiful in every way. I'm proud to share the distinguished Pantheon imprint with two other biographers whose work has been a model for mine: Richard Holmes and Geoff Dyer. I feel that I've come home.

I would also like to thank Nora Atlas, Patricia Bosworth, Anne Heller, Richard Cohen, Julia Markus, Daphne Merkin, Karen Pritzker, and Stacy Schiff, who read portions of the book at various stages in its development; my famously sharp-witted agent Binky Urban (I listened to the words of encouragement she left on my answering machine for years); the stalwarts of the Gotham Book Group; my dear children; and my brother Steve. I have managed to get almost to the end of a long writing career without mentioning him in print—his editorial acumen is evident on every page. Steve has an uncanny, virtually ventriloquistic ability to make me sound like myself and, when that's probably a bad idea, like someone I would like to be.

Notes

Readers are naturally curious to know where the writer came up with his sources, especially the more outlandish ones (for instance, my mother in conversation with a woman from Chicago at a beauty salon in La Jolla, California), and deserve to be spared the common experience of turning to the expected endnotes only to find what Mallarmé called *le vide papier que la blancheur défend.* (I quote this line of Mallarmé's, the only one I know, in order to annoy my brother, who read the manuscript with bristling attention to possible instances of pretension and argued me out of several other quotations in languages I barely know or don't know at all.) But I didn't want to weigh down my book with the scholarly apparatus of page-by-page notes. I have settled on a solution I came across in Leon Edel's biography of Henry James, where he provides citations for each chapter in the form of paragraphs listing his main sources. Edel explains: "A great deal of my documentation has come from unpublished diaries and letters; it is always difficult to source such materials minutely, but I have indicated where it is to be found." This has been my practice, too, adding the oral element of conversations conducted in parking lots, on beaches, in smoke-dense bars, and in the notable but unique instance mentioned above, a beauty salon. This is not a systematic bibliography. I have in general not made note of books referred to in the text that are readily available or still in print. Entire chapters go noteless, especially toward the end, when the autobiographical *I* elbows its way more aggressively into the text. I have also relied on my own sporadic but generally reliable journals. The only source I've omitted is the main one: memory. "Yet why not say what happened?" Robert Lowell asked in a late poem. Because you can't: you can only say what you *think* happened. I hope that has been enough. If you trust the writer's voice, you'll trust the writer's facts.

I

The Delmore Schwartz Papers repose in the Beinecke Library at Yale and contain twenty-nine boxes (23.3 linear feet), up from the six boxes I had to work with when I embarked on my biography of Delmore. These include, according to the library's catalog, drafts of poems, stories, "personal papers and effects, drawings, clippings, and printed material." The addition of Dwight's papers, those of Delmore's brother Kenneth, and the consolidation of documents housed at the Syracuse University Library largely account for this dramatic expansion of material; in 1981 I donated my own papers, collected from a wide variety of sources, to the Beinecke's linear footage of (a new coinage) Delmoreiana. Unless otherwise noted, quotations from Delmore's work can be found in the Delmore Schwartz Papers.

Delmore's own work has been sporadically in print, beginning with his collection of short stories, *The World Is a Wedding*, re-issued by New Directions in 1977 with a foreword by Irving Howe and an introduction by the present author. Since then collections of Delmore's poems and stories in various permutations have appeared with gratifying frequency, including *Letters of Delmore Schwartz*, selected and edited by Robert Phillips, with a foreword by Karl Shapiro (Ontario Review Press, 1984); *Successful Love and Other Stories* (Corinth Books, 1985); *Selected Essays of Delmore Schwartz*, edited by Donald A. Dike and David H. Zucker, with an appreciation by Dwight Macdonald (University of Chicago Press, 1985); *Portrait of Delmore: Journals and Notes of Delmore Schwartz*, edited and introduced by Elizabeth Pollet (Farrar, Straus & Giroux, 1986); *The Ego Is Always at the Wheel* (New Directions, 1987), an assemblage of "bagatelles" from the Yale collection, and *Last and Lost Poems of Delmore Schwartz* (1989), both edited by Delmore's executor, Robert Phillips; *Delmore Schwartz and James Laughlin: Selected Letters* (W. W. Norton, 1993); and *Screeno: Stories and Poems*, with an introduction by Cynthia Ozick (New Directions, 2004), featuring an unpublished story I found among Delmore's papers. On my table now (2016) is the latest, *Once and for All: The Best of Delmore Schwartz*, a newly minted anthology drawn from Delmore's criticism, essays, poems, stories, and letters, edited by Craig Owen Teicher with an introduction by John Ashbery (New Directions).

Not in print, alas, are *A Season in Hell*, his translation of Rimbaud's *En Saison en Enfer*, unconscionably inaccurate but not without a certain charm; *Genesis: Book One* (there would be no Book Two); and *Shenandoah*, the play that appeared in the short-lived Poet of the Month series (New Directions, 1941).

For those who wish to know more, my biography of Delmore has appeared in four editions: Farrar, Straus & Giroux (1977); Avon (1978); Harvest (1985); and Welcome Rain (2000).

II

Richard Ellmann's monumental *James Joyce*—no subtitle required—is available in numerous editions; I doubt it will be out of print as long as there *is* print. (I own the Oxford University Press paperback published in 1972.) But

I served my biographical apprenticeship under the spell of all of Ellmann's books; I single out here *Ulysses on the Liffey* (Faber & Faber, 1972), with its foldout facsimile of Joyce's outline of the novel, and his two superb books on Yeats: *The Identity of Yeats* (Faber, 1954); and *Yeats: The Man and the Masks*, first published in 1948, when the biographer was only thirty. *Golden Codgers: Biographical Speculations* (Oxford University Press, 1973) is a lively compilation of essays on George Eliot, Wilde, Joyce, and others in the pantheon of Modernism, supplemented by his thoughts on the genre he elevated into a literary art.

For a more intimate perspective on Ellmann's life at Oxford, see *London Lovers* by Barbara Hardy (Peter Owen, 1996).

III

Dwight was not a prolific writer, and the one book of his that still has a pulse is *Against the American Grain* (Vintage, 1962), the collection of miscellaneous essays that showcased the erudition, humor, wit, sixth sense for the phony, and occasional innocent malice that made him one of the significant intellectuals of his day. "My greatest vice is my easily aroused indignation," he once wrote: "also, I suppose, one of my great strengths." As the fictional Macdougal Macdermott in Mary McCarthy's *The Oasis* and Orlando Hutchins in Bellow's *Humboldt's Gift*, he came across as a stammering excitable figure; it's not until you read, or revisit, his essays that you get a sense of his range. Macdonald could write with equal ease about Hemingway and Frost, the *Encyclopaedia Britannica*, and in his classic "Masscult & Midcult," the leveling tendencies of American culture. For more about the man—there were no masks—turn to Michael Wreszin's excellent biography, *A Rebel in Defense of Tradition: The Life and Politics of Dwight Macdonald* (Basic Books, 1993); and *A Moral Temper: The Letters of Dwight Macdonald* (Ivan R. Dee, 2001), which contains a generous sample of the letters to me quoted in Chapter XV.

Lucasta Miller's quote comes from *The Brontë Myth* (Knopf, 2003).

IV

Leon Edel was Henry James's official keeper of the flame, and his five-volume biography, published over a period of twenty years by J. B. Lippincott, is not only the definitive life of James but one of the definitive "Lives" of the twentieth century. He also presided over the four volumes of James's letters, published in the decade from 1974 to 1984 by Belknap/Harvard. (His letter on the failure of his play *Guy Domville* is in volume three.) Like Ellmann, Edel was a shrewd commentator on his profession. In *Writing Lives: Principia Biographica* (W. W. Norton, 1987), he advanced his theory of the New Biography, making the case that biographers need to be vigilant about their own role in the narratives they create and that transference is a fundamental dynamic. *Literary Biography* (Indiana University Press, 1973) is a primer on how to write biography. See also Lyall H. Powers, "Leon Edel: The Life of a Biographer," *American Scholar* (Autumn 1997). His interview, "The Art of Biography," appeared in the winter 1985 issue of *The Paris Review*.

V

Larkin's ambivalence toward his executors, whom he advised to preserve or destroy his papers, depending on his mood, is described in *Philip Larkin: A Writer's Life*, by his authorized biographer, Andrew Motion. Further dilations on the subject can be found in *Selected Letters of Philip Larkin 1940–1985*, edited by Anthony Thwaite (Faber & Faber, 1992). The story of how Larkin's letters nearly disappeared is told in Andrew Motion's contribution to *Lives for Sale: Biographers' Tales*, edited by Mark Bostridge (Continuum, 2004).

Virginia Woolf's letters are contained in the six volumes of *Letters of Virginia Woolf*, edited by Nigel Nicolson and Joanne Trautmann (Harcourt Brace Jovanovich, 1975–80). My quotations are mostly from the last of these. I don't know where I got the quotation from Freud's taunting letter to his biographers. That Kafka directed his executor, Max Brod, to destroy his papers has been recounted by several traumatized biographers; the fullest instance is in the third volume of Reiner Stach's exhaustive and exhausting biography, *Kafka: The Years of Insight* (Princeton University Press, 2013). The best account of Thomas Hardy's determination to destroy his letters while preserving his legacy is in Claire Tomalin's *Thomas Hardy: The Time-Torn Man* (Penguin, 2006). Hardy wrote his own biography under the name of his wife, Florence—an ingenious solution to the problem of how to control your image before posterity.

VI

Shelley: The Pursuit, by Richard Holmes, is the triumphal biography of the post-Ellmann, -Edel, -Holroyd generation. I have the 1974 Penguin edition, festooned with urgent annotations ("incredible scene," "great writing"). I also recommend (too weak a word? *want to press upon the reader*) his two volumes of biographical memoir, *Sidetracks: Explorations of a Romantic Biographer* (HarperCollins 2000), and *Footsteps: Adventures of a Romantic Biographer* (Vintage, 1985). *Footsteps* emanates the feverish ardor of an obsessive for whom biography is "a haunting," "a pursuit," a quest for the "pre-biographical" element of self-identification. The other required book on Shelley (if you can find it) is by his friend Thomas Hogg, first published in 1854. It got poor reviews—Hogg was accused of being too hard on Shelley—and was abandoned after two volumes had appeared. A pity, as it really brings him alive.

Norman Sherry, *The Life of Graham Greene*, vol. 1, *1904–1939* (Penguin Books, 1989; two more would follow). See the Preface for Sherry's account of his doppelgänger feats. Jonathan Bate, *Ted Hughes: The Unauthorised Life* (Harper, 2015). James E. Breslin, *Mark Rothko: A Biography* (University of Chicago Press, 1993). Geoff Dyer, *Out of Sheer Rage: In the Shadow of D. H. Lawrence* (North Point Press/Farrar Straus & Giroux, 1997).

VII

My portrait of Philip Rahv is supplemented by *Literature and the Sixth Sense* (Harcourt Brace Jovanovich, 1970), a collection of his essays on James, Eliot, Freud, and others (Houghton Mifflin, 1969); and *Philip Rahv: Essays on Literature and Politics 1932–1972*, edited by Arabel J. Porter and Andrew J. Dvosin (Houghton Mifflin, 1978), which contains Mary McCarthy's touching essay on her former lover.

Gilchrist's biography of Blake is one of the six volumes that appeared in Richard Holmes's Classic Biographies series before it was mysteriously abandoned (HarperPerennial paperbacks, available only in England). The others were Johnson on Savage, Southey on Nelson, Godwin on Wollstonecraft, Scott on Zelide, and Defoe on Sheppard and Wilde.

I obtained Carlyle's biography of the poet John Sterling from a curious reprint house named Kessinger Publishing, which has no address or other identifying data; it's a facsimile of the edition published by Peter Fenelon Collier in 1897.

IX

Isaac Rosenfeld, *An Age of Enormity: Life and Writing in the Forties and Fifties* (World, 1962), was edited by Theodore Solotaroff and contains a preface by Bellow; his novel, *Passage from Home* (Meridian, 1961), was reprinted by Markus Weiner in 1988, with an introduction by Mark Shechner, who also edited a necessary volume, *Preserving the Hunger: An Isaac Rosenfeld Reader* (Wayne State University Press, 1988). Shechner's anthology collects, in addition to the best of Rosenfeld's essays, three stories originally written in Yiddish and a selection from his journals. See Steven J. Zipperstein's excellent *Rosenfeld's Lives: Fame, Oblivion, and the Furies of Writing* (Yale University Press, 2009). I must also acknowledge, with great reluctance, the retrieval of a few paragraphs about Rosenfeld from my primitive novel *The Great Pretender* (1986); readers curious to know more about this haunting figure—and others depicted in the book—should look elsewhere.

X

Plutarch's *Lives*, with an introduction by James Atlas (Modern Library Classics, two volumes, 2001); there's a handy one-volume edition in the Penguin Classics. See also Diogenes Laertius, *Lives of Eminent Philosophers*, vol. 1 (Loeb Classics, 2001); Suetonius, *Lives of the Caesars* (Oxford World's Classics, 2000); *Einhard and Notker the Stammerer: Two Lives of Charlemagne* (Penguin Classics, 1969). Giovanni Boccaccio, *Life of Dante*, foreword by A. N. Wilson (Hesperus Press, 2002); Boccaccio, *Famous Women* (I Tatti Renaissance Library, 2001); Vasari, *The Lives of the Artists* (Oxford Classics, 1998). *Aubrey's Brief Lives*, edited by Oliver Lawson Dick (David R. Godine, 1999), includes Edmund Wilson's authoritative essay on Aubrey. Izaac Walton, *The Lives of John Donne and George Herbert* (Harvard Classics, 1909) is one of the volumes on their Five-Foot Shelf. As for the massive, multivolume biographies of the Victorian Age, I have only "looked into" them (as Mayor Daley told a reporter who asked if he had read *Herzog*); A.O.J. Cockshut's *Truth to Life: The Art of Biography in the Nineteenth Century* is a fine scholarly crib.

There is much Johnsoniana (where does this *-iana* suffix come from? the papers of Johnson's close friend Hester Thrale are referred to as "Thraliana") in this chapter, but I thought it best to put Dr. Johnson and his biographer together, entwined as they were in life. Books about this literature-linked pair are in the notes to Chapter XIX.

XI

Strachey's *Eminent Victorians* remains in print (Penguin Classics), as does a one-volume edition of Michael Holroyd's masterly biography of Strachey (Penguin, 1971). "None ever wished it longer," Dr. Johnson said of *Paradise Lost*. This is not true of Holroyd's *Lytton Strachey;* even the fat two-volume edition published by William Heinemann in 1967 and 1968 left me hungry for more.

XII

Selected Letters of James Joyce, edited by Richard Ellmann (Viking, 1975). The erotic letters ("Fuck me naked with your hat and stockings on *only* flat on the floor with a crimson flower in your hole behind") are on pages 180–95, for those eager to go straight to the dirty bits.

For Johnson's purported struggles with S/M, I have relied heavily on Adam Gopnik, "Man of Fetters, Dr. Johnson and Mrs. Thrale," *New Yorker,* December 8, 2008. Gopnik cites Katherine C. Balderston, "Johnson's Vile Melancholy," in *The Age of Johnson*, edited by Frederick Whiley Hilles (Yale University Press, 1949); Balderston was a pioneer in this narrow but important field.

XV

There are two biographies of Edmund Wilson: Jeffrey Meyers's *Edmund Wilson: A Biography* (Houghton Mifflin, 1995); and, a decade later, Lewis Dabney's authorized *Edmund Wilson: A Life in Literature*, begun after I declined the assignment and completed twenty years later. Both are adequate. I doubt there will be a third.

Apart from the biographies of Bellow by Mark Harris, *Saul Bellow: Drumlin Woodchuck* (University of Georgia Press, 1980), and Ruth Miller, *Saul Bellow: A Biography of the Imagination* (St. Martin's Press, 1991), there is now a third: Zachary Leader's *The Life of Saul Bellow: To Fame and Fortune* (Knopf, 2015). A second volume is to follow. There are also two odd but revelatory memoirs, *Saul Bellow's Heart: A Son's Memoir*, by Greg Bellow (Bloomsbury, 2014); and *Handsome Is: Adventures with Saul Bellow* (Fromm International, 1997), by his agent Harriet Wasserman.

XVIII

Charles B. Strozier, *Heinz Kohut: The Making of a Psychoanalyst* (Farrar, Straus & Giroux, 2001). Kohut is the key to understanding Bellow: the work cited here, *The Analysis of the Self: A Systematic Approach to the Psychoanalytic Treatment of Narcissistic Personality Disorders*, was first published by the University of Chicago Press (1971) and has been reprinted in several editions.

XIX

The best introduction to Boswell is *The Heart of Boswell: Highlights from the Journals of James Boswell*, edited by Mark Harris (McGraw-Hill, 1981); Harris was the author of *Drumlin Woodchuck*, a winningly idiosyncratic biography of Bellow. *Boswell's London Journal 1762–1763*, edited by Frederick A. Pottle (McGraw-Hill, 1950); *Boswell's Edinburgh Journals 1767–1786*, edited by Hugh M. Milne (Mercat Press, Edinburgh, 2001); *Boswell in Holland 1763–1764*, edited by Frederick A. Pottle (McGraw-Hill, 1952). Frank Brady's two-volume biography, sensibly divided up into *The Earlier Years 1740–1769* and *The Later Years 1769–1795* (McGraw-Hill, 1976 and 1984); Peter Martin, *A Life of James Boswell* (Weidenfeld & Nicolson, 1999); D. B. Wyndham Lewis, *James Boswell: a short life* (Eyre & Spottiswoode, 1946). Note that this is *not* Wyndham Lewis the painter but some other person, identified by Wikipedia as "a British journalist, author and biographer, known for his humorous newspaper articles." *Boswell's Presumptuous Task*, by Adam Sisman, is a chronicle of how the greatest biography in English got written despite its author's virtually limitless capacity for self-destructive behavior (Hamish Hamilton, 2000). Another biography worth noting if not reading is *Johnson and Boswell: The Story of Their Lives*, by Hesketh Pearson (Harper and Brothers, 1958). Perhaps the oddest book about Boswell is by C. E. Vulliamy, who seems to have detested his subject—he described Boswell's journals as "a garbage-pie of the most extraordinary dimensions"—but it's about Boswell, so of course I read it anyway (Geoffrey Bles, 1932). Unless otherwise indicated, anecdotes about Boswell are from my eye-challenging unabridged edition of the *Life*, published in a single volume (J. M. Dent & Sons, 1933).

My edition of Macaulay's *Life of Samuel Johnson* (Atheneum, 1896) is, at 121 pages, a model of the short form. John Hawkins, Knt., *The Life of Samuel Johnson, LL.D.*, edited, abridged, and with an introduction by Bertram H. Davis (Macmillan, 1961); *English Men of Letters*, edited by John Morley (Harper & Brothers, no date given); *The Fortunes of Francis Barber: The True Story of the Jamaican Slave Who Became Samuel Johnson's Heir*, by Michael Bundock (Yale University Press, 2015); Christopher Hibbert, *The Personal History of Samuel Johnson* (Penguin, 1984); *Lives of the English Poets*, introduction by John Wain (Everyman Library, 1975). See also Richard Holmes's *Dr. Johnson & Mr. Savage*, a poignant and highly entertaining portrait of Johnson's friendship with the poet/murderer Richard Savage, with whom he used to perambulate about St. James's Square at all hours of the night. John Wain, the critic I mutely stood beside at a urinal in an Oxford pub, also wrote a fine biography of Johnson (Macmillan, 1974).

XXI

I thought of giving the reader a hand with the fragmented quotes that cluster around themes—biography is good, biography is bad—but decided against it when I remembered the unfathomable capacity of Google to identify a source from just two or three words, a feat as mysterious to me as the existence of black holes (or telephones, for that matter). Most of them were lodged in my memory and had never been written down; others, thanks to Google, I located through secondary sources. Joyce's coinage, "biografiends," which occurs on page 55 of *Finnegans Wake*, can be found in Ellmann's *Joyce*—and it's a good thing, since I never got that far. And when I looked up my tutor's felicitous phrase about "the wrought jar," Google informed me, "You've visited this page many times." I invite the reader to go there, too.

XXIII

Elizabeth Gaskell, *The Life of Charlotte Brontë*, introduction by John Wain (Penguin Classics, 1975). There is also a later edition, with an introduction by Elisabeth Jay, who wrote a biography of Mrs. Oliphant and, according to the author's note, "lives in Oxford with her two children." (But that was in 1997; they're probably grown by now.) Juliet Barker, *The Brontës: Wild Genius on the Moors* (St. Martin's Press, 1995), is a mammoth enterprise that comes in at 1003 pages, and I haven't read all of them, or even half; but it's one of the most detailed biographies ever written. Less demanding but equally informative is *Charlotte Brontë: The Evolution of Genius,* by Winifred Gérin (Oxford University Press, 1967).

Froude's Life of Carlyle was abridged and edited by John Clubbe (Ohio State University Press, 1979); or you could just read Julia Markus's *J. Anthony Froude: The Last Undiscovered Great Victorian,* which is both admirably lucid and of rational length (Scribner, 2005). This story is so strange that some readers may want to go back to the original sources, especially Alexander Carlyle's hotheaded defense of his uncle, *The Nemesis of Froude: A Rejoinder to James Anthony Froude's "My Relations with Carlyle"* (Bodley Head, 1903); and Froude's agonizing self-defense, *My Relations with Carlyle* (Longmans, Green, 1903).

The Table Talk and Omniana of Samuel Taylor Coleridge, with a note by Coventry Patmore (Oxford University Press, 1917), like a number of old books in my possession, bears the disheartening mark of de-accession: in this instance, by Sacramento Junior College. I also have a book on Latin biography stamped East Lake Community Library, Palm Harbor, Florida, and another that I can't seem to lay my hands on from some college in Texas. It makes me sad that these libraries didn't consider such interesting books worth keeping on their shelves, but at least they have found a safe haven on mine. The two best biographies on Frost are Jeffrey Meyers, *Robert Frost: A Biography* (Houghton Mifflin, 1996) and Jay Parini, *Robert Frost: A Life* (Holt, 1999). It was from Parini's afterword, a consideration of Frost and his biographers, that I learned of the essay by Donald G. Sheehy, "The Poet as Neurotic: The Official Biography of Robert Frost," in *American Literature* (October 1986).

Andrew Field, *VN: The Life and Art of Vladimir Nabokov* (Crown, 1977). Brian Boyd's biography of Nabokov was published in two volumes: *The Russian Years* and *The American Years* (Princeton University Press, 1990 and 1993). Boyd's *Stalking Nabokov: Selected Essays,* despite its menacing title, is an affectionate homage to his subject, whom he subjects to rather steely critical scrutiny but in a tone of unwavering admiration. Nabokov's complaint to Field is cited in Boyd's *The American Years,* p. 610.

Without wishing to prolong this informal bibliography, I can't resist mentioning *Aspects of Biography,* by Andre Maurois (D. Appleton, 1929); *The Craft of Literary Biography,* edited by Jeffrey Meyers (Schocken, 1985); and *Telling Lives: The Biographer's Art,* edited by Marc Pachter, with contributions from Justin Kaplan, Leon Edel, and Alfred Kazin, among others (New Republic Books, 1979).

Also, there's a lot of stuff I never got around to talking about, like Julian Hawthorne's uncanny biography of his father, Nathaniel, written in the first person, which makes you feel as if you're standing beside him (in Rome, he evokes "the murmurous plash" of the Trevi Fountain); and Leslie Stephen's two-volume *Studies of a Biographer*, with its leisurely, old-fashioned essays on Wordsworth and Gibbon, Jowett and Pascal. Now I never will, but I hope another biografiend will take up my flickering torch someday and rediscover them.

Index

Permissions Acknowledgments

Grateful acknowledgment is made to the following for permission to reprint unpublished and previously published material:

Susan E. Barrett: Excerpt of undated letter from William Christopher Barrett to James Atlas. Reprinted by permission of Susan E. Barrett.

Carcanet Press Limited: Excerpt from "To Bring the Dead to Life" from *Complete Poems in One Volume* by Robert Graves, edited by Patrick Quinn. Published in Great Britain by Carcanet Press Limited, London, in 2000. Reprinted by permission of Carcanet Press Limited.

Trina Doerfler: Excerpt from undated letters from Trina Doerfler to James Atlas. Reprinted by permission of Trina Doerfler.

Joseph Epstein, Literary Executor of Edward Shils: Excerpts from memos written by Edward Shils to James Atlas. Reprinted by permission of Joseph Epstein, Literary Executor of Edward Shils.

The Estate of Alfred Kazin: Excerpts of an undated letter and postcard from Alfred Kazin to James Atlas. Reprinted by permission of The Estate of Alfred Kazin.

The Estate of Isaac Rosenfeld: Excerpts from the Journal of Isaac Rosenfeld and an unpublished poem, "Grandfather sits in his armchair," by Isaac Rosenfeld. Reprinted by permission of The Estate of Isaac Rosenfeld.

Hoover Institution Archives: Excerpt of undated letter from Albert Glotzer to James Atlas. Copyright © Stanford University. Reprinted by permission of Hoover Institution Archives at Stanford University.

New Directions Publishing Corp.: Excerpts of "Calmly We Walk Through This April's Day," "During December's Death," "In The Naked Bed, In Plato's Cave," and "The Heavy Bear Who Goes With Me" from *Selected Poems* by Delmore Schwartz. Copyright © 1959 by Delmore Schwartz. Reprinted by permission of New Directions Publishing Corp.

Nick Macdonald: Excerpt from writings of Dwight Macdonald to James Atlas. Reprinted by permission of Nick Macdonald.

The Random House Group Limited: Excerpt from Lytton Strachey by

Michael Holroyd, published by Chatto & Windus. Reprinted by permission of The Random House Group Limited.

Robert Phillips, Literary Executor for The Estate of Delmore Schwartz: Excerpt of letter from Delmore Schwartz to Robert McCauley, dated October 7, 1961; excerpt of undated letter from Delmore Schwartz to Julian Sawyer; and letter from Delmore Schwartz to James Laughlin, dated 1951. Excerpts from journals and verse notebooks of Delmore Schwartz. Reprinted by permission of Robert Phillips, Literary Executor for The Estate of Delmore Schwartz.

University of Virginia Library: Excerpt from "Notes from Conversations with Robert Frost" by Lawrance Thompson. Reprinted by permission of the Manuscripts Department of the University of Virginia Library.

Illustration Credits

PAGE

Printed in the United States
by Baker & Taylor Publisher Services